CONFLICT AND UNITY

CONFLICT AND UNITY

An Introduction to Canadian Political Life

Roger Gibbins
Department of Political Science
University of Calgary

 METHUEN

Toronto   New York   London   Sydney   Auckland

To my students, who have taught me so much.

Copyright © 1985 by Methuen Publications
(A division of the Carswell Company Limited)

CANADIAN CATALOGUING IN PUBLICATION DATA

Gibbins, Roger, 1947–
  Conflict and unity

Includes bibliographies.
ISBN 0-458-98910-X

1. Canada–Politics and government.   2. Politics,
Practical–Canada.   I. Title.

JL65 1985.G52 1985   324′.0971   C84-099626-8

Design: The Dragon's Eye Press

Printed and bound in Canada

1 2 3 4   85   89 88 87 86

Acknowledgments

Len Norris cartoons reproduced by permission of the artist and *The Vancouver Sun*.

Roy Peterson cartoons reproduced by permission of the artist.

Excerpt from *The Public Philosophy*. Copyright © 1955 by Walter Lippman. Copyright renewed © 1983 by Walter Lippman. By permission of Little, Brown and Company in association with the Atlantic Monthly Press.

"How Big is Big?" and "The Costs of Democracy" reprinted by permission of The Canadian Press.

"Mending Wall," from *The Poetry of Robert Frost*, edited by Edward Connery Lathem. Copyright 1930, 1939, © 1969 by Holt, Rinehart and Winston. Copyright © 1958 by Robert Frost. Copyright © 1967 by Lesley Frost Ballantine. Reprinted by permission of Holt, Rinehart and Winston, Publishers.

Excerpt from James Eayrs, "Sharing a Continent: The Hard Issues," p. 93, *The United States and Canada*, James Sloan Dickey, ed. Englewood Cliffs, N.J.: Prentice-Hall, 1964. Reprinted by permission of The American Assembly, Columbia University, New York.

"W.L.M.K." from *Collected Poems of F.R. Scott* reprinted by permission of McClelland and Stewart Ltd., The Canadian Publishers.

Duncan Macpherson cartoons reprinted with permission of the Toronto Star Syndicate.

Phil Mallette cartoon reproduced by permission of the artist.

Andy Donato cartoon reproduced by permission of Canada Wide/Toronto Sun.

All material from Canadian government sources reproduced by permission of the Minister of Supply and Services Canada.

Contents

Preface

The completion of this project would not have been possible without a great deal of assistance and support. A leave fellowship, provided by the Killam Foundation in the fall of 1983, enabled me to get the writing underway. My colleagues in the Political Science department at the University of Calgary were a constant source of support, and the critical assessments provided by Don Barry, Mark Dickerson, Stan Drabek, Bohdan Harasymiw, Jim Keeley, Frank MacKinnon, Neil Nevitte, and John Woods, and, in particular, Tom Flanagan, were invaluable. The same can be said of the comments provided from outside the department by Howard Palmer, Tamara Palmer, Rick Ponting, and Nancy Sanford. Thomas Huang untangled a seemingly endless list of word-processing complications, while Glen Armstrong, Jeanette Derosario, and Carole Pesta assisted with the background research.

Special thanks must be extended to Peter Milroy, Editorial Director of the Academic Division of Methuen Publications, who first suggested the project and went on to provide unabated support and encouragement. Cathy Munro, Assistant Editor at Methuen, handled the complex task of copyright clearances and permissions with admirable patience, and Kate Forster's copy editing ironed out a wrinkled manuscript. Michael Atkinson, W.K. Bryden, Donald Smiley, Grace Skogstad, and Allan Tupper reviewed manuscript drafts for Methuen, and their comments improved the final product immeasurably.

Finally, I would like to thank my family for their support and sacrifice throughout the project. Without Isabel's assistance with the word processing, and without Christopher's and Daniel's tolerance of their father's preoccupation, the project would not have been possible.

To all of the above, I owe so much. While I take sole responsibility for the book's imperfections, its very existence is as much their accomplishment as it is my own.

CHAPTER ONE

Setting the Stage

"The political game is a great one to play. It is exciting even to watch; it brings with it disappointments and frustrations, but there are compensations in the acquaintances it brings, *in the friendships formed, and in the knowledge acquired of humanity, sometimes at its worst, more often at its best."* CHUBBY POWERS's *memoirs,* A Party Politician

This text provides an introduction to the complex and often tumultuous world of Canadian politics. Its focus is on what might be termed the *dynamics* of politics, the issues and conflicts which drive the political process. Woven into this analysis is a discussion of the institutional arenas within which political conflict takes place and the parties, leaders, and groups through which conflicting interests are mobilized.

Here it might be useful to compare politics with Canada's national game of hockey. On different levels we can think of hockey as a set of rules for playing a game; as a network of professional and community arenas (not to forget backyard rinks and frozen prairie ponds); and as a vast army of referees, league officials, timekeepers, scorekeepers, coaches, parent helpers, skate-tiers, and rink-cleaners who make the game possible. We can think of the Canadian political system in an analogous fashion. It encompasses a set of rules and procedures that govern elections, the legislative process, and the conduct of public officials. It encompasses, furthermore, a network of political arenas including Parliament, provincial legislatures, federal–provincial conferences, town councils, school boards, and community associations, and a multitude of federal, provincial, and municipal public servants who staff the bureaucratic infrastructure of government.

Hockey, however, also entails the competing teams, the stars and villains, the traditional league rivalries, the emotion of parents and fans, the bodychecks and

1

penalties, the referees and questionable calls. While to understand hockey one must know the rules of the game, it is the action—the teams, emotion, and conflict—that brings the sport alive. In this text, particular emphasis will be placed on the issues and conflicts which energize political life. The institutional arenas and rules of the game will not be neglected, but rather will be introduced through a study of the broader game of politics.

Like hockey, politics is a great spectator sport. We can read political news as we might read the sports pages, looking at the Gallup polls to determine the partisan point-spread and following political columnists as parties fire coaches, trade players, and combat dissension within their ranks. Politics, however, is much more than a spectator sport, for the political process moulds our lives and shapes our futures. It is thus imperative that we be active players as well as interested spectators. But if we are to be players, if we are to leave the sidelines and wade into the fray, we must first understand the game.

Conflict and Politics

To study politics is first and foremost to study conflict. Political systems are systems of conflict management for dividing up the spoils of public life among competing individuals, groups, and interests. In the words made famous by Harold Lasswell, the study of politics is the study of who gets what, when, where, and how. In democratic political systems, however, conflict is largely contained within well-established institutional arenas. The scope and intensity of conflict is limited by a general respect for the rules of the game, and by an overarching set of values or "political culture" that most, though not all, participants share. Democratic political systems in particular are characterized by their capacity to manage conflict without recourse to violence. In the words of American essayist H.L. Mencken, "voting is simply a way of determining which side is the stronger without putting it to the test of fighting."[1]

It is the conflictual character of politics that makes the political world not only so fascinating but also so difficult to understand. For every event that takes place, citizens are bombarded by competing and contradictory explanations. The heroes and villains of the piece are very much a function of who is speaking, of the partisan lenses through which we see the political world, of the ideological predispositions we bring to our analysis. Like beauty, much of the truth in politics lies in the eye of the beholder. It may be for this reason that the public school system conveys so little information about politics; educators choose to neglect political life rather than to send students and teachers into a partisan and ideological morass. At the college and university level we have no choice but to plunge into the morass. Fortunately, the discipline of political science provides a set of survival skills that makes the enterprise less risky, more fruitful, and considerably more enjoyable.

Observations on Political Life

Democratic politics has been the source of a good deal of sardonic commentary, as the following examples illustrate:

"Political language ... is designed to make lies sound truthful and murder respectable, and to give an appearance of solidarity to pure wind." GEORGE ORWELL, Politics and the English Language

"Politics and the fate of mankind are shaped by men without ideals and without greatness. Men who have greatness within them don't go in for politics." ALBERT CAMUS, French author and philosopher

"[Democratic politicians] advance politically only as they placate, appease, bribe, seduce, bamboozle, or otherwise manage to manipulate the demanding and threatening elements in their constituencies. The decisive consideration is not whether the proposition is good but whether it is popular—not whether it will work well and prove itself but whether the active talking constituents like it immediately. Politicians rationalize this servitude by saying that in a democracy public men are the servants of the people." WALTER LIPPMAN, The Public Philosophy

"In the trackless wastes of politics, men lose their purpose, and the stars by which they once steered vanish in the bottomless sky of other men's aspirations. They wander like nomads, from oasis to oasis, quenching their thirst from the wells of power and warming themselves by the abandoned fires of those who have come and gone before." DALTON CAMP, Gentlemen, Players and Politicians

"Democracy substitutes election by the incompetent many for appointment by the corrupt few." GEORGE BERNARD SHAW, British playwright

The conflictual nature of politics contributes to, even if it does not wholly explain, one of the more intriguing democratic paradoxes. Canadians are generally proud to be living in a democratic country. When we look at the world about us, our system of government sets us apart from our less fortunate counterparts in other countries, and in years past tens of thousands of Canadian servicemen have given their lives in defence of democracy. Yet at the same time, "politics" tends to be a very derogatory term in common usage. How often have you heard something dismissed as "mere politics"; how often are terms like "office politics" and "political connections" used to refer to the shady underside of life? (Robert Thompson, former leader of the national Social Credit party, even complained that Parliament was being turned into "a political arena"!) How often do you find in novels, movies, and television programs that politicians are the villains, thwarting the more honest endeavours of police officials, community groups, and private detectives? The paradoxical thing to note about this contempt for things political is that it extends to those very elements—election campaigns, political parties, interest groups, office-seeking politicians, and voting itself—that make democratic government possible.[2]

There is, it should be stressed, a positive side to political life. Throughout history people have banded together in political communities in order to achieve goals collectively that they could not achieve alone. Be those goals collective security from external foes or internal disorder, economic expansion, cultural enlightenment, or a sense of group identity, mission, and purpose which transcends and thus elevates the individual, political organization has provided an indispensable vehicle for their pursuit. It is because those things that transcend the individual are so integral to the human spirit that politics is so important, that, as Aristotle observed in the fourth century B.C., man is a political animal. It is also because conflict is so intrinsic to human existence that we need means of conflict resolution which stop short of clubbing each other over the head. Well-functioning democratic political systems do not eliminate conflict but reduce its intensity and effects to a level compatible with a civil society.

Observations on Political Life

Not surprisingly, practising politicians have a more positive view of their art than that possessed by the person on the street. It is a view, moreover, that captures an important element of the political experience.

"... politics is the science which teaches the people of a country to care for each other. If a mischievous individual were to attempt to cut off his neighbour's hand, would that neighbour's other hand and feet do well quietly to permit the amputation of the limb if they could hinder it? All will say, No. This then is politics. That part of our duty which teaches us to study the welfare of our whole country, and not to rest satisfied altho' our own household is well off when our neighbours are in difficulty and danger. The honest politician is he who gives all he can of his time and means to promote the public good, whose charity begins at home *but does not end there. The man who says he is no politician, is either ignorant of what he is saying, or a contemptible selfish creature, unworthy of the country or community of which he is a part." WILLIAM LYON MACKENZIE, The Colonial Advocate, June 27, 1833*

"I am asked—and I am speaking to Young Canada now—are there any rewards in public life? There are—not monetary, but there is a tremendous satisfaction in being able to say, 'I tried, I stood.'" JOHN G. DIEFENBAKER, 1967

It should also be stressed that conflict is not necessarily bad. As former Prime Minister Pierre Trudeau has urged, we should keep our differences: "creative tension, after all, gives society its very life and growth."[3] Thus, to describe the Canadian political system as conflictual is to recognize its human face.

There are a number of important questions about political conflict that merit consideration. Is our political system reasonably effective in handling the sources of conflict with which it must contend, or are there features of the political system which exacerbate rather than moderate conflict? Are there some forms of conflict that the system handles well, and others that it handles poorly or even creates? Have we become so preoccupied with certain conflicts that other important issues are pushed from the political agenda? Is the level of conflict so high that collective goals, including national unity and our survival as an independent country on the North American continent, are imperiled?

Underlying such questions is a concern for the integrative capacity of the Canadian political system, for its capacity to knit together often disparate regional and linguistic communities into a national whole. Here the conclusion advanced in the chapters that follow is generally positive. Although the Canadian political system has been confronted with an array of very difficult problems, the national community has endured and prospered. Perhaps of even greater importance, it has done so while maintaining the strength and vitality of subnational linguistic and regional communities.

The Canadian Conflict Agenda

If you were to take a copy of a major Canadian newspaper and list all the political disputes and issues raised within its pages, the list would be formidable even if you excluded those occurring outside Canada. It is the sheer volume of political information, and the complexity of so many issues, that can make the study of politics so daunting to students. How can one hope to make sense out of a political world that is so complex, and often so unfettered by logic or rationality? One answer is to go to, if not "back to," the basics, to address a relatively small handful of issues forming the bedrock of Canadian political life. In so doing, of course, many exciting and some important issues will be neglected. The pedagogical premise of this text, however, is that the "big issues" provide an essential backdrop against which one can place the welter of other issues that form the daily grist of politics.

What, then, are the big issues, the threads which must be followed if one is to untangle the knot of Canadian national politics? To a degree, the selection of any set of issues will be contentious and idiosyncratic; both writers and readers will differ as to what issues should be included. I would argue, however, that the five pursued in this text—language politics, regionalism, the redistribution of wealth, Canadian–American relations, and intergovernmental relations—share a fundamental importance to the Canadian political experience. While their relative importance can be debated, and while a case can undoubtedly be made for a more expansive set of issues, these five are essential to an understanding of Canadian

"What is in behind the little curtains . . . just in case anyone should ask me?"

Len Norris, *9th Annual*. Originally published in *The Vancouver Sun*, December 9, 1959

political life. All share deep historical roots, and none of the five is likely to slip from the nation's political agenda in the near future. Moreover, the five in combination provide a setting within which a much wider array of institutional and constitutional matters can be addressed.

The format of the text follows directly from the selection of these five central issues. Chapter Two provides a historical backdrop by looking at the Confederation agreement, and at the early emergence of the principal axes of Canadian political life. The five issues are then examined sequentially in Chapters Three through Seven. Chapter Eight looks at the Canadian party system, and the extent to which it reflects the principal lines of cleavage that have been identified. The concluding chapter is followed by five appendices covering the legislative process, the Government of Canada, the Constitution Act, and some pointers on how to write a term paper. A glossary provides brief definitions for the more technical terms used in the text. Each chapter provides study questions and suggested readings. The latter, it should be stressed, provide some modest acknowledgment of the parasitical nature of textbooks. A good text builds upon, and to a degree pillages, the wealth of facts, theories, and insights put together over time with great effort by the academic community. I am deeply indebted to my colleagues whose research cleared the land and broke the soil; this text is far more the fruit of their labours than my own.

By the time you reach the final chapter, there is little doubt that many questions will remain unanswered. For this I have no apologies; my hope is that your appetite for things political will have been whetted, not satiated. This text can do no more than create a portal upon the rich and fascinating vista of Canadian political life. As a student of politics, you must demand more. As a citizen you must be prepared to use your increased understanding as a bridge to active political participation. Not to participate in the political process is to abandon your fate to those who do, and who may not share your goals, ambitions, and dreams. As Plato warned in *The Republic*, "the punishment which the wise suffer, who refuse to take part in the government, is to live under the government of worse men."

Suggested Readings

1 For an excellent overview of post-war Canadian politics, see Robert Bothwell, Ian Drummond, and John English, *Canada Since 1945: Power, Politics, and Provincialism* (Toronto: University of Toronto Press, 1981).
2 For a more general historical overview, see J.L. Granatstein, Irving M. Abella, David J. Bercuson, R. Craig Brown, and H. Blair Neatby, *Twentieth Century Canada* (Toronto: McGraw-Hill Ryerson, 1983).

CHAPTER TWO

In the
Beginning . . .

The objective of this text is to introduce the reader to contemporary Canadian politics. Why, then, you might ask, do we begin in the distant past? Why is it important to delve into the pre-Confederation politics of the 1850s and 1860s, to dust off the Constitution Act of 1867?

Here it should be recognized that Canadians tend to be a very ahistorical people, believing, as one of my students wrote, that "Canada has very little history." Our reluctance to grapple with the past goes beyond the widely shared delusion that we are a new country—we are in fact one of the oldest countries in the world—to embrace two common assumptions. The first is that the past has little relevance for what is happening today. The second is that Canadian history is boring, lacking as it does the clash of armies and the fiery rhetoric of revolution. Neither assumption withstands serious examination. One has only to look at the slogan "je me souviens" on Quebec license plates to realize not only the relevance of the past but also the way in which history is woven into the cloth of contemporary political life. In some cases the weaving is done with deliberate intent to shade our appreciation of current events, to alter our perception of the political landscape. Thus our views of Canada, and of our province and its place in the national fabric, are in part historical artifacts that should be carefully inspected.

For those interested in contemporary Canadian politics the past provides a useful guide, highlighting important landmarks and identifying the winners and losers in political combat. As Canadian historian Donald Creighton has written:

The waves behind the vessel which is carrying humanity forward into the unknown ... can teach us where the winds of change are blowing and on what course the chief currents of our age are set. They can reveal to us the main direction of our voyage through time.[1]

For the political scientist it is the currents rather than the details of the past which are of particular importance, for they provide a clarity of perspective that is difficult to find amid the complexities of contemporary events. They allow us to identify the harmonies and conflicts which have shaped and continue to shape Canadian political life. If, as Creighton has written, there are no "tragic finalities" in Canadian politics but "only the endless repetitions of the same themes,"[2] then it is important to have some appreciation of the historical setting from which those themes have emerged.

The reader who is prepared to go beyond the brief synopsis of this chapter to a deeper exploration of the confederation era will find that Canadian political history is far from colourless. In Sir John A. Macdonald, the chief architect of Confederation and Canada's first prime minister, one finds a fascinating mix of political brilliance, statecraft, chicanery, human frailty, and personal charm. Even if the personalities of the day are put aside, the confederation era presents a fascinating tangle of political conflict and opportunity. The way in which that tangle was addressed by the fathers of confederation provides as good an introduction to political craftsmanship and applied political science as one is likely to encounter.

The Wit and Wisdom of Sir John A. Macdonald

There is no better advice for the after-dinner speaker in search of a humorous opening or the student in search of some adornment for a term paper than to rummage through the sayings of Sir John A. Macdonald. Colombo's Canadian Quotations (Edmonton: Hurtig, 1974) offers the following gems:

"The task of the politician is to climb the tree and shake down acorns for the pigs below."
• *In an exchange with Senator A.R. Dickey, who had promised to support Macdonald whenever he thought Macdonald was right, Macdonald replied: "That is no satisfaction. Anybody may support me when I am right. What I want is a man who will support me when I am wrong."*
• *"Given a Government with a big surplus, and a big majority and a weak Opposition, and you could debauch a committee of Archangels."*
• *"I will have no accord with the desire expressed in some quarters by any mode whatever there should be an attempt made to oppress the one language or to render it inferior to the other; I believe that would be impossible if it were tried, and it would be foolish and wicked if it were possible."*
• *"As for myself, my course is clear. A British subject I was born. A British subject I will die."*
• *"Let us be English or let us be French, but above all let us be Canadians."*
• *"Would you move away please, your breath smells terrible ... it smells like water."*

The politicians who drafted the confederation agreement and, in so doing, laid

Confederation was first proposed in 1858 by John A. Macdonald, left, and George-Etienne Cartier, one of the most famous teams of political leaders in Canada—Macdonald from Canada West and Cartier from Canada East.

Archives of Ontario

the foundations for the modern Canadian state, faced a formidable task. At the very least they had to accomplish the following objectives:

• They had to dissolve the 1840 marriage between Canada East (now Quebec) and Canada West (now Ontario) while at the same time reuniting the two in a larger political community. Thus the instrument of divorce had also to be the instrument of reconciliation.

• They had to hold at bay an American military threat and the threat of American territorial expansion in the West.

• They had to meet the demand from Canada West for representation by population while meeting the demand from Canada East that "rep-by-pop," and through it the domination of the Catholic francophone minority by the Protestant anglophone majority, not be imposed.

• While recognizing a strong commitment to local autonomy in the existing British North American colonies, they had to create a strong central government that would be able to take over colonial debt and attract the financing required for railway construction.

- They had to entice the Maritime colonies into a transcontinental union centred far from the Atlantic coast, a union in which Maritimers would at best play a supporting role.

Quite remarkably, the fathers of confederation were successful, and for this reason alone the confederation agreement warrants our attention as a fine example of political craftsmanship. We also find in the agreement the emergence in elementary form of what have become perennial features of Canadian political life: the tensions between anglophones and francophones, between the centre and the periphery, between Canada and the United States, between the provincial and federal governments, and between parliamentary institutions and federal principles. In the financial terms of union we find the origin of contemporary instruments for the regional redistribution of wealth. In short, for those readers trying to understand Canadian politics today, Confederation is a good place to start.

Factors Leading to Confederation

The road to Confederation can only be summarized here, with a more detailed account being left to the historians.[3] Our discussion focuses upon four factors commonly acknowledged to have played key roles in bringing about the confederation agreement: political stalemate in the Canadas, a two-pronged threat from the United States, economic imperatives, and, for lack of a better phrase, what might be termed the "national dream."

POLITICAL STALEMATE IN THE CANADAS

The 1760 conquest of Quebec by British forces set in motion a complex colonial interplay between the French and English communities in British North America. In 1774 the British Parliament passed the Quebec Act, which provided protection for the French language, French institutions, and the French civil law in what had become *British* North America. Beyond recognizing what has been termed "the French fact," the Act also extended the boundaries of the Quebec colony westward to the Great Lakes. Then, in the face of growing English settlement around the Great Lakes, Parliament passed the Constitutional Act of 1791 which divided Quebec into Upper Canada (now Ontario) and Lower Canada (now Quebec). The 1791 Act also provided for elected assemblies in each colony but not for responsible government; the political executive could not be turned out of office by a majority vote of the legislative assembly. Thus by 1791 the French-speaking inhabitants of British North America had received legislative recognition of their language and institutions along with an elected assembly in which they would exercise majority control.

In 1837 political unrest in both Upper and Lower Canada led to an investigation of the colonial situation by Lord Durham. In his *Report on the Affairs of British North America*, Durham made his famous observation on Canadian political life:

I expected to find a contest between a government and a people: I found two nations warring in the bosom of a single state: I found a struggle, not of principles, but of races....

Lord Durham's solution was straightforward; the French Canadians should be assimilated into what was then a smaller English Canadian community. It was a solution reflecting Durham's harsh assessment of French Canadians:

There can hardly be conceived a nationality more destitute of all that can invigorate and elevate a people, than that which is exhibited by the descendants of the French in Lower Canada, owing to their retaining their peculiar language and manners. They are a people with no history, and no literature.

Durham's solution abandoned the political accommodation that had been put in place following the conquest of New France, an accommodation in which British colonial control and economic influence coexisted in Lower Canada with the social dominance of the Catholic church and French language.

In partial response to the political unrest of 1837, Durham recommended that responsible government be implemented, that the executive's term of office be contingent upon continued majority support in the elected assembly. However, in order to ensure that responsible government did not fall under the control of French Canadian nationalists, and in order to promote the assimilation of French Canadians, Durham also recommended the colonial union of Upper and Lower Canada. This second recommendation was carried out through the 1840 Act of Union, which combined Upper and Lower Canada into a single British colony, the Province of Canada, with a single elected assembly. The Act further promoted the assimilation of French Canadians by making English the only official language of the new legislative assembly, and by giving Canada East and Canada West, as Lower Canada and Upper Canada were now called, equal representation in that assembly even though only 432,000 people lived in Canada West compared to 717,000 in Canada East. While the Canada East figure contained a significant number of English Canadians, the French Canadian population alone in Canada East exceeded the total population of Canada West.

Had the assimilationist objectives of the Act been achieved, Canada today would be a unilingual state with a fully assimilated French Canadian minority. In fact, they were not achieved. Acting as a bloc on matters of religion and language, French Canadians were able to protect their interests within the new legislative arena. French was reinstated as a language of legislative debate following an 1842 speech in French by Louis-Hippolyte Lafontaine. When faced with the demand that he speak in English, Lafontaine replied:

I am asked to pronounce in another language than my mother tongue the first speech that I have to make in this House. I distrust my ability to speak English. But I must inform the honourable members that even if my knowledge of English were as intimate as my knowledge of French, I should nevertheless make my first speech in the language of my French Canadian compatriots, if only to protest against the cruel injustice of the Union Act in trying to proscribe the mother tongue of half the population of Canada. I owe it to my compatriots; I owe it to myself.[4]

Thereafter French was used in the House, though it was not made an official language of parliamentary debate and record until 1848.

Although formally the two colonies had been merged into a single unit, in practice a form of linguistic and political duality emerged that foreshadowed the introduction of federalism in 1867. Indeed, as Careless argues, the continued existence of two Canadas, East and West, "... destroyed Durham's very idea of a complete blending of the two peoples."[5] Governmental coalitions were headed by leaders from both Canada East and Canada West, the team of George-Etienne Cartier and John A. Macdonald being the most famous. Legislation impinging upon linguistic or cultural interests required a double majority—a majority among members from both Canadas—to pass. The administration of the colony was carried out on a dual basis, with separate ministries for Canada West and Canada East. Macdonald, for example, served as Attorney General for Canada West, not for the colony as a whole.

Practical as these adaptations were, the colonial marriage of the two Canadas proved to be unworkable, or workable only within an atmosphere marked by cultural polarization, governmental instability, and a growing pettiness in public life. The introduction of responsible government in 1848 did little to improve the situation. Deadlock rather than accommodation set the tone of legislative politics, with eighteen different ministries holding office between 1841 and 1867. Double majorities were increasingly difficult to find as the linguistic and religious division between the two Canadas came to be further reinforced by economic rivalry between the transportation, banking, and manufacturing interests of Montreal (supported to a degree by Toronto, Kingston, Hamilton, and London) and the agrarian interests of western Ontario championed with such force by George Brown, editor of the *Toronto Globe*.

Of all the factors eroding the Act of Union, the most important was the shifting demographic balance between Canada East and Canada West. By 1851 Canada East no longer had the larger population; approximately 952,000 people lived in Canada West compared to 890,000 in Canada East. By 1861 the imbalance was even greater; 1,396,000 in Canada West compared to 1,112,000 in Canada

East. Not unreasonably, Canada West became increasingly restive with the equal representation embedded in the Act of Union. Agitation grew for the introduction of representation by population in order to give Canada West the legislative clout that its numbers seemed to warrant. In 1861, for example, George Brown wrote the following editorial in *The Toronto Globe*:

THE GLOBE is the unflinching advocate of REPRESENTATION BY POPULATION. By the present iniquitous system, Lower Canada sends the same number of Representatives to Parliament as Upper Canada, although Upper Canada has THREE HUNDRED THOUSAND SOULS more than Lower Canada, and contributes SEVEN DOLLARS to the general revenue for every THREE DOLLARS contributed by Lower Canada. By this system of injustice and the unanimity with which the French Canadians act together, the Representatives of the Lower Section not only administer the affairs of their own Province, but control those of Upper Canada as well.[6]

Just as reasonably, the French Canadians rejected representation by population. Stuck with the equal representation of the two Canadas despite their majority in 1841, they were quite happy to be stuck with it still when Canada East no longer had the majority.

While the failure of the Act of Union was clearly apparent by the late 1850s, proposals for reform foundered on the issue of representation by population. Stalemated within the colony, Canadian politicians began to seek an escape through territorial expansion which would make possible a more workable federal structure than could be attained with only two provinces.[7] Such expansion was indeed to provide the solution, but only in the wake of civil war in the United States and growing economic distress north of the American border.

THE AMERICAN THREAT

Throughout its history Canada has been buffeted by events in the United States. Indeed, the landmarks of early American history such as the revolution of 1776, the War of 1812, and the Civil War were also landmarks in Canadian history, with the Civil War providing a major impetus for Confederation.

When the American Civil War broke out in 1861 Canadian attitudes could best be described as anti-Northern and anti-Southern.[8] If anything, the former prevailed, not because Canadians sided with the South on the slavery issue, which they did not, but because the secession of the South would break up a growing American hegemony on the North American continent. When General Lee surrendered the Confederate forces in 1865, Canadian hopes for some future balance of strength on the continent were also lost. In the meantime, Canada had come to be seen in the northern states as decidedly pro-Southern and anti-Northern. Britain's support of the South during the war had soured perceptions of the

British North American colonies in the victorious North. Also, in 1864 a small Confederate raiding party crossed the border from the Canadian side and robbed the bank in St. Albans, Vermont. When the raiders fled back into Canada they were only briefly detained before being released with the bank money. It was a minor event in the war but one which the North had by no means forgotten when the war ended a year later.

Canadian–American tensions at the end of the Civil War were heightened on the Canadian side by the Fenian threat. The Fenians were Irish-American veterans of the Civil War who sought to free their native Ireland from British rule. As the Atlantic Ocean prevented any direct Fenian intervention in Ireland, an attack on the British presence in Canada was considered. As the *Song of the Fenian Brotherhood* proclaimed,

We are the Fenian Brotherhood, skilled in the art of war,
And we're going to fight for Ireland, the land that we adore.
Many battles have we won along with the boys in blue,
And we'll go and capture Canada, for we've nothing else to do.[9]

In retrospect, the Fenians have a comic-opera character that belies the very serious threat perceived by Canadians at the time. An anticipated Fenian invasion on St. Patrick's Day, 1866, led to the mobilization of 10,000 volunteers for the defence of Canada. A month later 1,500 Fenians did cross the border, to be repulsed in a brief battle in which nine Canadians were killed. More importantly, the Fenians constituted only the tip of a threatening iceberg—the largest army in the world was being demobilized in the American North, freeing thousands of trained soldiers who quite literally might have nothing else to do than to "go and capture Canada."

The American military threat was exacerbated by British indifference. It had always been assumed in Canada that any Canadian war with the United States would be an offshoot of a larger British–American conflict, and hence that Britain would come to Canada's defence. In the wake of the Civil War, however, a purely North American conflict seemed all too possible. For its part, the British government was more concerned with reducing the financial burden of colonial defence and resuming war-disrupted trading relations with the United States than with the defence of Canada. As Benjamin Disraeli, Chancellor of the Exchequer, wrote to the British Prime Minister Lord Derby in 1866:

it can never be our pretense or our policy to defend the Canadian frontier against the United States.... what is the use of these colonial deadweights which we do not govern?

If the British North American colonies were to defend themselves, they had little alternative but to band together in defence of a common foe. External threat has played a significant role in the formation of most of the world's federal unions,[10] and Canada was no exception.

As things turned out, the American military threat did not materialize. However, the resumption of American westward expansion across the continent, which had been curtailed not only by the war but by the pre-war debate over slavery,[11] posed an equally serious threat to Canadian interests. The creation of new American states had been checked by the political deadlock as to whether they would be slave-holding or free states, with neither the North nor the South prepared to accept any increase in the ranks of the other side. With the slavery issue settled by the Civil War, unbridled western expansion began to threaten the unoccupied prairie land lying to the north of the forty-ninth parallel. If American settlement were to preempt Canadian settlement, Canadians would be boxed into the small north-eastern corner of the continent, and their absorption into the United States would be only a matter of time.

Finally, it should be noted that a general fear of things American, quite apart from the specific threats of the Fenians, demobilization, and westward expansion, lay behind Confederation. As Wise and Brown conclude, "... it is not too much to say that the large measure of agreement among provincial leaders on the nature of and dangers from political *Americanism* constituted one of the unifying intellectual forces in the Confederation movement."[12]

ECONOMIC IMPERATIVES

In the 1840s British economic policy swung toward international free trade and away from the preferential imperial tariffs which had been designed to promote trade between Britain and her colonial possessions. On the positive side, the British liberalization of trade encouraged the establishment of responsible government in British North America. As Careless explains, "... now that the Old Colonial System was being abandoned, now that trade was freed and the colonies' economic life was not to be controlled, there seemed little reason to control their political life either."[13] Responsible government came to Nova Scotia and the Province of Canada in 1848, to Prince Edward Island in 1851, to New Brunswick in 1854, and to Newfoundland in 1855. On the negative side, the British abandonment of "imperial preferences" was a serious, almost devastating, blow. The repeal of the Corn Laws in 1846 ended a privileged British market for Canadian flour and grain, and preferential treatment for Canadian timber was also ended. In 1849 economic conditions were so bad in Montreal that over 1,000 merchants signed a manifesto urging annexation to the United States. In related riots the Quebec parliament buildings were burned and the British Governor of the colony was pelted with stones.

In order to replace lost British markets, Canadians sought reciprocal tariff reductions with the United States. Although Americans were initially cool to the idea, representations by the British government eventually brought them round to the Canadian side. The New England states were particularly enticed by the promised access to the entire North American fisheries.[14] The southern states were persuaded by the British Colonial Secretary, Lord Elgin, that rather than bringing about the annexation of Canada and thus upsetting the delicate free state–slave state balance, reciprocity would be the one thing that would allow the British North American colonies to resist the siren call of annexation. The eventual outcome was the 1854 Reciprocity Treaty which significantly increased north–south trade and revitalized the Canadian economy.

While the Reciprocity Treaty cushioned the young Canadian economy from the British drift toward free trade, it also made the Canadian economy more vulnerable than it had been to events in the United States. With the outbreak of the Civil War in 1861 and the character of Canadian sympathies in that war, the prospects for the treaty's survival looked bleak. As a consequence, the expected economic impact of the treaty's termination became a major consideration in the discussions leading toward Confederation. Almost wholly dependent on trade with Britain and the United States, yet facing a hostile political climate in both countries, the British North American colonies were caught between a rock and a hard place. The creation, through confederation, of a free trade zone on the northern half of the continent offered the only prospect of economic relief. When the Reciprocity Treaty was cancelled in 1866, the new Canadian economic community was largely in place.

Economic factors played a particularly important role in the Maritime colonies, where they helped offset popular opposition to Confederation. By opening up a lucrative trade with the United States, the Reciprocity Treaty had launched the golden age of "iron men and wooden ships" in the Maritimes, an age in which the colonies were oriented toward the sea, Britain, New England, and the West Indies. As Rawlyk and Brown explain,[15] "it is difficult to imagine a people less concerned in their enterprise or vision with the interior of North America than were the Maritimers at the mid-way point in the nineteenth century." However, with the looming loss of reciprocity, the onset of technological change that was making wooden ships, if not iron men, obsolete, escalating debts associated with extensive railway construction, and with the ever-growing importance of a rail-fed continental economy, confederation became an increasingly attractive economic, if not emotional, enterprise.

Maritime Opposition to Confederation

In 1865 the pro-confederation Tilley government in New Brunswick fought an election on the issue of Confederation, and was soundly defeated. This lesson was not lost on the pro-confederation government in Nova Scotia, which avoided any electoral confrontation until Confederation was a fait accompli. When provincial and federal elections were held in Nova Scotia during the fall of 1867, pro-confederation candidates went down to massive defeat; anti-confederates captured thirty-six of the thirty-eight provincial seats and eighteen of the nineteen federal seats. Yet while Confederation was far from popular, to many it seemed an economic necessity.

For many French Canadians, Confederation promised the economic growth which was essential if emigration from Quebec into the New England states was to be stemmed.[16] More generally, Confederation provided the political foundation for a dynamic and expansionist capitalist state. Intrinsic to this vision was the construction of new railways that would connect the Maritimes to the continental economy, open up new markets for central Canadian manufacturers, and fend off the northward expansion of Americans in the West. Confederation would also enable existing railway debt to be taken over by the new central government; Easterbrook and Aitken go so far as to argue that the assumption of railway debts by the central government was "a prerequisite for the formation of the dominion."[17] Thus as Nicol and Whalley note in their irreverent history, "in Canada as in no other country the ties that bind are five feet long and creosoted."[18] More important is Pierre Berton's reminder, in the title of his history of the CPR, that the railways were part and parcel of a more encompassing "national dream."[19]

THE NATIONAL DREAM

It is easy to emphasize the negative in discussions of Confederation, to conclude that Confederation came about because of external threat and anti-colonial sentiment in Great Britain, because English and French Canadians could not work together within a single colonial government, because the economy was distressed and no one was willing or able to shoulder the debts associated with railway construction. This negative tone figures prominently in the writings of Canadian political scientists and historians. French Canadian historian Jean-Charles Bonenfant, for example, writes:

Confederation was achieved because English Canadians had to exist with French Canadians, and the latter could not then become independent. The great majority of nations have been formed, not by people who desired intensely to live together, but rather by people who could not live separately.[20]

Bonenfant's sentiment is echoed in historian Arthur Lower's now-famous comment on Confederation:

Some peoples are born nations, some achieve nationhood and others have nationhood thrust upon them. Canadians seem to be among these latter.[21]

This tone is very different from that associated with the founding of the United States. It also places insufficient emphasis on the positive appeal of Confederation, on the "national dream" of a new transcontinental state stretching from sea to sea—*a mari usque ad mare*—across the northern half of the continent. It was a bold vision given that the British North American colonies contained just over three million people, and given the much larger nation to the south pursuing its self-proclaimed manifest destiny of continental expansion. Thomas D'Arcy McGee, who was particularly concerned with American expansion, gave expression to the national dream in an 1860 speech to the House of Assembly in Quebec City:

I see in the not remote distance, one great nationality bound, like the shield of Achilles, by the blue rim of ocean—I see it quartered into many communities—each disposing of its internal affairs—but all bound together by free institutions, free intercourse, and free commerce; of industrious, contented, moral men, free in name and in fact, men capable of maintaining, in peace and in war, a constitution worthy of such a country.

Admittedly, the territorial expansion embodied in the national dream was championed primarily by the banking, transportation, and manufacturing interests of central Canada who stood to gain most from the creation of new hinterlands to the east and west, and who sought a firmer governmental base to support the massive debt engendered by territorial expansion. There was, however, a grander vision than commercial exploitation, a vision bordering on imperialism. Note, for example, an editorial on western expansion which appeared in the *Toronto Globe* on January 22, 1863:

If Canada acquires this territory, it will rise in a few years from a position of a small and weak province to be the greatest colony any country has ever possessed, able to take its place among the empires of the earth. The wealth of 400,000 square miles of territory will flow through our waters and be gathered by our merchants, manufacturers and agriculturalists. Our sons will occupy the chief places of this vast territory, we will form its institutions, supply its rulers, teach its schools, fill its stores, run its mills, navigate its streams. Every article of European manufacture, every pound of tropical produce will pass through our stores. Our seminaries of learning will be filled by its people. Our cities will be the centres of its business and education, its wealth and refinement. It will afford fields of enterprise for our youth....

While it may be difficult from our contemporary perspective to see Canadians as imperialists, the sentiment captured above played an important role in forging the Canadian state.

Those who sought to build a new transcontinental nation had to face some harsh practical realities. Across the British North American colonies there was a strong, parochial attachment to local autonomy. In the Maritimes, where Prince

Edward Island struggled to avoid the clutches of "imperialistic" Nova Scotia, there was little enthusiasm for being swallowed by the new Canadian whale. For the Catholic francophones in Canada East, cultural autonomy from the Canadian Protestant (and anglophone) majority was an essential condition for entry into Confederation. In Canada West "local control of local affairs"—or freeing the Protestant majority from the shackles imposed by the Act of Union—was a longstanding plank of the Liberal–Reform movement. The trick, then, was to maintain or, in the case of Canada East and West, enhance local autonomy while at the same time creating a new national government strong enough to deal with the awesome tasks of territorial expansion and defence, to create a new Canadian nationality without submerging any of the constituent cultural or regional parts. The solution was found in the marriage of British parliamentary institutions to the American innovation of federalism.

The Constitution Act of 1867

On July 1, 1867, the British North America Act—now the Constitution Act, 1867—was proclaimed and the embryonic Canadian state came into being. While at the time it encompassed only Nova Scotia, New Brunswick, and the southern portions of what are now Quebec and Ontario, the Constitution Act established the basic constitutional framework for the larger Canadian state that was to come. As new territories and provinces were added, that framework remained intact. Indeed, it continues to provide the basic constitutional skeleton for the Canadian federal state, though that skeleton was augmented in 1982 by the Charter of Rights and Freedoms, an amending formula, and the constitutional recognition of aboriginal peoples. Paradoxically, however, to understand the Act it is best to begin with what it was not.

An Important Change in Terminology

The basic constitutional framework of the Canadian federal state was put into place by the British North America Act of 1867. Between 1871 and 1975 the BNA Act was amended eighteen times, with the amendments being identified by year. Thus we had, for example, the BNA Act of 1886 and the BNA Act of 1930.

With the proclamation of the Constitution Act, 1982, the original BNA Act and its subsequent amendments were renamed. The British North America Act, 1867, is now the Constitution Act, 1867, and all amendments to the BNA Act have also been renamed. Hence, for example, the BNA Act, 1871, is now the Constitution Act, 1871.

Convention at Charlottetown, Prince Edward Island, to consider the union of the British North American Colonies, 1864. (John A. Macdonald seated, centre of photograph.)

Public Archives Canada/C733

WHAT DID *NOT* HAPPEN IN 1867

The 1867 Constitution Act did not emerge suddenly as a dramatic or revolutionary document, but rather emerged through an extended series of intercolonial negotiations. The confederation proposal was first broached in 1858 by the Macdonald–Cartier administration in the hope that a broader community would end the Union government's political impasse. When its major opponent, George Brown, endorsed the proposal in 1864, Canadian politicians sought an opportunity to present it to the Maritime colonies. The opportunity came that year when the Nova Scotia legislature called for a conference to discuss Maritime union. When the governments of New Brunswick, Nova Scotia, and Prince Edward Island agreed to meet in Charlottetown in early September, the coalition government in Canada asked to send a delegation. Through the leadership of John A. Macdonald, the Canadian delegation was able to have discussion of Maritime union shelved in favour of debate on the Canadian proposal for a broader union. After ten days of talks the delegates agreed to continue the following month in Quebec City. From the Quebec conference emerged a series of resolutions which were to form the core of the Constitution Act. Following approval of the Quebec resolutions by the governments of Nova Scotia, New Brunswick, and Canada, a final conference was held in London in December 1866 to work out the details of the new legislation with the British government.

The Constitution Act, it must be stressed, was not a declaration of Canadian independence; it was a British law passed by the Parliament of the United Kingdom. Canadians at the time did not seriously consider any alternative to remaining a colony within the British Empire. The Constitution Act simply regrouped three British North American colonies into a single colony and provided means for the eventual absorption of other British colonial possessions in North America into the new Canadian colony. Independence was to evolve more slowly. While Canada's independence was acknowledged by the Balfour Declaration of 1926 and formally recognized by Britain in the 1931 Statute of Westminster, it was not until 1946 that the Canadian Citizenship Act was passed, 1949 that the Supreme Court of Canada became the final court of appeal, 1950 that the first Canadian Governor General was appointed, 1965 that Canada had its own flag, and 1982 that the country's constitution was patriated.

There was no ringing rhetoric in the Constitution Act, nothing analogous to the American Declaration of Independence—"We hold these truths to be self-evident, that all men are created equal, that they are endowed by their Creator with certain unalienable Rights, that among these are Life, Liberty and the pursuit of Happiness"—or the opening words of the American Constitution—"We the People of the United States, in Order to form a more perfect Union, establish Justice, insure domestic Tranquility, provide for the common defence, promote the general Welfare, and secure the Blessings of Liberty to ourselves and our Posterity, do ordain and establish this Constitution for the United States of America." The Constitution Act began in a far more prosaic fashion: "Whereas the Provinces of Canada, Nova Scotia, and New Brunswick, have expressed their desire to be federally united into one Dominion under the Crown of the United Kingdom of Great Britain and Ireland, with a Constitution similar in principle to that of the United Kingdom: And whereas such a Union would conduce to the welfare of the Provinces and promote the interests of the British Empire: And whereas ...." This is not the sort of phrase that one shouts from the barricades or that school children memorize to give them a sense of their constitutional heritage. As Nicols and Whalley note, "in the entire history of literate man, no people has ever found endearing a document that began with 'Whereas.' "[22]

Confederation was not wrested from the unwilling hands of the British government. At the time colonial sentiment was weak in Britain, the consensus being that colonies were costing more than they were worth and that the colonies should be encouraged to carry their own weight. Indeed, the British government played an important role in bringing about confederation by closing off any alternative solution to the economic problems faced by the Maritime colonies;

Britain was unwilling to negotiate a reciprocity agreement with the United States that did not include Canada, and would not discuss Maritime union apart from some broader union with Canada. Thus Canadians were assuming responsibilities that Britain was only too willing to shed. The Canadian negotiators who came to London in December 1866 met general indifference rather than opposition. On March 1, 1867, a *Times of London* editorial stated that "we look to Confederation as the means of relieving this country from much expense and much embarrassment."[23] The contrast with the American revolution in the 1770s could not be more complete.

Lastly, the Constitution Act did not provide a complete constitution for Canada. A large part of the constitution remained unwritten, covered only by the opening phrase "with a Constitution similar in principle to that of the United Kingdom." In practice this meant that Canada adopted British parliamentary institutions and the conventions of responsible government, that the provinces other than Quebec adopted British common law, and that Canadians were able to draw upon centuries of British parliamentary tradition. (As John Diefenbaker declared, "the warp and woof of our constitution are the golden threads of our British heritage.")[24] The Act itself was primarily concerned with those aspects of Canadian government which were not similar to the United Kingdom's, such as the definition of Canada's colonial relationship, the establishment of new national and provincial governments, the federal division of powers, the fiscal relationship between the two levels of government, and the protection of language and educational rights.

WHAT DID HAPPEN IN 1867

The Constitution Act of 1867 divided the former colony of Canada into Quebec and Ontario, and then combined Quebec, Ontario, Nova Scotia, and New Brunswick into a single British colony, the Dominion of Canada. Section 146 also provided for the eventual entry of Newfoundland, Prince Edward Island, British Columbia, Rupert's Land, and the North-West Territories into the Dominion. The Act spelled out Canada's colonial relationship in a detailed description of the powers of Britain's representative in Canada, the Governor General. New national legislative institutions—the House of Commons and the Senate—were created, and their method of election and appointment was described. A national judicial system was created, and the financial obligations of the federal government to the provinces were described. Section 145 called for an immediate start to the construction of the Intercolonial Railway linking the St. Lawrence Valley to Halifax.

In many respects the key sections of the Constitution Act were those which put into place a federal system of government by specifying the division of powers between the national and provincial governments. It is here that the Act drew from American constitutional innovations and, to a degree, from the bifurcated administrative experience of the Province of Canada. It is here also that we find the most dramatic departure from British constitutional principles. Those principles, however, were not fully rejected nor was federalism fully embraced. The result was an awkward marriage of parliamentary institutions and federalism that was not to prove a complete success.

Federalism

Federal systems divide the powers of the state between two levels of government, both of which govern the same people and the same territory. The government at each level is elected directly by the people. Thus, for example, the national government is chosen by the people of Canada, not by the provincial governments or legislatures, and its impact on the Canadian people is not mediated by the provincial governments.[25] In theory, each level of government should have at least one area in which it is sovereign, in which the other level of government cannot legislate. There must also be a written contract specifying the federal division of powers—in the case of Canada the Constitution Act of 1867—which cannot be unilaterally altered by either level of government. Finally, there must be some impartial means of settling any disputes which might arise over the meaning of that contract. In Canada this was provided first by the Judicial Committee of the Privy Council (*see Glossary*) and, after 1949, by the Supreme Court of Canada.

The federal division of powers was set forth in a number of sections within the Constitution Act, the most important of which were Section 91, which specified the powers of Parliament, and Section 92, which specified those of the provincial legislatures. In a very general sense the two sections gave Parliament control over national economic management (public debt, regulation of trade and commerce, legal tender, banking) while giving the provincial legislatures control over matters "of a merely local or private Nature in the Province." This division was designed to free the new national government from the sectarian conflict that had crippled the Union government while providing it with the economic leverage thought to be essential for territorial expansion. By assigning the major areas of French–English conflict to the jurisdiction of the provinces, such conflict could be swept under the provincial rug, leaving Ottawa free to meet the challenges of national economic development.

Areas of sectarian conflict included "property and civil rights," which Section 92 assigned to the provinces, and education, which Section 93 also assigned to the provinces, albeit with important constraints imposed to protect the educational interests of the Protestant minority in Quebec. Section 95 gave Ottawa and the provinces concurrent jurisdiction—both could be legislatively active—over agriculture and immigration with the proviso that should provincial legislation be "repugnant to any Act of the Parliament of Canada," the national legislation would be paramount. Section 109 assigned "all lands, mines, minerals and royalties belonging to the several provinces ..." to the provinces. It is this section, along with article 5 in Section 92 ("the management and sale of the Public Lands belonging to the Province, and of the timber and wood thereon") which established the provincial ownership of natural resources, a constitutional principle that has played a critical role in the evolution of the Canadian federal state.

It was the federal division of powers that reconciled Canada West's demand for representation by population with Canada East's opposition to rep-by-pop. The terms of that reconciliation can be illustrated by the constitutional treatment of education. By assigning education to provincial jurisdiction, the Constitution Act put Quebec's educational system beyond the legislative reach of a national majority that was both anglophone and Protestant. This in turn meant that rep-by-pop within Parliament was acceptable to French Canadians because Parliament, with its anglophone Protestant majority, was constitutionally prohibited from infringing upon the provincial control of education. Rep-by-pop within Quebec was also acceptable, as Catholic francophones made up a clear majority of the Quebec population, and were thus assured of political control in Quebec's National Assembly. In a more general sense, then, and to the extent that minority concerns are assigned to provincial jurisdiction, federalism blunts the inherent danger that majority rule poses to minorities.

It should be stressed, however, that federalism protects only certain kinds of minorities under certain conditions. It only works if *national minorities* are also *provincial majorities*, as was the case for French Canadians living within Quebec. The federal division of powers provides no formal protection for minority group members who live outside the province where their group is a majority, such as French Canadians living outside Quebec. The minority protections embedded in the Constitution Act, apart from the division of powers itself, applied to the English minority within Quebec rather than to the French minority outside Quebec. As noted above, Section 93 provided protection for Protestant schools in Quebec. Section 133 provided for the use of both French and English in the Quebec legislature and courts, and for the representation of the English minority in both the Canadian Senate and the Quebec National Assembly. At the time of Confederation, provincial autonomy for Quebec was seen as the key safeguard for French Canadian interests, with little attention being paid to the French Canadian minorities in other provinces.[26] It was only *after* Confederation, Silver argues, that these minorities were brought to the attention of Quebec by "the harassment of the Métis in the North-West, the dismantling of Catholic separate school systems in New Brunswick, Prince Edward Island and the prairie provinces, the disestablishment of the French language on the prairies, [and] the attempt to eliminate French from Ontario schools."[27]

The protection of minorities through the federal division of powers is limited in a second way: it does not extend to minorities which have sharply different interests from the majority in matters of *national jurisdiction*. However, in well-designed federal systems this risk is reduced, though not eliminated, by other protections such as the equal representation in legislative assemblies regardless of population (as in the American Senate) and cabinet representation.

This discussion should not leave the impression that the federal division of powers is watertight, for it is not. Take, for example, the contemporary issue of jurisdictional control over post-secondary education, a matter of particular concern for students and professors. Initially, the issue seems quite clear; Section 93 of the Constitution Act assigns education to the provinces. However, although the federal government cannot *legislate* in the educational field, there are no constitutional limitations on its *spending power*. We find, then, that since the early 1960s Ottawa has been paying approximately half the cost of the advanced education provided through provincial institutions. In 1984 Ottawa's contribution came to about $4 billion. The research activities of Canadian academics, apart from their base salaries, are by and large funded not by the provinces but by Ottawa through agencies such as the Social Sciences and Humanities Research Council and the National Research Council. Here Ottawa's 1984 contribution came to approximately $400 million. To the extent that universities can be seen as providing *manpower training* rather than *education*, the constitutional door is potentially opened for direct involvement by the national government. Finally, both levels of government provide financial support for students, though perhaps not to the degree that readers might wish. In 1984 the national government allocated $150 million for student aid. Thus the practice of federalism is far more complex than one might suspect from an inspection of constitutional documents.

Some matters are explicitly assigned to neither level of government. The 1867 Constitution Act, for example, did not mention telecommunications or the disposal of nuclear wastes, lapses for which the politicians of the day can surely be excused. In Canada it is often argued that the opening clause of Section 91 gives such *residual powers* (*see Glossary*) to the national government: "It shall be lawful for the Queen, by and with the advice and consent of the Senate and House of Commons, to make laws for the peace, order, and good government of Canada, in relation to all matters not coming within the classes of subjects by this Act assigned exclusively to the Legislatures of the Provinces...." Over time, however, the courts have interpreted the peace, order, and good government clause somewhat narrowly, restricting its application to emergency conditions or situations in which a clear *national interest* can be demonstrated. At the same time, the property and civil rights clause in Section 92 has been broadly interpreted so as to verge upon a residual powers clause. Other clauses can also be used to lodge powers which were not specified in the original division of powers. Consumer protection, which did not weigh heavily in the confederation debates, can be seen as falling under Parliament's responsibility for trade and commerce or under the responsibility of provincial legislatures for property and civil rights.

Federalism, it should be pointed out, acts as a constraint on the supremacy of Parliament. In Britain, Parliament is supreme: "there is no higher legislative authority; no court can declare Acts of Parliament to be invalid; there is no limit to Parliament's sphere of legislation; and no Parliament can legally bind its successor, or be bound by its predecessor."[28] In Canada, however, parliamentary supremacy has been limited in a number of ways. Until the passage of the Statute of Westminster in 1931 Canada remained a British colony. Thus the supremacy of the Canadian Parliament was in theory limited by Britain, though in practice this limitation was of little if any consequence. More importantly, the doctrine of parliamentary supremacy does not enable Parliament to encroach upon provincial fields of jurisdiction. Within those fields, parliamentary supremacy rests within the provincial legislative assemblies.[29]

What remains to be seen is the extent to which the Charter of Rights and Freedoms will further restrict the supremacy of Parliament and of the provincial legislatures. For the first time, the Charter permits court challenges to the constitutionality of Acts of Parliament (or Acts passed by provincial legislatures) on grounds other than an alleged transgression of the federal division of powers. With respect to rights laid out within the Charter, then, Parliament and the provincial legislatures are not supreme. At the same time, Section 1 of the Charter guarantees the rights and freedoms set forth within it "subject only to such reasonable limits prescribed by law as can be demonstrably justified in a free and democratic society." This clause would *appear* to reassert the principle of parliamentary supremacy. The "notwithstanding" provision of Section 33, moreover, enables legislatures to override many Charter rights for up to a five-year (renewable) period: "Parliament or the legislature of a province may expressly declare in an Act of Parliament or of the legislature, as the case may be, that the Act or a provision thereof shall operate notwithstanding a provision included in Section 2 or Sections 7 to 15 of this Charter." Section 33 has been used wholesale by the Quebec National Assembly to exempt Quebec legislation from the Charter.

To bring this discussion of federalism to a close, it is useful to reiterate how federalism provided a solution to the perplexing problems facing Canadian politicians in the 1860s. The factors that led to confederation—political deadlock, the American threat, economic distress, and the national dream—did not dictate a *federal* constitution. Federalism was dictated by the conflict over representation by population, by a widespread desire to protect local autonomy, and by the need to create a strong national government without mangling the cultural and regional components of the new Canadian state. Federalism permitted rep-by-pop while giving the French Canadian minority, or at least those French Canadians living in Quebec, constitutional protection from the Anglo-Canadian majority. It created a strong national government while maintaining local autonomy in a number of important jurisdictional domains, and it laid the foundations for a new Canadian nationality without doing violence to the regional and cultural roots of the Canadian population. Federalism accomplished this by restricting the exercise of majority rule through parliamentary institutions.

Responsible Government

The term *responsible government* defines the relationship of cabinet ministers to the House, to the Crown, and to each other. Collectively the cabinet is responsible to the House of Commons in that the government must maintain the support of a majority of MPs if it is to continue in office. If cabinet loses the "confidence" of the House through a specific "want of confidence" or non-confidence vote, or through the defeat of a major government bill, unwritten constitutional convention calls for the government to tender its resignation. In practice, the prime minister would usually ask the Governor General for the "dissolution" of Parliament, and would go to the people in a general election. Thus, while the House can defeat a government, it cannot choose a new one.

Parliamentary Defeat and Responsible Government

The convention requiring the resignation of the government following its defeat in the House is open to interpretation. In February 1968, the minority Liberal government of Lester Pearson was defeated in the House through carelessness. Prime Minister Pearson, who had announced his retirement, was on holidays, and many prominent Liberal MPs were out of Ottawa campaigning for the upcoming Liberal leadership convention. When a vote was called in the House, the remaining Liberal MPs were outvoted, and the government was defeated. A strict application of the doctrine of responsible government would have dictated the resignation of the government and the dissolution of Parliament. This would have pitched the leaderless and ill-prepared Liberals into a national campaign against a rejuvenated Conservative party and its

new leader, Robert Stanfield.

The Liberals, however, argued that the defeat in the House was a mistake, and did not constitute a true loss of confidence in the government. To prove this point the government introduced a formal vote of confidence in the House the next day. By this time Pearson was back from holidays, all leadership candidates and other absent MPs were in the House and, with the support of the Créditistes, the confidence motion was passed.

If the opposition parties had boycotted the House when the vote of confidence was called, if they had insisted that the government had been defeated and that an election should be called, it is unlikely that the Pearson stratagem would have worked. However, the Conservative leader decided that an election should not be forced at that time. As a consequence *the House continued to sit, the Liberals chose a new leader less than two months later, and the new leader, Pierre Elliott Trudeau, promptly called a national election. The Liberals swept to victory, and the Conservatives were to wait eleven years before briefly winning power in June 1979. In politics, nice guys finish last.*

This episode could have provided an important precedent for the House that might have loosened the bonds of party discipline. If governments were deemed to fall only on explicit votes of non-confidence, as has become the parliamentary convention in Great Britain, then government back-benchers would be less compelled to support government legislation come hell or high water. However, the precedent was not picked up, and the importance of party discipline was not eroded.

Individually, cabinet ministers are responsible for the conduct of their departments, and must answer for their departments on the floor of the House. Cabinet ministers are also responsible to the Crown, who formally appoints them, and to the prime minister, who in reality appoints them. Finally, cabinet ministers are collectively responsible to one another. Like the Three Musketeers, the cabinet operates on the principle of one for all and all for one. Cabinet speaks with a single voice, and thus once a decision has been made all ministers are expected to endorse that decision publicly even though they may have strenuously opposed it behind cabinet doors. As a consequence, any one minister speaks with the full weight of cabinet behind him.

Collective responsibility necessitates that cabinet proceedings be secret, and indeed ministers are bound to secrecy through their Privy Council oath. Secrecy in turn facilitates both frank discussion within cabinet and a facade of government cohesion for the external political environment. Collective responsibility also means that the House cannot oust a single minister but can only defeat the government as a whole. (While the prime minister can dismiss individual ministers, this is seldom done.) Nor can government backbenchers publicly promote the sacking of a specific minister, for an attack on one minister is an attack on the full cabinet. From the perspective of opposition parties, collective responsibility is all to the good, for it allows them to tar the whole government with a bad ministerial brush.

In reality, responsible government is constrained by the inability of the House to change governments without an intervening election, and by the fact that party leaders and thus indirectly prime ministers are selected by national party conventions lying beyond the control of the House. It is also constrained by strong party discipline. If the governing party controls a majority of seats in the House, it will not be defeated on a vote of confidence. The government will remain in office until the prime minister decides to go to the people, or until its constitutional term expires. As Hockin concludes, "ever since the ascendancy of mass, disciplined political parties in Canada was confirmed in 1878, the ... notion of responsible government, except for its legal accuracy, has grown increasingly unhelpful as a way to understand day-to-day parliamentary activity and its role in policy-making."[30]

Representative Democracy

The Canadian political system provides citizens with few opportunities to vote directly on matters of public policy. The instruments of direct democracy — referenda and plebiscites — are virtually unknown in national or provincial politics; the 1980 sovereignty-association referendum in Quebec, discussed in the next chapter, is very much the exception to the rule. Canadians have opted instead for a system of *representative democracy* in which the policy preferences of citizens are filtered through elected assemblies. Rather than govern directly, we elect representatives who govern in our place. If we are unhappy with the way in which our representatives interpret our policy preferences, we can retaliate through the electoral process but we cannot directly assume legislative power. The Canadian electorate makes governments, not laws.

Public Support for Direct Democracy

In a national survey conducted in the fall of 1978 (The Gallup Report, December 9, 1978), 82 percent of the respondents stated that they would be in favour of a vote among the general public being held on the issue of capital punishment. Only 12 percent opposed such a vote.

However, on matters where the divergence between Parliament and public opinion was less clear-cut (Parliament abolished capital punish-ment despite overwhelming public support for its retention), there appeared to be less interest in direct democracy. When asked what specific issues apart from capital punishment "might best be settled by holding a referendum or popular vote," 12 percent mentioned Quebec's separation or language issues, 3 percent constitutional change, 2 percent the right to strike, 2 percent prison reform, and 17 percent a host of other issues.

The term *representative democracy* can also be taken to mean that political institutions should be broadly reflective of the electorate in their composition, that politicians should not only represent their constituents in the sense of a lawyer representing his or her clients but should also, in the aggregate, constitute a broad cross-section of Canadian society. To a degree this form of representation is provided by the structure of parliamentary institutions. There is rough regional equality in the Senate, each province is assured of a proportionate number of seats in the House, and the francophone majority in most Quebec ridings ensures that francophones within Quebec are well represented in the House of Commons. In other respects Parliament is much less representative, with MPs and Senators tending to have higher incomes, more formal education and higher-status occupations than the citizens they represent. Provincially, the situation is no different: "in every province, provincial MLAs, like federal MPs, are a socioeconomic and demographic elite."[31]

Nowhere is the House of Commons less representative of the Canadian population than in its gender composition. In the eleven elections from 1940 to 1972 only sixteen women MPs were elected, less than 1 percent of the House membership for the period.[32] While more women MPs have been elected in recent years, their share of the total House membership is still small. In the 1980 election only fifteen (5 percent) of the elected MPs were women while twenty-eight women (10 percent) were elected in the 1984 general election. Nor is the situation any better in the provinces where, in 1977, only 4 percent of the elected members were women.[33]

Apart from a growing concern over the underrepresentation of women in public life, the fact that elected politicians tend to come from a socioeconomic and demographic elite has been the source of little political controversy in Canada. This may reflect an understandable normative ambivalence on whether political institutions *should* encompass a cross-section of the general population. It is not clear, for example, that we are poorly served by legislators who are better educated than the norm, or who are more likely to come from professional or managerial than from manual or unskilled occupations. There is much less ambivalence, however, on the representative character of the cabinet. It is in cabinet building that we see the full flowering of this second form of representative democracy.

Prime ministers strive for cabinets which, if not *proportionally* representative, contain at least representatives from the major sectors of the electorate. Ideally, all Canadians can find their reflection somewhere within the ranks of the cabinet. More practically, prime ministers face the following representational demands:

• With the possible exception of Prince Edward Island, there must be a minister appointed from each province. If the governing party has only one MP from a given province, he or she will be appointed regardless of ability. If the governing party failed to elect any MPs in a given province, Senators from the missing provinces can be appointed to fill the void. Of the initial cabinet appointments made between 1945 and 1976, 35 percent came from Ontario, which contained approximately 34 percent of the national population. Quebec had 31 percent of the initial appointees and 28 percent of the national population, Atlantic Canada 14 percent of the appointees and 10 percent of the population, and the West 20 percent of the appointees with 28 percent of the national population.[34]

• Not only must each province be represented, but Ontario generally has more ministers than Quebec, Quebec more than any province other than Ontario, and so forth.

• Francophones must be adequately represented. If there is an insufficient number of francophone MPs in the government caucus, Quebec Senators can be appointed.

• Since John Diefenbaker's appointment of Ellen Fairclough, Canada's first female cabinet minister, women must be represented in the cabinet.

• Major regions within the larger provinces must be represented. For example, Ottawa and the Niagara Peninsula–Hamilton area are both traditionally represented in the cabinet.

• The cabinet should include a representative of the English-speaking population of Quebec and a representative of the French-speaking population outside Quebec, the latter usually coming from Ontario.

• There must be some visible representation of the roughly 30 percent of the Canadian population which is of neither French nor English ancestry.

Quite apart from these considerations, the prime minister must provide cabinet representation for the major factions within his own party, as cabinet building is carried out with an eye to party as well as national unity.

These representational demands make the task of cabinet building a daunting one. There is only limited room to consider the ability of potential ministers apart from their representational characteristics. The fortunate choices are those individuals who can represent several segments of the Canadian population, such as a woman MP from Quebec with a non-French ethnic background. Even then, however, there is considerable pressure to expand the size of the cabinet to ensure that no major group is left out.

The Meaning of Confederation

In a country's history, there are certain *formative events* which have an importance reaching far beyond their time and place.[35] Confederation was such an event, setting in place institutions which to this day shape the unfolding of political life in Canada. Confederation also plays an important role in debates over the direction Canada should follow in the years ahead, for, to an extent, we all try to anchor our claims and visions in the past, portraying them as the inevitable outcome of historical forces set in motion by older and, if our thinking concurs, wiser men.

It is therefore useful to examine the *meaning* of Confederation, to go beyond the terms of the 1867 Constitution Act to their intent. What vision guided the politicians of the 1860s; what aspirations were they trying to achieve through dry and convoluted constitutional phrases? Here we must recognize, though, that most political events are ambiguous, open to widely divergent interpretations, and Confederation is no exception. The search for meaning is handicapped by a lack of consensus among the founding fathers themselves, by a contentious historical record, and by a human tendency to bend the historical record to fit the political needs of today.

Evidence that the intent of Confederation was to create a federal system with a strong central government and relatively subordinate provincial governments is provided by the terms of the Constitution Act and the argumentation on their behalf by John A. Macdonald. Here it must be remembered that the confederation agreement was reached against the tragic backdrop of the American Civil War. While Canadians were prepared to adopt a federal system, and indeed had little choice in the matter, they were not prepared to adopt the specifics of an American model which had failed to prevent the calamity of civil war. Thus we find in the 1860s repeated references to the failure of American federalism and the lessons to be learned from that failure. At the 1864 Quebec conference Macdonald argued that "we must have a strong Central Government with all authority except what is given to the local governments in each Province, and avoid the errors of the American constitution."[36] The point where the American Constitution broke down, Macdonald argued, was in the assignment of residual powers to the states and to the people rather than to the national government. The "peace, order, and good government" clause was the product of Macdonald's concern.

To Canadians like Macdonald, the principal weakness of the American federal system was that the states had been given too much power. The lesson for Canada was that the national government should be strengthened vis-à-vis the provinces. That the founding fathers set out to do just that seems apparent from a number of the Constitution Act provisions:

• The Act assigned what were thought to be the "great subjects of legislation" to Parliament; the provincial legislatures were restricted primarily to matters of a "merely local or private nature."
• Parliament was given the power to raise money by "any Mode or System of Taxation" while the provincial legislatures were restricted to direct taxation and federal subsidies.
• The Act gave Parliament paramountcy (*see Glossary*) in areas of concurrent jurisdiction.
• Parliament was given the declaratory power to make laws in relation to "such works as, although wholly situate within the province, are before or after their execution declared by the Parliament of Canada to be for the general advantage of Canada or for the advantage of two or more provinces."
• The Act gave Parliament the power to make criminal law, with a national criminal code being the consequence, and gave the national government the power to appoint all superior court justices.
• The national government was given the power to appoint Lieutenant-Governors who were to serve as a national check on the provincial governments just as

the Governor General was to serve as an imperial check on the government of Canada. The Lieutenant-Governor had the power to withhold assent from provincial legislation, and to reserve such legislation for acceptance or rejection by the national government.

• Senators were to be appointed by the federal government, and not by the provinces.

• The Act gave Parliament the power to disallow provincial legislation—to prevent it from coming into effect—even when such legislation was wholly within the provincial legislative domain.

As Smiley explains, "in terms of both the provisions of the Act and the expectations of those who framed it, the provinces were to be in precisely the same constitutional relationship to the federal government as the individual colonies of British North America had been to the Imperial authorities."[37] Indeed, the federal government's power to intervene in the constitutional domain of the provincial legislatures was so extensive that some federal scholars have been reluctant to describe the Constitution Act of 1867 as a federal document, preferring instead the term "quasi-federal."[38]

This view of Confederation, however, has not gone unchallenged. A.I. Silver presents rather persuasive evidence that French Canadians did *not* see Confederation "... as a national unification transforming a scattered collection of colonies into a single people under a strong national government."[39] Rather, Confederation was endorsed because it was seen to protect the autonomy and separateness of Quebec. Silver points out that the assignment of matters of a "merely local or private matter" to the provinces was interpreted in Quebec as a recognition of, and not a diminution of, provincial autonomy. The mid-1860s attitude of the French Canadian press toward Confederation can be encapsulated by the following editorial statement appearing in *Le Courrier de St-Hyacinthe*: "We want a confederation in which the federal principle will be applied in its fullest sense— one which will give the central power control over only general questions in no way affecting the interests of each separate section, while leaving to the local legislatures everything which concerns our particular interests."[40] Confederation was supported, then, because it would free Quebec from Upper Canada, and give French Canadians autonomous control over their local affairs. As E.-P. Taché explained in 1864, the national government would have enough power "to do away with some of the internal hindrances to trade, and to unite the Provinces for mutual defence," but it would be the provinces to which people would look for the protection of their liberty, rights, and privileges.[41]

Silver, then, argues that at the time of Confederation, Macdonald's vision was not characteristic of French Canada. More recently, *compact theories* have emerged to provide historical support for bicultural and, even more recently, province-centred visions of the Canadian federal state. Bicultural compact theorists do not dispute the letter of the Constitution Act but focus instead on its spirit. Confederation, they argue, was the result of an implicit but nonetheless very real bicultural compact between the French and English communities. Without that compact Confederation would not have occurred and thus the meaning of Confederation is revealed more by that compact than by the letter of the Constitution Act. While there may be little compact evidence in the Act itself, evidence can be found in subsequent legislation such as the 1869 Act for the Temporary Government of Rupert's Land, the Manitoba Act of 1870, and the North-West Territories Act of 1875.[42]

Bicultural compact theories emerged in Quebec during the 1930s, and came to play a significant role in debates on the place of Quebec in Canada, and on the status of the French language outside Quebec. They have also been highly contentious, with critics charging that they distort if not falsify the historical record. One of the most outspoken critics had been the historian Donald Creighton, who has concluded that the evidence against the two-nation theory of confederation is overwhelming:

It is obvious that the last thing the Fathers of Confederation wanted to do was to perpetuate duality; they hoped, through confederation, to escape from it entirely ... . There was nothing in ... the British North America Act which remotely approached a general declaration of principle that Canada was to be a bilingual or bicultural nation.[43]

Critics of the bicultural compact have not been confined to English Canada. In its background paper for the 1980 sovereignty-association referendum, the Parti Québécois government declared:

Under the terms of the British North America Act, Quebec is not the homeland of a nation, but merely a province among the others.... Nowhere in the Act is there a talk of an alliance between two founding peoples, or of a pact between two nations....[44]

Compact theories have also been tied to classical models of federalism in which federal constitutions are seen as legal contracts. If the Constitution Act is seen as a contract, one can ask whom the contract was between or among. Since the national government did not exist prior to 1867, it can be argued that the contract was among the provinces, and that the provincial governments are the legitimate custodians of the constitution. In this view there is no acknowledgment of a subordinate role for the provincial legislatures, as the letter of the Constitution Act might suggest. As Stevenson points out, the lack of public ratification of the confederation agreement has strengthened compact interpretations. Confederation, after all, was a governmental rather than a popular product, portrayed at the time as a treaty among governments.[45] As the only governments in existence at the time were the provincial governments, the compact interpretation gains weight.

The Confederation Legacy

The boundaries of the Canadian state have greatly expanded since 1870. In 1870 Manitoba entered Confederation, and both the North-West Territories and Rupert's Land were acquired by Canada. On the promise of a transcontinental railroad British Columbia joined in 1871, as did Prince Edward Island two years later in the wake of a poor harvest, economic recession, and railway debt. In 1880 Canada acquired the Arctic islands, and in 1905 Alberta and Saskatchewan became the eighth and ninth Canadian provinces. In 1912 Ontario and Quebec nearly doubled in size as their boundaries were expanded to the north, and in 1949 Newfoundland became Canada's tenth province.

Canada, of course, has changed in countless other ways as well. Our population has increased from just over three million at the time of Confederation to twenty-five million in 1985. No longer a frontier society, Canada has become a modern industrialized state. No longer rural and agrarian, we live in a highly urbanized and technologically dependent society. Yet the massive changes that have occurred have not rendered Confederation irrelevant for an understanding of contemporary Canadian politics. The Constitution Act of 1867 continues to provide the *federal* skeleton for the Canadian state. The political institutions put into place by the confederation agreement continue to provide the arenas within which much of our political life occurs. While Confederation did not provide a straitjacket for the political evolution of the Canadian state, it set the stage, provided the institutional props, and supplied many of the dramatic themes.

The fathers of confederation grappled with very difficult political problems. To the extent that these problems are still with us—to the extent, for example, that linguistic tension remains and that we enjoy only a precarious independence from the United States—one might be tempted to conclude that Confederation was a failure. Such a conclusion, however, would be harsh. One must remember that the confederation agreement created a political community that has experienced quite remarkable stability, domestic peace and material prosperity. Moreover, the problems that Canadians confronted in the 1860s are not ones that can ever be eliminated; at best they can be moderated and contained, their burden to the community lightened but not removed. As British Prime Minister James Callaghan said in 1978, you can never reach the promised land, but only march toward it. The fact that we are still here as a country to grapple with the same problems that faced the fathers of confederation pays no small compliment to their work.

Suggested Readings

1 Michel Brunet, "The Historical Background of Quebec's Challenge to Canadian Unity," in Dale C. Thompson, ed., *Quebec Society and Politics* (Toronto: McClelland and Stewart, 1973), pp. 39–51.

2 For a discussion of the compact theory, see Ramsay Cook, *Canada and the French Canadian Question* (Toronto: Macmillan, 1976).

3 For an illustration of the historical debate on the compact theory see Ralph Heintzman, "The Spirit of Confederation: Professor Creighton, Biculturalism, and the Use of History," *Canadian Historical Review*, September 1971, pp. 245–75; and D.J. Hall, "The Spirit of Confederation: Ralph Heintzman, Professor Creighton, and the Bicultural Compact Theory," *Journal of Canadian Studies*, November 1974, pp. 24–43.

4 For a discussion of Nova Scotia's opposition to Confederation see Colin D. Howell, "Nova Scotia's Protest Tradition and the Search for a Meaningful Federalism" in David Jay Bercuson, ed., *Canada and the Burden of Unity* (Toronto: Macmillan, 1977), pp. 169–91.

5 Rod Preece, "The Political Wisdom of Sir John A. Macdonald," *Canadian Journal of Political Science* xvii:3 (September 1984), pp. 459–86.

6 G.A. Rawlyk and Doug Brown, "The Historical Framework of the Maritimes and Confederation," in G.A. Rawlyk, ed., *The Atlantic Provinces and the Problems of Confederation* (St. John's: Breakwater, 1979), pp. 1–47.

7 A.I. Silver, *The French-Canadian Idea of Confederation, 1864–1900* (Toronto: University of Toronto Press, 1982).

8 Peter B. Waite, *The Life and Times of Confederation* (Toronto: University of Toronto Press, 1962); and *The Confederation Debates in the Province of Canada, 1865* (Toronto: McClelland and Stewart, 1963).

Study Questions

1 In light of the limited defence provided by the division of powers for French Canadians living outside Quebec, how would you assess the protection provided by the federal division for English Canadians living inside Quebec? In what ways are the two situations analogous? In which ways are they not?

2 If your province was entering Confederation today, would your provincial government seek a different division of powers? If so, what would be the difference? What about you personally; would you favour a different division of powers, and, if so, what would the difference be?

3 Take a careful look at the federal division of powers outlined in Sections 91 and 92 of the Constitution Act, 1867. Given that division, which level of government do you think would have primary responsibility in the following fields: acid rain, the control of nuclear wastes, the regulation of professional sports, consumer protection, lotteries, medicare, and pollution control for automobile exhausts. In each case, to what extent does the formal division of powers provide a useful practical guide?

CHAPTER THREE

Language Politics

Two features of Canadian society have been of unsurpassed importance in shaping the contours of political life. The first is the existence of a large *francophone minority* which, over the last hundred years, has made up between a quarter and a third of the national population. The second is the concentration of that minority within Quebec, where a solid *francophone majority* controls the provincial government. In conjunction, these two features have generated a complex pattern of language politics weaving together the tensions between the anglophone national majority and the francophone national minority, between the Quebec and national governments, between the francophone majority and the anglophone minority within Quebec, and between francophone minorities and anglophone majorities within the other nine provinces.

FIGURE 3.1

Linguistic Composition (Mother Tongue) of Canada and Quebec (1981)

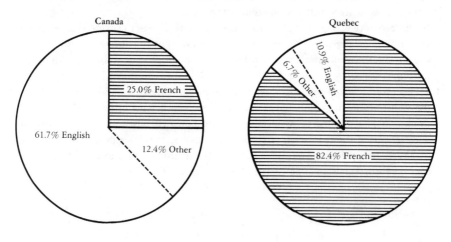

The examination of Canadian language politics can be compared to opening a carved set of Russian dolls; within the first doll is another, and within that another, and so forth until one is left with a table covered in doll parts but no doll. Like the set of dolls, the components of language politics are nested within one another. Thus we must consider not only each component in turn but the interplay among them in coming to grips with the language policies pursued by the governments of Canada, Quebec, and the other nine provinces. The controversies that have swirled about these policies provide a useful window through which to view the broader Canadian political process.

In tackling this chapter, the reader should be cautioned that language forms only part of the complex relationship between the French and English communities in Canada. Historically, that relationship was founded on the religious division between Catholics and Protestants; language per se was important largely as a carrier of religious and cultural values. In today's more secular society, however, language has come increasingly to the fore. As René Lévesque wrote in 1968:

At the core of the Québécois personality is the fact that we speak French. Everything else depends on this one essential element and follows from it or leads us infallibly back to it.[1]

While cultural, class, and religious differences are by no means absent between the two linguistic communities, it is largely in terms of the status of the French language that one can define the place of Quebec and French Canadians within the broader fabric of Canadian life.

Although conflict emerges as the dominant theme in a discussion of language politics, the two linguistic communities have coexisted without bloodshed and without the assimilation of the francophone minority. The survival of the "French Fact" in Canada speaks well not only for French Canadians' tenacious defence of their language and culture, but for the political system's ability to maintain workable compromises in very contentious policy areas.

The Linguistic Composition of Canada

Over the years the linguistic composition of Canada has been reasonably stable. Figure 3.2 shows that since 1931 the percentage of Canada's population whose mother tongue (the language spoken most often at home when the individual was a child) is French has varied within a range of only 3 percent. (These data were not available prior to the 1931 census.) Figure 3.2 also shows that Quebec's share of the national population, a share roughly equivalent to the *combined* populations of Newfoundland, Prince Edward Island, Nova Scotia, New Brunswick, Manitoba, Saskatchewan, and Alberta, has been reasonably stable. It is important to note, however, that between 1966 and 1981 Quebec's share of the national population dropped by almost 3 percent.

FIGURE 3.2

Quebec and French Mother Tongue Shares of the National Population

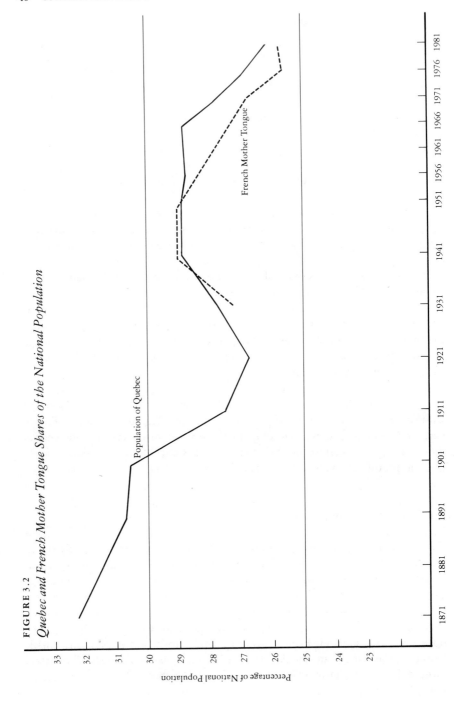

In many ways it is quite remarkable that Quebec has retained more than a quarter of the national population, and that more than one Canadian in four is of French mother tongue. The present French Canadian population of over six million has evolved almost entirely from the seventy thousand French settlers who remained in Canada after the "conquest" of New France in 1760.[2] Immigration from France virtually ceased in 1760, just as immigration from other countries was getting underway. Soon francophones became a minority within the British North American colonies, though they remained a majority in what is now Quebec. Immigrants from countries other than France tended to settle outside Quebec in part because economic opportunities were better and land was more readily available, in part because of the closed nature of the French Canadian community, and in part because, if one had to acquire a new language, English was of greater economic currency in North America than was French. (For many immigrants, Canada was little more than a stopover on their way to the United States.) For every immigrant who settled in Quebec, three to four settled in Ontario.[3] Yet regardless of where they settled, immigrants were either anglophones to start with or overwhelmingly adopted English rather than French upon their arrival in Canada.[4] Joy found that by the 1961 census 91 percent of the pre-war immigrants spoke English only, 7 percent spoke both French and English, and only 1 percent spoke only French, the same proportion that spoke neither official language.[5] Thus immigration worked to erode the proportionate contribution of both Quebec and francophones to the national population.

Figure 3.3 provides a simplified illustration (*not* drawn to scale) of the factors determining Quebec's share of the national population. In the past Quebec, like other provinces, faced a steady loss of population through out-migration, a loss attesting to the geographical mobility that Canadians enjoy. In Quebec's case, however, out-migration was primarily to the United States rather than to other provinces. Quebec migrants, for example, played a relatively minor role in the settlement of the Canadian West. For every one person who moved from Quebec to the West before 1931, six moved to the West from Ontario and eight moved from Quebec to the United States.[6] Thus most of those who left Quebec were lost not only to Quebec but to French Canada. Without the infusion of migration, francophone communities outside Quebec were left exposed to the assimilationist pressure of the anglophone majority. As Joy concludes, "the great exodus of French Canadians toward the United States was one of the decisive factors contributing to the supremacy of the English language in Canada."[7]

Out-migration from Quebec was offset not by immigration into the province from abroad or from other provinces, but by a high birth rate reflecting the rural character of the Quebec population, the dominance of the Catholic religion, and a cultural ethos which linked a high birth rate to the very survival of French Canada. With respect to this last point, Joy cites the eulogy in a Beauce County newspaper for a Monsieur Philippon who, when he died at the age of 96, left six

FIGURE 3.3

Factors Affecting Quebec's Share of Canada's Population

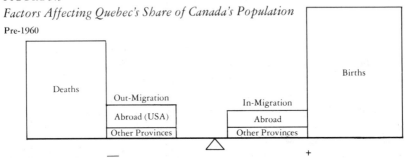

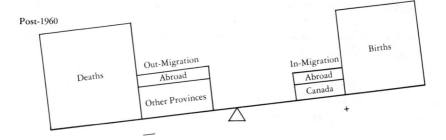

hundred descendants: "the grandfather of Mr. Philippon met an honorable death at the Battle of the Plains of Abraham; his grandson has well revenged this death by adding, through his own efforts, an entire parish to French Canada."[8] This *revanche des berceaux*, or revenge of the cradle, played a critical role in maintaining Quebec's share of the national population in the face of the "fatal hemorrhage" of French Canadians into the New England states and the steady flow of overseas emigration into Ontario and the West.

By the 1960s, however, Quebec's demographic balance was upset by a number of changes. Perhaps of greatest importance was a decline in the birthrate. Although in 1931 Quebec's birthrate had been 40 percent greater than that for the country as a whole, this advantage declined to 35 percent in 1941, 26 percent in 1951, 9 percent in 1961, and 6 percent in 1966.[9] By 1971 Quebec's birthrate had fallen below the national average, and by the mid-1970s it was the lowest in Canada. In the early 1980s the birthrate, already well below the rate necessary to maintain a stable population, was still falling. At the same time, the Quebec language legislation discussed below and intensified Québécois nationalism increased emigration from Quebec's anglophone community and reduced even further in-migration from other provinces and countries. In 1982, the most recent year for which data are available, Quebec was the only province to experience a net loss when both interprovincial and international migration were taken into account; 9,000 more people left the province during the year than moved in.[10] Between 1966 and 1976, 306,200 people left Quebec for other parts of Canada while only 168,700 moved into Quebec from the other provinces.[11] Given that 63 percent of those who *left* were of English mother tongue (another 8 percent were of neither French nor English mother tongue) and that 42 percent of those who *moved to* Quebec were of French mother tongue, the pattern of interprovincial migration works to strengthen, not weaken, the country's linguistic division.

In combination, these demographic changes have begun to erode significantly Quebec's share of the national population, a process likely to accelerate in the years ahead. This erosion has in turn strengthened nationalist arguments in Quebec. In its 1979 proposal for sovereignty-association, the government of Quebec stated that it would be an illusion to believe that francophones could in the future play a determining role in the Government of Canada:

On the contrary, they will be more and more a minority and English Canada will find it increasingly easy to govern without them.... Given these prospects ... Quebecers feel it is urgent to take action before it is too late.[12]

From this perspective, the longer Quebec stays in Canada the weaker her demographic and political position will be, and thus the more difficult it will be to negotiate favourable terms through which Confederation might be dissolved.

THE LINGUISTIC COMPOSITION OF QUEBEC

Immigration into Canada has posed a dual linguistic problem for Quebec: it has reduced Quebec's share of the national population, and, to the limited extent that immigrants have come to Quebec, they have threatened to erode the province's francophone majority. The proportion of immigrants adopting English rather than French has been only slightly less in Quebec than for Canada as a whole. René Lévesque estimated that of the 620,000 immigrants who came to Quebec between 1945 and 1966 (only 8 percent of whom came from France), 80 percent were absorbed into the anglophone population.[13] Quebec's principal linguistic "battleground" has been Montreal, where the west end of the island has been predominantly English, the east end predominantly French, and the middle the principal locale for immigrant settlement. It is in that middle community where the important choice between Canada's official languages has been made.

TABLE 3.1

Percentage of Quebec Population with French Mother Tongue

1931	79.7%
1941	81.6
1951	82.5
1961	81.2
1971	80.7
1976	80.0
1981	82.4

As Table 3.1 shows, however, the French language has more than held its own in Quebec despite the problems associated with immigration. Anglophones are increasingly confined to the Montreal area, though significant enclaves still exist in the eastern townships, the upper Ottawa Valley, and Hull. Anglophones are more likely than in the past to be recent immigrants to Canada. Between 1971 and 1981, the proportion of Quebecers speaking English at home declined from 14.7 percent to 12.7 percent while the proportion speaking French increased from 80.8 percent to 82.5 percent.[14] The proportion of students attending French schools increased from 83.4 percent in 1976–77 to 87.5 percent in 1982–83, and is expected to reach between 91 percent and 92 percent by 1993–94.[15] Here it should be noted, though, that the very factors which are strengthening the French language in Quebec (primarily an anglophone exodus) are undercutting the demographic strength of Quebec in Canada.

THE LINGUISTIC COMPOSITION OF CANADA OUTSIDE QUEBEC

The Canadian population outside Quebec is often referred to as "English Canada," a term that neglects both anglophones within Quebec and francophones outside Quebec, groups which play critical roles in Canadian language politics. It also distorts our perception of the non-French community, which has become progressively less English, more ethnically diverse or multi-cultural, and more *Canadian* over time.[16] Whereas 88 percent of the non-French population was of British descent in 1871, that proportion has fallen to only 60 percent today. Yet, while "English Canada" is much more heterogeneous in its regional, ethnic, and religious composition than is "French Canada," this greater heterogeneity has not affected the supremacy of the English language outside Quebec.

The 942,080 Canadians of French mother tongue living outside Quebec at the time of the 1981 census made up only 5.3 percent non-Quebec population. This proportion has declined from 7.8 percent in 1941, and is expected to decline further in the years ahead.[17] In the past, Canada was sprinkled with French

Canadian communities whose relatively self-contained educational, social, and religious institutions preserved the French language. Today, that isolation has disappeared in the face of social and technological change, and the linguistic assimilation of francophones has been progressive and far-reaching. (A possible exception here is the Acadian community in New Brunswick.) Even the small proportion of non-Quebec residents whose mother tongue is French overstates the strength of the French language outside Quebec, as many such Canadians have been or are being assimilated into the anglophone community. When anglophones and francophones have come into contact anywhere across the country, linguistic assimilation has favoured anglophones except in those cases where francophones make up more than 95 percent of the population.[18]

The linguistic trends inside and outside Quebec reveal that *linguistic segregation is increasing* in Canada. The francophone proportion of Quebec's population is increasing, and will continue to increase, while the francophone proportion of the non-Quebec population is decreasing, and will continue to decrease. As a consequence, Canada's francophone population is increasingly concentrated within Quebec. (In the 1981 census, 96 percent of those who spoke only French, 56 percent of those who spoke both French and English, and 77 percent of the two groups combined resided in Quebec.) This trend of linguistic segregation threatens francophone minorities outside Quebec and the anglophone minority inside that province, and raises concerns about the long-term viability of national policies to promote bilingualism. As Smiley notes,

The ongoing territorial separation ... means that a decreasing proportion of Canadians experience duality as an important circumstance of daily life.... Because of this, the resistance of most non-francophones to a view that the essential nature of their country is dualistic is understandable....[19]

While the national linguistic split may be approximately three to one, anglophones to francophones, nobody lives in such a community. As Table 3.2 shows, we live in provincial communities where the linguistic balance is much more lopsided. Our local communities are likely to be even more homogeneous in their linguistic composition. Thus the national "average" has little resemblance to the linguistic reality that most Canadians experience.

QUEBECOIS, ANGLO-QUEBECERS, AND FRENCH CANADIANS

Through the use of a set diagram incorporating two overlapping segments of the Canadian population—those living in Quebec and those whose mother tongue is French—Figure 3.4 illustrates the three linguistic groups around which this chapter will be structured. The largest group is the Québécois, defined here as the francophone residents of Quebec. This, of course, is a rather barren definition,

TABLE 3.2

Linguistic Composition of Canada, 1981 Census

	English only	French only	Both English and French	Neither English nor French
Canada	66.9%	16.6%	15.3%	1.2%
Newfoundland	97.6	<.1	2.3	<.1
Prince Edward Island	91.7	.2	8.1	<.1
Nova Scotia	92.3	.2	7.4	.1
New Brunswick	60.5	13.0	26.5	.1
Quebec	6.7	60.1	32.4	.8
Ontario	86.7	.7	10.8	1.7
Manitoba	90.3	.3	7.9	1.5
Saskatchewan	94.6	.1	4.6	.8
Alberta	92.4	.2	6.4	1.0
British Columbia	92.8	.1	5.7	1.4
Territories	83.9	.1	6.7	9.3

and the reader should be aware of the emotional baggage associated with the term. René Lévesque, for example, began his independence manifesto with the statement "We are *Québécois*," and then elaborated: "what that means first and foremost—and if need be, all that it means—is that we are attached to this one corner of the earth where we can be completely ourselves: this Quebec, the only place where we have the unmistakable feeling that 'here we can really be at home'."[20]

Anglo-Quebecers, a residual category made up of Quebec residents whose mother tongue is other than French, form the second largest group. This increasingly heterogeneous group encompasses the descendants of United Empire Loyalists whose roots in the province go back to the 1770s, more recent immigrants to Quebec who have assimilated into the English rather than into the French linguistic community, and those anglophones who have moved to Quebec from other provinces. The third group is made up of those of French mother tongue living outside Quebec. With the emergence of "Québécois" as a group identity, the term "French Canadian" has come to be more specifically identified with these non-Quebec francophones. Interestingly, the federally funded organization for this group is called *Francophones hors Quebec*, a label that describes the group by what it is not rather than by reference to a more positive, national affiliation such as is embodied in the term French Canadian. A fourth, and the smallest, group (not shown in Figure 3.4), composed of bilingual Canadians whose mother tongue

FIGURE 3.4

The Three Nodes of Linguistic Politics

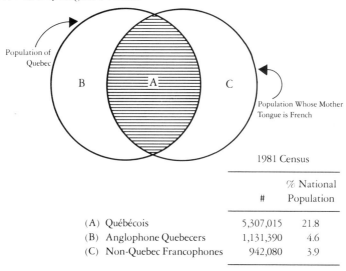

| | 1981 Census | |
	#	% National Population
(A) Québécois	5,307,015	21.8
(B) Anglophone Quebecers	1,131,390	4.6
(C) Non-Quebec Francophones	942,080	3.9

is English rather than French, is now beginning to emerge as an important political constituency.

The Québécois

In order to set the stage for a discussion of language policy in Quebec, some historical background is needed. This will be provided through a brief look at the Union Nationale government of Maurice Duplessis, the Quiet Revolution, and the Parti Québécois.

DUPLESSIS AND THE UNION NATIONALE

Revolutionary change must be measured against the benchmark of the past, the essence of the new being the negation of the old. For the Quiet Revolution of the 1960s, that benchmark became the Duplessis years, "la Grande Noirceur" (the "great darkness" or the "dark ages"). Yet we also find in the Duplessis years one of the more enduring features of Quebec life—the use of the provincial state to protect Québécois interests and to hold at bay the national anglophone community and its perceived political agent, the Government of Canada.

The Duplessis years began with the victory of the Union Nationale in the 1936 provincial election. The victory had been put together by a coalition of nationalist and Conservative elements, with control of the new party quickly coming to rest in the hands of Maurice Duplessis, who was to lead the party until his death in 1959. Although the Union Nationale was defeated in 1939, it rebounded to win large majorities in 1944, 1948, 1952, and 1956 before narrowly losing to the Liberals in 1960. With a platform stressing Quebec nationalism, Catholic values, and strident anti-communism, the party's electoral appeal extended outward from its heartland in rural and small-town Quebec to encompass a majority of the francophone constituencies in Montreal and Quebec City.

The Union Nationale's first defeat in 1939 helped establish its long-term success. Duplessis called the election three weeks after the outbreak of the Second World War, contending "... that the federal government was using the sweeping powers it possessed under the War Measures Act as a pretext for curtailing the rights of the province under the British North America Act."[21] (Here we have an example of the Canadian tendency to perceive the world through the narrow prism of federal–provincial relations!) Quite rightly, Duplessis's campaign was seen as a direct challenge to the national war effort, and Ottawa was quick to respond. The Quebec ministers in Mackenzie King's Liberal government took the unusual step of campaigning in the provincial election, stating that they were the only barrier to military conscription (see Chapter Eight), and that they would resign from the federal cabinet if Duplessis won. Faced with this prospect and the certainty of conscription should the Conservatives form the national Government, the Quebec voters elected sixty-nine Liberals and only fourteen Union Nationale candidates. However, it proved to be a Pyrrhic victory for the provincial Liberals when the King government was eventually forced to impose conscription despite intense opposition from Quebec. In the 1944 provincial election the Union Nationale became the nationalist vessel into which anti-conscription sentiment was poured, and the party captured forty-eight seats compared to thirty-seven for the Liberals.

The Second World War and the post-war expansion of the federal government (see Chapter Seven) threatened the constitutional autonomy of Quebec, the protection of which has been a primary objective for Quebec governments from Confederation to the 1980s. Although he clothed it in the garb of Quebec nationalism, Duplessis defended a classic vision of the federal state; the provinces should be sovereign and autonomous within their own constitutional domain. At the 1950 federal–provincial conference, Duplessis stated: "I definitely and firmly believe that Canada is and should always be a federation of autonomous provinces,"[22] a stance he placed before the provincal electorate in the campaigns of 1948, 1952, and 1956.

Duplessis defended provincial autonomy in the face of a variety of federal incursions including unemployment insurance, family allowances, a national plan of hospital insurance, and the construction of the Trans-Canada Highway. Following the expiration of wartime tax agreements, Ottawa and Quebec clashed on the collection and share of personal and corporate income taxes. Duplessis also cam-

Le Chef, Maurice Duplessis, leader of the Union Nationale from 1936 until his death in 1959.

Canapress Photo Service

paigned against federal immigration policy, post-war loans to the United Kingdom, and foreign aid to developing countries. In the 1948 provincial campaign, the Union Nationale slogan was *"Les liberaux donnent aux étrangers; Duplessis donne a sa province."*

Duplessis, in step with most nationalist Quebec intellectuals of his time, opposed the expansion of the provincial state on ideological grounds as much as he opposed the expansion of the federal state on constitutional grounds. Schools, hospitals, and social services remained almost entirely in private, mostly church, hands. The growth of the Quebec provincial state, a quite different matter than the constitutional defence of its legislative domain, was to await and characterize the Quiet Revolution.

Although Duplessis was vigilant to the point of extremism in warding off constitutional intrusions by Ottawa, his governments actively encouraged the intrusion of Anglo-Canadian and American capital into the Quebec economy through low taxes and royalties, and through a legislative environment that crippled provincial trade unions. The Duplessis government and the anglophone business elite enjoyed a close and mutually beneficial working relationship. The business community gave Duplessis full authority within the political arena in return for freedom from state intervention and a restrained trade union movement.[23] The relationship was cemented by generous campaign contributions which fuelled the legendary Union Nationale patronage machine.[24] Duplessism, which Clift describes as "the corruption of the social and personal bonds which people in traditional societies have towards one another," was part of the Union Nationale legacy.[25]

While a close relationship between the business community and provincial governments was not unusual in Canada, it had the effect in Quebec of reinforcing the linguistic segmentation of the provincial economy. This segmentation was captured in the expression "capital speaks English and labour speaks French." Capital and labour were bridged by bilingual supervisors and foremen drawn almost exclusively from the francophone community. Thus the class division inherent in any industrialized society reinforced and was reinforced by the linguistic cleavage. Here it should be stressed, however, that Duplessis was not without supporters among the francophone elite, many of whom believed that distinctive French Canadian cultural values could only be preserved through isolation from the secular and anglophone world of commerce. Duplessis, in an explicit political alliance with the Catholic church, stuck to the tacit bargain that followed the Treaty of Paris: economic control would rest in English hands while control over social and cultural affairs would rest with the Catholic Church. As a consequence, the economic horizon for Quebec francophones was restricted.

For the many Quebec intellectuals and labour leaders radicalized during the Asbestos strike (*see Glossary*) in 1949, and for those Canadians outside the province who followed Quebec affairs, Duplessis symbolized an old, almost archaic, Quebec. His death in 1959, followed by the defeat of the Union Nationale government a year later, strengthened this symbolic role; he became the antithesis to, and thus helped define, the Quiet Revolution. The excesses of his administration—the authoritarianism, the patronage machine and electoral corruption, the political influence of the Catholic church, the antediluvian approach to trade unions—came to be highlighted while the important threads of continuity in his constitutional stance, threads reaching back to the confederation agreement and forward to the Parti Québécois, were often overlooked.

THE QUIET REVOLUTION

The 1960 election of Jean Lesage's Liberal government marks the onset of the "Quiet Revolution," an event of mythological proportions in Quebec. The "revolution" was not so much in the social underpinnings of Quebec, which had been in a state of transition since the 1930s, as it was in the province's state of mind. It was in the "beliefs about the purpose and character of society and polity," as McRoberts and Posgate describe it, that the change was "so profound and far-reaching that we can see how many would have found it 'revolutionary.' "[26] Even in this respect, however, the extent of change should not be exaggerated.[27] To call the Quiet Revolution the "springtime of Quebec," a phrase that has become commonplace, is to exaggerate the seasonal change and to understate the threads of continuity which link Quebec's past, present, and future.

The Quiet Revolution entailed an acceptance of the modern economic order and an enthusiasm for urban life. Gone was the cultural nostalgia for the values of a rural society long since departed. More importantly, the Quiet Revolution was to address the linguistic stratification of Quebec. In a province where 80 percent of the population was of French mother tongue, those who spoke only English earned substantially more on average than those who spoke only French *or those who were bilingual.* One could debate whether this reflected a host of cultural values and economic choices made by generations of francophone and anglophone Quebecers, whether it reflected economic reality on a continent where the vast majority of the population was anglophone, or whether it reflected the raw edge of corporate power. It is clear, however, that the apparent injustice of a situation in which the language of the majority was an economic burden lay at the root of the language legislation that was to emerge from the Quiet Revolution.

Linguistic tension grew in step with the Quiet Revolution's secularization of Quebec society. In the past, the Catholic church had played a dominant role in the province. It controlled the educational system (apart from the Protestant schools) and most social services, was a central actor in the trade union movement, and had a pervasive influence in political affairs. By 1960 this influence was on the wane as the Church withdrew from an active role in political affairs and as many Quebecers withdrew from the Church. At the onset of the Quiet Revolution more than 80 percent of the Catholic population of Quebec (which was more than 80 percent of the Quebec population) went to Mass every Sunday; by 1983 the attendance rate had fallen to only 25 percent.[28] With the decline of the church, the protection of the French language and cultural values passed from clerical hands to the secular hands of the provincial state.

The most important short-term impact of secularization came with the 1964 transfer of control over education from the Church to the Quebec Ministry of Education, a transfer associated with the modernization of the educational curriculum and a rapid growth in the proportion of students pursuing post-secondary education. No longer were post-secondary students channelled through the classical colleges into the three traditional francophone occupations—law, medicine, and the clergy—where they could work in French and without entanglement in the English business community. Graduates began to emerge with degrees in business administration, the social sciences, engineering, and communications. No longer rejected, the modern economy was being embraced.

English, however, was the language of work in that economy, at least at the levels to which the new graduates aspired. If one chose to or could work only in French, the limited employment opportunities in the private sector were not commensurate with the skills newly acquired from the secularized educational system. Immersion in the English work environment was equally unattractive given the personal cost of learning a second language, the handicap of operating in a second language, and the perceived danger of absorbing anglophone cultural values embedded in the workplace. From this dilemma came the pressure for legislation that would turn the ability to speak French into an economic asset and shift the burden of bilingualism from the francophone majority in Quebec to the anglophone minority.

Another alternative for young francophone graduates was to pursue a career within the Quebec public service, where French was the language of work. In the face of limited employment prospects in the private sector, educational reform thus promoted a rapidly expanding public service staffed with young, aggressive, well-trained, and highly ambitious people, similar in most respects to the reader. They were to spearhead Quebec's bureaucratic assault on the Canadian federal system, an assault designed to shift jurisdictional responsibilities *and the accompanying career opportunities* from Ottawa to Quebec City.[29] In a related move the leadership of René Lévesque, then Minister of Natural Resources in the Lesage government, led in 1962 to the creation of Hydro-Québec through the nationalization of the province's privately owned electric power companies. Upon nationalization French replaced English as the language of work, and Hydro-Québec became the showpiece for francophone managerial and technological competence, and an important employment pole for nationalistic francophones.

It was the new Québécois middle class—the bureaucrats, writers, artists, intellectuals, teachers, musicians, technocrats, communications experts, and business managers—who derived the greatest personal benefits from the Quiet Revolution, and who stood the most to gain from independence.[30] (Not coincidentally, such individuals outside Quebec are the ones who stand to gain the most from Canadian policies of cultural nationalism vis-à-vis the United States.) The benefits of nationalism are rarely distributed evenly across social classes, and Quebec was to prove no exception. Within Quebec, trade union leaders have argued that the replacement of an anglophone managerial class with a francophone managerial class is not enough, that for a true revolution to occur there must also be a redistribution of wealth across social classes. To date, however, the primary income redistribution arising from the Quiet Revolution has been between anglophones and francophones rather than among social classes in the francophone community.

Before the Quiet Revolution, Quebec nationalism had been defensive in character, a bulwark for *la foi, la langue, la race* (faith, language, and race). Distinctive cultural values embedded in the Catholic religion and French language were to be protected by the federal division of powers and by the isolation of French Canadians from the commercialism of the English world. By 1960, however, both forms of protection were breaking down. The federal government was encroaching upon Quebec's political autonomy, and the modern mass media had breached the cultural walls of "Fortress Quebec." In this environment nationalism based on *la survivance* was not enough, and the theme of the Quiet Revolution became *la rattrapage*, the desire to catch up to the modern world, to make up for the winter of the Duplessis years. Here Jean Blain referred to the *déblocage* of the sixties, "the progress of Quebec at a more normal rate towards the ideals familiar to every modern society."[31] For some, particularly those associated with the Quebec Liberal party, the rejection of the Duplessis era led to the rejection of nationalism itself. For others, nationalism became more outward looking, expressing a new sense of confidence that Quebec could compete on equal terms in the modern social and economic order. For all, *la langue* rather than *la foi* or *la race* became the overarching concern.[32]

The Quiet Revolution initially had a positive reception outside Quebec, where it was assumed that *rattrapage* would strengthen national unity by moving Quebec into the Canadian and North American mainstreams, and that the language divide could be bridged by a national commitment to bilingualism. In fact, the Quiet Revolution exacerbated language conflict both inside and outside the province as francophones sought to establish French as one of the two national languages in Canada and as the dominant language in Quebec. Because of its *étatist* orientation, in which the provincial state was seen as the principal vehicle for *rattrapage*, the Quiet Revolution also posed a fundamental challenge to the Canadian federal system. As Mallory explained in 1971, it was to the provincial state that Quebec leaders looked for economic development, social change, and career opportunities; "for them, these things must be done by their own French-Canadian state of Quebec, and not by Ottawa."[33]

The Liberal campaign slogan in the 1962 provincial election—"*maîtres chez nous*" or "masters in our own house"—became the slogan of the Quiet Revolution. For some, this meant the rollback of federal intrusions into the provincial legislative domain and the search for greater fiscal transfers to the Quebec government so that it could meet its growing legislative commitments. Yet for many Québécois, rollbacks were not enough, for the existing house, as defined by the federal division of powers, was too small. If, they argued, the Quebec government was to meet its responsibilities as the "national" government for French Canada, Quebec needed at the very least a restructured federal system with expanded provincial powers. This would still mean, however, that some important decisions would continue to be made by the federal government in which francophones were a minority, and a shrinking minority at that. For those who believed that "national" decisions should be made within the context of Quebec rather than Canada, any federal limitation on "*maîtres chez nous*" was unacceptable. In this sense, the independence movement can be seen as a logical, though not a necessary, extension of the Quiet Revolution.

This growing unrest with the federal status quo began to cause considerable unease outside Quebec. There were no comfortable answers to *the* political question of the late 1960s and 1970s: "what does Quebec want?"[34] Those French Canadians who defended the federal system and who sought to exercise the power of French Canada through the government in Ottawa—people like Jean Chrétien, Marc Lalonde, Jean Marchand, Gérard Pelletier, and Pierre Trudeau—asked for a national commitment to bilingualism that many English Canadians were not prepared to make. Demands from the government of Quebec for a radically restructured federal system touched off a much broader assault by other provincial governments on the powers of the national government. Of greatest concern was the growing support in Quebec for independence, for the dismantling of the Canadian state. Independence, it should be stressed, was seen not as a Quebec issue but as a direct threat to the very survival of Canada. As John Meisel wrote in 1973, "for many English Canadians the internal threat to the continuation of Canada is emotionally and in every other way the equivalent of the challenge to their own survival experienced by most French Canadian nationalists."[35]

INDEPENDENCE AND THE PARTI QUEBECOIS

Although there had been sporadic agitation for Quebec's independence since the Rebellion of 1837, only in the 1960s did independence emerge as a serious option commanding a reasonable degree of popular support, a broad intellectual following, and the backing of organized political parties. Indeed, the 1960s witnessed a plethora of separatist groups, some of which sought Quebec's independence as a means to a fundamental transformation of the social and economic order. Here it should be noted that such groups, and indeed the Quiet Revolution, reflected in part a broader current of social and political unrest sweeping across North America and western Europe, a current incorporating student radicalism, the American civil rights movement, opposition to the war in Vietnam, and early manifestations of the ecology and feminist movements.

The first and most important of the early independence groups, the *Rassemblement pour l'Independence nationale* (RIN), emerged only months after the Liberal victory in 1960. Other groups, while enjoying less popular support, achieved a high public profile through the use of terrorist tactics. Quebec politics during the 1960s were marked by bombs, politically motivated robberies, and extremist rhetoric borrowing heavily from radical movements in the United States, Cuba, and across the Third World.[36] Quebec was portrayed as a colony (or a colony within a colony, depending upon one's perception of the Canadian–American relationship) destined, like other colonies in the Third World, for national liberation.[37] Repeated reference was made to the fact that the General Assembly of the United Nations was rapidly filling with countries that were smaller, less populous and much poorer than Quebec.

While the colonial analogy continues to inform political debate on the place of Quebec in Canada, the radical stage of the independence movement was brought to a close by two events. The first was the founding of the Parti Québécois in 1967. Led by René Lévesque, the PQ grew out of the *Mouvement Souveraineté-Association* and retained sovereignty-association as the foundation for its political platform. After the RIN was disbanded and largely absorbed by the PQ in 1968, the PQ dominated the independence movement, though smaller, more radical groups remained. In Lévesque, a former broadcast journalist, the independence movement had found an inspired and inspiring leader. A seasoned politician and master communicator, Lévesque was able to orchestrate the ideologically diverse independence movement. He was the ideal foil for the province's most popular federalist spokesman, Pierre Trudeau. Lévesque was also effective in carrying the case for independence into English Canada. Unlike most of his contemporaries, Lévesque tried to show that Quebec's independence would be to the advantage of English Canada, that it would free the English Canadian majority from continual compromise with the French Canadian minority. The rejection of independence, he argued, would mean perpetual wrangling "over everything and over nothing"; it would mean "the sterilization of two collective personalities which, having squandered the most precious part of their potential, would weaken each other so completely that they would have no other choice but to drown themselves in the ample bosom of 'America.'"[38]

The second event was the October 1970 kidnapping of James Cross, British Trade Commissioner in Montreal, and Pierre Laporte, Quebec's Minister of Labour, by the FLQ (Front de Libération du Québec). Cross was eventually freed but Laporte was killed, the first political murder in Canada since the 1868 assassination of MP Thomas D'Arcy McGee by an Irish nationalist. The kidnappings and associated political turmoil came to be known as the "October Crisis," in response to which the federal government imposed the War Measures Act, giving law enforcement agencies extraordinary powers of search and arrest. The Canadian Armed Forces took on a highly visible role in guarding political leaders and public institutions, membership in the FLQ was declared a post facto crime, and over four hundred people were arrested in Quebec, none of whom were linked to the kidnappings.

While the imposition of the War Measures Act enjoyed strong public support at the time, even in Quebec, it has subsequently been the topic of intense and generally critical debate.[39] However, regardless of the merits of the federal response, the October Crisis did mark the disappearance of terrorist factions within the Quebec independence movement. Whether violence was dropped for strategic reasons, given Ottawa's demonstrated willingness to counter force with superior force,[40] or out of a sense of revulsion toward the excesses of the FLQ is not clear. What is clear is that in the wake of the October Crisis the electoral aspirations of the Parti Québécois became virtually the exclusive concern of what had been an ideologically diverse and somewhat fragmented independence movement.

In the 1970 provincial election the Parti Québécois captured 23 percent of the popular vote but elected only 7 members in the 110-seat National Assembly. In 1973 the PQ won only 6 seats, compared to 102 seats for the Liberals, though its share of the popular vote increased to 30 percent. On November 15, 1976, the PQ increased its vote again to 41 percent and captured 71 seats while 26 seats were won by the Liberals, 11 by the Union Nationale, and one each by the *Ralliement des créditistes* and by the *Parti national populaire*. For the first time, a government had been elected which was committed to the withdrawal of Quebec from the federation. Ironically, however, the PQ's success stemmed as much from its promise *not* to secede, or at least not to interpet its election as an endorsation of independence, as it did from the party's support for independence.[41]

In the 1976 campaign the Parti Québécois had promised that a referendum on sovereignty-association would be held before any steps were taken toward independence. This strategy of *étapisme* (independence by stages) was based on public opinion polls which showed that support for the PQ and its leader ran consistently ahead of support for independence. It would enable voters to support the PQ while reserving judgment on independence. By postponing the decision on independence, the PQ assumed that time and demography were on its side, given that opposition to independence was most widespread among older voters and that support was strongest among the younger Québécois, many of whom were not yet in the electorate.

Sovereignty-Association

The term sovereignty-association *binds together the goal of political independence (or sovereignty) for Quebec with both a recognition and acceptance of Quebec's economic integration with the rest of Canada. Its closest model comes from the European Economic Community, wherein still-sovereign states pursue coordinated and integrated economic policies.*

The proposal for sovereignty-association calls for Quebec and Canada-minus-Quebec to negotiate a series of agreements designed to preserve the existing benefits of economic association. Such agreements might yield a common tariff union, a common currency, the free flow of goods, people, and capital, and joint economic institu- *tions such as a central bank. These agreements, however, would take the form of treaties between sovereign states, and hence would be flexible and adaptable rather than constitutional in character. The government of Quebec would be the only national government for Quebecers. Quebec residents would not elect representatives to Parliament, but instead would be represented in Ottawa by the Quebec government.*

Sovereignty-association would provide an equal partnership between Quebec and the rest of Canada, a partnership based on diplomatic norms of equality between sovereign states. Quebec would continue to enjoy the economic benefits of the larger Canadian union (as would other provinces) without being reduced to minority status within the Canadian state. In essence, then, sovereignty-association would preserve economic linkages while creating a new form of political association.

Sovereignty-association is easier to grasp as a concept than as a process. Before the terms of association could be agreed upon, Quebec would have to declare its independence or sovereignty Yet it would be difficult for Quebecers to endorse sovereignty before the terms of association were known.

For almost four years after the election of the PQ government, Canadians inside and outside Quebec waited for the referendum shoe to drop. In late 1979, Premier Lévesque set the stage with an emotional call to the people of Quebec, describing a yes vote in the forthcoming referendum as "... the only road that can open up the horizon and guarantee us a free, proud and adult national existence."[42] When the referendum was held on May 20, 1980, voters were not asked if they supported independence per se, but whether or not they supported the Quebec government entering into sovereignty-association negotiations with Ottawa, the final and at that point unknown pact being left for voter approval in a subsequent referendum. The intense referendum campaign, however, addressed the broader issue of independence rather than the specific question that was posed. The *"oui"* forces favoured independence in some fashion and at some time, though the immediate consequences of a yes vote were not at all clear. The *"non"* forces, united by the slogan *"mon non est québécois,"* favoured the retention of Canadian federalism, though not necessarily the federal arrangements in place at the time.[43] Indeed, the *"non"* campaign explicitly linked a no vote in the referendum to the promise of a "renewed federalism," the specifics of which were not set forth. The campaign engaged all political forces within Quebec, including the seventy-four Quebec Liberal MPs led by Jean Chrétien and Prime Minister Trudeau. To an important degree the contest was personalized—Lévesque against Trudeau and Quebec Liberal leader Claude Ryan—making it a battle not only between competing visions of Quebec's future but between those leaders who, over the last decade, had symbolized and fought for those competing visions.

In the end, 60 percent voted no and 40 percent voted yes; the sovereignty-association proposal had been defeated. Although the *"oui"* camp captured close to 50 percent of the francophone vote, little attempt was made to claim a moral victory. The independence forces, however, had not been routed. In April 1981, the PQ government was reelected with an *increased* majority. In March 1982, an opinion poll conducted for *La Presse* found 28 percent of Quebecers supported sovereignty-association and an additional 13 percent supported outright independence; among francophones alone the total reached 48 percent.[44] While the emotional pitch of the independence debate has been lowered in the years since the referendum, the debate itself continues.

Pierre Elliott Trudeau, elected in 1968 as the leader of the Liberal Party and the Prime Minister of Canada, was a strong advocate of a bilingual Canada and a forceful opponent of the independence movement in Quebec.

Canapress Photo Service

René Lévesque, founder of the Parti Québécois, led his party to victory in the 1976 Quebec provincial election but failed to carry Quebec in the 1980 referendum on sovereignty-association.

Canapress Photo Service

QUEBEC LANGUAGE LEGISLATION

Although francophones in Quebec made up 80 percent of the population and controlled the electoral process at the onset of the Quiet Revolution, they earned considerably less than anglophones in the province and shouldered virtually the entire burden of bilingualism. Initially, little was done to overcome the linguistic income gap, and anglophone domination of the provincial economy continued unabated.[45] Yet the discrepancy between the political power and the economic subservience of the Québécois was inherently unstable. Some legislative response was inevitable.

In essence, Quebec language legislation would try to make French the language of work within the province; to make French more visible on signs, billboards, and advertisements; and to ensure that immigrants to Quebec assimilated into the francophone majority. All of these objectives were seen as essential if francophones were to enjoy a full range of economic opportunities, and if the French language and culture were to be kept afloat on the North American anglophone sea. The primary concern lay with the francophone majority in Quebec and not with francophone minorities in other provinces, who were in any event beyond the legislative reach of the Quebec National Assembly.

The first major piece of language legislation was steered through the National Assembly by Robert Bourassa's Liberal government in 1974. Bill 22 declared French to be the "official language" of Quebec. It also required students who wished to enroll in schools where English was the language of instruction to pass an English proficiency test, a measure designed to channel the children of immigrants into French schools. Bill 22 encouraged the use of French in the workplace by stating that contracts with the provincial government might hinge upon "*francisation*." Businesses, however, were not forced to adopt French as the language of work.

Bill 22 was strenuously attacked by Québécois nationalists, who argued that it did not go far enough, and by the English and immigrant communities, who argued that it went too far. The most contentious aspect of the legislation was the English proficiency requirement limiting the freedom of parents to send their children to the school of their choice. As it turned out, Bill 22 had little impact on the pattern of school enrolments, in part because the English proficiency barrier could be overcome by immigrant parents who made the effort, and in part because the legislation did not prevent francophone parents from enrolling their children in English schools.[46] In the 1973–74 school year, before Bill 22 came into effect, 16.0 percent of pre-college students were enrolled in schools where the language of instruction was English; with the passage of Bill 22, this proportion marginally *increased* over the next three years.[47]

In 1977 the new Parti Québécois government passed Bill 101, Quebec's French Language Charter (*Charte de la langue francaise*). Bill 101 did not depart from the principles of Bill 22 so much as it strengthened both their application and their extension into the Quebec society.[48] French was reaffirmed as the official language of Quebec,[49] official bilingualism was rejected, and the only legislative reference to English was the passing mention of "other languages" in use in Quebec. English-language schooling was restricted to children with at least one parent educated in English *in Quebec*, to children who were attending an English school when Bill 101 came into effect, to children who had a brother or sister already in an English school, and to children whose parents were living in Quebec in 1977 but were educated in English elsewhere. Thus immigrants, people moving into Quebec from elsewhere in Canada, *and Quebec francophones* were denied educational freedom of choice. In order to strengthen the visibility of French, all public signs and advertisements were to be in French only. Municipalities, school boards, and hospitals, many of which were in English communities serving a largely anglophone clientele, were required to use French as the internal language of communication. The right to work in French was given legislative support, and firms employing more than one hundred people were required to establish labour–management francisation committees. (The legal requirements for francisation, however, could be met by improving the French-language skills of anglophone employees rather than by hiring or promoting francophones.) *L'Office de la langue francaise* was established to oversee the legislation, and its more zealous officials became known as the "tongue troopers."

In late 1983 the Quebec National Assembly moved to relax some of the provisions of Bill 101. Limited recognition was given to Quebec's English community by an addition to the preamble stating that the Assembly pursues the objective of making French Quebec's official and working language "in a spirit of justice and openness, and showing respect for the institutions of the English Quebec community and of ethnic minorities, whose precious contribution to the development of Quebec it recognizes." English educational rights were extended to children from those provinces which offered French schooling similar to the level of English schooling provided in Quebec. Only New Brunswick qualified at the time, but Ontario, the province from which Quebec employers would be most likely to recruit, could well qualify in the future. Students who had spent at least three years in an English-language high school in Quebec no longer had to pass a French proficiency test to practise as professionals in the province. Local institutions were no longer required to operate internally in French or to ensure that all employees spoke French, as long as French-language services could be provided. Bilingual signs were allowed, but only for stores specializing in products "typical of a foreign country or particular ethnic group." Under the terms of the legislation, English Canadians did not qualify as a "particular ethnic group."

These amendments appeared to enjoy broad support from the francophone community. In a 1983 poll conducted for *Alliance Quebec*, the political arm of the English-language community in Quebec, 71 percent of the francophone respondents supported the right of anglophones who move to Quebec to have their children educated in English, 72 percent would allow other languages to accompany French on public signs, and 89 percent would allow anglophone institutions to function internally in English.[50]

Legislative protection of the French language in Quebec has been so successful that by the 1990s it may no longer be required. In 1983 Camille Laurin, Quebec's Minister of Education, predicted that in eight to ten years the objectives of Bill 101 would be reached, and that in the future legislative protection may instead be required for minority languages, including English.[51] Anglophones remaining in the province are increasingly bilingual and are more prone to use French in the workplace. Public opinion polls have shown that the proportion of English mother tongue respondents who spoke only English on the job has fallen from 64 percent in 1971 to only 32 percent in 1982.[52]

Though successful, Quebec's language legislation has been contentious in many respects. Its educational provisions, which give precedence to the collective interests of the francophone majority over individual freedom of choice, have been the source of bitter confrontations. (Nationalist policies, no matter what the government of origin, generally involve restrictions on individual freedom of choice, restrictions justified by reference to the greater collective or national good.) Even though francisation has not been extended to corporate head offices and centres of research and development, and even though many exceptions have been granted, it has probably impaired economic growth. It is likely that language legislation has also curtailed migration into the province, be it from other parts of Canada or abroad, and has thus marginally eroded Quebec's demographic weight within the Canadian community. Language legislation has entailed extensive government intervention into the economy and society in order to curtail what had been the progressive erosion of French in the preexisting linguistic "free market." By far the most serious conflict, however, has been with the bilingualism policies of the Canadian government and their entrenchment within the Charter of Rights and Freedoms.

On July 26, 1984, a unanimous ruling of the Supreme Court struck down the "Quebec clause" in Bill 101 which required parents (or at least one parent) to have received their primary education *in English in Quebec* before their children could attend English schools in Quebec. In upholding the 1982 decision by the Quebec Court of Appeal, the Supreme Court ruled that the Bill 101 provision was inconsistent with Section 23 of the Charter of Rights and Freedoms, the so-called "Canada clause" which guarantees Canadian citizens the right to educate their children in their language—whether English or French—anywhere in Canada where numbers permit. In its case before the Supreme Court, the government of Quebec recognized the inconsistency but argued that the Bill 101 provision was consistent with Article One of the Charter, which states that the rights and freedoms guaranteed by the Charter are subject to "such reasonable limits prescribed by law as can be demonstrably justified in a free and democratic society." The Quebec submission concluded that the limitation placed on English education in Quebec "is reasonable because it is the expression of a collective right of the francophone majority—vulnerable because it is a minority in Canada and only constitutes 2.5 per cent of the population of North America—to assure its rightful cultural security." The Supreme Court did not concur, ruling that all English Canadian citizens have the right to have their children educated in English in Quebec.

The Supreme Court ruling is unlikely to have a dramatic effect on Quebec. Firms may find it easier to recruit in English Canada, though not in the United States. For immigrant children in Quebec, Bill 101's provisions have not been altered by the Supreme Court ruling. Nor has the educational situation been altered for francophone families in Quebec, as the Charter provisions do not extend the right of an English education to the children of francophone parents. Prior to the Supreme Court ruling, a study for the *Conseil de la langue francaise* by demographer Michel Paille predicted that the application of the Canada clause would increase the proportion of Quebec students attending English schools only from 13.1 to 13.5 percent.[53] As Liberal MNA Richard French said at the time of the ruling,

The future of the French language is not going to be played out in the courtroom or in the classroom—but in front of a TV set and a computer screen. If you compare the importance of this decision with the importance of cablevision in Chicoutimi with American TV channels, or the impact of Boy George and Michael Jackson on the Quebec record industry, or the importance of English as the language of international technology, you are talking about another order of magnitude.[54]

Regardless of its practical importance, the Supreme Court ruling is of great symbolic importance. In a policy area of vital concern to the Quebec government, the Charter, which has yet to be endorsed by the Quebec government, prevailed over legislation passed by the Quebec National Assembly.

Anglo Quebec

Historically, Quebec's anglophones carried far greater weight than their numbers warranted. A minority within Quebec, albeit one with deep historical roots, they were able to draw upon the political power of the anglophone national majority and the cultural power of an overwhelming continental majority. Anglophones formed the economic elite in Quebec, though by no means were all Quebec anglophones part of that elite. They were the representatives of Anglo-Canadian and American capital and, in a crude sense, had the power and political protection that money can buy.[55] Anglophones also formed a sizable electoral constituency in Quebec that could be ignored only at considerable political risk. Finally, anglophone, or, more accurately, Protestant, educational institutions were constitutionally protected through Sections 93.2 and 93.3 of the Constitution Act of 1867.

Whether the historic position of Quebec anglophones can best be described as privileged, or whether it was little more than the consequence of a free market economy in which anglophones were more active participants than francophones, is not a question that can be settled here. What is clear in retrospect, however, is that their position was precarious. It was inevitable that at some point the large francophone majority would use its democratic control of the provincial political system to redress the linguistic disparities in wealth and economic opportunity. What was needed before this could occur was a more positive outlook toward state intervention in the economic order, and an altered political perspective in which Anglo-Quebecers were seen less in a Canadian context (as part of the national *majority*) and more in a Québécois context (as a provincial *minority*). The Quiet Revolution provided both.

In the wake of the Quiet Revolution and the coming to power of the Parti Québécois a decade later, Quebec anglophones underwent a dramatic transformation. They became strangers, if not imperialists, in their own land, *"les autres"* in a province vibrating to the themes of Québécois nationalism. Anglophones took up the uncomfortable garments of minority status being shed by Quebec francophones. Their relative wealth became a political stigma, and their contribution to the province was stripped of symbolic recognition as Quebec was recast as a Québécois and francophone society. Their grip on the province's business community was loosened, though not broken, by language legislation and educational reform. Many left Quebec to seek a more hospitable social and linguistic climate elsewhere in Canada. The remaining community was no longer *English* Canadian, as it had largely been in the past, but was far more diverse in its ethnic composition. It was more accurately described as a residual population of those whose mother tongue was not French, cast together and bound together by the province's language legislation.

Here it is interesting to note that Quebec's language legislation has also increased the heterogeneity of the francophone community. Such legislation has separated language and culture, with the French language becoming the primary language of communication for all cultures in Quebec. Whereas in the past francophones shared a common history, culture, and religious orientation, this will be less and less so in the future as the francophone community expands to encompass the totality of the Quebec society. Historical events like the Conquest may lose their integrative and symbolic force as a growing proportion of the francophone community comes to find its roots in a quite different historical setting.

Quebec's language legislation has set in motion a modest redistribution of economic opportunities and social advantage in which middle-class francophones have been the principal winners, and Quebec anglophones the principal losers. To defend their linguistic interests, Quebec's anglophones must rely upon their declining economic and demographic power, their cultural identification with the North American mainstream, and the language policies of the national government. However, those policies, to which we now turn, are directed more to the protection of the French language outside Quebec than to the protection of either official language within Quebec.

French Canadians and Canadian Bilingualism

Beyond the provincial jurisdiction of Quebec, language conflict has taken two forms. The first has occurred when the interests of French Canada, broadly conceived, have clashed with those of the English Canadian majority. Apart from the conscription crises (discussed in Chapter Eight) and the 1885 execution of Louis Riel following the North-West Rebellion, (*see Glossary*) this first form of conflict has been surprisingly rare.

In English Canada Riel's execution was seen as just and deserved. Prime Minister Macdonald's statement that "he shall hang though every dog in Quebec bark in his favour" captured the more moderate reaction while *The Toronto Star* (May 18, 1885) wrote: "Strangle Riel with the French flag! That is the only use that rag can have in the country." In Quebec, the reaction was dramatically different. Israel Tarte, a prominent Quebec Liberal, predicted that "at the moment when the corpse of Riel falls through the trap and twists in convulsions of agony, at that moment an abyss will be dug that will separate Quebec from English-speaking Canada, especially Ontario."[56] Tarte's prediction was borne out as 40,000 French Canadians took to the streets to burn Macdonald in effigy.

It is often assumed in Canadian political folklore that the French Canadian reaction to Riel's execution set in motion a political realignment that persisted into the 1980s. Honoré Mercier, who declared that "the murder of Riel was a declaration of war upon French-Canadian influence in Confederation," formed the Parti National and, in 1886, drove the provincial Conservatives from power in Quebec.[57] Wilfrid Laurier, who said "had I been born on the banks of the Saskatchewan I myself would have shouldered a musket," became leader of the national Liberal party and, in 1896, inaugurated a Quebec-based Liberal dynasty that was to dominate Canadian politics for most of the next ninety years.[58] While electoral statistics suggest that the role of Riel's execution has been exaggerated in explanations of both Liberal success and Conservative failure in Quebec,[59] the execution has nonetheless become an important symbol in the mythology of Canadian partisan politics.

The second form of conflict has centred on the language and educational rights of French Canadian minorities outside Quebec, with the "Manitoba Schools Question" providing a good example.[60] In 1890 the Manitoba legislature abolished the existing denominational school system, which included Catholic schools using French as the language of instruction, and replaced it with a non-sectarian public system in which English was to be the sole language of instruction. Franco-Manitobans, with ecclesiastical support from the Catholic church in Quebec, urged the Conservative government in Ottawa to disallow (*see Glossary*) the provincial legislation. The government demurred, pending an appeal to the Judicial Committee of the Privy Council. When that appeal upheld the provincial legislation, Ottawa was urged to pass remedial legislation (*see Glossary*) restoring the dual school system. This demand was deflected onto the Canadian Supreme Court, which ruled that Parliament could not pass such legislation, and then onto the Judicial Committee, which ruled that it could.

All this set the stage for the 1896 general election campaign in which the Conservatives promised remedial legislation, believing that the consequent losses in English Canada (twenty-one Conservative seats were in fact lost) could be offset by gains in Quebec, where remedial legislation was strongly supported. However, although the Liberals opposed remedial legislation and incurred the wrath of the Catholic church by doing so, Laurier's appeal to his fellow French Canadians was too great. The Liberals captured forty-nine Quebec seats, a gain of fourteen from 1891, and won the election.

In the Manitoba Schools Question, Laurier charted a constitutional course similar in principle to that followed by Quebec governments over the next ninety years. Because Laurier attached great importance to the federal division of powers in the protection of French Canada, he opposed remedial legislation as a threat to provincial autonomy. If remedial legislation was used in the short term to protect Franco-Manitobans, in the long term it could facilitate the intrusion of the English Canadian national majority into the affairs of Quebec. With respect to the use of remedial legislation, Franco-Manitobans had to be sacrificed to the greater good of provincial autonomy. Laurier did, however, work out a practical compromise with the Manitoba government.

Conflict over minority education rights returns us to a basic limitation in the federal protection of minority interests. In the specific case of French Canada, federalism provides protection *to the extent that* French Canadian interests fall within the provincial domain and *because* French Canadians form a majority in Quebec. The federal division of powers provides protection to national minorities which can be recast as provincial majorities; it provides no protection per se within the domain of the national government, and no protection for French Canadian provincial minorities. Given these limitations, it is not surprising that many French Canadians have sought protection within "Fortress Quebec," defending and where possible expanding the powers of *their* government. Nor should it be surprising that this strategy is rejected by French Canadians living in other parts of Canada, for whom Quebec is at best a fickle ally. However, it has also been rejected by a significant number of French Canadians within Quebec who see the fulfillment of French Canada taking place within the Dominion rather than within the more narrow confines of Quebec. It is this perspective that is closely associated with the writings and political leadership of Pierre Elliott Trudeau.

In reaction to the claustrophobic Duplessis years, many French Canadians sought an expanded national vision in which French and English Canada would coexist in an equal partnership rather than as the "two solitudes" so vividly portrayed by novelist Hugh MacLennan in 1945. This vision was captured and documented by the Royal Commission on Bilingualism and Biculturalism which had been established in 1963 by Prime Minister Lester Pearson "to inquire into and report upon the existing state of bilingualism and biculturalism in Canada and to recommend what steps should be taken to develop the Canadian Confederation on the basis of an equal partnership between the two founding races...." Chaired by André Laurendeau and Davidson Dunton, the B & B Commission laid the foundations for national bilingualism. However, while its call for the equality of the English and French languages—for a *bilingual* Canada—was accepted, its call for the equality of the English and French societies—for a *bicultural* Canada—was not. In its response to the commission the federal government separated the threads of language and culture which the Commissioners had woven into a single strand, arguing that *multiculturalism within a bilingual framework* was the vision which best captured the demographic reality of modern Canada.

In 1966, Prime Minister Pearson started the federal public service down what was to be a rocky road toward full bilingualism. Then in July 1969, Parliament passed the Official Languages Act which declared English and French to be Canada's official languages, guaranteed all citizens the right to communicate with the federal government in the official language of their choice, enabled employees of the federal government to work in the official language of their choice, and provided funds for second-language education across Canada.[61] Official bilingualism had arrived.

Although national bilingualism had been set in motion by Lester Pearson, it has been more closely identified with the personality and career of Pierre Trudeau, whose government introduced the 1969 Official Languages Act. His flawless command of both languages epitomized the bilingual ideal, and bilingualism was a central concern, at times even a preoccupation, of the governments he led. In *Grits*, Christina McCall-Newman captures the Trudeau image, if not mythology, in the following passage: "above all he was perfectly bilingual, with his French father and his English mother, his Jesuit education at home and his post-graduate education abroad, the pan-Canadian the country had been looking for, who fused the French and English into one, a kind of racial hermaphrodite, the unmatchable bicultural man."[62] Bilingualism was to Trudeau "... as the CPR was to John A. Macdonald, his instrument for building a continent-wide country out of a huddled group of provinces."[63]

Initially, bilingualism was well received in English Canada. It was seen as a necessary response to the Quiet Revolution and the growing independence movement in Quebec. Given the role that young francophones were beginning to play as nationalist pointmen within the Quebec public service, it seemed essential that countervailing career opportunities be opened up for francophones in Ottawa. More generally, if French Canadians were to be bottled up in Quebec by their language, the appeal of independence would be difficult to counter. Bilingualism appeared to be the price of national unity. It might also be speculated that national bilingualism played a significant role in the resurgent Canadian nationalism of the period (see Chapter Six). At a time when the British connection no longer played a very useful role in setting Canada apart from the United States, Canada's bilingual character came to satisfy the same nationalistic need.

For many English Canadians growing uneasy about the independence movement in Quebec, Trudeau was the champion they sought, the leader who would stand up to the separatists and defend Canada in a way that no anglophone of the times could do, at least in Quebec. This role was dramatically illustrated on the eve of the 1968 federal election, when Trudeau reviewed Montreal's St. Jean-Baptiste Day parade. As separatist demonstrators threw bottles at the reviewing stand, and as other dignitaries fled, Trudeau stood alone, unmoved and defiant. It was a moment of personal courage and dramatic political symbolism that anointed the new prime minister as Canada's champion against the *indépendantistes*.

Yet this role was easily misunderstood, for although Trudeau opposed the *indépendantistes* and the more extreme constitutional demands of Quebec governments, he vigorously promoted the extension of the French presence throughout the institutional fabric of the Canadian society. In its own way, Trudeau's vision of Canada was no less sweeping in the demands that it would make upon English Canadians than was the vision held by René Lévesque. As Gwyn argues, although "Trudeau and Lévesque are the heroes of opposing armies ... each has fought for his people, the French Canadians, even though Lévesque's francophones are limited to those within Quebec while Trudeau's vision encompasses all in Canada whose mother tongue is French."[64] As Gwyn goes on to argue, Trudeau sought to extend the French fact across Canada while Lévesque sought to consolidate and defend it within Quebec. In either case, English Canadians faced the linguistic transformation of their society.

Official bilingualism was not new in Canada. Section 133 of the 1867 Constitution Act provided for the use of both English and French in Parliament, the courts of Canada, and the legislature and courts of Quebec. Thus on Parliament Hill both languages were used in debate and Hansard. All Acts of Parliament appeared in both languages, and even the prayer beginning each sitting day was read by the Speaker in English and French on alternate days. Bilingual stamps appeared in 1927, bilingual currency in 1936, and in 1962 Prime Minister Diefenbaker introduced bilingual federal cheques and simultaneous translation in Parliament. Such forms of bilingualism, it must be emphasized, were virtually cost-free to English

Canadians. The effect of the Official Languages Act was to extend parliamentary equality into the wider society, to broaden the scope of state intervention in the language field, and thus to intrude in a more direct and visible fashion into the lives of Canadians. All federal government signs and publications began to appear in both languages. Consumer products were required to carry bilingual labels, and airline passengers were told to buckle up in English and French. In short, Ottawa was increasing the visibility of French across Canada, albeit in a bilingual context, in a manner analogous to the Quebec government's efforts to increase the visibility of French in Quebec, albeit in a unilingual context.

When Trudeau worked in the Privy Council Office in the early 1950s, during the time when Louis St. Laurent was serving as Canada's second French Canadian prime minister, he witnessed what Christina McCall-Newman has described as an "unbelievable fight" to have a sign put up in the East Block reading *"Bureau du Premier Ministre"* as well as "Prime Minister's Office."[65] In retrospect, opposition to such an innocuous proposal, particularly during the tenure of a French Canadian prime minister, almost defies comprehension given the extent to which the Official Languages Act has transformed the linguistic face of Canada.

Bilingualism had its most immediate impact on the federal public service. The *institutional* bilingualism embodied in the Official Languages Act was designed so that *individuals* would not have to be bilingual—Canadians would be able to communicate with the national government in the official language of their choice. Bilingual institutions meant, however, a bilingual public service. Before the reforms launched by Prime Minister Pearson, English had been *the* language of work in the federal public service. Francophones were proportionately underrepresented in Ottawa, with underrepresentation increasing as one moved up through the ranks. Virtually the only bilingual public servants were those of French mother tongue. As senior positions demanded a skilled and even artful use of language, francophones were placed at a double disadvantage. Not only did they have to absorb the costs of learning a second language but, in having to function in their second language, they often appeared less subtle, less sensitive, and thus less competent than their anglophone compatriots.

With the introduction of bilingualism, knowledge of French became a career asset rather than a liability; anglophones now faced limited career mobility unless they learned French. Although the majority of public service positions were not designated as bilingual, the senior positions and thus implicitly the middle-rank positions from which senior managers were drawn, were so designated. To ease the transition to bilingualism, French-language training was made available in 1973 for anglophones holding positions which had been designated as bilingual. For thousands of anglophones, many of whom were senior officials at the peak of their careers, this meant months of being reduced to the status of secondary students, struggling with the acquisition of a new language. (By the 1980s French-language training was being phased out, with greater reliance being placed on an

"Darling, I am just a poor civil servant . . . cheri, je ne suis qu'un pauvre fonction-
naire . . . but I love you . . . mais je vous aime beaucoup . . . will you . . . voulez-vous . . ."

Len Norris, *15th Annual*. Originally published in *The Vancouver Sun*, April 15, 1966

adequate knowledge of both official languages prior to initial recruitment.)

Bilingualism has resulted in an increase in the number of francophones employed within the federal public service. The 1984 report of Canada's Official
Languages Commissioner shows that the proportion of francophones has risen to
27 percent from 21 percent in 1965, and that the proportion in senior positions
has risen from 17 percent to 25 percent over the same period. This increase
reflects the fact that during the Trudeau governments bilingualism was associated
with the growth of "French Power" in Ottawa, a phenomenon marked by the
emergence of highly visible and influential French Canadian ministers, deputy
ministers, heads of crown corporations, and senior advisors. At the same time, a
knowledge of both official languages became increasingly useful outside the
government for the leaders of professional organizations, interest groups, and
cultural associations claiming to be national in character. In short, bilingualism
became almost a prerequisite for individuals hoping to scale the peaks of Canadian political life.

Bilingualism was also associated with the widespread symbolic transformation of Canadian public life that began with the creation of a Canadian flag in the mid-1960s to replace the Union Jack and Red Ensign. Symbols grounded in only one of the two linguistic communities, such as the coat-of-arms on mail boxes, were replaced by symbols which might include not only French Canadians but also Canadians of neither British nor French descent. The names of government departments and agencies were changed to ones that could be easily expressed in either official language, and thus we had Transport Canada/Transports Canada, Post Canada/Postes Canada, Lotto Canada and so forth. Even metrification—the introduction of a "French system of measurement"—was seen by many as an extension of bilingualism. The national anthem was increasingly sung in its bilingual version, to the accompaniment of boos from some sports fans in English Canada.

The Official Languages Act captured an important if contentious tenet of Canadian life. If French Canadians were to be *Canadians*, then not only Quebec but also Canada would have to be the home of the French language. As Henri Bourassa wrote in 1912:

we deserve better than to be considered like the savages of the old reservations and to be told: "Remain in Quebec, continue to stagnate in ignorance, you are at home there; but elsewhere you must become English. No, we have the right to be French in language; we have the right to be Catholics in faith; we have the right to be free by the constitution. We are Canadians before all; and we have the right to enjoy these rights throughout the whole expanse of Confederation.[66]

Although Bourassa's logic is persuasive, it is not surprising that bilingualism encountered opposition in English Canada. The national majority was being asked to accept major change for the sake of the national minority, change that included a significant redistribution of status between the English and French communities. To many, bilingualism was seen not as the foundation for a stronger pan-Canadian nationalism but as an assault on the country's British heritage. Opposition was particularly intense in the more multicultural West where the French Canadian minority tended to be seen in a regional rather than national context. While in the latter context French Canadians made up almost a third of the national population, in a regional context they were outnumbered by many of the ethnic groups who had settled the West and who had adopted the English language in the process.

Although bilingualism affected the career opportunities of a substantial number of anglophones, it may be the threat to one's status that best explains the intensity of opposition among individuals who were untouched in any practical or objective sense in the introduction of bilingualism. For others, their opposition was not to bilingualism per se but to what they saw as Ottawa's excessive pre-

occupation with bilingualism and the consequent neglect of economic and regional concerns. In this respect Dalton Camp argues that the politics of bilingualism
intensified regional and intergovernmental strains within the national community:

The persistence and growing pervasiveness of bilingualism had alienated English Canadians from their federal government, turning them inwards to more familiar, compatible
and nearer political jurisdictions in the provinces.... The government of Canada had lost
its constituency.[67]

The surprising thing about opposition to bilingualism is that it failed to find a
champion within the party system. Apart from a few dissenting voices among
Progressive Conservative MPs, the major parties locked arms on the Official
Languages Act. In the subsequent elections voters were not given a choice between parties supporting and opposing bilingualism. Conservative leaders Robert
Stanfield and Joe Clark, whose party potentially had the most to gain from cater-
ing to anti-French sentiment given its then-bleak electoral prospects in Quebec,
were adamant in their support of bilingualism. Outside the party system, the
opponents of bilingualism who found their way into the media encountered a
consistently hostile reception. They tended to be treated as bigots and political
Neanderthals rather than as citizens with legitimate concerns about the direction
of national policy. Even a hard-line position against Quebec separatism became
difficult to express in a public forum.[68]

Bilingualism for the North

In June 1984, official bilingualism came
into effect in the northern territories.
The Yukon and Northwest Territories
Acts were amended to read that "English and French are the official
languages of the Territories and have
equal status and equal rights and
privileges as to their use in all institutions of the council and government
of the Territories."

The 1981 census showed that only
635 people or 2.7 percent of the
Northwest Territories' population of
45,000 spoke French at home. There
were 225 people in the Yukon who said
they spoke French in their homes.

When the amendments were first
introduced, Richard Nerysoo, the
Northwest Territories government
leader, said they would be a "serious
infringement" on the constitutional
authority of his government. They
were also strongly opposed by Yukon
government leader Chris Pearson, who
called them a return to colonialism.

The deliberate exclusion of potentially divisive issues from public debate and
electoral competition by political and social elites is termed "consociationalism."

A consociational democracy can be defined as one "... with subcultural cleavages tending towards immobilism and instability but which is deliberately turned into a stable system by the leaders of the major subcultures."[69] In the case of French–English relations, consociationalism has helped shape an asymmetrical national debate. While in Quebec the debate has ranged freely over the full range of alternatives, from support for the federal status quo to the advocacy of complete independence, in English Canada it has been far more restricted. Rarely has it encompassed the creation of a unilingual anglophone state including Quebec, the use of force to suppress Quebec's independence, or the welcomed departure of Quebec. Persons holding such views have not been encouraged to join in the debate over Quebec's place in Canada; they confront an elite consensus that national unity must be maintained, and that bilingualism is essential to do so.

The national policy of bilingualism has created a new linguistic constituency that, in turn, provides important political support for that policy. Historically, only a small fraction of the Canadian population—12.7 percent between 1931 and 1971—has been bilingual, and of those 60 percent lived in Quebec, with only 8 percent of the non-Quebec population being bilingual.[70] The vast majority of bilinguals were those of French mother tongue who had learned English for reasons of employment, or who were in the process of being assimilated into the English Canadian community. Bilinguals of English mother tongue were a rare breed. With the passage of the Official Languages Act, however, knowledge of French became an economic asset for anglophones while unilingualism could eventually mean "a life sentence to job immobility."[71] As a result, an explosive growth in French immersion programs has occurred across the country, programs which cater largely to an English mother tongue clientele. In the lower grades outside Quebec, anglophone immersion students now outnumber French mother tongue students who are receiving their education in French. It is interesting to note, however, that at the same time immersion enrolments have been increasing, the overall proportion of students outside Quebec who are taking French has been decreasing. *Thus French language education has become a more intensive experience for a smaller proportion of the student body.*[72] As a result we may be developing, for the first time in our history, "... a distinct social elite of young, upper-middle-class, bilingual graduates."[73] This elite will form a powerful lobby for the national bilingualism policies from which it derives its elite status.

Bilingualism Pays!

A study for the Economic Council of Canada has shown that in 1980 bilingual individuals earned more. Across Canada, bilingual men earned 11 percent more than unilingual men, and bilingual women earned 12 percent more than unilingual women. The gap was greatest in Quebec, but still averaged 6 percent for both sexes outside Quebec. The gap has been growing over time. (Cited in Jeffrey Simpson, "The Bilingual Edge," The Globe and Mail, *National Edition, February 24, 1984, p. 6.)*

The bilingual elite may also prove to be a source of tension within the political system. When Newfoundland MP John Crosbie ran for the leadership of the national Progessive Conservative party in 1983, his lack of French proved to be an insurmountable problem. Crosbie's reaction on the campaign trail is worthy of note:

There are over 20 million of us who are unilingual English or French ... I don't think that the 3.7 million who are bilingual should suddenly think themselves some kind of aristocracy and leaders can come only from their small group.[74]

Don Braid of the *Edmonton Journal* called Crosbie's comments a "burst of insight." For this "self-satisfied ruling elite," Braid charged,

Bilingualism has become a ritual chant ... they demand it of national leaders, thus guaranteeing their continued membership in the club. They dismiss dissenters as red-necked bigots and intellectual lightweights, while exercising a powerful bigotry of their own.[75]

Public opinion surveys reveal that support for second-language education is greater inside Quebec than elsewhere in Canada. In a Gallup survey conducted in August 1983, 76 percent of the national sample wanted English taught as a compulsory subject in French Canada while 58 percent favoured French as a compulsory subject in English Canada, proportions virtually unchanged from a Gallup survey conducted in 1974.[76] In Quebec alone, 88 percent of the respondents supported compulsory English in Quebec schools and 86 percent supported compulsory French in non-Quebec schools. Among non-Quebec respondents, 71 percent favoured compulsory English in Quebec while only 48 percent favoured compulsory French outside Quebec.

The existence of national language legislation has increased pressure from francophone minorities for bilingual access to provincial programs and, in some cases, recognition of French as an official language. In New Brunswick, English and French are now constitutionally entrenched as official languages. In Ontario, where francophones make up less than 5 percent of the population, most government services are provided in both English and French, and every French-speaking student has been guaranteed the right to an education in French. French-language rights, however, are enshrined in provincial statutes only and not in the constitution. The Ontario government has resisted calls for constitutional entrenchment, arguing that the backlash which might result could jeopardize francophone interests within the province.

In 1979 the Supreme Court of Canada ruled that 1890 Manitoba legislation making English the province's only official language was unconstitutional. (The provincial legislation violated the terms of the 1870 Manitoba Act, passed by the Parliament of Canada, which had brought Manitoba into Confederation.) This ruling threw into question the constitutionality of 14,000 pages of laws, written only in English, that have been passed since 1890. While the final consequences of this ruling are still being worked out through both the courts and Manitoba's political system, the outcome will include a legal and constitutional status for French in Manitoba quite different from that in the other western provinces.

The steps toward bilingualism that have been taken in many of the English Canadian provinces are important to note. Historically, English Canadian provincial governments have been far less sympathetic toward provincial francophone minorities than Ottawa has been toward the national francophone minority. This is not surprising, given that the provincial minorities have been proportionately much smaller than the national minority. What is perhaps more surprising, and more lamentable, has been the reluctance of the national government to defend the interests of francophone minorities against anglophone and Protestant provincial majorities.[77] Historian W.L. Morton has argued that this reluctance has forced French Canadians to turn to the Quebec provincial state for protection, and has thus made an important contribution to the ongoing constitutional tension between the Quebec and federal governments.[78]

National bilingualism draws its political support from a diverse constituency that includes French Canadians living outside Quebec, Anglo-Quebecers, a substantial proportion of French Canadians living inside Quebec, the new anglophone bilinguals who have invested heavily in their own bilingualism or that of their children, and those English Canadians who believe that bilingualism, like it or not, is essential to the survival of Canada. It is a powerful coalition that commands the support of all three major parties and the social, economic, and cultural elites from which they in turn draw their support. Ironically, however, the coalition finds itself confronting the Quebec government and its nationalist Québécois supporters. While it might be thought that Ottawa's legislation to protect the francophone national minority and, to a lesser degree, the francophone provincial minorities outside Quebec would complement Quebec's legislation to protect the francophone majority in Quebec, this has not been the case.

To understand why the language policies of Ottawa and Quebec collide, we must go back to basic policy objectives. The Official Languages Act was designed to create a sense of security for francophones within Canada comparable to their sense of security within Quebec. This was to be achieved by strengthening the French language within national institutions and by increasing the visibility of French in the society at large. The Act and the entrenchment of language rights within the Charter protect the language rights of *individuals* — all Canadians, inside or outside Quebec, anglophone or francophone, have the *same* language rights based on their common Canadian citizenship. In practice, however, the language guarantees are of greatest relevance for linguistic *minorities*, be they francophones outside Quebec or anglophones inside. They are of less relevance for the francophone *majority* in Quebec, to which Bill 101 is addressed. Indeed, by protecting the anglophone minority in Quebec, they may even threaten the linguistic interests of the francophone majority.

Language Provisions in the Canadian Charter of Rights and Freedoms

The 1969 Official Languages Act has now been "constitutionalized" in Sections 16 to 20 of the Charter of Rights and Freedoms.
Section 16(1) of the Charter states that "English and French are the official languages of Canada and have equality of status and equal rights and privileges as to their use in all institutions of the Parliament and government of Canada." Section 16(2) extends this provision to the legislature and government of New Brunswick.

Sections 17 and 18 establish the equality of English and French in the proceedings of Parliament and the New Brunswick legislature (debate, statutes, records, journals) while Sections 19(1) and 19(2) state that "either English or French may be used by any person in, or in any pleading in or process issuing from" any court established by Parliament or any court of New Brunswick.

Section 20(1) states that "any member of the public in Canada has the right to communicate with, and to receive available services from, any head or central office of an institution of the Parliament or government of Canada in English or French, and has the same right with respect to any other office of any such institution

where (a) there is a significant demand for communications with and services from that office in such language; or (b) due to the nature of the office, it is reasonable that communications with and services from that office be available in both English and French."
Section 23 of the Charter goes beyond the Official Languages Act to state that, where numbers warrant, "citizens of Canada (a) whose first language learned and still understood is that of the English or French linguistic minority population of the province in which they reside, or (b) who have received their primary school instruction in Canada in English or French and reside in a province where the language in which they received that instruction is the language of the English or French linguistic minority population of the province, have the right to have their children receive primary and secondary school instruction in that language in that province."
Section 23(2) states that "citizens of Canada of whom any child has received or is receiving primary or secondary school instruction in English or French in Canada, have the right to have all their children receive primary and secondary school instruction in the same language."

The language policies of Ottawa and Quebec rest on different philosophical foundations. Ottawa's policies assert language rights as individual rights, indeed as fundamental human rights; the primary concern is with the protection of linguistic *minorities*. Quebec's policies promote collective interests even to the point of restricting the linguistic choices of individuals; the primary concern is with the protection of the province's linguistic *majority*. While Ottawa's policies promote a bilingual Canada, those of Quebec promote a unilingual Quebec. In so doing, Quebec's language policies may erode public support in English Canada for bilingualism. Unfortunately, any backlash would further support the rationale of Bill 101, compounding the vicious circle that bedevils language politics in Canada.

French Canada, Quebec, and the Canadian Federal State

Two linguistic features of Canada are of vital importance to an understanding of Canadian federalism: that in the country at large, more than one Canadian in four is of French mother tongue, and that francophones constitute a clear majority in the second-largest province. Hence the ongoing conflict between the linguistic majorities of Canada and Quebec. The basic question is this: which government best speaks for French Canada? Is it the Government of Canada, which encompasses all French Canadians, but within which French Canadians are a minority, albeit a large and influential minority? Or is it the Government of Quebec, which encompasses only 80 percent of the French Canadian population, along with a significant non-French element, but within which French Canadians form a majority?

In many respects, of course, both governments do and must speak for French Canada. The problem is that they speak for overlapping but nonetheless quite distinct communities. The linguistic concerns of *French Canadians* (primarily the protection of minority interests in the face of a national and nine provincial anglophone majorities) are quite different from the linguistic concerns of the *Québécois* (primarily the promotion of majority interests which may run counter to those of the linguistic minority in Quebec) even though the latter make up 80 percent of the former. The resulting clash of language legislation is a specific manifestation of a more fundamental issue, for we often find that the governments of Canada and Quebec articulate conflicting visions of French Canada. The question again becomes who speaks for French Canada, particularly when the two visions differ as dramatically as they did under the governments of Pierre Trudeau and René Lévesque. Here it is useful to note that within the space of a year (1980) the Quebec electorate defeated the sovereignty-association proposal in a referendum, reelected the Parti Québécois government with an increased majority, and elected Liberals in seventy-four of the seventy-five federal ridings. During this period Trudeau and Lévesque both enjoyed strong personal and political support in Quebec, as did their competing visions of French Canada.

A number of factors have combined to create a chronic uncertainty over the place of French Canada within the broader Canadian community. Quebec's declining share of the national population has raised fears that, over the long run, Quebec's and therefore French Canada's power within the national political community will be eroded. The demolinguistic transformation of Canada, in which Quebec is becoming progressively francophone and the rest of Canada is becoming progressively anglophone, raises concerns about the long-term survival of Anglo-Quebecers, French Canada outside Quebec, and the bilingual policies of the federal government. Finally, there is ongoing constitutional tension arising from the conflicting demands for a strong national government that can protect French Canadian interests outside Quebec, and a strong provincial government that can more fully protect and promote the francophone majority inside Quebec.

This tension was addressed during the 1960s and 1970s by the argument that because Quebec was not a province like the others in a linguistic or cultural sense, neither should it be a province like the others in a constitutional sense. Rather, it should be given a special status and an expanded legislative domain. The catch was that any strengthening of *Quebec's* powers would be at the expense of *French Canada's* power in the national government. The gains of the francophone majority in Quebec would be at the expense of the francophone minority in Canada, and at the particular expense of francophone minorities outside Quebec. Special status would also place Quebec MPs in an untenable position. As the Quebec government argued in its position paper on sovereignty-association, how could Quebec MPs

vote on federal laws that would apply to all of Canada except Quebec? How could they impose on Canadians taxes that Quebecers would not pay? And how could the prime minister or cabinet ministers come from Quebec, where many federal programs would not apply?[79]

Given that special status for Quebec was emphatically rejected by other provincial governments and by Prime Minister Trudeau, it is not surprising that the special status argument failed to carry the constitutional field. However, its central point, that Quebec is *not* a province like the others, cannot be easily set aside even though there is no clear way of giving constitutional expression to this difference.

In the short run, English Canadians have accepted a system that combines very substantial French Canadian power in Ottawa with a strong and assertive provincial government in Quebec. However, any constitutional strengthening of that provincial government could well lead to the demand for reduced French Canadian power in Ottawa. The central problem remains: how can Quebec be given powers commensurate with its role as the heartland of French Canada without giving the other provinces the same powers, and thus weakening the national government, the position of francophone minorities, and the prospects for national unity?

The last twenty-five years have witnessed a great deal of turmoil over the place of Quebec within the Canadian federal system. The debate was brought to a head in May 1980, when the sovereignty-association proposal was defeated, and in April 1982 when the Constitution Act was proclaimed without any special recognition of Quebec, without the approval of the Quebec government, and without any change in the federal division of powers. While the linguistic rights of individuals have been recognized in the Charter, the duality of the Canadian community still lacks constitutional recognition. Yet it remains the preeminent fact of Canadian political life.

Suggested Readings

1 Sheila Arnopoulous and Dominique Clift, *The English Fact in Quebec* (Montreal: McGill-Queen's University Press, 1980).
2 For excellent overviews of much of the material covered in this chapter, see David R. Cameron, "Dualism and the Concept of National Unity," in John H. Redekop, ed., *Approaches to Canadian Politics*, 2nd ed. (Scarborough: Prentice-Hall, 1983), pp. 233–50; and Reginald A. Whitaker, "The Quebec Cauldron," in Michael S. Whittington and Glen Williams, eds., *Canadian Politics in the 1980s*, 2nd ed. (Toronto: Methuen, 1984), pp. 33–57.
3 Donald G. Cartwright, *Official Language Populations in Canada: Patterns and Contacts*, Occasional Paper No. 16, The Institute for Research on Public Policy, July 1980.
4 Lowell Clark, ed., *The Manitoba School Question: Majority Rule or Minority Rights?* (Toronto: Copp Clark, 1968).
5 Dominique Clift, *Quebec Nationalism in Crisis* (Montreal: McGill-Queen's University Press, 1982).
6 For a chronology and analysis of Quebec language policy, see William D. Coleman, "From Bill 22 to Bill 101: The Politics of Language Under the Parti Québécois," *Canadian Journal of Political Science* XIV:3 (September 1981), pp. 459–86.
7 Susan Crean and Marcel Rioux, *Two Nations: An Essay on the Culture and Politics of Canada and Quebec in a World of American Pre-eminence* (Toronto: James Lorimer, 1983).
8 Alain G. Gagnon, ed., *Quebec: State and Society* (Toronto: Methuen, 1984).
9 Richard Gwyn, *The Northern Magus: Pierre Trudeau and the Canadians* (Toronto: McClelland and Stewart, 1980).
10 For an excellent overview of Quebec politics and society, see Kenneth McRoberts and Dale Posgate, *Quebec: Social Change and Political Crisis*, rev. ed. (Toronto: McClelland and Stewart, 1980).
11 Denis Moniere, *Ideologies in Quebec: The Historical Development*, trans. Richard Howard (Toronto: University of Toronto Press, 1981).
12 Maurice Pinard and Richard Hamilton, "The Parti Québécois Comes to Power: An

Analysis of the 1976 Quebec Election," *Canadian Journal of Political Science* xi:4 (December 1978), pp. 739–76.

13 Jean Provencher, *René Lévesque: Portrait of a Québécois*, trans. David Ellis (Toronto: Gage, 1975).

14 Herbert F. Quinn, *The Union Nationale: A Study in Quebec Nationalism* (Toronto: University of Toronto Press, 1963).

15 For a vigorous Québécois nationalist perspective on the material covered in this chapter, see Marcel Rioux, *Quebec In Question*, trans. James Boake (Toronto: James Lorimer, 1978).

16 Susan Mann Trofimenkoff, *The Dream of Nation: A Social and Intellectual History of Quebec* (Toronto: Macmillan, 1982).

17 Ronald Wardhaugh, *Language and Nationhood: The Canadian Experience* (Vancouver: New Star Books, 1983).

Study Questions

1 The last twenty years have witnessed extensive discussion of the federal division of powers. Are there powers which the people of Quebec would like to see transferred to the provincial governments, and which residents of other provinces would like to see remain with the national government in Ottawa? If so, how would you explain such different perspectives on the division of powers?

2 In the late 1970s, David R. Cameron described *dualism* as "the view which holds that the most significant cleavage in Canadian society is the line dividing English from French, and which identifies as the major challenge to domestic statecraft the establishment of harmonious and just relations between the English-speaking and French-speaking communities of Canada." ("Dualism and the Concept of National Unity" in John H. Redekop, ed., *Approaches to Canadian Politics* (Scarborough: Prentice-Hall, 1978), p. 237). As we enter the late 1980s, do you feel that a dualist view is still appropriate? If so, why? If not, what other cleavages rival that between the English and French communities?

CHAPTER FOUR

Regional Politics

To many foreign observers, the fact that Confederation is widely evaluated from the particular point of view of how given provinces have fared over the years is a remarkable feature of Canadian life. In other countries, cleavages such as social class, religion, race or creed have been of decisive importance to the collective lives of citizens. In Canada, how much the people of any given province have participated in the benefits of the federation, or shared its losses, has been at the forefront of our politics.[1]

It is not surprising that Canadians have an acute sense of territory and geography. Many of the symbols used to convey a sense of the country to non-Canadians and Canadians alike are rooted in geography: Peggy's Cove, Niagara Falls, the Great Lakes, the solitary splendour of the Canadian Shield captured in the paintings of the Group of Seven, the sweep of the prairies, the majestic Rocky Mountains, the blending of sea and air along the rain forest of the West Coast, and the vast silence of the Canadian North are intrinsic to the Canadian identity. Other symbols including the maple leaf, Canada geese, and the beaver are drawn from the land itself rather than from its human population. Yet many of the geographical features which give Canada definition—the Rockies, the Shield, the Atlantic Ocean and Gulf of St. Lawrence—also carve up the country into territorially defined subnational communities and contribute to the strength of subnational attachments. Geographical barriers make it difficult for Canadians to come to grips with the country as a whole, for residents of the East Coast, for example, to have an emotional handle on the "miles and miles of miles and miles" that make up the prairie West.

Given all this, we might well expect regional identities and regional conflict to play major roles in Canadian political life. We readily assume that in a vast, transcontinental society with a federal constitution designed to give political expression to territorial communities, regionalism will be a persistent feature. Regionalism is attributed to the simple facts of size and diversity, and to the not-so-simple fact of federalism, even though in the equally vast, diverse, *and federal* society to the south, regional conflict is both less prevalent and less disruptive.[2] As former Prime Minister William Lyon Mackenzie King observed, "if some countries have too much history, we have too much geography."[3]

On closer inspection, however, this line of argument is less convincing. It does not explain why regional conflict in Canada appears to be increasing over time[4] while in other western, industrialized countries there has been a marked and progressive decline in territorially based political conflict.[5] A further complication is that regional differences within the Canadian *society* appear to be waning at the same time that they are waxing within the political system. While lifestyles in Toronto, Halifax, Edmonton, Charlottetown, and Brandon are by no means identical, the differences are less acute today than they were in the past. It seems that no matter where Canadians live they can watch *The Journal*, shop at Canadian Tire, eat at McDonald's, subscribe to the same pay-TV channels, drink the same beer, and read *The Globe and Mail*. Thus the argument that regionalism within the political system reflects regional divisions within the underlying society has become less tenable over time.

Just as the Quiet Revolution led Quebec into the mainstream of Canadian life while at the same time increasing political conflict between Quebec and the broader Canadian community, so too has the regional homogenization of Canada in the wake of technological and industrial change been associated with increased regional conflict. The implication that one can draw from this is that the primary roots of regional conflict are to be found in the nature of the political system itself, and that regional variations in social characteristics are of secondary importance. While there are pronounced regional variations in the distribution of natural resources and the nature of economic activity, even here it can be argued that the study of regional conflict is primarily a study of *political* cause and effect.

Before exploring this thesis further, some guidelines must be established. Our principal focus will be upon the intrusion of territory—of territorial interests, identifications and conflicts—into *national* political life. Little attention will be paid to intraprovincial territorial conflicts such as those between Vancouver and the interior communities of British Columbia, between northern Ontario and the "golden horseshoe" stretching along the shore of Lake Ontario, between St. John's and the outports of Newfoundland. While these can be of critical importance in shaping the contours of provincial politics, their national impact is less pronounced. Nor will Quebec be brought into the regional analysis. Although in some respects Quebec constitutes a region analogous to other regions in Canada, the differences that set Quebec apart are of greater magnitude than those which set the English Canadian regions apart from one another. Given that Quebec has been discussed in Chapter Three, and given the analytical distortions that can arise in trying to pack Quebec into a regional framework, the focus of this chapter will be upon regional divisions *within English Canada* with particular attention being paid to the two regional peripheries—the four Atlantic provinces east of Quebec and the four provinces west of Ontario. A final exclusion concerns the northern territories which, while forming Canada's largest region, contain only 0.3 percent of the national population.

A troublesome conceptual problem in the discussion of regionalism comes from the unavoidable confusion between "provinces" and "regions." Terms such as "western Canada," "Atlantic Canada" or "the Maritimes" imply the existence of a transprovincial community sharing at the very least a common territorial interest, political perspective, or economic orientation. The reality of such regional communities, however, is a matter of contentious debate. As the former premier of Prince Edward Island, Alex Campbell, stressed in a 1977 address, the regional community is in many ways an artifact:

The only people who consider Atlantic Canada as a region are those who live outside Atlantic Canada, the planners and bureaucrats in Ottawa, the newscasters in Toronto, and the airline executives in Montreal. We in Atlantic Canada have not yet made the decision to develop as a region. We are four separate, competitive, jealous, and parochial provinces.... I suggest to you that we do not have a regional identity; we do not have regional bonds; we do not have regional strategies....

With respect to western Canada, British Columbia is often portrayed, particularly by its residents, as a region quite apart from the prairie west, a region with a very different physical terrain, economic base, settlement pattern, and political history.

The complexities of regional analysis can perhaps best be illustrated by the three prairie provinces.[6] Initially the three were bound together as a regional community by a common wheat economy and by the shared experiences, characteristics, and frustrations of an agrarian frontier. The three constituted a region because of what they shared in common, and because what they shared clearly set them apart from other areas in Canada. Then, in the decades following the Depression and the Second World War, the prairie region began to come unstitched as the importance of the wheat economy declined and as the regional economy diversified. Heterogeneity among the three prairie provinces increased while at the same time regional differences between the prairies and other parts of Canada decreased. Yet, while Alberta and Manitoba may share less in common today than in the past, and while life in Edmonton, Saskatoon, or Winnipeg may be more like life in Toronto, Hamilton, or Halifax than in the past, regional commonalities have not disappeared. They include, but are not limited to, a sense of alienation from the national government, an economic reliance on the exploitation of natural resources, and a marked dependency on unstable foreign markets for those resources. In a similar fashion, one can identify points of commonality across the Atlantic provinces, including, but again not limited to, a concern with out-migration, a fragile and often depressed economic base, a coastal environment and, to a degree, an economic reliance on the sea that is not shared by other Canadians, even those on the west coast.

A regional analysis, therefore, must be alert to shared characteristics among provinces, and in particular to shared characteristics that set off one region from another. At the same time we must be alert to provincial variations within commonly used regional units of analysis such as "the West" or "the Maritimes." While at some times and in some circumstances regional themes dominate the territorial dimension of Canadian political life, at other times and in other circumstances disparate provincial interests do so.

Demographic Profile

Figure 4.1 plots the regional composition of the Canadian population from 1871 to 1981. The most dramatic change came with the settlement of the Canadian West. Between 1901 and 1931, that region's share of the national population rose from 12.1 percent to 29.5 percent. Then, with the onset of the Great Depression, which was accompanied on the prairies by drought, grasshoppers, and the collapse of foreign grain markets, the West's share of the national population began a slide that was not arrested until the mid-1960s. Although the region's share of the national population increased between 1971 and 1981, at the decade's end it was still marginally below the 1931 peak.[7]

The westward shift in population at the turn of the century was reflected in part by the *relative* decline of Atlantic Canada. While the West was being settled during the first three decades of this century, the proportion of the national population living in the three Maritime provinces fell from 16.7 percent to 9.6 percent. The addition of Newfoundland in 1949 proved only a temporary respite in the progressive demographic decline of Atlantic Canada. It is interesting to note, however, that while Atlantic Canada lost approximately 10,000 people to other parts of Canada between June 1, 1981, and May 31, 1982, the region *gained* over 8,000 people during the next year and over 4,000 in the 1983–84 period. Nova Scotia showed the largest net in-migration, with over 70 percent of the incoming population arriving from Alberta.[8]

Perhaps the most striking features about Figure 4.1 are the demographic strength and resiliency of the centre. While, as the last chapter noted, Quebec's share of the national population has declined somewhat in recent years, and while Ontario's share was eroded by the growth of the West in the early part of the twentieth century, the centre has held. Ontario's share of the national population has rebounded from a low of 32.8 percent in 1951 to over 35 percent in 1981. Quebec and Ontario's combined share reached its lowest point—60.3 percent—in

FIGURE 4.1

Regional Distribution of the Canadian Population

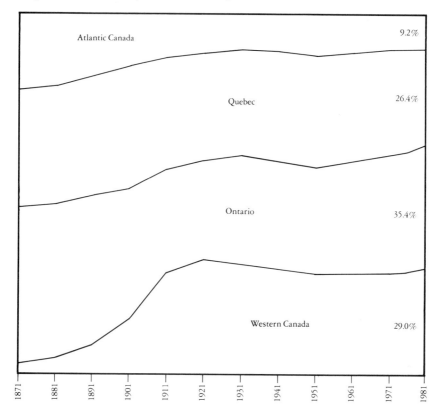

1921. Since that time it has fluctuated between 61 and 63 percent. Overall, then, Canada's demographic structure has been surprisingly stable, particularly since the Depression brought the agricultural settlement of the prairie West to a close.

Such stability has been less evident within Atlantic Canada and the West. As Figure 4.2 illustrates, a major change in the Atlantic region came with the addition of Newfoundland in 1949. The other shifts, including the gradual erosion of P.E.I.'s share of the regional population, have been more modest. Within the West there has been a steady westward shift in population since the onset of the Depression. Provincial differences in growth rates have been dramatic. From 1931 to 1981, British Columbia's population increased by 395 percent and Alberta's by 306 percent, while Manitoba's population grew by only 47 percent and Saskatchewan's by a minuscule 5 percent. (This translates into a net increase of 46,528 people in Saskatchewan compared to 2,050,204 in British Columbia!) As a

FIGURE 4.2
Provincial Distributions of Regional Populations

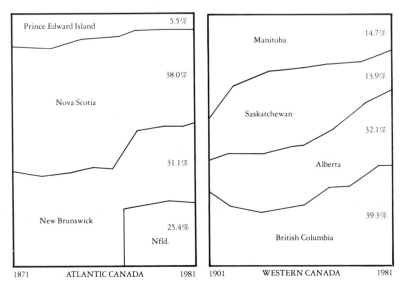

consequence of this westward shift, 71 percent of the regional population resided in the two westernmost provinces in 1981, compared to only 47 percent in 1931.

The Regions

Before turning to a more general discussion of regional dynamics within Canadian political life, it is useful to look in some detail at the major regional communities within English Canada.

ATLANTIC CANADA

At the time of Confederation, "Atlantic Canada" did not exist. It would be another six years before Prince Edward Island joined the Dominion, and eighty-two years before Newfoundland would expand "the Maritimes" to "Atlantic Canada." In the early years after Confederation, the region was marked by strong local and provincial loyalties which precluded any regional sense of community. As Forbes has noted, "... there was relatively little in the long history of the Maritimes to provide a truly collective historical experience, either actual or mythological, through which the people might develop a strong regional consciousness."[9] In the short run, Forbes argues, Confederation was an alternative to regional unity or consciousness; "the identification with the nation at the higher level and with the cultural group, economic interest, province, or local community at the lower seemed to leave little reason for interest in or loyalty to a Maritime region."[10] Over the longer run, Confederation and the ongoing struggle over "better terms" (*see Glossary*) for the Maritimes were to provide just such a regional bond.

The Maritimes in Historical Perspective

Confederation was greeted with a general lack of enthusiasm by the people of Nova Scotia and New Brunswick. Opposition was particularly pronounced in Nova Scotia, where a government pledged to repeal Nova Scotia's entry was elected almost before the ink was dry on the 1867 Constitution Act. However, the repeal movement was short-lived. Joseph Howe, the leading spokesman for repeal, joined Macdonald's national cabinet after failing to win British support, and by 1870 the movement had collapsed.

The entry of Prince Edward Island into the Dominion in 1873 was also accompanied by little enthusiasm: "most Islanders met the end of their independent history with bitter resignation and, as was the case in the other two Maritime Provinces, the legacy of resentment against those responsible remained."[11] The end came in the wake of British pressure, an economic recession coupled with a poor harvest, an impending financial crisis precipitated by overly ambitious plans for a provincial railway, and the patient courtship of the Canadian government.

The years between P.E.I.'s entry and the First World War saw the progressive "Canadianization" of the Maritime economy. This integration into the national economy yielded substantial regional benefits even though that economy's centre of gravity came increasingly to rest in Ontario and Quebec. Maritime manufacturing industries shared in the economic prosperity generated by the settlement of the Canadian West. The protective tariffs of the National Policy (*see Glossary*) and favourable freight rates on the Intercolonial Railway gave particular impetus to the Nova Scotia coal and steel industries, an impetus that was sustained by the industrial demands of the First World War.

Canadianization, however, was not complete. Other sectors of the Maritime economy—agriculture, forestry, and fisheries—were less successfully integrated into the national economy. Because they relied on continental and international markets, they benefited less from the protective tariffs of the National Policy. Tensions developed between indigenous entrepreneurs and industries, on the one hand, and the increased presence of national economic interests, based in Ontario and Montreal, on the other. As a consequence the region was not bound together by a dominant economic interest, as the West was to be bound together by the grain trade. When common economic interests did exist, they frequently resulted in intense intraregional rivalry and jealousy. Here the conflicts between the ports of Halifax, Nova Scotia, and Saint John, New Brunswick, took on legendary proportions. Taken together, the diversity of economic interests and intraregional competition reduced the leverage of the Maritimes on national economic policy and hampered efforts to achieve better economic terms within Confederation. As Forbes explains:

In trying to represent the diverse interests of their constituents Maritime politicians were often found quarrelling among themselves and attempting to influence national policy in different directions. This left them at a definite disadvantage in competing with regions having more clearly defined communities of interest.[12]

Such regions included not only Ontario and the interests of its manufacturing sector, but also the emerging agricultural West.

These early years also witnessed the political integration of the Maritimes into the broader Canadian party system, with the Conservative and Liberal parties sinking deep roots into the region. The major exception to this integration, though not to the dominance of the national parties, came with a flareup of the Nova Scotia Repeal Movement in 1886–87. Faced with economic distress and federal reluctance to endorse better terms for the province, W.S. Fielding's Liberal government introduced and passed a resolution proposing that "the financial and commercial interests of the people of Nova Scotia, New Brunswick and Prince Edward Island would be advanced by these provinces withdrawing from the Canadian federation and uniting under one government." While the repeal agitation reflected "a deep and widespread, though not perhaps overwhelming, sense of grievance with their place in the new nation,"[13] the call for secession was more a matter of rhetoric and ritual, born out of frustration rather than serious intent. Certainly regional unification was not of great appeal in Nova Scotia or elsewhere.

Although the Fielding government was reelected shortly after the legislative resolution was passed, its reelection was not widely interpreted as a mandate for secession. Nor was secession taken up by Nova Scotia's MPs, and within the year it had fallen from the political agenda. The lack of support from the province's federal representatives is of particular importance. Rawlyk and Brown argue that "in the only arena where regional grievances could be effectively redressed, the House of Commons in Ottawa, Nova Scotians as well as other Maritime Members of Parliament willingly sacrificed their regional interests on the altar of party loyalty."[14] This clash between party loyalty in the House on the one hand and effective regional representation on the other was to become a focal point of western Canadian political discontent in the years ahead, and was to result in a major challenge to and transformation of the national party system. No such challenge emerged in the Maritimes as a legacy of the Repeal Movement.

The first two decades of the twentieth century were prosperous ones for the Maritimes as the explosive rate of settlement in the prairie West created a strong demand for the industrial products of Ontario and the Maritimes. Yet the settlement of the West also opened up interregional conflict between the West and the Maritimes. This is a conflict that western Canadians have all but ignored, focusing

FIGURE 4.3

Number of Seats in the House of Commons

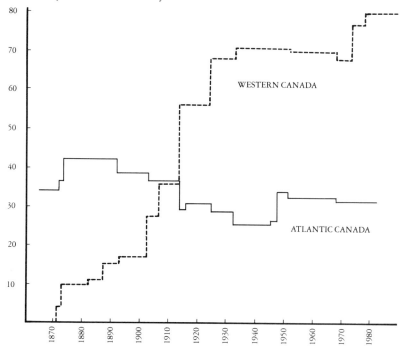

their attention instead on the regional conflict between the West and central Canada, a conflict in which the West could be unambiguously portrayed as the victim. The facts that the growth of the West came in part at the expense of the Maritimes, and that the interests of the western regional periphery were at times at odds with those of the eastern periphery, have not received adequate attention.

Interregional conflict between the Maritimes and the West was fed from several sources. First, population growth in the West led to a regional redistribution of seats in the House of Commons which had the appearance and to a degree the reality of *taking* seats from the Maritimes and *giving* them to the West. Figure 4.3 shows the growth of western representation in the House and the corresponding decline in Maritime representation, a decline that was not only proportionate but also absolute. Thus as Maritime seats disappeared, regional residents were provided with dramatic evidence of their declining role in the national political community, and of their eclipse by the ascendant West.

Secondly, the two regions were at loggerheads over the 1905 transfer of federal Crown lands (*see Glossary*) in the North-West Territories when Saskatchewan and Alberta were created, and when the provincial boundaries of Manitoba were greatly expanded. As Forbes explains, the West and the Maritimes lodged mutually exclusive claims: "the prairie case rested on the contention that the public lands had always belonged legally to the provinces, the Maritime one on the assumption that they belonged to the Dominion."[15] Maritimers argued that the original members of the Dominion were entitled to compensation for the "loss" of public lands, a *national* resource, to the prairie provinces. This argument was linked to a broader sense of regional grievance, for not only did the prairie provinces benefit from the transfer of Crown lands, but, in 1912, so too did Quebec and Ontario when their provincial boundaries were expanded. The Maritime provinces were left not only without new land, because there was none available on the east coast, but with a diminished share of a diminished national resource. In addition, Maritimers felt that the federal government had provided unreasonably generous financial subsidies to the new western provinces. For example, quite apart from land transfers, the federal subsidy to the Saskatchewan government was set at approximately three times that of the Nova Scotia subsidy even though at the time Nova Scotia had twice Saskatchewan's population.[16]

There was, then, a not-unfounded feeling that the settlement of the West was occurring at the expense of the Maritimes, and that its long-term consequence would be a diminished role for the Maritimes in the Canadian community. This concern apparently aroused little interest or empathy in the West. When disputes arose over freight rates, western politicians vigorously pursued their own regional interests with little regard to the potentially negative impact on Maritime industries. In a more general sense, the mythology that grew up around western settlement grated upon the Maritimes. As Forbes explains, "the thesis which was then becoming widely accepted, that independence, economic and social progress, and even democracy itself were the products of a new and dynamic agrarian frontier, implied an unflattering role for the Maritimes."[17]

Regional unease with the ascendancy of the West and the consequent decline of the Maritimes combined with other sources of political discontent in the *Maritime Rights Movement*, an umbrella label applied to the regional protest which swept across the Maritimes between 1919 and 1927. Other sources included labour unrest and a broad-gauge interest in social reform which, in the West, was expressed through the Social Gospel (*see Glossary*). While regional discontent was accentuated by the onset of an economic recession in 1920, its roots were "... firmly grounded among the deepest concerns and aspirations of the people — aspirations of a political, economic, social, and cultural nature which were seriously threatened by the relative decline of the Maritime provinces in the Canadian Dominion."[18] It was hoped that the political strength that would come through regional unity could correct the injustices being inflicted upon the Maritimes by the federal government and, through the federal government, by other regions. The Maritime Rights Movement was a continuation of the quest for better terms within Confederation, for the protection of a region being eroded by the growth of the West and the increased concentration of economic activity in the central Canadian provinces.

The regional plight of the Maritimes came to be symbolized by the Intercolonial Railway. The ICR, which linked the Maritimes to central Canadian markets and trade, was a direct legacy of Confederation. Based in the Maritimes, it was well-attuned to the special economic and political interests of the region, and its rate structure was designed to further those interests. As a consequence, however, the ICR was dependent upon federal subsidies which in turn were attacked by competing regional interests outside the Maritimes. In 1919 the federal government was instrumental in moving the Intercolonial headquarters from Moncton to Toronto, and in 1923 the ICR was absorbed into the new Canadian National Railway system. The transfer of the ICR headquarters was a stunning blow not only because of the employment loss, but because of the more important loss of regional control. The operation of the railway and its freight rate structure would now be determined by external management remote from the myriad regional interests clustered around the ICR. Rawlyk and Brown conclude that "the integration of the Intercolonial into a national railway system, in which management was neither sympathetic nor knowledgeable concerning Maritime problems, spelled disaster for Maritime business."[19]

The Maritime Rights Movement culminated in the 1925 appointment of a federal Royal Commission to provide a full hearing of regional grievances. The Commission, chaired by Sir Andrew Rae Duncan, was successful in venting regional discontent, and in 1926 the Commission released a generally sympathetic report. The report itself, promises by the federal government to act on its recommendations, and the economic recovery of 1927 brought the Maritime Rights Movement to a close. (At the Federal–Provincial Conference held that year, interregional tensions were also eased as the Maritime provinces supported the West's demand for the provincial ownership of natural resources[20] and the western provinces supported the Maritime quest for enhanced intergovernmental and freight rate subsidies.) While the movement had not resulted in any significant progress toward the political unification of the Maritimes, it had helped foster a regional consciousness and identity that were to persist.

Newfoundland

Whether this regional consciousness and identity extend to include Newfoundland is a matter of ongoing and contentious debate. In the 1860s Newfoundlanders, faced with a vulnerable economy and widespread poverty, came up against the Canadian drive to Confederation. Although Newfoundland delegates did not attend the 1864 Charlottetown conference, they did attend the subsequent conference in Quebec City where Newfoundland was offered generally favourable financial terms of entry. However, Canadian politicians were not as insistent in their courtship of Newfoundland as they had been in the case of Nova Scotia and New

Brunswick. Given opposition to Confederation by economic elites in St. John's, and given the fact that little of Newfoundland's trade was with the Canadian mainland, Confederation was rejected despite considerable British pressure. In 1869 an election was fought on the issue, with Confederation supporters winning nine seats and their opponents twenty-one. The island's sentiment was nicely captured by a song popularized during the campaign:

Hurrah for our own native isle, Newfoundland!
Not a stranger shall hold one inch of its strand!
Her face turns to Britain, her back to the gulf.
Come near at your peril, Canadian wolf![21]

The Canadian wolf took heed, and union was not considered again until 1895 when a severe recession led to unsuccessful talks with the Canadian government on financial terms of entry. In 1934, when responsible government in Newfoundland came to an end in the wake of near economic collapse, union with Canada, which at the time was also in the throes of the Great Depression, was not considered. Instead, the reins of government were passed to an appointed six-man commission, three of the commissioners coming from Newfoundland and three from Great Britain. The commission remained in place to steer Newfoundland through the wartime prosperity brought by American and Canadian airfields. The war years, as Campbell and Rawlyk conclude, "... forced Newfoundland into the mainstream of North American life and ... resulted in both a dramatic rise in the existing standard of living and also in the benchmark of expectations."[22]

With the end of the war and the departure of Allied airmen, the British government took a major step on the road to the island's union with Canada. The decision was made to hold a referendum on Newfoundland's future, and a convention was called to set the terms of the referendum. Initially, union with Canada was not to be one of the options. However, in the face of protest mobilized by broadcaster Joey Smallwood and sympathetically received by the British government, union was included along with retention of commission government and a return to responsible government under the British crown. The first round of the referendum narrowed the choice to union with Canada or a return to responsible government. On July 22, 1948, 52.4 percent of those voting opted for confederation with Canada, and on March 31, 1949, Newfoundland became Canada's tenth province. Eighty-five years after the Charlottetown conference, Confederation was complete.

Smallwood went on to dominate Newfoundland politics for the next twenty years. His passionate support for Canada and his success in entrenching the Liberal party on the island were to cement the relationship between Newfoundland and the broader Canadian community. Yet that relationship was not without difficulties as Newfoundland came to represent, albeit in exaggerated form, the pattern of dependency that was increasingly characteristic of Atlantic Canada. Newfoundland was the net recipient of fiscal transfers from the national government, transfers which flowed through equalization payments (*see Glossary*), unemployment insurance, welfare payments, and regional development grants. In fact, intergovernmental transfers alone came to account for roughly half the provincial budget. Such transfers to Newfoundland and to the Atlantic region in general could be borne by the national community because of the region's small and declining share of the national population. At the same time, they have stopped well short of providing economic prosperity. Newfoundland, for example, suffers chronically from the country's highest unemployment rates.

The end of dependency has been a persistent but elusive goal of Newfoundland political leaders. Prospects brightened considerably in the 1970s with the discovery of the Hibernia oil field off the east coast of Newfoundland. Hibernia, however, touched off a bitter jurisdictional battle between the Newfoundland and Canadian governments. In essence, Premier Brian Peckford's provincial government claimed the same ownership and thus control of offshore resources that other provinces, and most particularly Alberta, exercised over continental resources. The revenues which would eventually flow from Hibernia were to be used to lift Newfoundland from the ranks of the have-not provinces, to transform Newfoundland as oil had transformed Alberta. For its part, the Liberal government in Ottawa claimed that offshore resources fell under the jurisdiction of the federal government, that oil revenues should replace rather than build upon equalization payments, and that once Newfoundland's provincial revenues reached the national average, the federal take of natural resource revenue should be greatly increased. Also at issue was the pace of Hibernia's development; should it be set by the needs of the provincial or the national community?

The specific battle over offshore resources was fought out against the general backdrop of the constitutional struggle over patriation. It was also associated with the emergence of separatist sentiment within the province. Surveys by Memorial University political scientist Mark Graesser in 1982 and November 1983 revealed that 19 percent and 18 percent respectively of the provincial respondents were prepared to endorse independence "if that were the only way for the province to control its resources." However, the Party for an Independent Newfoundland, headed by Charlie Devine, failed to mobilize anywhere near that level of public support.

The offshore dispute bounced around in the political arena for some time. Prior to his victory in the 1979 federal election, Conservative leader Joe Clark stated that, if elected, a Conservative government would transfer ownership of offshore resources to the provinces. However, no action was taken before the Clark government was replaced by a less sympathetic Liberal government in the 1980 general election. With the resolution of the constitutional debate over patriation, the Newfoundland government referred the offshore dispute to the provincial

TABLE 4.1
Regional Sentiment in Atlantic Canada

In the fall of 1978 the Task Force on National Unity commissioned a comprehensive public opinion survey of the Atlantic region. Directed by Professors George Perlin and George Rawlyk, both from Queen's University, the survey encompassed 1,939 respondents. Although a number of years have since passed, it still stands as the most detailed snapshot available of political opinion in the region. While there has undoubtedly been some change in opinion since 1978, there is little reason to expect that the broad parameters sketched in by the questions below have been altered to any substantial degree.

		Atlantic Canada	Nfld.	P.E.I.	N.S.	N.B.
1. "Overall, would you say that Confederation has been a good thing or a bad thing for this province?"	Good thing	84%	90%	80%	80%	84%
	Bad thing	7	4	10	8	6
	Both	1	1	1	1	1
	Don't know/ no opinion	9	4	10	12	9
2. "Some people say that the way Confederation was set up gives all the advantages to Ontario. Other people say that is not true. What do you think?"	True	24%	17%	21%	25%	27%
	Not true	59	60	60	59	58
	Don't know/ no opinion	17	22	19	16	15

3. "Do you feel you belong to a group that hasn't got a fair deal out of federal government policy?"	Yes	28%	29%	22%	29%	27%
	No	67	65	74	65	68
	Don't know/ no opinion	6	6	4	6	5
4. "In term of their incomes and standard of living, on average, do you think people in Ontario are better off, about the same, or worse off than people here in (name of province)?"	Better off	62%	61%	73%	63%	59%
	About the same	27	23	22	28	30
	Worse off	5	7	1	4	6
	Don't know/ no opinion	6	9	4	4	5
5. "Some people think that more of the power to make decisions should be taken from the federal government and given to the provincial governments. Other people would rather keep things as they are. What do you think?"	Decentralize	38%	32%	38%	41%	39%
	Status quo	50	55	47	50	49
	Don't know/ no opinion	11	14	14	9	12

Supreme Court. When the Newfoundland court ruled in favour of Ottawa, the ruling was appealed to the Supreme Court of Canada. In February 1984, the Supreme Court ruled that jurisdiction over offshore resources lay with the federal government. Newfoundland's claim that it had retained ownership of the continental shelf upon entering Canada in 1949 was rejected.

In April 1984, the Supreme Court also upheld a 1969 contract between Newfoundland and Quebec Hydro which has enabled Quebec to capture the great bulk of the power and profits from the Churchill Falls power development in Labrador. The sixty-five-year contract, through which Quebec Hydro currently buys power at the Labrador border for approximately $3 per megawatt hour and sells it to New England utilities at approximately $90 per megawatt hour, contained no provisions for price increases. As a consequence, Quebec Hydro netted approximately $800 million in 1983, compared to only $8 million captured by Newfoundland from a resource lying within its provincial boundaries. This decision, coupled with the offshore decision and federal control of the Atlantic fisheries industry, serves to reinforce the preexisting pattern of provincial dependency.

The Atlantic Region
The dispute over offshore resources illustrates the deep fissures that can exist between Atlantic Canada and the broader national community. It also illustrates the differences that can exist within the region itself. Nova Scotia, for example, reached an amicable agreement with the federal government over the development of offshore natural gas deposits, an agreement ensuring a considerable measure of both national and provincial control over resource development and access to subsequent revenues.[23] Certainly the relationship between New Brunswick and Ottawa, or between Ottawa and Prince Edward Island, has not been marked by the degree of intergovernmental discord that has come to characterize the Newfoundland–Ottawa relationship over recent years.

Table 4.1 demonstrates a very high level of support for Confederation among Atlantic Canadians surveyed in 1978. While a significant number agreed that "the way Confederation was set up gives all the advantages to Ontario," they were outnumbered more than two to one by those who disagreed. Fewer than 30 percent agreed that they belonged "to a group that hasn't got a fair deal out of federal government policy," even though 61 percent felt that people in Ontario were better off than were people in their own province. A majority of respondents also supported the federal status quo, with only 32 percent supporting a more decentralized federal system in which more power would be given to the provincial governments. Finally, it is interesting to note the very limited intraregional variation in the table. Opinion varied little from one province to the next, suggesting a regional perspective on political life transcending one's provincial residence.

Since the end of the Second World War Atlantic Canada has become increasingly marginal to the national economy.[24] Interlocking economic and demographic decline has in turn eroded the region's position within the national political community. While the development of offshore resources may forestall any further erosion, the prospects for a dramatic reversal in the region's fortunes are not bright. Yet to date the national fabric has not been seriously strained by regional discontent, at least within the three Maritime provinces. As Rawlyk and Brown conclude, "in a fascinating twist of a complex relationship, the region of Canada which was once most vociferously opposed to Confederation has become one of its most ardent and committed supporters."[25] Atlantic Canadians have not challenged the basic institutional or constitutional structure of the Canadian federal state, and have not allowed regional discontent to dampen their electoral support for the two mainline national parties. The political necessity of protecting local and conflicting subregional interests, the economic competition among the Atlantic provinces,[26] a declining share of the national population, a widespread dependency on transfer payments from the federal government (discussed in Chapter Five), and powerful regional spokesmen within the federal cabinet, including such figures as John Crosbie, Romeo LeBlanc, Allan MacEachen, and Jack Pickersgill, have all served to contain regional discontent, and to set Atlantic Canada in sharp contrast to the Canadian West.

WESTERN CANADA

In a narrow sense, Confederation was the amalgamation of existing British North American colonies into a single colonial unit, Canada. In a broader sense, it was also the vehicle through which a new and unsettled region could be developed, a region whose resources were believed to be immense. This region was the prairie West, stretching over a thousand miles from the western edge of the Canadian Shield to the Rocky Mountains.

Even before Confederation, the prairie West assumed an important place in the Canadian national vision. Note, for instance, an editorial that appeared in the Toronto *Globe* on March 6, 1862:[27]

When the territory [the West] belongs to Canada, when its navigable waters are traversed for a few years by vessels, and lines of travel are permanently established, when settlements are formed in favourable locations throughout the territory, it will not be difficult by grants of land to secure the construction of a railway across the plains and through the mountains.... If we set about the work of opening the territory at once, we shall win the race [against the United States, which was pushing steadily westward].... It is an empire we have in view, and its whole export and import trade will be concentrated in the hands of Canadian merchants and manufacturers if we strike for it now.

To a large degree, the West has fulfilled even the most optimistic visions of early

Canadians. Yet it has done so through prolonged and often acrimonious regional conflict, the seeds of which are to be found in the above quote. The conflict between *national* interests and the more narrow economic interests of Central Canada, on the one hand, and the regional aspirations of those who settled the prairie West, on the other, has not been easily resolved. Indeed, contemporary western alienation provides ample testimony that a resolution still eludes Canadians over a hundred years after settlement began to spread across the prairies.

To explain the contemporary nature of political life in western Canada, we must first sketch in, with very broad strokes, the region's historical evolution. Here it must be recognized that there have been two quite different Wests—the prairie West encompassing Manitoba, Saskatchewan, and Alberta, and, across the mountain divide, British Columbia. The settlement history of British Columbia, its economic foundations and political history have been very different from those of the prairie provinces. For this reason, our initial discussion focuses on the prairie West alone and its incorporation into the Canadian union.

The Prairie West in Historical Perspective

For many Canadians, Confederation was the key that would unlock the riches of the North-West and, in so doing, stimulate economic growth and prosperity in central Canada. The key, however, was very slow in turning. A world-wide economic depression in the 1870s and 1880s stemmed the tide of immigration to the New World and, for those who did come, open land was still available in the United States. There was in fact considerable skepticism that the prairie climate and terrain would support agricultural settlement. Nevertheless, the rail system that was to transport western resources to world markets and settlers to the West was put in place while incremental settlement spread across Manitoba and westward along the CPR tracks and the North Saskatchewan valley.

The long-anticipated settlement boom began in the late 1890s as the depression lifted, large-scale immigration resumed, and free land in the United States all but disappeared. The success of early settlers and the introduction of new and hardier strains of wheat put the earlier skepticism about prairie agriculture to rest. In the single decade from 1901 to 1911 the prairie population rose from 419,000 to 1,328,000, an increase of over 316 percent in only ten years. When Prime Minister Wilfrid Laurier declared in 1904 that the twentieth century belonged to Canada, he reflected the sense of optimism that seized the "last, best West," as the prairies were described in the promotional literature of the Canadian Pacific Railway and federal government.

While the settlement of the West is a saga that cannot be recounted in any detail here, there are a number of features that should be noted given their impact on Canadian political life. Although the West was settled in large part by the westward migration of Canadians, and in particular by those from Ontario, many settlers came to the West from Europe and the United States. They had spent little if any time in other parts of Canada, and had limited exposure to the political values, institutions and parties of the central Canadian heartland. Thus the prairie population had *relatively* shallow roots in Canadian political soil and, more particularly, in the mainstream Conservative and Liberal parties. In the economic crises to come, western Canadians were, as a consequence, open to new political ideas and quite prepared to abandon the traditional parties in order to support more radical, regional parties.

The prairie population was also set apart by its ethnic composition. In the 1931 census, which marked the ethnic crystallization of the prairie community, only 56.5 percent of the residents were of British or French descent, compared to 80.1 percent for Canada as a whole and 82.7 percent for Ontario. The prairie population was marked by large numbers of German, Scandinavian, Ukrainian, Dutch, Polish, Russian, and American settlers. With that diversity came a multiplicity of religions, languages, and cultures, giving the prairies a uniquely multicultural cast. French Canadians made up only 5.8 percent of the prairie population in 1931, a proportion surpassed by those of German, Ukrainian, and Scandinavian descent. This demographic feature has been of long-lasting political importance. It helps explain why French Canadians have often been seen as simply another ethnic minority, and a relatively small one at that, and why the *regional* rather than *national* size of the French Canadian population has dominated prairie reactions to bilingualism and biculturalism. Moreover, in the historical process of assimilating a linguistically diverse immigrant population, the protection of the French language was often seen as an unwelcome shield behind which other ethnic groups might seek protection from assimilationist pressures. In combination, these demographic features help account for widespread opposition in the West to dualist interpretations of Canadian political life.

Although the prairie population was demographically diverse, it was pulled together by the wheat economy. Unlike the Maritime provinces, the prairie provinces shared a common and overriding set of economic interests. The wheat economy, which touched the lives of virtually every inhabitant, bound the prairie provinces into a single economic unit within which individuals shared essentially the same environment, interests, and problems. The wheat economy forged a "regional way of life,"[28] facilitated the political integration of the prairie West, and set the region apart from central Canada to the east and British Columbia to the West.

Prairie agriculture was a precarious undertaking at the best of times. Farmers were dependent upon an uncertain and often harsh climate, and upon volatile foreign markets lying beyond their control. (While the Canadian economy at large was dependent upon volatile foreign markets, no other region exported as much or was dependent on such a narrow market base.) Wheat was not a crop that could be sold on the local or even Canadian market. It had to be sold—through the middlemen in the grain trade—on distant foreign markets, and shipped across Canada and the Atlantic Ocean on a monopolistic transportation system. The wheat economy was afflicted by cycles of boom and bust determined by the state of European markets and the size of the Canadian crop, both beyond the control of the prairie farmer.

The nature of prairie agriculture led to a litany of economic grievances. These included tariff protection for central Canadian manufacturers, which increased the price western Canadians had to pay for consumer goods and farm machinery while their own crops sold on the unprotected international market; transportation bottlenecks; freight rates which were seen to be excessive; inequities in the grading and marketing of grain; and the frustrations of a debtor frontier toward the central Canadian financial institutions which loaned badly needed capital, collected the interest, and, when times were tough, foreclosed on the family farm.

Economic Alienation

It is a longstanding tenet of western alienation that the federal government has been at best indifferent to the economic woes of the West, and at worst a major contributor to those woes through national tariff and freight rate policies.

As economist Kenneth Norrie has pointed out, however, the West is a relatively sparsely populated economic hinterland within both the Canadian and North American market economies. As many of its economic grievances, such as the lack of secondary manufacturing and economic diversification, arise from the region's location in these market economies, they

"... must be interpreted as dissatisfaction with a market economy rather than with discriminatory policies of the federal government."[29] *Norrie goes on to argue that the negative effects of federal policies have been exaggerated, and to question whether even the most supportive national policies would be able to overcome market forces and encourage any substantial increase in manufacturing and secondary industry in the prairie West. While extensive government intervention in the market economy would be a necessary condition, it may not prove to be a sufficient condition.*

These economic grievances generated in turn a regional set of political grievances embodied in the term *western alienation*.[30] Apart from the specific economic grievances mentioned above, western alienation reflected the belief that the West's contribution to the national economy was not being sufficiently acknowledged. At the time, wheat was a mainstay of the national as well as the regional economy. As Mallory has pointed out, "almost the whole Canadian economy was vitally affected by, and organized around, the movement of the annual grain crop into world markets."[31] While that movement supported the national railway system, which in turn bound the new country together and

The Milch Cow

Grain Growers Guide, December 15, 1915. Glenbow Archives, Calgary

provided essential western Canadian markets for the industries of central Canada, the West received few compensations from national policies on tariffs and freight rates. At the heart of the matter lay the belief, and essentially the reality, that western Canadians lacked the political muscle commensurate with their contribution to the national economy. The region found itself in a quasi-colonial position vis-à-vis central Canada and the national government, and the specific economic problems that confronted the West were attributed in large part to the region's political impotence. Thus their solution required a regional assault on the political and institutional status quo.

The quest for political reform followed a number of paths, including support for national opposition parties; the creation of new, regionally based parties that would, it was hoped, be more attuned to western Canadian interests; the rejection of the party system altogether and the advocacy of non-partisan forms of government; and the advocacy of changes in the rules of the House of Commons which would weaken party discipline and make MPs the agents of their constituents rather than of their parties. The quest, then, lacked a clear focus; westerners were divided among those who sought simply a change in government, those who sought new, regionally based parties, and those who rejected the party system altogether. The regional critique of parliamentary institutions was hesitant and inconsistent. For example, while party discipline was assailed, Parliament itself was venerated without a clear recognition that party discipline is an essential feature of parliamentary democracy. The desire to weaken party discipline was not coupled with practical proposals for alternate institutional arrangements that would have sustained parliamentary democracy after the key prop of party discipline had been removed.[32]

Perhaps the most significant thing about western agrarian protest is that it failed to have any substantive impact on the *institutional* fabric of the Canadian federal state before the Great Depression transformed the face of the West. Although the Depression, which began in 1929, reached its peak in the mid-1930s and lingered on until the start of the Second World War, was a major economic shock for the country at large, its impact on the prairies was particularly catastrophic. The collapse of world trade devastated the export-based prairie grain economy. Accompanying the collapse in markets came drought, grasshoppers, and high winds which stripped the topsoil from the land, creating the immense duststorms of the "dirty thirties." The debt accumulated in the good years as farmers expanded their holdings and improved their equipment became a crushing burden in the 1930s. When crops could be grown they often could not be sold, or could be sold only at a price insufficient to cover the costs of production and transportation. Farmers frequently had no choice but to plough their crops under and hope for better times "next year." For many others in "next year country" the only alternative was to leave both the land and the region as debts mounted and the banks foreclosed.

The Depression redefined the place of the prairie West in Canada. Prior to the 1930s, the prairies had been the magnet drawing immigration into Canada. With the onset of the Depression and the Second World War, immigration slowed to a trickle. When it resumed after 1945, the prairie West was bypassed. Unsettled agricultural land had all but disappeared, and grain prices were low. The grain economy had become more capital-intensive, offered fewer employment opportunities, and was costly to enter for new farmers. Post-war immigrants, primarily from urban backgrounds, had skills ill-suited for prairie agriculture. In addition, the prairie West, struggling to recover from the devastation of the Depression, was no longer seen as a region of promise and new beginnings. Even a passing familiarity with the Depression was sufficient to deter all but the most masochistic immigrants from settling on the prairies.

The end of in-migration to the region, the out-migration of hundreds of thousands of prairie residents during the Depression, and the increasing mechanization of prairie agriculture all combined to undercut the region's population base and political power. Western agriculture also became less central to the Canadian economy; even though more grain than ever was being produced, the grain economy's proportionate share of the national economy steadily declined. As fewer people produced more and more with less and less economic impact, the prairie West drifted toward the margins of Canadian life.

The New West

As the "old," agrarian West declined, a "new West" was beginning to emerge. Its birth was marked by the discovery and commercial development of the Leduc oil field in Alberta during the late 1940s and early 1950s. The new West, like the old, was based on natural resources, but these now included oil, natural gas, potash, coal, and uranium. The *relative*, but not *absolute*, decline of agriculture and the broadened resource base brought the prairie economy more into line with that of British Columbia, and laid the foundation for a broader political region than had existed in the past. (The resource base of the British Columbia economy encompassed not only forestry and the Pacific fisheries but also coal, natural gas, hydroelectric power, and a variety of minerals including copper, lead, molybdenum, and zinc.) Although resting on a broader base, the new regional economy was similar to the old in that it was heavily dependent upon foreign markets and highly variable world prices. The "boom and bust" problems of the wheat economy were inherited, moderated to a degree, but not surmounted.

The new West developed slowly at first, with British Columbia being the primary growth pole and population magnet. Then, after 1973, escalating world prices for oil fuelled rapid growth in the Alberta and, to a lesser degree, Saskatchewan economies. The face of the new West was urban rather than rural, its features coming from the skylines of Vancouver, Calgary, and Edmonton rather than from the silhouettes of grain elevators against the prairie sky. The spirit of the region was marked by the aggressive boosterism of communities on the move and on the make. Migration into the region accelerated as thousands of Canadians packed their belongings into U-haul trailers and moved to the West in search of a slice of the natural resource pie. Once again the West seemed to be at the cutting edge of Canadian society, and the smouldering coals of political discontent burst into flame.

During the 1970s and early 1980s, western alienation was fuelled from a number of sources. Provincial governments in the West, growing rapidly in size and bureaucratic expertise, challenged the federal government's management of national economic policy and sought to roll back federal intrusions into provincial fields of jurisdiction. National bilingualism policies found an unsympathetic and at times hostile audience in the multicultural West, a reaction that was in large part symptomatic of a more general frustration that Ottawa's preoccupation with national unity problems stemming from Quebec pushed western concerns off the nation's political agenda. Note a 1979 speech by Stan Roberts, then president of the Canada West Foundation (*see Glossary*):

The new fury of the Westerner demonstrates itself when it strikes home that Quebec's six million plus citizens have turned the country on its collective ear and created an enormous attention to their problems by the election of a péquiste government, while the West's six million plus citizens (still) can't be heard over the rush and scramble to accommodate Quebec. Sometimes the West's frustration and rage is misconstrued as anti-Quebec in nature. It is not. It is, in most cases, envy of Quebec's political prowess combined with fury at the West's own impotence on the national scene.[33]

Of greatest importance, however, was the lack of elected western representation within the national government, and thus the inability of westerners to see their own regional reflection in national institutions.

As Figure 4.4 illustrates, there have been dramatic swings in western Canadian representation on the government side of the House of Commons, dramatic in comparison with the more stable pattern in Atlantic Canada. The highwater mark came in 1958 when the West moved overwhelmingly into the Progressive Conservative camp, and when John Diefenbaker swept the region and the country in the largest Canadian electoral landslide ever. While Diefenbaker's appeal was undeniably national in 1958, it was particularly strong in the prairie West. As Denis Smith explains,

He gave to the Prairies for the first time in their history the same sense of dynamic and central participation in nation-building that his predecessor, John A. Macdonald, had given to central Canada after 1867.... [his policies] were policies of national integration that typified the prairie conception of Canada.[34]

When other regions swung back to the Liberals in the early 1960s the West stood pat, and with Diefenbaker's defeat in 1963 western representation on the government side of the House fell to precariously low levels. The situation was particularly bleak on the prairies. Of the sixty-five western Liberal MPs elected in the 1963, 1965, 1968, 1972, and 1974 general elections, only twenty-three came from the three prairie provinces. In 1979 the Progressive Conservatives formed a minority government in which the West enjoyed strong representation. The Conservative leader, Joe Clark, was the first Canadian prime minister born in the West. Only nine months later, however, the Conservatives were defeated and replaced by a majority Liberal government. In that election only two Liberal MPs were elected west of Ontario, both in Manitoba. The West had been all but shut out of the national government.

The lack of elected representation in the national government was at odds with the growing economic muscle of the West and the region's burgeoning share of the national population. It was irksome to westerners that a majority government could be elected before a single ballot was counted west of Ontario, as had happened in 1980. (When this happened again in 1984, but with the West on the winning side, it evoked little comment!) The practical cost of regional exclusion from the national government was driven home, at least to Albertans, by the federal response to rising world oil prices in 1973–74, by the introduction of the National Energy Program in the fall of 1980, and the related and acrimonious conflict between the national and Alberta governments over the price structure for Canadian oil and natural gas.

FIGURE 4.4

MPs Elected to the Government Side of the House

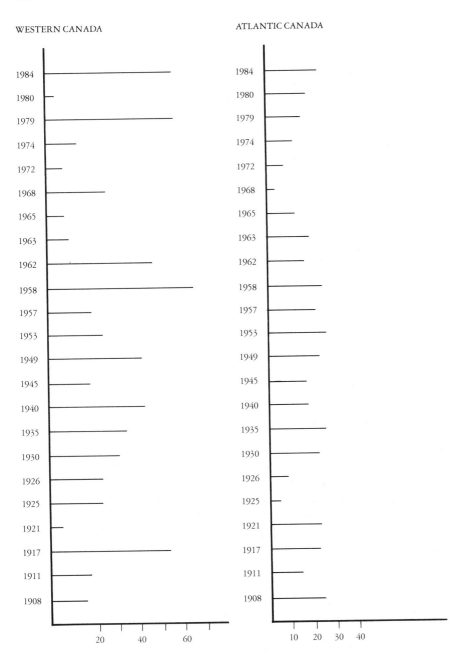

FIGURE 4.5

Western Alienation

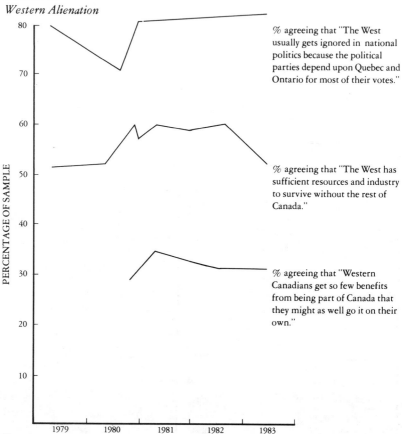

These data are taken from a series of public opinion polls conducted for the Canada West Foundation, Calgary, Alberta. For details, see the Foundation's *Opinion Update* series.

The extent of western alienation during this period is traced out in Figure 4.5. At its peak, nearly a third of western Canadians agreed with the statement that "western Canadians get so little out of Confederation that they might as well go it on their own." Throughout this time, levels of western alienation tended to be higher in Alberta and British Columbia than they were in Saskatchewan and Manitoba, though the sentiment was far from absent in the eastern half of the region. Alienation was also much more pronounced among Conservatives than among Liberals, with New Democrats occupying an intermediate position. As Table 4.2 shows, discontent with the regional distribution of costs and benefits by the Canadian federal system is not confined to the West. There is, however, a clear east–west gradient to such discontent that sharply differentiates the political climates of the Atlantic and western regional peripheries.

TABLE 4.2

Regional Variations in the Perceived Costs of Federalism
1979 National Election Study

Percentage of respondents believing that their province or region pays undue costs or receives less than its fair share of benefits in the federal system:

Atlantic Canada	32%
Newfoundland	23
Prince Edward Island	14
Nova Scotia	39
New Brunswick	34
Quebec	38
Ontario	46
Western Canada	56
Manitoba	48
Saskatchewan	43
Alberta	62
British Columbia	58

Source: This table is derived from Figure 2.4 in Harold D. Clarke, Jane Jenson, Lawrence LeDuc, and John H. Pammett, *Absent Mandate: The Politics of Discontent in Canada* (Toronto: Gage, 1984), p. 44.

Western alienation, it should be stressed, cannot be equated with support for western separatism. While it is true that during the early 1980s separatist parties emerged for the first time in western Canada, they were able to attract only marginal support. In the absence of a federal election, separatist candidates ran provincially, where they played a minor role at best in the provincial elections held in Saskatchewan and Manitoba, and no role whatsoever in the British Columbia election. Only in Alberta did the Western Canada Concept make a mark by electing an MLA in a provincial by-election and by capturing 11 percent of the popular vote in the subsequent provincial election. In that election, however, the sitting WCC member was defeated as the governing Conservatives picked up seventy-five of the seventy-nine seats. In the aftermath, the various separatist parties entered a period of disarray and declining public support from which they have not begun to emerge. In the short term at least, prospects for a separatist revival have been crushed by the outcome of the 1984 federal election.

In a tactical sense, western Canadians sometimes drew a parallel between their own situation and that faced by the residents of Quebec who, the argument went, had used the threat of separatism to extract political and economic concessions from the national government. Only if western Canadians were prepared to play the same game, the argument continued, would Ottawa pay attention to the complaints and aspirations of the West. The Quebec analogy failed to recognize that many Québécois had much more than a tactical commitment to independence, that for many independence was a positive goal and not simply a club with which to beat concessions out of Ottawa. More importantly, it failed to recognize the essential core of western alienation.

Despite alarmingly high levels of western alienation in the late 1970s and early 1980s, the separatist option failed to attract significant public support. In ten surveys tracked by the Canada West Foundation between mid-1979 and mid-1980, support for separatism averaged only 6.6 percent across the region. Even this figure may overstate the true level of separatist support, as support for separatism was used by some respondents as a vehicle for expressing the intensity of one's frustration rather than as a positive endorsation of an independent West. Unlike the Québécois, who have sought to ward off assimilation, western Canadians have sought integration into the Canadian political, economic, and social mainstreams. In the words of the late W.L. Morton, the region's foremost historian:

the West has been defined as a colonial society seeking equality in Confederation. That equality was sought in order that the West should be like, not different from the rest of Canada.[35]

Western alienation captures the frustration that integration has been incomplete, that western Canada has failed to play a role in the nation's life commensurate with the region's resources, potential, and aspirations. Western Canadians want in, not out. Even among separatists the cry has been: "we are not separating, it is Canada that is abandoning the West." Thus western alienation was not a vociferous expression of a regional or provincial identity, but rather the expression of a frustrated Canadian identity.

At its peak, then, western alienation represented a demand by the "new West" for greater recognition within the nation's political and economic fabric. This demand came to a head in the political struggle over the patriation of Canada's constitution, a struggle that took place at a time when the federal government had but two elected representatives from western Canada. When the dust had settled on the patriation battle and the Constitution Act had been proclaimed, little had been done to redress long-standing western grievances.[36] Admittedly, provincial control over natural resources was strengthened through the addition of Section 92A—"Non-Renewable Natural Resources, Forestry Resources and Electrical Energy"—to the Constitution Act, and the new amending formula was modelled after western proposals. However, parliamentary institutions had not been reformed so as to provide more effective and more visible regional representation in Ottawa.

The West has not been able to impose its own political vision upon the Canadian federal state despite a nearly unbroken tradition of regional political discontent reaching back a hundred years. Its chance to do so seemed better than ever during the patriation negotiations: the West's economy was strong, its population was growing relative to the nation as a whole, its provincial governments were led by popular and articulate leaders. Since that time the western economy has softened, and there has been significant out-migration from the West in general and from Alberta in particular. The "new West" is no longer ascendant, and western discontent no longer evokes a sense of national urgency.

There is an important lesson to be learned from the western Canadian experience over the last ten years. Once all was said and done, once the price of oil had gone up and down again, once thousands had moved into the region and left again, *the centre held.* The West remained on the national periphery, a region rich in resources and territory, but with a relatively small and widely dispersed population. The lesson is this: regional discontent will *not* be overcome by dramatic shifts in the regional location of people and industry. In the short and at least intermediate runs, the Canadian economic and demographic landscapes are immutable. Marked differences in the regional distribution of natural resources, population, and industry will remain, and will continue to generate tension within the national political system. Thus, if we recognize regional discontent as a problem and seek solutions, we must look to the way in which we conduct our political affairs. The solutions are to be found in leaders and parties, in regionally attuned developmental policies.[37] Such policies, however, will require national institutions and parties that are sensitive to regional peculiarities, interests, and aspirations. While neither institutional reform nor party reform will necessarily result in more regionally attuned national policies,[38] they remain of central importance to the resolution of regional discontent.

The Political Economy of Regionalism

The argument that regionalism has institutional rather than geographical roots is one that is developed at length within the political economy literature. Note, for example, the following discussion by Wallace Clement:

> *Regionalism is but one expression of more deeply rooted inequalities and social problems in Canada. Any dominant class creates problems through its very existence and actions; one such problem is regionalism. To suggest that regional inequalities are "natural"*

ignores the realities of power and the control some men have over the lives of others. Thus a detailed analysis of the current structure of regionalism would show that it is not the product of some natural phenomenon like geography or resources or even historical accident; rather, it is the product of a series of actions and institutions created and alterable by man.[39]

Clement goes on to argue that primary importance should be attached

*to economic institutions and the
impact of class. Thus it is not "Ontario"
that dominates Canada: "it is the
capitalist class and its operating arm in
the economy, the economic elite, which
has always performed and continues to
perform this task."[40] Political factors
such as the federal structure of the
Canadian state, take on a somewhat
secondary role:*

But do ... political boundaries

*really explain regionalism in
Canada? Are the real regional
splits not based more on economics than politics? ... While political fragmentation aggravates
regionalism, it is not itself the
cause of regionalism. That cause
must be found in the uneven
economic development of the
country and the branch-plant
structure of corporate capitalism.*[41]

During the 1970s and early 1980s, Pierre Trudeau served as the lightning rod for western Canadian political discontent. It is appropriate, then, that in one of his last public speeches as Canada's prime minister, Trudeau should capture the essence of western Canadian discontent. Speaking before the Quebec wing of the federal Liberal party on March 31, 1984, Prime Minister Trudeau made the following statement:

No Canada can exist without the support of this province. Remind yourselves of that during the leadership race to elect my successor, during the coming election. Quebec is strong. Quebec can decide who will govern this country, but more importantly how this country will be governed.

Western Canadians would not challenge that statement. Their frustration stemmed from the fact that Canadian leaders could not make a similar statement about the West despite the fact that more people lived in the West than in Quebec, and that the West made a greater contribution to the national economy. The result was not discontent with Canada per se but with the Canadian political system, discontent that bound four rather disparate provinces into a single regional community, and which helped to make regionalism a pervasive and enduring feature of Canadian political life.

In the 1984 federal election campaign, a great deal of symbolic attention was paid to the West by all three major parties. The Conservatives and New Democrats appealed to what has now become their traditional constituency within the region, while John Turner made the rebuilding of the Liberal party in the West a central plank in his campaign, one he emphasized through his decision to run for election in the riding of Vancouver Quadra. Following the election, the West had fifty-eight MPs on the government side of the House, compared to only two MPs following the 1980 election, and enjoyed strong representation within the Mulroney cabinet. Thus the circumstances could not be better for the disappearance of western alienation from the nation's political agenda. To the extent that western alienation persists despite such favourable conditions, we will have evidence that its roots are to be found more in the nature of political institutions, in relatively immutable features of the economy, even in geography per se than in the party system and the regional insensitivities of national leaders.

ONTARIO

Embodied within western alienation lies a polarity which is fundamental to an understanding of both political life in western Canada and the dynamics of regionalism more broadly conceived. That polarity pits the region against "Central Canada," against the "East" or "Upper Canada" (a term more common to political discourse in Atlantic Canada than in the West). While the terms "Central Canada" and "the East" are often used to include Quebec, it is Ontario that forms the regional pivot for Canadian political life.

By any measure other than geographical size, Ontario is Canada's largest "region." Indeed, we find within Ontario a concentration of people, wealth, industry, and cultural activity that sets Canada sharply apart from the American federal system to the south. Ontario contains over 35 percent of the national population—California, the largest state in the United States, contains less than 10 percent of the national population—and forms the economic heartland of Canada. Ontario's domination of the Canadian economy far surpasses that exercised by any single state in the United States, be it New York, Illinois, Michigan, California, or Texas. Toronto dominates English Canadian cultural life to a far greater extent than any one city is able to do in the United States; there is no ready Canadian equivalent to the cultural competition between New York, Boston, Los Angeles, San Francisco, and Washington, to name but a few. Ontario, moreover, is the site of Canada's largest city *and of the national capital*. While the American capital is located in the District of Columbia, outside the boundaries of any state, Ottawa's location reinforces Ontario's position at the centre of Canadian life.

It may seem odd, then, that the analysis of regionalism in Canada largely neglects Ontario. When the term *regionalism* is used in reference to Ontario the focus is usually upon territorial divisions within the province—on conflict, for example, between northern Ontario and the "golden horseshoe"—rather than upon Ontario's position in national political life. Conventional political discourse rarely treats Ontario as one of the many Canadian regions. Joe Clark is considered to have made a major strategic blunder in his 1983 bid to retain the leadership of the national Conservative party when he declared that should Ontario Premier Bill Davis run for the leadership, Davis would be seen as "a regional candidate." In a retrospective look at the leadership campaign, Ron Graham concluded that "however true that observation was, the heart of Ontario is not won by treating it as less than the centre of the universe."[42] The study of regionalism in Canada has been primarily the study of the regional peripheries, with the central Canadian linchpin placed aside.

How do we explain a regional analysis which all but ignores Canada's largest and most influential region? Why is Ontario little more than a residual term in the regional analysis of Canadian political life? In part, the answers have to do with the manner in which regionalism is conceived. The analytical focus is not on the relationship *among* the various regions that make up the Canadian community, but rather *between* the centre and the periphery. In this context, the centre ceases to be a region like other regions and instead takes on the colouration of the whole. It is the *metropolis* to the regional *hinterlands*.[43] Given Ontario's size and weight within the national community and its central location, the identification of the regional part, Ontario, with the national whole, Canada, is understandable. To illustrate the point in very simplistic terms, it is at least conceivable to imagine Quebec, Newfoundland, or the West separating from Canada. It is inconceivable to imagine Ontario separating; Ontario *is* Canada to a degree that no other region can claim.

To cast the argument in more political terms, Ontario's share of the national electorate is sufficient to ensure at least adequate representation within the national government. In fact, since the end of the Second World War there has not been a national government with fewer than thirty-five Ontario MPs, with the average being close to fifty. (In 1984, sixty-seven Conservative MPs were elected from Ontario.) Ontario traditionally has more representatives in the federal cabinet than any other province, and the majority of Canadian prime ministers, including Macdonald, Mackenzie, Borden, King, Meighen, and Pearson, have held seats in Ontario. There is, then, a ready identification of Ontario with the national government, an identification reinforced by the location of the national capital. This does not mean a lack of intergovernmental conflict between Ottawa and the Ontario provincial government in Queen's Park, nor does it mean that the composition of the national government always reflects the wishes of the Ontario electorate. What it does mean is that Ontario cannot be shut out of the national government in the way in which both Quebec and the West have been in the past. It means, furthermore, that the "national interest" as articulated by Ottawa will reflect in large part the national interest as perceived by the voters of Ontario. (The close fit between the "National Policy" introduced in 1878, and essentially retained ever since, and the economic interests of Ontario manufacturers cannot be seen as coincidental.) In this vitally important respect Ontario is not a region like the others, and the difference tends to place the province outside the framework of regional analysis.

Regional and National Identifications

Lodged within the above discussion of Ontario is the assumption that regional and national identifications overlap in the province, that there is no conflict between being an "Ontarian" and being a Canadian, that one is simply the expression of the other. In other parts of the country, however, a harmonious relationship between regional and national identities cannot be so readily assumed.

CONFLICTING EXPECTATIONS

There is little reason to doubt that the great majority of Canadians are strongly attached to their country. While it might be argued that nationalism in Canada is less intense than in some other countries, this is not to question the existence of a strong bond between Canadians and their country. There is also little reason to doubt that Canadians are characterized by strong regional attachments, that where we live *within* Canada shapes our personal identity, our sense of who and what we are. What is less clear is how national and regional identifications interrelate.

For many observers of the national scene, regional identities are the building blocks of the Canadian national identity. Historian J.M.S. Careless, for example, writes that "what has been sought and to some degree achieved [in Canada] is not really unification or consolidation, but the articulation of regional patterns in one transcontinental state."[44] Regional identities, in other words, are found at the core of the Canadian *national* identity. This line of thought has been given political expression in former Prime Minister Joe Clark's description of Canada as a "community of communities." It also found expression, to cite but one of many possible examples, in speeches by Alberta Premier Peter Lougheed in the political debate leading up to the patriation of the Canadian constitution. Rankled by the charge that his vigorous defence of Alberta interests was in some sense "un-Canadian," Lougheed asserted that to defend Alberta was to defend Canada, that one's Canadian identity could be legitimately expressed through a strong provincial identity. To the premier there was no intrinsic conflict between regional and national identities; they were more appropriately seen as different but complementary modes of expressing one's attachment to Canada.

This conclusion is not universally accepted. The counterargument has been made that regional identities, or at the very least *strong* regional identities, constitute a corrosive influence on the strength and vitality of Canadian nationalism. It is as if individuals have only so much loyalty to parcel out, that there is a "zero-sum" relationship between national and regional identifications in which a gain by one entails a corresponding loss by the other. While one can, for example, be both a British Columbian and a Canadian, one can only be strongly attached to British Columbia at the expense of one's sense of attachment to the country as a whole. Those who perceive, and who are concerned about, a relatively weak sense of Canadian nationalism often finger regionalism as the cause; Canadians are accused of putting the regional cart before the Canadian horse, of being preoccupied with narrow regional interests while the larger interests of Canada are ignored. For others, the strength of regional identifications is seen as the consequence rather than the cause of a weak sense of Canadian nationalism; regional identifications fill the vacuum left by the absence of a more dynamic Canadian nationalism.

THE EVIDENCE

Over the last decade, opinion surveys have explored citizen identifications at some length. By far the clearest finding has been that *regional* identities, as opposed to *provincial* or *national* identities, are very weak. At issue here is the extent to which people in Atlantic Canada and the West identify with the broader region rather than with its provincial components or the larger nation. In the 1978 Perlin and Rawlyk study of opinion in Atlantic Canada, respondents were asked the following question: "Do you think of yourself first as a Canadian, as a Maritimer or as a (Newfoundlander, Prince Edward Islander, Nova Scotian, New Brunswicker)?" Across the region, only 6 percent of the respondents first chose a Maritime identity. When a similar question was posed to western Canadian respondents in 1982, less than 8 percent identified themselves as "western Canadians."[45] Neither finding demonstrates that respondents lack regional identities or that these are unimportant. They do suggest, however, that regional identities pale in importance compared to the identifications citizens have with their province and their country. They also suggest that pan-provincial regional identities may come into full blossom only within the political environment, that the terms "western Canada" and "Atlantic Canada" have a political resonance that they lack in other spheres of life.

It is not coincidental that the identifications which lack a corresponding governmental structure are the weakest. As Alan Cairns has argued, governments are not passive reflectors of their social environment.[46] They are actively involved in shaping that environment, in moulding the contours of citizen identifications as they seek to maximize political support. Thus our sense of being a Canadian, and of being a resident of a specific province, is nurtured by our federal and provincial governments respectively. No government exists, however, to nurture one's sense of being a western Canadian or an Atlantic Canadian. There are no *regional* flags, holidays, ceremonies, capitals, or symbols. It is not surprising, then, that few western Canadians or Atlantic Canadians see themselves *first* in regional terms.

Repeated surveys have found that when respondents are asked to choose between national and provincial identifications, the former prevail by a wide margin. In the Perlin and Rawlyk study, 62 percent of those selecting either a national or a provincial identification selected the former, while 38 percent said

TABLE 4.3
Provincial Variation in Citizen Identifications, April 1983

"Do you think of yourself *first* as a Canadian or as a Newfoundlander/Nova Scotian/New Brunswicker/Prince Edward Islander/Quebecer/Ontarian/Manitoban/Saskatchewanian/Albertan/British Columbian?

	Canadian	Provincial Identification	Both Equally
Newfoundland	42%	47%	11%
Prince Edward Island	57	38	5
Nova Scotia	65	30	5
New Brunswick	78	18	3
Quebec	50	34	15
Ontario	93	5	1
Manitoba	85	11	2
Saskatchewan	73	14	12
Alberta	71	12	16
British Columbia	72	14	14

(Table excludes the 0.7% of the sample who failed to answer the question, and the 1.2% who cited identifications other than national or provincial.)

that they thought of themselves first in provincial terms. In a December 1980 national telephone survey, the Carleton School of Journalism asked 1,275 respondents the following question: "Where does your first loyalty lie—with Canada or with the province in which you live?" Nationally, 74 percent chose Canada and 26 percent their province. The ratio was 66 percent to 34 percent in the Atlantic provinces, 53 percent to 47 percent in Quebec, 90 percent to 10 percent in Ontario, and 80 percent to 20 percent in the West.

A final illustration of this point is provided by Table 4.3. The data in the table are derived from a national survey conducted by the author in April 1983. Overall, 73 percent of the respondents said that they thought of themselves first as Canadians, 17 percent first as provincial residents, 8 percent refused to choose or stated an equal preference, and 2 percent did not have an opinion. The interesting aspect of Table 4.3 is the marked provincial variation. Thus we find, for example, that while 93 percent of the Ontario respondents identified themselves as Canadians first, in Newfoundland a plurality of respondents identified themselves as Newfoundlanders first. Although Table 4.3 does not mean that provincial identities are absent in Ontario, it does support the conclusion drawn above that provincial and national identifications overlap to a greater extent in Ontario than they do elsewhere in the country. At the same time, national identities elsewhere are far from weak. In the West, 74 percent of the respondents identified themselves as Canadians first even though western alienation was very pronounced at the time.

The finding that national rather than provincial identifications tend to prevail in most parts of the country is an important one, but it does not address the relationship between the two identifications. While hard information on the nature of that relationship is neither abundant nor clear-cut, what there is suggests that national and provincial identifications are not in conflict and may even be mutually reinforcing to a modest degree.

In an analysis of the 1974 national election survey, the "feeling thermometer" scores assigned by respondents to Canada and the various provinces were found to be *positively* correlated; relatively positive assessments of one's country and province tended to hang together, as did relatively negative assessments of the two.[47] As the correlation was weak and, under some statistical conditions, inconsistent, the authors stopped short of concluding that national and provincial identifications were mutually reinforcing. They did conclude that "in simple affective terms, liking one's own region does not seem to be a deterrent to liking Canada as a whole."[48] This conclusion was supported in a subsequent analysis of the 1974 data by David Elkins. While Elkins notes that Canadians have a "deep and abiding" sense of place extending to their local area, province, and country at large, and that this sense of place has heightened over time, the various identities are not competitive.[49] Indeed, those respondents who were the most sensitive to regional considerations had the strongest sense of themselves as Canadians. Thus Elkins concludes that the assumption that provincial identities override a sense of nationalism or national identity "is totally unwarranted, except in the case of a minority of Quebec French respondents with separatist sentiments."[50] Far from precluding a national identity, regional identities are best seen as partial identities within a grander, more diverse whole. Here it is also interesting to note that in the 1974 survey regional sensitivity was positively correlated with generally high levels of knowledge about Canada, with a familiarity with several parts of Canada, and with a preference for the federal government over provincial governments.

Before leaving this discussion, a number of methodological points should be made. The first is that research to date may be distorting reality by asking the wrong questions. When, for example, respondents are asked if they "first think of themselves as Canadians or New Brunswickers," they are being placed in a forced-choice situation. Yet if national and provincial identifications are not competitive, the forced choice does not square with the psychological reality of respondents. For many and perhaps most Canadians, national and regional identities may be two sides of the same coin. This point was captured in the slogan of those Quebecers opposed to the 1980 Quebec referendum on sovereignty-association; "mon non est Québécois" emphatically rejects the proposition that one must or can choose between Canadian and provincial identities. In the words of John

Holmes, "it is in the Canadian tradition for citizens to want to preserve the Canadian framework in order to live more securely as Quebeckers or Nova Scotians or British Columbians."[51]

Secondly, regional identities take on a mythical, almost lyrical, character that makes empirical measurement difficult. Richard Allen, for example, has described the Canadian West as "a region of the mind," an evocative and in many ways compelling phrase which nevertheless provides little guidance for empirical research.[52] Historian Douglas Francis evokes the same imagery, arguing that there is an aspect of the West's history

... which transcends the decisions of politicians, the intricate workings of the economy, and the daily activities of its peoples; it exists in the mind. The history of the West has often been governed as much by what people imagined the region to be as the "reality" itself.[53]

Survey researchers have yet to design instruments of sufficient sensitivity to capture the richness of regional imagery and identification implied in this passage. Until they do, a firm understanding of the relationship between national and regional identifications will have to wait.

The Political Roots of Regional Discontent

National communities such as Canada are made up of countless competing groups and interests, only some of which are territorially based. To a large degree, the political system reflects these competing groups and interests; it is the arena within which competition is played out. As discussed above, however, it is more than the arena, more than a passive reflection of social conflict. The political system shapes the pattern of conflict by moderating some of its forms while exaggerating others.

The specific manner in which the political system shapes social conflict depends upon the nature of political institutions. As the American political scientist E.E. Schattschneider observed,

all forms of political organization have a bias in favour of the exploitation of some kinds of conflict and the suppression of others because organization is the mobilization of bias. Some issues are organized into politics while others are organized out.[54]

We might ask, then, whether there is an institutional bias to the way in which the Canadian political system handles regional conflict. Is regionalism organized into or out of Canadian political life? Do Canadian political institutions moderate regional conflict, building bridges across regional divisions and thereby integrating a large and regionally diverse national community, or do they exacerbate regional conflict? Is regional conflict more intense and more pervasive within the political system than within the society itself? Does our regional location shape our political outlook more than it shapes our social mores or economic beliefs? To address such questions, we must begin with a look at federalism and federal institutions.

Federalism can be seen as a political device to reconcile the potentially conflicting interests of national majorities and territorially bounded minorities. It provides a check on the national majority in some instances while permitting reasonably unfettered majority rule in others. To understand just how this is accomplished, it is useful to draw a distinction between *interstate* and *intrastate* federalism.

The term *interstate federalism* refers initially to the federal division of powers. Minority interests, or at least the interests of those minorities which can be reconstituted as provincial majorities, can be protected from the national majority through the federal division of powers. To the extent that provincial governments have jurisdiction over matters of minority concern, the weight of the national majority cannot be brought into play. In practice, though, we find that a clear division of powers has been impossible and even inconvenient to maintain. Thus the meaning of interstate federalism has been extended to encompass the protection of minority interests by provincial governments in the intergovernmental arena. The major characteristic of contemporary interstate federalism is the representation of regional interests *to* the national government by provincial governments, rather than the representation of such interests *within* the institutions of the national government by national politicians.

This latter form of representation is referred to as *intrastate federalism*. In part, intrastate federalism can be seen as an alternative to interstate federalism. The need for provincial governments to represent regional interests to the national government, as opposed to their more narrow governmental interests, is reduced if such interests receive full expression within national institutions. Intrastate federalism can also be seen as an essential complement to interstate federalism. While the federal division of powers provides significant protection for minority interests, communities may still have important regional stakes in those fields falling within the jurisdiction of the national government. If effective means of intrastate representation are not built into national institutions, regional conflict can be intensified by national policies which fail to take full account of regional concerns, sensitivities, and peculiarities.

Intrastate and interstate federalisms shape political conflict in quite different ways. Intrastate federalism emphasizes the national dimension of conflict by channelling it through the institutions of the central government, whereas interstate federalism emphasizes the regional dimension of conflict by channelling it through intergovernmental relations. As a general rule of thumb, there are more

TABLE 4.4
Provincial Senate Representation

Province	1981 Population	No. of Senators	Population per Senator
Ontario	8,625,107	24	359,000
Quebec	6,438,403	24	268,000
British Columbia	2,744,467	6	457,000
Alberta	2,237,724	6	373,000
Manitoba	1,026,241	6	171,000
Saskatchewan	968,313	6	161,000
Nova Scotia	847,442	10	85,000
New Brunswick	696,403	10	70,000
Newfoundland	567,681	6	95,000
Prince Edward Island	122,506	4	31,000
Northwest Territories	45,741	1	46,000
Yukon	23,153	1	23,000

incentives for conflict resolution in the intragovernmental arenas of intrastate federalism than exist within the intergovernmental arenas of interstate federalism.

The Constitution Act of 1867 tried to marry British parliamentary institutions, which had evolved within a small and relatively homogeneous country, to the American innovation of federalism, which had evolved to meet the political demands of a large and territorially segmented society. The marriage was not fully consummated. While the federal division of powers—interstate federalism—was put into place, national parliamentary institutions were not adequately modified to accommodate the needs of intrastate federalism, to provide for the representation of regional interests by national politicians within national institutions. The cost has been a political system that does not handle regional conflict as well as it might.

Canadian parliamentary institutions frustrate intrastate federalism in a variety of ways, with the nature of the Senate perhaps heading the list. All federal systems have a bicameral or two-chamber legislature, with one chamber based on representation by population and the other based on territorial representation in which disproportionate weight is given to territorial units with relatively small populations. In the Canadian case, the House of Commons is based on representation by population, while the Senate incorporates representation by territory. As a federal institution, however, the Senate is badly flawed. Initially, the Senate provided equal *regional* representation; twenty-four seats each were assigned to Ontario, Quebec, and the Atlantic region. When the West was recognized as a Senatorial district, it too was given twenty-four seats. While premised on a certain rationality, this system has produced over time a pattern of *provincial* representation within the Senate that is almost haphazard, as Table 4.4 illustrates. Although in general smaller provinces are overrepresented in the Senate, the pattern is not consistent. The populations of British Columbia and Alberta, for example, are *underrepresented*, not overrepresented, relative to the population of Ontario.

A far more serious flaw comes from the fact that the Senate is an appointed, not an elected, institution. Unfortunately, but perhaps inevitably, the appointment process and hence the Senate have fallen into disrepute. Appointment to the Senate is seen primarily as a reward for party service, as a means of paying off political debts and removing deadwood from active political life. While this perception is not always justified, it is correct often enough to tarnish even the most worthy Senate appointment. More importantly, an appointed Senate lacks political legitimacy within a democratic system. As a consequence it is unable to challenge effectively the majority will of the House of Commons, should it be inclined to do so. There is, then, no effective balancing of majority interests (expressed through the House of Commons) and regional interests (expressed through the Senate). It is the House, and the House alone, that dominates the national legislative process. While this should not imply that the Senate fails to perform useful legislative functions, those functions do not include providing effective regional representation.

The institutional characteristics of the House also close off rather than facilitate regional representation. Here the principal culprit is party discipline, one of the most striking and important features of modern parliamentary government. In the early decades following Confederation, party discipline was much looser, a reasonable number of MPs were elected as independents, and many MPs behaved as such within the House. Today, the prospects of an independent candidate being elected are little better than those of the proverbial snowball, as the national parties and their leaders dominate election campaigns.[55] Within the House, opportunities for independent action are rare. The House is organized along party lines, the MP is elected in large part as a party symbol, and both the MP's career within the House and fate in the next election are yoked to the electoral fate of the party.

In a classic commentary written shortly before the Second World War, Richard Crossman characterized the British House in the following terms: "one can say that the scale of ethics in parliamentary democracy today is roughly that your conscience comes last, your constituency second, and your party requirements come first."[56] There would be little quarrel in applying Crossman's characterization to the contemporary Canadian House. As Robert Jackson and Michael Atkinson maintain, "... the overriding fact of parliamentary life is the existence of persistent and powerful political parties, and members of parliament are encouraged to regard party cohesion as more important than freedom of action in the House."[57]

Party discipline on the government side of the House is essential given the conventions of responsible government. If backbenchers—government MPs who are not members of the cabinet—were to vote against the government, more than the specific bill would be at stake. The very survival of the government would hang in the balance. The price of defeat in the House, followed by dissolution and an uncertain general election, is so high that government MPs have no choice but to follow the cabinet through hell or high water. For opposition parties, the conventions of responsible government per se do not impose rigid party discipline. Opposition MPs can break party ranks without immediate impact on the composition of the government, though to do so in a minority government situation might deny one's party the opportunity to defeat the government. It is nevertheless important for opposition parties to maintain a united front in the House. If the Leader of the Opposition wages a spirited attack against a government bill, it is awkward if some members of his party then support the bill in the House. To the extent that opposition parties try to present themselves to the electorate as alternative governments, disunity within the House can tarnish this image. Thus both opposition and government MPs who break party ranks do so at considerable risk to their political careers.

The individual responsible for making sure that MPs are in the House to vote when needed, and that they vote correctly, is the party Whip. The name is an unfortunate one in that it suggests the coercive enforcement of party discipline. While coercion is not entirely absent, party cohesion is maintained by a variety of other factors. In writing about his experiences as a Liberal backbencher, Mark MacGuigan, former Justice Minister in the Trudeau government, dismissed heavy-handed pressure as a factor in maintaining party discipline, arguing that a more compelling factor was

the desire to get along with and to be well thought of by one's closest associates. It is, in other words, an in-group feeling that is generated by constant association, a common philosophy, and the desire to keep the party strong.[58]

Party discipline follows from the conventions of responsible government, from a very human desire to be a good team player, from the rewards that follow from party loyalty including a chance at a cabinet appointment, from peer pressure, from a willingness to follow the leader of one's party despite disagreement on particular policies, and from an understandable belief among long-time partisans that what is best for their party is also best for their country. It is hard to imagine a government member who would feel so strongly about a specific piece of legislation that he would be prepared to see the country fall into the hands of the opposition.

The point to be stressed, then, is not that party discipline is a malignant growth within Parliament that should be removed, nor that MPs are little more than robots with little effective freedom of action. Private channels of protest do exist, including the weekly caucus meeting where dissension can be safely and at times effectively vented behind closed doors. To a degree, public dissension is possible in speeches outside the House. MPs can lobby members of the cabinet on behalf of constituency interests. "Free votes," where MPs are not bound by party discipline and where the fate of the government is not held to be at stake, do occur, though they are generally restricted to issues with a heavy moral content, such as capital punishment, where party discipline would be difficult to maintain even if imposed. The committee system also provides an opportunity for MPs to question at least the details of government legislation.

Nevertheless, in the final analysis MPs cannot place the interests of their region above the interests of their party. Thus, if the two should clash, the MP may be seen by his or her constituents as having sold out, as having forsaken the role of *regional representative*. Unfortunately, much of the representational work that MPs may do, such as speaking out in caucus meetings and bending the ears of parliamentary colleagues and cabinet ministers, takes place in private, out of sight of constituents. The public image of the MP may be that of a slave to party discipline at the expense of regional interests, while the private reality may be that of a spirited and indefatigable champion of regional interests. It is not that party discipline prevents regional representation, but rather that it inhibits dramatic *public* displays of regional representation in action. The MP cannot stand on the floor of the House and insist that the regional interest must prevail, that he or she will not budge. For such histrionics, voters must look to their provincial premier.

The manner in which parliamentary conventions inhibit public forms of regional representation takes us to regional representation within the federal cabinet. From the time of the Confederation debates in the 1860s, cabinet has been seen as the first line of regional defence in Ottawa.[59] Ideally, the cabinet contains representatives not only from the ten provinces but also from the major regions within the larger provinces. It should be noted, however, that while the appearance of the cabinet reflects an overriding concern with regional representation, the reality of regional representation takes place far from the public eye. Cabinet ministers are bound not only by party discipline but also by the cabinet conventions of secrecy and collective responsibility. Thus while vigorous regional representation may take place behind the closed doors of cabinet, in public all ministers support cabinet policy. This places regional residents in a difficult position should the cabinet announce policies at odds with their perceived regional interest. In public, their regional representative in cabinet has no alternative but to endorse and defend the government. In private, any number of things could have happened: the minister may have fought hard for the region but lost, traded a regional loss on one policy for a regional gain on another, been convinced that on this particular issue the national interest or the interest of some other region should prevail, been asleep at the switch, or sold his or her region and constituents down the river. The problem is that voters have no way of determining which in fact took place. For the *public* defence of regional interests, voters are likely to take more satisfaction from their provincial premier, who is unhampered by party discipline, collective responsibility, or cabinet secrecy.

Cabinet Representation

In 1978, when the Trudeau government had been in power for over ten years and largely with the same cast of ministers, a Gallup survey asked a national sample of Canadians the following question: "Apart from Prime Minister Trudeau, do you happen to recall the name of a cabinet minister in Ottawa?"

Only 33 percent of the respondents could name a minister and correctly identify his or her portfolio. A further 14 percent were able to name a minister, but could not correctly identify the portfolio. Nineteen percent mentioned the name of an individual who in fact was not in the cabinet, and 34 percent would not even venture a guess!

These findings raise some doubt as to the importance Canadians attach to regional representation within the federal cabinet. If many Canadians are unaware of who is even in the cabinet, it is doubtful that they think of particular ministers as "their man (or woman) in Ottawa." This suggests in turn that the much higher profile of provincial premiers, relative to that of cabinet ministers, greatly enhances the representative role of premiers within the national political process. The Gallup Report, *October 28, 1978.*

When the problems attendant upon regional representation in the Senate, House, and cabinet are taken together, and when they are considered in conjunction with the frequent inability of parties to elect candidates from all regions of the country (discussed in Chapter Eight), it seems fair to conclude that intrastate federalism in Canada is at best impaired. Partly though not entirely as a consequence, there has been a growing emphasis on the interstate representation and protection of regional interests. More and more, the provincial premiers and their governments have come to be seen as the primary line of regional defence *within the national political process.* This emphasis on interstate federalism is not cost free. It greatly inflates the role of provincial premiers, giving them a national prominence not envisioned in the original federal design. The resolution of regional conflict is removed from the parliamentary arena and placed in the more abrasive intergovernmental arena. An overreliance on interstate federalism undermines the role of MPs, stripping them of an important function which is then divested to the premiers. It can inflame intergovernmental conflict, allowing governments to present what may be a governmental struggle over resources, programs, and prestige as a regional conflict.

"During the course of this election campaign, it has not been my intention to give anyone the impression that Easterners are a festering horde of greedy-eyed, furry little demons and fat, pompous robber-barons who would like nothing better than to sneak into my beloved Alberta in the dead of night and rob me blind. If this impression has inadvertently been presented, it is, indeed, truly unfortunate."

Phil Mallette, *Globe and Mail*, March 13, 1979

This is not to suggest that provincial governments do not have the responsibility to speak out for their province. The problem arises from the lack of an effective counterbalance from national politicians. Instead of a multiplicity of regional voices, articulating a variety of regional perspectives, the stage is dominated by the premiers. The regional voices of Senators and MPs have been muted by the institutional constraints within which they must work. Thus parliamentary institutions, despite their other virtues, fail to provide a forum for the resolution of regional conflict, conflict which has been deflected into the intergovernmental arena.

It was frustration with both impaired intrastate channels of regional representation and the intergovernmental conflict that results from an excessive reliance on interstate representation that lay behind the search for institutional reform that preoccupied governments, special task forces, policy institutes, and political scientists for much of the late 1970s and early 1980s. Given the regional role that second chambers play in other federal systems, it is not surprising that much of that search has focused upon Senate reform,[60] though other institutions were not neglected. Procedural reform of the House of Commons has been pursued on a periodic basis, and electoral reform has been frequently proposed.[61] About the only reform that has been definitely ruled out is the amalgamation of the existing provinces in the eastern and western peripheries into larger and, in theory, more powerful provincial units.

In 1970 a Royal Commission headed by John J. Deutsch reported in favour of Maritime union. However, even though the commission reported a public opinion survey in which 64 percent of the respondents were in favour of "a complete union into a single province,"[62] the recommendation failed to generate significant political support. In the 1978 Perlin and Rawlyk survey, only 31 percent of the respondents supported while 59 percent opposed "the joining together of Newfoundland, Nova Scotia, Prince Edward Island, and New Brunswick in one big Atlantic province, with just one government for all four." A 1970 conference held in Lethbridge, Alberta, to discuss the formation of a single prairie province generated such compelling arguments *against* union that the idea quickly vanished, never to reappear.[63] It seems clear that any serious proposal for institutional reform will have to accept the existing provincial boundaries as given. The smaller provinces are no more likely to join together than the larger ones are to subdivide.

The quest for institutional reform has not been hobbled by a lack of alternatives. If anything, the very multiplicity of reform options poses more of a problem. If significant institutional reform is to occur, reform of the magnitude of an elected Senate, two conditions will have to be met. The first is that the costs of regional conflict must come to be seen as intolerable, or at least sufficiently onerous so as to seriously impair the performance of the national government and to threaten the stability of the political community. Second, Canadians must come to believe that only institutional reform offers a solution to regional discontent, that a solution is not to be found in a new leader, a new party, or a new government. Although the first condition was approached during the later Trudeau governments, the second has not been met. Given the results of the 1984 general election, it is not likely to be met in the near future. Therefore to describe regional conflict as something akin to a cancer in the Canadian body politic that should be removed by institutional surgery would be to overstate the problem that most Canadians perceive. While to describe it as a mere wart or mole would be to understate the problem, an analogy might be found in arthritis. The condition can be painful and limiting but, with no satisfactory cure in sight, we can get by.

The National Interest

While it is important to understand the political roots of regional conflict in Canada, the impression should not be left that such conflict is *entirely* an artifact of flawed institutions and flawed political leadership. The regions of Canada are different in their resources, in their population base, and in their industrial organization. These differences produce conflicting regional interests and aspirations, which are reflected in turn within the political system.[64] Many features of the Canadian landscape, furthermore, lie beyond the reach, or largely beyond the reach, of political institutions, reformed or otherwise. Institutional reform will not move oil from the prairie sedimentary basin to the Canadian shield, or the pulp forests of Ontario and Quebec to Prince Edward Island. Nor will it dramatically affect the regional location of the Canadian population, the rate of unemployment in Newfoundland, and the concentration of industrial activity in central Canada.[65]

As Paul Phillips notes, "for most of the country outside of the industrial heartland, economic fortunes rest directly on the fortuitous distribution of climate, geography and natural wealth, and on the state of foreign markets, none of which respond much to Canadian policies."[66] The dependency on volatile foreign markets exposes the Canadian economy to sharp and unpredictable dislocations which are often regionally specific in their effects, both positive and negative. For example, the impact of the Depression was more catastrophic on the prairies than it was elsewhere, just as escalating world prices for oil in the 1970s conveyed widely divergent benefits and costs on the Canadian provinces. As Richard Simeon explains,

exogenous economic factors like the energy crisis have a highly differential regional impact. Because the domestic economy is so regionalized, this impact sharpens internal divisions; it is disintegrative rather than unifying ... the territorially specific location of resources combines with their allocation to the provinces to maximize regional conflict.[67]

Although governments cannot move resources and can do little to control foreign markets, they can transfer the revenues that come from resource development and cushion the impact of foreign markets. Within the context of a national economy, regional dislocations need not be as severe as they might otherwise be nor economic specialization as risky. Regions whose markets have gone soft can ride out the storm, sheltered by those sectors of the national economy that remain strong. As we will see in the next chapter, however, the redistributive mechanisms that are required can be complex and politically contentious. They also bring us up against conflicting visions of the national interest.

Discussions of regionalism often boil down to arguments over which should prevail: regional interests or "the national interest"? When the question is put in this form, the answer in a democratic country seems obvious. The national interest should prevail, given that it reflects the aspirations of a larger number of citizens. However, to oppose regional and national interests is to simplify grossly an interesting and difficult problem.

There are essentially three issues at stake in discussions of the national interest. The first is the extent to which the national majority should prevail, an issue that arose in last chapter's discussion of English–French relations. On this point, Pierre Trudeau has been an emphatic spokesman for the supremacy of the national will:

If Canada is indeed to be a nation, there must be a national will which is something more than the lowest common denominator among the desires of the provincial governments. And when there is a conflict ... between the national will and the provincial will, the national will must prevail. Otherwise, we are not a nation.[68]

Yet when Canadians adopted a federal system of government, they rejected the assumption that the national majority should always prevail. The essence of federalism is that on at least some issues, in at least some circumstances, the will of the national majority will be *constitutionally frustrated*. A political system is not federal if it is predetermined that national majorities will prevail over provincial majorities should the two collide. As the Canadian political system is thoroughly federal in principle and design, it cannot be assumed that the national majority *should* prevail. The perception that the national majority *will* prevail, the principles of federalism notwithstanding, lies close to the heart of regional discontent. Note, for example, Dalton Camp's distillation of the political sentiment he found in British Columbia:

Where the wealth is found, the numbers are still few; where the numbers are found, so too are the looters, carpetbaggers and welfare indolents. And since democracy is the rule of numbers, the pillage of the West seems certain.[69]

In federal systems, numbers alone should not rule.

The second issue is who should articulate the national interest or, if there are several articulations, which one should prevail. The House of Commons, with representatives from every nook and cranny of the country elected through a system that ensures the equal weighting of individuals and the proportionate weighting of provincial populations, is certainly a claimant. (From a Québécois perspective the House may be rejected, and the Quebec *National* Assembly endorsed, for just those reasons.) If it is to be the House, how do we deal with the fact that Ontario and Quebec jointly determine the composition of the national government, that the House is organized along party lines, that when the House speaks it is actually the governing party speaking, and that important groups may lack adequate representation on the government side of the House? (Those who seek institutional reform, such as a popularly elected Senate, are frequently concerned with the ability of parliamentary institutions to articulate the national interest in an authoritative manner.) Should provincial governments be involved in the articulation of the national interest? Should it be the governments of Canada, rather than one level of government alone? If so, what would be the appropriate institutional mechanism for orchestrating the voice of eleven governments? How would we handle conflicts between governments, such as arose during the early 1980s when the Alberta government argued that higher oil prices were in the national interest while the federal government argued just the reverse?

The third issue has to do with the way in which we conceptualize the "national interest." Is it something that transcends regional interests, or is it best seen as something that faithfully reflects regional interests? Is the whole greater than the sum of its parts, or is the whole equal to the sum of its parts? Ironically, one of the most colourful statements in support of a transcendent national interest came from the West's most successful politician, John Diefenbaker:

We shall never build the nation which our potential resources make possible by dividing ourselves into anglophones, francophones, multiculturalphones, or whatever kind of phoneys you choose. I say Canadians, first, last and always.[70]

This issue takes us back to the nature of Canadian society. Is Canada best seen as a community of communities, or is there a national community that in some meaningful way transcends its regional components?

These are not easy questions to answer. They do reveal, however, that the articulation of the national interest in a regionally diverse federal state is never straightforward and seldom non-contentious. To appeal to the national interest in the resolution of regional conflict is to duck a set of issues which adds much of the flavour to Canadian political life.

Suggested Readings

1 David G. Alexander, *Atlantic Canada and Confederation: Essays in Canadian Political Economy*, comp. Eric W. Sager, Lewis R. Fischer, and Stuart O. Pierson (Toronto: University of Toronto Press, 1983).

2 Herman Bakvis, *Federalism and the Organization of Political Life: Canada in Comparative Perspective* (Kingston: Institute of Intergovernmental Relations, Queen's University, 1981).

3 For a comparative look at regional issues in western and Atlantic Canada, see David Jay Bercuson, ed., *Canada and the Burden of Unity* (Toronto: Macmillan, 1977).

4 J.F. Conway, *The West: A History of a Region in Confederation* (Toronto: James Lorimer, 1983).

5 David J. Elkins and Richard Simeon, eds., *Small Worlds: Province and Parties in Canadian Political Life* (Toronto: Methuen, 1980).

6 Ernest R. Forbes, *The Maritime Rights Movement, 1919–1927: A Study in Canadian Regionalism* (Montreal: McGill-Queen's University Press, 1979).

7 Roger Gibbins, *Regionalism: Territorial Politics in Canada and the United States* (Toronto: Butterworths, 1982); and *Prairie Politics and Society: Regionalism in Decline* (Toronto: Butterworths, 1980).

8 Donald S. MacDonald, ed., *Government and Politics of Ontario* (Toronto: Macmillan, 1975).

9 Ralph Matthews, *The Creation of Regional Dependency* (Toronto: University of Toronto Press, 1983).

10 Paul Phillips, *Regional Disparities*, rev. ed. (Toronto: James Lorimer, 1982).

11 G.A. Rawlyk, ed., *The Atlantic Provinces and the Problems of Confederation* (St. John's: Breakwater, 1979).

12 John Richards and Larry Pratt, *Prairie Capitalism: Power and Influence in the New West* (Toronto: McClelland and Stewart, 1979).

Study Questions

1 How would *you* answer the survey question discussed in this chapter: "Do you think of yourself first as a Canadian or as a Manitoban, Ontarian, Nova Scotian or whatever?" In your own case, how would you describe the relationship between national and provincial identifications?

2 How would you characterize your own province in terms of the costs and benefits of Confederation? Compared to other provinces, has your own province done relatively well or relatively poorly? Do you find the cost–benefit approach to be a useful one, or do you find it difficult to apply to your own or other provinces?

3 Trace out the history of your province's representation on the government side of the House of Commons and within the federal cabinet. How has your province fared compared to others?

4 Have there been occasions in the past when the national interest, as articulated by Parliament, has been clearly at odds with the majority interest within your province? If so, how was the conflict resolved? Are there such conflicts at present, or can such conflicts be seen on the political horizon?

5 What would you propose as the best method of articulating the national interest? How would you defend this choice?

CHAPTER FIVE

Redistributive Politics

Governments provide many programs which are of roughly equal benefit to all citizens. The security benefits provided by national defence, for example, vary little across regions, gender groupings, or generations. Many other programs, however, provide more selective benefits: assistance for the disabled, low-cost student loans, tariff protection for the textile industry, and family allowance cheques for Canadians with dependent children provide but a few examples. Even in the field of national defence, significant selective benefits flow from the location of military bases and the procurement of military supplies. While we all may benefit from one form or another of such selective benefits, this is not to say that on balance the benefits of government are equally or randomly dispersed across the population. Indeed, a more realistic assumption would be that benefits are not equally dispersed, and that an essential element of political life is the contest over the benefits of government, the struggle to divide up the spoils of public life.

Government programs are supported by taxation and, just as the benefits of government are not evenly distributed, neither is the tax load or what might be termed the burden of government. Some pay more, both absolutely and relative to the benefits they receive in return, while some pay less. Thus a second essential element in political life is the contest over the burden of government. Just as citizens and, for that matter, corporations try to maximize their return from government programs, so too do they try to minimize their tax load, shifting that burden where possible onto other shoulders.

Both of these elements blend into the *redistributive activities* of modern governments. Simply put, governments no longer accept, if they ever did, the distribution of wealth that would occur through an unhindered free market. The free market is constrained in countless ways: individuals too old or too incapacitated to work are nonetheless provided with a minimal income, universities are subsidized

131

so that students do not have to pay the market cost of their education, domestic industries are protected from "unfair" foreign competition. In Chapter Three we discussed the redistributive impact of language policies in Quebec and within the federal public service. In this chapter our primary focus is on the redistribution of income among individuals and across regional communities, two redistributive domains widely recognized as being central to Canadian political life. As a 1970 position paper on income security stated:

We believe the Government of Canada must have the power to redistribute income, between persons and between provinces, if it is to equalize opportunity across the country.... The "sense of a Canadian community" is at once the source of income redistribution between people and regions in Canada and the result of such measures.[1]

In its exploration of redistributive politics, this chapter addresses three basic topics. The first is the evolution and redistributive impact of the modern welfare state. Given that the redistributive impact turns out to be very modest, the chapter then examines why individual disparities in income have not played a larger role in Canadian political life. Thirdly, the chapter examines the redistribution of income and economic opportunities across the regional communities of Canada. Throughout, the primary focus will be upon the redistributive role of the national government and national policies. However, it should be borne in mind that provincial governments are also actively involved in redistributive policies, and that provincial governments are central players in the administration and guidance of the Canadian welfare state. The territorial dispersion of economic activity, both across Canada and within provincial boundaries, is also of acute concern to provincial governments. The national focus of this chapter, then, provides but the flavour of redistributive politics in the Canadian setting.

The Canadian Welfare State

The emergence of the welfare state was marked by a shift in social responsibility from the private to the public sector. Prior to its emergence, individuals were dependent upon their own resources, the support of an extended family, and, in the extreme, private charity in meeting the contingencies of unemployment, illness, injury, and old age. Today, while private means of support have not disappeared, they have been supplemented and in some cases dwarfed by state activity. The emergence of the welfare state has been associated with greatly increased public expenditures on education, health care, and social assistance. This growth, it should be stressed, has been characteristic of all western, industrialized states. The emergence of the welfare state is not a phenomenon restricted to Canada alone.

THE EVOLUTION OF THE CANADIAN WELFARE STATE

Prior to the Great Depression of the 1930s (*see Glossary*), only a very limited redistributive role had been prescribed for government. It was assumed that most people could thrive in the free market, and that those who did not had largely themselves to blame. Both success and failure were attributed to characteristics of the individual. Those who succeeded did so because they were frugal, restrained in their passions, and committed to the work ethic. Those who failed did so because of a lack of hard work, because they squandered their financial and human resources, because their lack of self-restraint led to alcohol abuse and the crippling financial load of large families. Although it was recognized that some individuals could not compete for reasons beyond their control, including physical and mental disabilities and extreme old age, it was assumed that they were small enough in numbers to be sustained through private charity and the support of extended families. In essence, then, the free market was to run its course, the strong were to survive and thrive, and the weak were to fall by the wayside.

The Depression had a profound impact on this ideology. By the millions, North Americans who believed in the work ethic, who believed that only the lazy need go without work, were unable to find employment. In the face of the magnitude of the Depression's economic collapse, explanations of economic success and failure based on individual characteristics lost much, though not all, of their force. It became evident that the root problem lay beyond the control of the individual, that in the throes of the Depression individuals were not the captains of their fate. Government intervention in the economic order became more acceptable when it came to be perceived that the economy could not cure its own ills, or could do so only at an unacceptable social and political cost.

With the end of the Depression came the Second World War and massive governmental intervention in the economy. Somewhat unexpectedly, that intervention coincided with economic prosperity and a reasonably equitable sharing of the war's economic burden. Thus at the war's end, government intervention was seen in a more positive ideological light. Indeed, it was called for by many in order to ward off both an expected post-war recession and the growing left-of-centre electoral threat to the incumbent Liberal government posed by the Co-operative Commonwealth Federation (*see Glossary*). When both this acceptance of government intervention and the altered views of poverty that emerged from the Depression were combined with the new Keynesian emphasis on interpersonal transfers as an essential tool for economic management, the stage was set for the full blossoming of the modern welfare state.

Although the welfare state is primarily seen as a collection of social programs, it also has an important economic component. James Rice argues that acceptance of the welfare state, particularly by business interests, hinged upon the prior acceptance of Keynesian economics, that the welfare state was born at the end of the Second World War when "... the government realized that it could use social policies as a means of economic management."[2] It was the marriage of the welfare function and the economic management function, Rice maintains, that created business support for the expansion of social programs which the welfare state entailed.[3] In 1945, the federal government's White Paper on Employment and Income recommended the stabilization and, in some cases, the subsidization of consumer expenditures through transfer payments to persons. Large-scale social programs, it was argued, would allow the government to stimulate the economy when private demand faltered, as it was feared would happen at the end of the war. Here historian Donald Creighton argues that the social programs of the new welfare state—veteran's benefits, family allowances, unemployment insurance, increased old age pensions—were designed to distribute purchasing power as widely as possible, to "... put money into the hands of people who could be counted on to spend and keep on spending."[4] The welfare state thus came to provide much of the fuel, if not the engine, for post-war economic growth.

John Maynard Keynes (1883–1946)

When the Great Depression struck in 1929, the initial response of western governments was based on the economic model of the family. Just as families curtail expenditures when times are bad, governments slashed public expenditures. Thus funds for social assistance became increasingly scarce at a time when the need for social assistance was desperate.

Yet as public spending was cut, the Depression only deepened. Then, in 1936, John Maynard Keynes published The General Theory of Employment, Interest and Money *which crystallized a radical alternative for public expenditures. Keynes argued that government spending was not analogous to family spending, and that government spending should be* increased *when the private economy faltered.*

By increasing public spending

and/or decreasing taxes when times were bad (and by decreasing public spending and/or increasing taxes when times were good) governments could moderate the swings in the business cycle. Public spending could compensate for a decline in private demand. It could stimulate the economy, create jobs and eliminate troughs in the business cycle that had been exaggerated by government cutbacks in the past. If governments wanted to provide an immediate stimulus to the economy, then social programs provided a way of transferring purchasing power to those who, in Creighton's words, "could be counted on to spend and keep on spending." Thus, payments to the poor, the elderly, and the unemployed became important tools of economic management.

Marxist interpretations of the welfare state go beyond recognizing its role in economic management. Finkel, for example, argues that the welfare state "... was devised by governments that wished to preserve the power of the ruling class but saw that power threatened by working-class militancy directed against an economic system that seemed unable to provide jobs or security."[5] Whether or not one chooses to accept this interpretation, it is clear that the economic stability fostered by the welfare state made an important contribution to Canada's postwar political stability.

A variety of other factors, rooted in a rapidly changing social and economic environment, also contributed to the emergence of the Canadian welfare state. With urbanization and industrialization came a new set of social problems that overwhelmed the resources of the family and private charity. In an urban setting and wage economy, those who could not earn a wage—the elderly, children, and the handicapped—were no longer seen as productive members of the family unit but were redefined as economic burdens.[6] As the modern economy came to require a well-trained labour force, the state moved to create wider access to post-secondary education through a massive increase in funding for public universities, colleges, and technical institutes. Ideological changes set in motion by the Depression continued to shape the evolution of the welfare state. It was increasingly accepted that old age, mental or physical disability, the poverty of one's parents, or the inability of the economy to provide full employment should not deny individuals adequate food, shelter, and medical attention. In short, it came to be accepted that the government should provide assistance to those unable to fend for themselves, and that basic educational and medical services should be universally available to citizens regardless of their income or that of their parents. While the welfare state did not provide "cradle to grave" security, it left individuals much less exposed to the vagaries of the economy and the afflictions of life.

The embryonic Canadian welfare state can be seen in the 1914 Ontario Workmen's Compensation Act, the 1916 Mother's Allowances in Manitoba, the federal Old Age Pensions Act of 1927 which provided modest pensions to those in need, and the introduction of national unemployment insurance in 1941. The full flowering of the welfare state came with the end of the Second World War and the introduction of Family Allowance payments to the mothers of dependent children (1945), universal old age pensions (1951), national hospital insurance (1958), the Canada and Quebec Pension Plans as important supplements to the Old Age Pension (1965), national medicare (1968), the progressive expansion in the coverage of Unemployment Insurance and Workers' Compensation, and massive public expenditures on schools, universities, and technical institutes. In 1966 the Canada Assistance Plan provided an umbrella for a variety of social assistance programs including Old Age Assistance, Blind Persons Allowances, Disabled Allowances, child care, and aid for needy mothers. The federal government committed itself to pay 50 percent of the cost for all provincial programs falling under this umbrella, with the terms of coverage being set by the provincial governments. In total, these and other programs have created safety nets which protect Canadians from the more extreme hardships that might otherwise be imposed by injury, sickness, unemployment, and old age.

It should also be noted that the introduction of the welfare state had a significant impact on Canadian federalism. The fields of government that were most germane to the welfare state—education, health care, and social services—fell largely within the jurisdictional domain of the provinces. Thus the consequent growth of government in those fields tipped the federal balance toward the provinces as provincial governments came to supply a host of new programs and services to Canadian citizens. To the extent that the federal government was a major player, its contributions had to be channelled through federal–provincial programs. This resulted in increased intergovernmental friction over federal intrusions into the provincial domain, an increasingly complex set of federal–provincial fiscal arrangements, and growing fears on the part of the federal government that its contributions to the programs of the welfare state were not sufficiently appreciated by the electorate. (These results are explored in detail in Chapter Seven.) In addition, the central role of provincial governments meant that if the programs of the welfare state were to be available in roughly equal measure to all Canadians, discrepancies among the provinces' fiscal resources would have to be ironed out. We return to this point in the latter part of the chapter.

THE GROWTH OF GOVERNMENT

The emergence of the welfare state took place in step with a dramatic increase in the size of government. As Table 5.1 shows, government spending as a percentage of the country's Gross National Product—the total of all goods and services produced within the country—increased by two-thirds in the thirty years following the end of the Second World War. There was a corresponding rise in both the tax load and the governmental contribution to personal income. Public sector employment also increased, though by much more modest proportions. From 1961 to 1975, the share of the Canadian labour force employed by all governments, including school boards and hospital boards, increased from 22.2 percent to 23.8 percent.[7] This compares to an increase from 18.9 percent to 20.6 percent in the United States, and from 22.4 percent to 27.4 percent in the United Kingdom over the same period. In the Canadian case there was actually a proportionate *decline* in public sector employment at the federal level which was offset by growth at the provincial and municipal levels. This reflects a more general Canadian trend in which, by any measure, the growth of government has been greater at the provincial and municipal levels than it has at the federal level.

In assessing the linkage between the emergence of the welfare state and the growth of government there are a number of points to keep in mind. The first is

TABLE 5.1

The Growth of Government

Government spending as a % of GNP

5-year averages	Total	Exhaustive expenditures	Transfer expenditures	Share of personal income originating directly in government*	Total taxes as % GNP
1947–51	23.1	13.3	9.8	3.7	23.4
1952–56	26.5	17.7	8.7	4.4	23.4
1957–61	28.9	18.2	10.7	6.4	23.6
1962–66	30.3	19.7	10.6	9.1	25.7
1967–71	34.9	22.0	12.7	13.1	30.2
1972–76	38.7	23.1	15.7	13.9	32.3

*Includes wages, salaries and transfer payments.

Source: Richard M. Bird, in collaboration with Meyer W. Bucovetsky and David K. Foot, *The Growth of Public Sector Employment in Canada* (Montreal: Institute for Research on Public Policy, 1979), pp. 9 and 23.

that modern governments have grown for many reasons quite apart from the emergence of the welfare state. In the United States, for example, though not in Canada, much of the growth is attributable to rising military expenditures. More generally, much of what we think of as "big government" entails government regulation of and intervention in the economy. Neither is necessarily associated with the welfare state, though both serve to blunt what might otherwise be the raw edge of capitalism. It should also be noted that much of the growth has come about through an increase in transfer payments rather than exhaustive expenditures.

The distinction between transfer payments and exhaustive expenditures is an important one. Transfer payments entail monies that are redistributed by, but not ultimately spent by, governments.[8] Pensions, social assistance, and family allowance payments all constitute government expenditures, but the money involved is spent by private citizens in a manner which they determine. Exhaustive expenditures, on the other hand, entail monies which are ultimately spent by governments on salaries, roads, equipment, or whatever. From 1947 to 1977, 22.6 percent of all government expenditures in Canada were transfer payments to individuals, a proportion that has been increasing over time.[9] Indeed, in a rather complex economic argument, Bird maintains that in recent years the growth of government has been somewhat of an illusion, that since 1967 "the proportion of the economy's real goods and services 'used up' by the government sector [exhaustive expenditures] in the course of its activities has actually *declined* slightly."[10]

How Big is Big?

Figures from the Organization for Economic Co-operation and Development in Paris show that government in Canada takes up only an average share of the economy — though these figures do not include spending by state-owned corporations such as Petro-Canada.

Federal, provincial, and local governments in 1980 accounted for 40.7 percent of Canada's $320 billion gross domestic product, the total of all goods and services produced in the country.

In other words, for every $100 spent in the economy, $40 came from one level of government or another.

Although the comparable figure was only 33.2 percent in the United States and 32 percent in Japan, in the United Kingdom it was 44.6 percent, in Italy 45.6 percent, in France 46.2 percent, and in West Germany 46.9 percent. In Sweden, probably the most highly socialized democracy in the world, it was 65.7 percent. Edison Stewart, "Government: How big is too big?," Calgary Herald, April 13, 1983, p. C1.

INCOME DISPARITIES

There is a vast gulf between the rich and the poor in Canada. Peter C. Newman, who has chronicled Canadian wealth in his books *The Canadian Establishment* and *The Acquisitors*, offers example after example of a level of affluence beyond the wildest dreams of most Canadians: the Ontario magnate who had his own private eighteen-hole golf course constructed, complete with resident pro, after being grazed by a duffer's ball on a less exclusive course; the Vancouver millionaire who donated $275,000 to the YMCA for two racquetball courts that would be reserved exclusively for him at 5:00 P.M. for the rest of his life; and another Vancouver millionaire who paid Billy Carter, brother of the then U.S. President Jimmy Carter, $28,000 to jump off a diving board with a red rose clenched in his teeth. In more academic analyses, Canadian sociologists have documented a small, homogeneous, and relatively cohesive corporate elite in Canada that enjoys great wealth and exercises even greater economic power.[11]

At the other end of the scale we find that approximately four million Canadians — or one Canadian in six — live on incomes below the "poverty line."[12] The poverty line presently used in Canada is defined as the point below which 58.5 percent or more of family income is spent on the essentials of life: food, shelter, and clothing. The actual dollar figure varies according to family size and location, with higher incomes being required for large families and in urban areas. For example, the March 1984 poverty line was set at $7,322 for a single individual living in rural Canada and at $20,136 for a family of four living in a metropolitan area with a population of 500,000 or more.[13] Poverty is thus defined in relative rather than absolute terms. To be poor in this relative sense is not necessarily to be destitute or to be without adequate shelter, food, and clothing. Here it should also be noted that, *in a relative sense*, the poor will always be with us. As relative poverty cannot be eliminated, the important questions concern the absolute conditions faced by those at the bottom of the income scale.

The location of the official poverty line can be a contentious matter, for the line establishes the parameters of poverty; it defines how many Canadians are poor. There can be considerable debate as to whether individuals near the poverty line are in fact "poor," and whether the line should be moved up or down. Here it is useful to note an important observation made by the National Council of Welfare:

... the debate over what is the *right* poverty line and the *real* number of poor people contributes little if anything to an understanding of the economic situation of low-income Canadians. Poverty lines only establish the upper limit of the low-income population. Most poor Canadians—all welfare recipients, almost all minimum wage workers, and the majority of single elderly persons and single-parent families led by women—live on incomes that are hundreds and more often thousands of dollars under the poverty line. Few people would regard these incomes as adequate by any standard.[14]

Arguments over the placement of the poverty line should not obscure the reality of poverty in Canada, or the fact that a significant number of Canadians would fall below even the most frugal placement.

Poverty is not randomly distributed in Canada. It is twice as prevalent in rural areas as it is in urban areas, though most of the poor live in urban areas as that is where most Canadians live.[15] The incidence of poverty is higher in Atlantic Canada and Quebec, though in absolute terms there are more low-income Canadians living in Ontario than in any other province.[16] The incidence is particularly high among the elderly and within Canada's aboriginal population. Of great importance is the fact that many, and in some estimates the majority, of Canadian poor are the "working poor," those who experience close to full employment and yet do not earn enough to raise themselves and their families above the poverty line.[17]

Many of the factors associated with poverty apply with particular force to women, with the consequence that over two-thirds of Canada's poor are women.[18] As women live longer and are generally entitled to lower pension benefits, old age poses a greater threat to income security. The loss of a spouse through death or divorce carries a greater income threat to women than to men. As Bryan observes, more than half of all married women between the ages of fifty-five and sixty-four have no income at all, and have been described as being "only one man away from poverty."[19] Women who do work generally earn lower incomes than do men.

Single-parent families are more likely to be headed by women than by men, and to experience a high incidence of poverty.

INCOME REDISTRIBUTION AND THE WELFARE STATE

It is a common assumption that the welfare state has been associated with a significant shift in income from the relatively affluent to the relatively poor, and that the income disparities discussed above have been reduced though by no means eliminated. The very term "welfare" carries this connotation. In fact, however, *the emergence of the welfare state and the growth of government with which the welfare state has been associated have not led to any significant redistribution of income.* The popular image of the welfare state as Robin Hood writ large is not supported by the available evidence.

The distribution of income among individuals has remained virtually unchanged since 1951.[20] Despite the growth of government and the profusion of social programs which collectively make up the welfare state, the poorest fifth of the Canadian population received the same proportion of the national income in 1981—4 percent—as it did in 1951.[21] Nor has the income position of the wealthiest fifth been significantly eroded; they received 42 percent of the total personal income in 1981 compared to 43 percent in 1951. Social benefits, it is important to note, have increased and have come to play a larger role in the income of relatively impoverished Canadians. They accounted for 57 percent of the 1981 income for the poorest fifth of Canadians, as opposed to only 29 percent in 1951. This increased flow of social benefits, however, has not resulted in any greater equality among income groups.

In an extensive analysis of income redistribution, Gillespie concluded that "in Canada, at least, a larger state has not led to a more egalitarian state."[22] Transfer programs have stabilized rather than significantly altered the distribution of income. Gillespie argues that while the poor gained ground in the 1960s, they lost ground during the 1970s. The rich, on the other hand, not only gained ground during the 1960s but held that ground during the 1970s. The relative improvement of the rich, Gillespie finds, has been at the expense of the median and upper-middle income groups.[23] Gillespie's findings are supported by St. Laurent, who found that between 1951 and 1971 the distribution of income in Canada became *less* rather than more equal.[24] Hence Smiley's critically important conclusion: "... the extension of the public sector has no inevitable disposition to further communitarian and egalitarian values."[25]

The lack of any significant redistributive impact from the welfare state can be traced to a number of factors. Many of the programs associated with the welfare state are social *insurance* programs which are supported by taxpayer contributions and have not been designed to redistribute income. Unemployment Insurance, Workers' Compensation, and the Canada and Quebec Pension Plans, for

"Burglar? How d'you know it isn't just some Ottawa civil servant taking from the rich to give to the poor?"

Len Norris, *20th Annual*. Originally published in *The Vancouver Sun*, December 2, 1970

example, are designed to provide protection against income loss due to temporary unemployment, injury, or age. They are *not* designed to shift income from the relatively affluent to the relatively poor, and thus we should not be surprised if they fail to do so. The redistributive impact of other programs such as Family and Youth Allowances, Veterans' Allowances, and Old Age Security is blunted by the fact that such programs are universalistic in their coverage; payments are made to the rich as well as to the poor. Universalistic programs account for more than 80 percent of the income security expenditures administered by Ottawa's flagship of the welfare state, the Department of Health and Welfare.[26]

Overall, government spending provides greater benefits to those at the bottom of the income scale than to those at the top.[27] Some major programs, however, may actually provide greater benefits for the relatively well-to-do. For example, an individual earning $50,000 is required to make the maximum contribution of $169.20 a year to the Canada Pension Plan. Because CPP contributions are a deduction in the calculation of one's taxable income, $87.71 of that individual's contribution is recovered as a tax saving. *The net contribution* is thus only $81.49, for which the individual is entitled to 100 percent of the pension. An individual making $6,000 per year, an income sufficiently low that no income tax would be paid, is required to contribute $90 a year, for which he or she receives no tax saving and is entitled to only 58 percent of the pension!

In an analogous fashion, while all Canadians are covered by medicare, that coverage tends to be utilized more frequently and more extensively by the relatively affluent. Government support for secondary and post-secondary education can also be seen as a transfer payment from the relatively poor to the relatively affluent.[28] While in theory a university education is made available to all at a cost well below its market value, in practice it is the sons and daughters of the relatively affluent who are more likely to attend university. Thus, to the extent that programs associated with the welfare state are used more extensively by the well-to-do, such programs may actually redistribute wealth in the opposite direction to what we might expect.

The factors discussed to this point have dealt primarily with government expenditures. The redistributive impact of the welfare state cannot be assessed, however, by looking at its programs and services alone. We must also examine how such expenditures are financed through the tax system, expenditures and taxation being two sides of the same redistributive coin.

THE TAX SYSTEM

Our necessarily brief discussion of the tax system begins with income taxes, which were first introduced as a temporary measure during the First World War. Until the end of the Second World War and the emergence of the welfare state, they played a relatively modest role in the Canadian tax picture. In 1930, for example, only 3 to 4 percent of Canadians earned enough to be subjected to income taxes.[29] Then, as the costs of government increased, so too did the reach of income taxes. They have become the most visible form of taxation and a major source of revenue for both the federal and provincial governments. They have also become the symbol of a national commitment to the redistribution of wealth, to the principle that the relatively well-to-do should carry a proportionately larger share of the burden of government than should the relatively disadvantaged. The reality, however, is more complex than the principle would suggest.

Income taxes are only one form of tax paid by Canadians. There are also property taxes (paid directly by homeowners and indirectly by renters), sales taxes, excise taxes, licence fees, user fees for such things as national parks, and special taxes levied on selected consumer items. Taxes, for example, increase the cost of a litre of gas by about 60 percent, alcoholic beverages by about 100 percent, and cigarettes by approximately 140 percent. When all taxes are taken into account, income taxes alone account for only 30–35 percent of the total Canadian tax load.[30]

The income tax is a *progressive tax*; the tax rate increases with income. As people make more money, they pay more taxes not only in an absolute sense but also in a proportionate sense. Most other forms of taxation are *regressive*; as incomes rise, individuals pay a smaller and smaller share of their income. For example, an individual who smokes two packages of cigarettes a day pays approximately $1.75 a day or $640 a year in taxes. If that individual makes $20,000 a year, the effective "tax rate" is 3.2 percent; if he or she makes $50,000 a year, the tax rate drops to 1.3 percent. Our *tax system* combines the progressive income tax with a wide variety of regressive taxes.

It should be emphasized that income taxes not only form the smaller of the two components, but are also less progressive than is often assumed. Many of the tax breaks which are in theory open to all Canadians in fact convey far greater benefits to those with high incomes. For example, the tax-savings from registered retirement savings plans, research development tax credits, and child-care expenses all increase as income increases. A 1981 study by the Department of Finance concluded that taxpayers making more than $100,000 were able to shave their taxes by $46,000 while taxpayers making between $10,000 and $15,000 were able to reduce theirs by only $771.[31] In 1982, 239 Canadians who earned more than $250,000 in that year paid no income tax whatsoever![32] We find, then, that marginal tax rates increase much more slowly in fact than they do on paper, and may actually *fall* among individuals with very high incomes. On balance, income taxes have little redistributive effect. In 1981, income taxes alone reduced the income share of the top fifth of Canadian families from 42 percent to 40 percent, and increased the income share of the bottom fifth from 4 percent to 5 percent.[33]

Tax Expenditures

Government budgets contain detailed information on taxes collected and revenue spent. However, they fail to capture an important form of government spending, and an important redistributive instrument, called the tax expenditure. Tax expenditures are not monies paid out by the government but rather are revenues forgone through the provision of tax deductions and allowances. The difference between regular government expenditures and tax expenditures can be illustrated by two redistributive programs directed toward taxpayers with dependent children.

At present, my family receives family allowance cheques worth $689 per annum. This is a government expenditure, and it shows up in the federal budget under the Family Allowance Program. Taxed at a marginal rate of 30 percent, the family allowance cheques constitute a net transfer payment of $482 to my family.

I am also entitled to a deduction of $1,420 from my taxable income for my two dependent children. Again at a marginal tax rate of 30 percent, this represents a net saving of $426. (If I did not have children I would be paying $426 *a year more in taxes.) This $426 is a tax expenditure; it is tax income forgone rather than an expenditure identified with a particular program and department.*

Tax expenditures entail a massive amount of money. In 1979, the Joe Clark Conservative government estimated that the Government of Canada "spent" close to $30 billion on more than a hundred tax expenditures, compared with a regular budget of approximately $50 billion. Tax expenditures can thus have a very substantial redistributive effect. Yet because

they are much less visible than other governmental expenditures and, not coincidentally, subject to less parliamentary scrutiny, their redistributive effects are more difficult to document. Thus the tax system redistributes income through tax expenditures without Canadians being fully aware of the extent of the redistribution, or of the net losers and beneficiaries. Taxpayers may mutter about and search for "loopholes" without realizing the sweeping impact that tax expenditures may have on the redistribution of income in Canada.

Given that income taxes are not as progressive as they appear on paper, and that the bulk of the tax load borne by Canadians comes through a variety of regressive taxes, it should not be surprising that the tax system as a whole does not redistribute income from the relatively affluent to the relatively poor. Indeed, the tax system is *regressive* over the upper and lower income brackets—the higher one's income, the lower the tax rate—while being mildly progressive across middle income groups.[34] On balance, then, the mildly progressive impact of government expenditures—the programs and services of the welfare state—are cancelled out by a mildly regressive tax system. As Bryan concludes, it is these offsetting effects which help explain why there has been so little change in the distribution of income over the past thirty years.[35]

The discussion to this point should not leave the impression that there has been no improvement in the lot of the poor as a consequence of the welfare state. In absolute terms, the poor are better off in Canada today than they were in the past, even though their relative position has not changed. Numerous programs significantly enhance the quality of life of the relatively disadvantaged even if they do not shift income per se. Such programs would include medicare, assistance in many provinces for the purchase of pharmaceutical drugs, counselling programs of various kinds, rental assistance, employment training grants, and subsidized daycare facilities. Nor should we understate the importance of income security programs and the protection they provide against injury, illness, unemployment, and old age. Indeed, it is primarily such protection that the welfare state was designed to provide. That the Canadian welfare state has not redistributed income is not a mark of failure. The welfare state was never intended to remove inequality from the Canadian society, but rather to ensure that those near the bottom were spared destitution, that Canadians would enjoy a reasonable degree of security against the contingencies of life, and that all Canadians would have access to such things as medical care and educational opportunities.

Class Conflict and Party Politics

In the *Communist Manifesto*, published in 1848, Karl Marx argued that class conflict was *the* basic feature of political life. "Political power," the *Manifesto* declared, "is merely the organized power of one class for oppressing another." In Canada, the income disparities discussed above have *not* played a central role in political life. Class conflict has not been entirely absent; radical parties such as the Communist Party of Canada and the Marxist–Leninists, the 1919 Winnipeg General Strike (*see Glossary*), labour unrest in Quebec, and agrarian unrest in western Canada provide only a few examples of its emergence onto the political stage. Nevertheless, when one looks at the major issues that have dominated Canadian political life, class conflict has not been among them.

If one's analytical perspective is grounded in the political left, the absence of more robust class politics can be explained by the nature of the Canadian state. The state is seen not as a neutral arena within which class interests compete, but rather as an instrument of the dominant capitalist class. As such, the state acts to restrict the full expression and political organization of class interests, apart from those of the dominant class, and thus moderates class conflict. From this perspective, the welfare state becomes an effective means of "pacifying" deprived individuals within the society.[36] Where this fails, the coercive power of the state can be brought into play.

A substantial body of literature has examined the Canadian economic elite and its proximity to the centres of political power.[37] This literature confirms a good deal of mobility between corporate and political elites, along with extensive interpersonal ties based on kinship, marriage, club memberships, and common ethnic and educational backgrounds. The strength of economic elites within both the Conservative and Liberal parties, it could be argued, effectively precludes the expression of class interests other than those of the capitalist class in party competition. Hence the lack of class conflict in the electoral arena may reflect not the reality of class among Canadian voters, but rather the reality of the capitalist state and the linkage between economic and political power that it embodies.

Throughout this century, parties have existed which have offered a class analysis of political life and programs of reform based upon that analysis. On the whole, however, they have been bit players on the political stage. Although some, such as the Communist Party of Canada, have endured over time, most have not touched the political lives of the great majority of Canadians in any meaningful way. To the extent that the political left has had a significant impact on Canadian party politics, that impact has come through the New Democratic Party and its predecessor, the Co-operative Commonwealth Federation. While there is no questioning the radical stance adopted by the early CCF, there is also no question that the CCF mellowed over time, and that the radical legacy inherited by the NDP had been diluted by the end of the Depression and by the frustration of electoral defeat.

The Regina Manifesto

At its first national convention, held in July 1933, the CCF set forth its program in the Regina Manifesto. The Manifesto began with a ringing condemnation of the status quo:

> We aim to replace the present capitalist system, with its inherent injustice and inhumanity, by a social order from which the domination and exploitation of one class by another will be eliminated, in which economic planning will supersede unregulated private enterprise and competition, and in which genuine democratic self-government, based upon economic equality, will be possible. The present order is marked by glaring inequalities of wealth and opportunity, by chaotic waste and instability; and in an age of plenty it condemns the great mass of the people to poverty and in- security. Power has become more and more concentrated into the hands of a small irresponsible minority of financiers and indus- trialists and to their predatory interests the majority are habitually sacrificed.... We believe that these evils can be removed only in a planned and socialized economy in which our natural resources and the principal means of production and distribution are owned, controlled and operated by the people.

The Manifesto closed with equal fire:

> No CCF Government will rest content until it has eradicated capi- talism and put into operation the full program of socialized planning which will lead to the establishment in Canada of the Co-operative Commonwealth.

The NDP, which replaced the CCF in 1961, certainly stands to the political left of its major rivals, the Liberal and Conservative parties. Yet it would be incorrect to assume that the NDP embraces a radical critique of Canadian society. Although the NDP has provided a political vehicle for organized labour in Canada, the unions themselves have seldom offered a radical challenge to the Canadian economic order, and the majority of union members support the Liberal and Conservative parties rather than the NDP. In the late 1960s the Waffle faction within the NDP called for "an independent socialist Canada" and "a truly socialist party," but the Wafflers failed to carry the NDP, much less the country. Brodie and Jenson conclude that the political analysis put forward by the NDP owes more to populism— to the defence of the ordinary individual against corporate interests—than it does to social democracy, much less any more radical socialist analysis.[38] In its 1972 federal campaign, Brodie and Jenson argue, the NDP offered Canadians "a fairer, more just, and more equitable capitalism" while launching a populist attack on Corporate Welfare Bums.[39] In the 1974 federal election the NDP campaign slogan was "People Matter More," not exactly the kind of phrase that revolutionaries might hurl from the barricades. The 1984 campaign, with its slogan "Mainstreet not Bay Street," was built around the NDP's role in protecting the "average Canadian," a category from which few voters were excluded.

The Conservative and Liberal parties, which between them attract more than 75 percent of the popular vote, do not differ significantly with respect to redistributive policies.[40] Nor do they draw upon different bases of class support within the electorate. The correlates between voting behavior and social class are modest at best, and are dwarfed by the correlates with regional, religious, or ethnic characteristics.[41] Thus Brodie and Jenson conclude that while the politics of class may be part of the Canadian reality, the electoral organization of classes is not.[42]

Interestingly, however, Brodie and Jenson take the very absence of class differences among the parties as evidence for the existence of class politics in Canada.[43] "Political parties," they argue, "shape the interpretation of what aspects of social relations should be considered political, how politics should be conducted, what the boundaries of political discussion most properly may be and what kinds of conflicts can be resolved through the political process."[44] From this perspective the Conservative and Liberal parties have structured the Canadian political agenda so as to conceal class conflict behind an artificial emphasis on linguistic, religious, and regional conflict. Brodie and Jenson maintain that "the most successful exercise of capitalist class domination occurs when conflict between the classes is simply 'defined away' by ethnic, religious or other social differences."[45] Thus the very absence of any conclusive evidence of class politics in studies of voting behaviour confirms the very existence of class politics:

The absence of class cleavages in electoral politics should *not* be taken to imply that elections are, as institutions, devoid of class content or importance in class struggle. The electoral organization of class relations occurs if the bourgeois parties, for whatever reasons, can successfully maintain an ideological and organizational dominance which defines politics in non-class terms. It is precisely non-class definitions of politics which disorganize the subordinate classes and place some limits on their demands on private capital.[46]

This argument draws our attention to the important role that political parties and party competition can play in setting the terms of the political agenda. To offer a more complete explanation for the location of redistributive politics on the Canadian agenda, to explain why income disparities have not had a greater impact on Canadian political life, we turn now to five additional factors which have tempered class politics in Canada.

THE AMBIGUITY OF CLASS LINES

If political life were to be organized along class lines, we would need a workable class division of the Canadian population. For a number of reasons, such a division is difficult to accomplish whether we employ subjective or objective definitions of social class. As Johnson points out, this latter distinction is a critical one:

There is, in all likelihood, no greater point of division between non-Marxist and Marxist intellectuals in North America than that which arises over the definition, importance, and purpose of the study of class. Primary to this division is the degree to which the non-Marxist (or "liberal") intellectual depends upon the measurement of the subjective attitudes of individuals as his basis of analysis. In contrast, the Marxist measures or defines his categories by the objective situation of those studied.[47]

Let us look first at the measurement of subjective attitudes.

Most Canadians have at best a weak "class consciousness." They do not think of themselves in class terms and do not identify with a particular social class.[48] For example, in the 1968 and 1974 national election studies, only 39 percent and 45 percent of the respondents respectively said that they considered themselves as belonging to a social class.[49] Immediately after the 1979 federal election, respondents in the national post-election survey were asked the following question: "Which of the five social classes would you say you were in—upper class, upper-middle class, middle class, working class, or lower class?[50] Fully 58.5 percent of the respondents refused to or could not locate themselves within one of the five class categories provided. Of those who did answer the question, 58.4 percent described themselves as middle class, 25.0 percent as working class, 13.3 percent as upper-middle class, 2.8 percent as lower class and 0.5 percent as upper class. In total, then, 82 percent of the national respondents either did not adopt a class location or used the most innocuous and indistinct class category—the middle class.

Admittedly, survey questions which ask respondents to identify their class position are fraught with a number of methodological problems.[51] Respondents may use the class terminology provided by the question without it having any real meaning or resonance. In the social setting of the interview, it is easier simply to seize upon one of the answers provided than to admit that you do not understand what the interviewer is talking about. What are termed "ego effects," or the respondent's use of the survey question to enhance his or her own social standing, may distort class measurements if respondents attribute a higher class position to themselves than others would accord them.[52] In more general terms, there is reason to suspect that responses to forced-choice questions, in which respondents are asked into which of three, four, or five classes they fall, probably overstate the degree of class consciousness within the Canadian population. Although such problems do not negate the usefulness of the concept of social class, they do complicate its empirical application.

The understandable tendency of respondents to inflate their class position takes us to objective definitions of social class, for only if we have objective criteria can we argue that individuals are "wrong" in their self-placements. In part, what is at issue here is whether our social status is as we perceive it to be or as others perceive it to be. If I see myself as "middle class" but others see me as "lower-middle class" or "working class," am I wrong or are they wrong? Perhaps more importantly, if I fail to see myself in class terms at all, am I reflecting the reality or failing to see the reality of Canadian class structures?[53]

Objective definitions of social class are structural; an individual's class position is defined by reference to his or her relationship to the means of production. In the initial Marxist terminology three basic classes were identified in capitalist societies: (1) the bourgeoisie or capitalists, who owned the means of production and purchased labour; (2) the petite bourgeoisie, such as craftsmen and farmers, who both owned and operated the means of production; and (3) the proletariat, who did not own the means of production and who sold their labour in the marketplace. This classification is of much less use within modern industrial societies. It provides little assistance, for example, in enabling us to make analytical distinctions among stockbrokers, teachers, veterinarians, models, bureaucrats, rock stars, hockey players, plumbers, chartered accountants, lawyers, real estate agents, media personalities, academics, computer programmers, car salesmen, ministers (either clerical or political), doctors, and pharmacists. In short, the very complexity of modern societies makes it difficult to draw class lines. While the top and bottom of the class structure may be relatively easy to identify, there remains a very large and poorly differentiated middle.

The problems associated with objective definitions of social class can be illustrated by the methodological problems that confront survey researchers trying to measure the social class of respondents. Here it is useful to pause for a moment and think of those attributes which contribute in some significant way to the class position of individuals. At the very least we would want to include income, occupation, and education. Even these three, however, are not perfectly correlated. Thus we must deal with individuals with high formal educations but relatively modest incomes (academics and clerics might be included here) and those with modest educations but high incomes, a group that includes many businessmen, professional athletes, and some skilled tradesmen. We might also want to include some assessment of the respondent's dwelling place and personal possessions, and perhaps even more subjective measures such as the respondent's use of language or knowledge of the arts. Combining such multiple and inconsistent measures into a single index of social class is an extremely difficult task.

Nor do the problems end there. If occupation is used as a measure of class, what do we do about the woman who is employed within the house? Simply assigning her a class position equal to her husband's seems iffy—does a judge's spouse have the same social standing as a judge?—but then neither is her husband's occupation irrelevant to her own class position. How does one handle retired people: do they carry the status of their previous occupation (or occupations), or is their status fundamentally altered by retirement? What do we do with the tremendous variance that can exist within occupational groupings? Certainly business people are not interchangeable in their class position, nor are lawyers, doctors, mechanics, athletes, musicians, civil servants, or construction workers. Dividing up the population also means deciding how many classes are to be used—deciding into how many pieces the social pie should be cut—and how cutpoints between the various classes are to be determined.

These methodological problems confound the use of class concepts for the analysis of political life in Canada, be that analysis by academics or by the average Canadian trying to make some sense out of a complex social and political reality. Such problems only increase when we consider that, to a significant degree, class lines are fluid rather than fixed.

Income and the Determination of Social Class

Measurement problems in survey research are particularly acute when it comes to income, a variable of critical importance in any discussion of social class.

For a start, many respondents understandably will not reveal their income to interviewers. Other respondents, the number of which is impossible to estimate, will lie or at least exaggerate. Sometimes the researcher may suspect a lie, as I did when one of my respondents—an unemployed, nineteen-year-old male living in a rundown boarding house—reported a yearly income of $60,000. It is difficult, however, for the interviewer simply to fill in the "correct" income.

Considerable confusion can arise from the differences between before-tax and after-tax income, and between personal and family income. A housewife, for

example, may know to the penny the family's net income without knowing or caring about the gross income. To many wage-earners, income before taxes or before deductions means little; it is the take-home pay that counts. Many people keep track of their income by their hourly, weekly, or monthly wage, and experience some difficulty converting this into the annual income requested by the interviewer.

Income figures, when obtained, must then be adjusted for the number of dependants and the age of respondents. A young, unattached woman earning $30,000 a year has a very different class position than does a forty-year-old man earning the same income, but with a non-working wife and five dependent children.

SOCIAL MOBILITY

The political importance of social class depends in large part on the rigidity or permeability of class lines. If individuals feel trapped at birth, if they feel that no matter how hard they work their chances to rise in the world are restricted by their social background and that of their parents, then class-based political action becomes more likely. People may decide that the only way their own position in the world will be improved is if the position of all people like themselves is improved, and that will require collective political action. If, on the other hand, the society is seen to be relatively open, if individuals can climb to, or at least toward, the top on the basis of their own effort, if the channels of upward mobility such as educational institutions are open to all, *then class-based politics becomes less likely*. If solo ascent is possible, there is little point in dragging along one's class compatriots.

The belief in social mobility—the belief that class boundaries are fluid, that individuals rise and fall in the social order because of their own effort, that the peaks of Canadian social and economic life are relatively accessible to individuals with talent and ambition—forms an important part of our cultural mythology. Like all myths which survive over time, those embedded within the notion of social mobility enjoy some correspondence to reality, though, again like all myths, they simplify that reality and brush aside conflicting details.

In a general sense, social mobility can be defined as "who gets what chances to rise or to fall, and under which conditions."[54] More specifically, Figure 5.1 presents three forms of social mobility which, in combination, capture a good part of the Canadian mythology and reality. The first panel illustrates individual social mobility, or the ability of individuals to rise through social strata by their own efforts, pulling themselves up by their own bootstraps. (The "strata" lines in the figure are used only to position the individual relative to the surrounding society; they are not meant to suggest distinct class lines or divisions.) It is this form of mobility which is central to the mythology, but it is the second panel that captures a larger part of the reality. In that panel, the position of the individual improves over time because the entire society moves upward over time. For example, the Canadian society of the 1980s is a far wealthier society than that of the 1940s, with individuals having access to a wide range of private and public goods that were unavailable in the past. Thus individuals can gain in an absolute sense without any *relative change* in their social position. In the second panel of Figure 5.1 the individual has "moved up in the world" only because the world has moved up; he or she has been swept along by the general improvement in the society.

In the third panel of Figure 5.1, we find mobility across generations; the parents' position does not change over time but that of their child does. Parents may find a great deal of satisfaction in seeing their sons and daughters succeed in the world, satisfaction that may offset discontent with their own more limited mobility. Thus the parents who work hard at manual jobs in order to send a son or daughter to university can believe that "the system works" when the child graduates as a doctor, an engineer, or even a political scientist! Children may also measure their own progress by reference to their parents; have they come up or down in the world from the social status achieved by their parents?

FIGURE 5.1
Models of Social Mobility

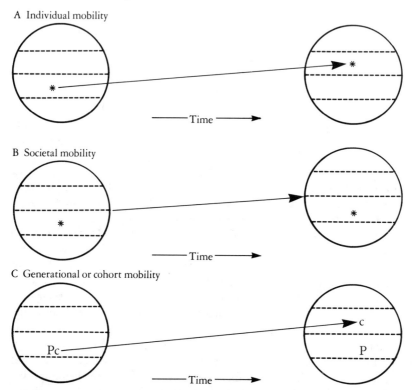

A Individual mobility

B Societal mobility

C Generational or cohort mobility

It should be stressed that the three forms of social mobility illustrated in Figure 5.1 may be difficult for individuals to untangle. An individual who appears to be moving up in the world through his or her own efforts may in fact be carried along by the upward movement of the society, the absolute gain of the society being misinterpreted as relative gain for the individual. Societal mobility may be mistaken for generational mobility; the father who takes pride in the fact that his daughter received a university degree while he himself received only a grade twelve education may not realize that today's university degree is the functional equivalent of his high school diploma. The father who worked as a labourer may be pleased to see his daughter pursuing a white-collar career as a data-entry specialist, without realizing that the labouring jobs of his generation are disappearing and that data-entry may be the new functional equivalent. Thus while both individual and generational mobility unquestionably exist, their importance tends to be exaggerated under conditions of general societal improvement. As our lives improve we are likely to attribute that improvement to our own efforts rather than to broader patterns of social change, just as when our children succeed we are likely to attribute that success to their own stellar characters and to the upbringing that they were so fortunate to receive.

Mobility, it should be stressed, can run both ways. Individuals can fall as well as rise in the world, the general standard of living for the society can fall as it did during the Depression, and many children will be less successful than their parents. Individual mobility may be dependent upon collective action. Organizations such as trade unions, ethnic associations, feminist groups, and provincial governments can play an important role in determining the success or failure of group members. Here Strauss points out the importance of collective factors in the mobility experienced by individual Americans: "while many citizens have shrewdly hitched their individual stars to rising industries, towns, and regions, other Americans have been caught in the decline of entire regions, towns, and industries."[55] To regard individuals in either case as masters of their own fate, Strauss argues, turns a blind analytical eye to the important role of collective factors.

In its various forms, social mobility contributes to the appearance of Canada as a classless society, or at least as a society in which social status is fluid. With respect to that fluidity, a great deal of importance is attached to education. If educational opportunities are open to all, and if education is the golden key to social mobility, then the educational system in general and the universities in particular come to play a central role. Here reality conveys a more somber message. Forcese, to cite but one example, concludes that

... the educational system favours the already privileged, and screens out the already disadvantaged. Rather than defeating stratification, formal education is a cause of persisting and increasingly rigid stratification.[56]

There is little question that the reality of social mobility is less than the mythology suggests. From a political economy perspective, Wallace Clement argues that despite the changes of the last two decades,

... Canada has not fulfilled its promise as a society with equal opportunity. As long as corporate power is allowed to remain in its present concentrated state, there is no hope for equality of opportunity or condition in Canada.[57]

It is not clear, however, that the mythology of social mobility has been seriously eroded by the conclusions of social scientists, or that its moderating impact on class conflict has abated. What is clear is that the mythology of social mobility blunts the appeal of those who would try to organize political life along class lines.

Lotteries and Social Mobility

Social mobility holds out the promise that "anyone can become a millionaire." In fact, of course, few can, and those most likely to do so are those born to wealth. Today, however, the dream has been rekindled and vigorously marketed by the fifteen lotteries run by the governments of Canada.

Lotteries were legalized by a 1969 amendment to the Criminal Code, and the first major lottery was launched by the federal government in 1973 in order to raise revenue for the 1976 Montreal Olympics. Since the termination of the federal government's Sports Pool in 1984, the provincial governments have exclusive control over this form of voluntary taxation. In 1983, Canadians spent $1.3 billion on the fifteen provincial lotteries, with Loto-Quebec earning a net profit of $223 million on sales of $662 million and Wintario earning $44 million on sales of $197 million.

Lottery regulations require that winners be publicly identified. One consequence of this is that players can see people like themselves who have won. To date, few winners have been found among prominent businesspeople, doctors, engineers, and lawyers. Thus the public image of the lottery is one in which the "ordinary Canadian" can suddenly be catapulted into the ranks of the millionaires. Lottery advertising plays upon this image, and indirectly upon the mythology of social mobility. Through lotteries, anyone can become a millionaire, though the odds of winning the grand prize in the 6/49 Lottery are 13,983,816 to one.

Lotteries, it can be argued, diminish class conflict by providing a few people with the means, and large numbers of people with the dream, of dramatic social mobility. As long as some individuals can make it, perhaps for as little as a one-dollar investment, the fact that most do not becomes more tolerable. The random chance of the lottery even introduces an element of fairness into a system which, in other ways, may not provide equal rewards for equal labour.

CROSS-CUTTING CLEAVAGES

One explanation for the relative weakness of class politics in Canada is that Canadians and Canadian political parties have been preoccupied with other issues. Thus, for example, one might argue that linguistic and/or regional conflict have pushed class conflict down, if not off, the political agenda. While at first glance this explanation may not seem to take us very far, as it does not say *why* other issues have been more important, it takes on additional weight when we consider how other issues have tended to *cross-cut rather than reinforce* class cleavages.

Figure 5.2 presents three models of a hypothetical society in which individuals differ from one another in only two respects: income and religion. In all other respects—age, gender, place of residence—individuals are indistinguishable from one another. In the first model the income and religious cleavages *cross-cut* one

FIGURE 5.2
Cross-Cutting and Reinforcing Cleavages

A Cross-cutting cleavages

B Overlapping cleavages

C Reinforcing cleavages

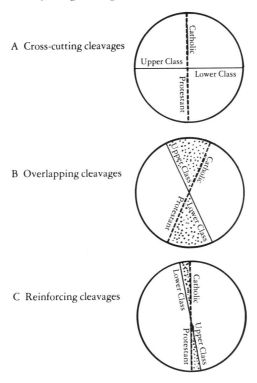

another. The fact that an individual is a Catholic tells you nothing about that individual's income, just as knowledge of the individual's income provides no indication of religious preference. Low-income individuals are as likely to be Protestant as they are to be Catholic. In this model, class conflict is moderated by the cross-cutting religious cleavage, assuming that the religious cleavage is politically salient. Low-income Protestants find their hostility to the high-income individuals moderated by the fact that many of their religious compatriots also enjoy high incomes. If one shares a common bond with members of *both* one's class (defined here in an income sense alone) and one's religion, then either intense class conflict or religious conflict can be disquieting.

In the second model the income and religious cleavages *overlap* to a significant degree. The majority of Catholics have high incomes, just as a majority of Protestants have low incomes. Thus to a degree religious and class conflicts within the political system will tend to reinforce one another; Protestants will conflict with Catholics not only because the latter are of a different religion but also because they have higher incomes. However, conflict will also be moderated by those individuals who fall within the shaded segments of the model. While the majority of low-income individuals are Protestants, and a majority of high-income individuals are Catholics, there are significant minorities of high-income Protestants and low-income Catholics. These minorities signify the extent to which the two cleavages are cross-cutting rather than reinforcing.

If we turn to the third model in Figure 5.2, the income and religious cleavages *reinforce* one another to a much greater degree. Virtually all low-income individuals are Protestants, and virtually all high-income individuals are Catholics. As a consequence, political conflicts are likely to be more intense here than in the other two models. The religious cleavage reinforces that of income, just as the income cleavage reinforces that of religion.

In the Canadian case, there are a number of cleavages which have tended to cross-cut that arising from social class. Prior to the Quiet Revolution in Quebec, for example, the linguistic cleavage effectively immobilized class-based politics within the province. As Quinn has observed,

> ... in a society where an ethnic minority [within Canada] has reason to believe that its interests as a distinct cultural group are threatened, the struggle to defend and protect those interests tends to become the dominant issue in politics and encourages the growth of strong nationalistic sentiments. As a result, purely economic issues, which ordinarily play an important role in any capitalist society, are likely to be pushed into the background.[58]

With the onset of the Quiet Revolution, class and linguistic conflict became reinforcing as political attention was focused on the income differential between francophones and anglophones. For Canada at large, however, linguistic and class cleavages are predominantly cross-cutting. It is unlikely, for instance, that a blue-collar worker in British Columbia feels more in common with francophone blue-collar workers in Quebec than with other British Columbians occupying different class positions. At least within the political realm, there has been little evidence of individuals across the country putting aside linguistic differences in order to pursue class interests held in common.

Within English Canada, regional conflict cross-cuts class conflict. When, for example, there is conflict between the energy-producing and energy-consuming provinces on the price of oil or natural gas, the class interest that a white-collar professional in Alberta might share with a white-collar professional in Toronto tends to be submerged beneath a common regional interest shared with other Albertans of whatever economic status. In a related example, oil workers in Alberta, Saskatchewan, Newfoundland, and the Northwest Territories may share a common class position, but the issue of more immediate concern may well be the regional location of oil exploration. In general, when class lines are cross-cut by regional cleavages, the mobilization of class interests within the national political system is rendered difficult. Given the pervasiveness and saliency of regional conflict, this conclusion is of considerable importance.

Federalism complicates the orchestration of class politics by introducing intergovernmental conflict into the political system, conflict which can cross-cut and overshadow political conflict based on class interests, and which can reinforce the regional effects noted above. It is for this reason, Richards and Pratt argue, that the Canadian left has been marked by impatience with both provincialism and federalism itself: "indeed, [the left's] dominant tradition, apart from its incorrigible penchant for sectarianism, is one of unabashed centralism, expressed as the belief that only a powerful federal government armed with overriding legislative and financial powers can regulate modern industrial capitalism and set in motion the transition towards a socialist society."[59] In recent years this tradition has abated somewhat as provincial New Democrats in the West have sought a greater reconciliation between social democratic principles and the political realities of a federal state with strong subnational loyalties and provincial governments.

In a landmark article on regional conflict in Canada, Richard Simeon pointed out that disadvantaged citizens face a choice among competing explanations for their status: "a poor New Brunswick logger may explain his poverty by saying he is disadvantaged because he is a New Brunswicker, or because he speaks French, or because loggers everywhere always get a poor deal."[60] The choice, Simeon argues, will have important consequences for which axis of political conflict— regional, linguistic, or class—will come to the fore. To date, the first two choices facing Simeon's logger have prevailed, and in doing so have preempted political conflict based more on class than on regional or linguistic lines. Here one might speculate, however, that the 1984 election of a national government with strong support across the regions and within both linguistic communities sets the stage for a more ideologically structured political agenda. The composition of the Conservative government may reduce the saliency of regional and linguistic cleavages, and thus may open the door for a more free-wheeling ideological debate than has been characteristic of Canadian political life in the past.

POLITICAL RESOURCES

In democratic political systems it is reasonable to expect that governments will be responsive to the pressure exerted upon them by citizens. Yet if the old cliché is true that the squeaky wheel gets the grease, it is also true that effective squeaking requires political resources. Such resources are not evenly distributed across the population.

Numbers do count in democratic politics, and the force of numbers is a key political resource. However, relatively small groups can offset a lack of numbers through other resources, including an educated and articulate leadership, ready access to and favourable treatment by the media, geographical concentration so that the group's vote is brought to bear in specific constituencies rather than being thinly dispersed across the country, the support of provincial governments, alliances within the domestic political arena, foreign allies, and economic power. Perhaps the key resource is money, which can be parlayed into a variety of other political resources. This is not to suggest that money can be equated with political power, but rather that it plays a critical role in the mobilization and effective use of other political resources.

This suggests in turn that the relatively affluent in Canada have the political resources, largely because they have the financial wherewithal, to protect their interests within the political system. There is nothing surprising about such a conclusion. It is important to stress, however, that the poor in Canada are poor not only in financial terms but also in terms of those resources which are essential to the exercise of political power. In part this explains why their interests are not fully articulated, and why the debate on income redistribution has not played a larger role in Canadian political life.

The Political Organization of Welfare Recipients

Several years ago an association was formed in Calgary to promote the rights and interests of local welfare recipients. The organizational problems faced by this group, problems which shortly led to its demise, illustrate in microcosm the political problems facing the poor.

One of the first problems the group faced was identifying its clientele. Many potential members were difficult to contact because they did not have telephones or fixed addresses. Others did not want it to be known by neighbours that they were receiving welfare, and shunned any public identification with a welfare rights group. Still others did not want to associate with the "sort of people" who were welfare recipients. They saw their own dependency on welfare as a temporary condition, and they shared with the broader society a negative perception of the "typical" welfare recipient.

Meetings were difficult to arrange. People could not be reached due to a lack

of a telephone or irregular hours. Many single parents could not get or could not afford babysitters. A meeting place was difficult to find as most group members did not have large enough homes or enough chairs, coffee cups, and so forth. A meeting time was difficult to find as many members had part-time employment at irregular hours.

If all these hurdles could be overcome, meetings were difficult to conduct. Few members had had any experience running meetings, and few were familiar with conventional rules of order. Procedural and substantive criticisms were often taken as personal attacks, and tempers frequently ran high. Effective chairpersons were rare.

Decisions made by the group were hard to implement. Implementation often required money, a detailed knowledge of the relevant political and bureaucratic environments, and well-honed interpersonal skills, all of which were in short supply. Throughout, then, the group was hobbled by severe organizational handicaps. These were largely a consequence or manifestation of the economic position of the group's members and clientele, and they pre-

cluded any effective political action to improve that position. As a consequence of their poverty, group members lacked the political resources to challenge their economic position in society.

The political system does not compensate individuals for their lack of economic resources, but rather compounds their problem. It is not that the system is stacked against the poor per se. It is stacked against those who lack political resources, and such people are far more likely to be poor than to be rich. Harold Laski, a famous British political scientist and major figure in the London School of Economics, once wrote that "the meek will not inherit the earth unless they are prepared to fight for their meekness." Within the conventional political arena, that fight is a difficult one to wage for economically and hence politically impoverished groups.

EXTERNAL INFLUENCES

The Canadian society is very open to the external world, not only in terms of trade and immigration but also with respect to ideological currents and the flow of political ideas. As a consequence, the way in which Canadians see the political world is strongly influenced by American and, to a lesser extent, western European ideologies.

Canada shares with the United States, the world's largest and most successful capitalist society, a dominant liberal ideology which emphasizes personal freedom and individual rights. Liberalism assumes that the primary allocation of wealth within the society occurs through the private sector, while at the same time recognizing that an unregulated free market can deny individuals equal opportunity to pursue private gain. Thus market intervention is accepted in order to promote equality of opportunity, to shelter those who cannot compete for reasons of age or incapacity, and to correct for distortions that might occur as a result of racial, religious, or sexual discrimination. Liberalism, then, accepts a substantial redistributive role for government while relying upon the private sector as the primary mechanism for the generation and distribution of wealth. At the same time it is resistant to class analysis in any form. To the extent that Canadians see the political world through such ideological spectacles, the class organization of political life is impeded.

The influence of both Britain and the United States on Canadian life has tended to obscure Canadian extremes of wealth and poverty. Britain's aristocratic heritage has generated a host of class symbols including titles, landed estates, the Oxbridge accent, and school ties which have no ready equivalent in Canada. It is not that wealthy Canadians do not exist, but rather that they are not so readily identified.

Because the wealthy individuals featured in the mass media followed by most Canadians are Americans, we know far more about the comings and goings of the American rich than we do of the Canadian rich. The very obscurity of Canadian wealth, it can be argued, diminishes class conflict. The most visible targets of class hostility are found outside rather than inside the country. In a similar fashion, many of the images Canadians have of poverty are lodged outside the country, in the slums of London, the urban decay of the United States, and the appalling poverty of many Third World countries. The reality of Canadian poverty is thus obscured, and its impact on Canadian political life diminished.

In the international community there are many socialist countries which offer radically different models of redistributive politics. To date, however, such models have played little role in Canadian political life. In part this is attributable to the military tension which exists between the Soviet bloc and the NATO alliance, in which Canada is an active member. More importantly, American hostility to socialism in general and to the Soviet Union in particular has been so intense that it has washed over into the Canadian political culture. While Canadians may not accept the American world view holus bolus, it has sufficient credibility and penetration to cast socialist models beyond the pale of conventional Canadian political discourse.[61]

To summarize, much of Canada's external environment consists of an impoverished Third World, a continental neighbour within which class-based political cleavages are relatively weak and anti-communism is strong, socialist states posing a serious military threat, and Great Britain with its aristocratic symbols of wealth and power. Within this international context, the Canadian extremes of poverty and wealth tend to pale. Perhaps more importantly, neither end of the Canadian income spectrum is exposed to the full light of the media, which instead reflects images of wealth and poverty lodged beyond Canadian borders.

Inequality in the distribution of human resources is inevitable. Some individuals will always be stronger, quicker, more intelligent, and more aggressive. Largely as a consequence, inequality in the distribution of wealth is also inevitable, and indeed there is no evidence that Canadians would prefer an egalitarian or even a more egalitarian society. There is no expectation that the modest political equality of one person/one vote should be transformed into economic equality.

There is, however, public support for at least a modest redistributive role for Canadian governments. Equality of opportunity is a highly prized value, and thus government intervention to ensure that everyone has an equal chance to compete is widely endorsed. While there is no expectation that everyone can or should win, it is assumed that everyone should at least be in the race and should be as unencumbered as possible by discrimination stemming from race, national or ethnic origin, colour, religion, sex, age, or mental or physical disabilities. There is widespread political support for greater security for those at the bottom of the economic scale, for the basic programs of the welfare state, and for the principle of the progressive income tax.

At the same time, there is little support for any substantial redistribution of wealth among individuals, and little political concern that no such redistribution has taken place over the past thirty years. While the Canadian welfare state has provided greater security for all Canadians, it has not redistributed wealth to any significant degree, and there is little evidence that most Canadians see this as a failure. Continued income disparities have been tolerated, or at the very least have not come to the fore in political life. Indeed, Canadians appear to be more willing to tolerate large income disparities among individuals than they have been to tolerate more modest income disparities among regions.

The Redistribution of Wealth Across Regions

As we have observed in Chapter Four, the regions of Canada differ significantly in their natural and human resources. Such differences are reflected in marked regional variations in personal income, as Figure 5.3 illustrates. Regional differences in both resources and personal income lead in turn to marked differences in the fiscal resources available to Canada's ten provincial governments.

In the absence of government intervention, the mobility of people and capital is the natural consequence of such regional variations. People will tend to move to those locations where employment prospects are the most promising and where government programs are the most richly endowed. In regions where resources are limited, both wages and the level of government services will fall, encouraging further out-migration until some equilibrium is established, with low wages drawing in new investment capital. To provide but one example, the United States has experienced pronounced internal shifts in the regional distribution of its population. These have included not only the westward shift involved in the initial settlement of the continent, but also shifts from the rural South to the industrial cities of the Northeast and then, in more recent years, the shift from the Northeast and "frost-belt" states to the "sun-belt" states of the American South and Southwest. The mobility of both people and capital has been an acknowledged feature of the American experience, and an accepted response to changing economic circumstances across the regions of the United States.

The Canadian experience has also witnessed substantial regional migrations. As Chapter Three noted, out-migration, albeit mostly to the United States rather than to other parts of Canada, played an important role in the demographic evolution of Quebec. As we observed in Chapter Four, regional migrations have been of great importance in the histories of both Atlantic Canada and the West. In Canada, however, there has been less acceptance than in the United States of individual mobility as a response to regional differences in economic potential. Federal and provincial governments have intervened in a variety of ways to shore up regional communities and thus reduce the need for regional migration. Here three broad strategies have been employed: fiscal transfers from the national

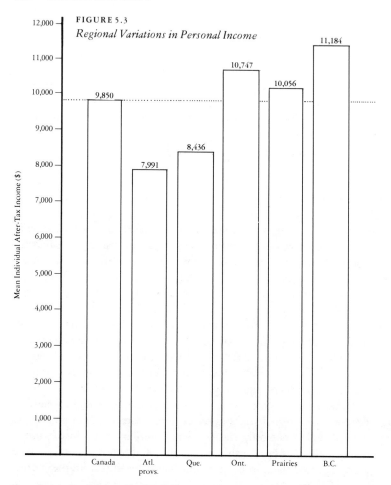

FIGURE 5.3

Regional Variations in Personal Income

Mean Individual After-Tax Income ($)

Canada	9,850
Atl. provs.	7,991
Que.	8,436
Ont.	10,747
Prairies	10,056
B.C.	11,184

Source: Statistics Canada, *Income After Tax. Distributions by Size in Canada, 1981* (Ottawa: Supply and Services, April 1984).

treasury to provincial governments in relatively depressed regions; redistributive programs run through the departments of the federal government; and "province-building" strategies pursued by provincial governments. Each of these will be examined in turn.

INTERGOVERNMENTAL TRANSFERS AND EQUALIZATION

Intergovernmental transfers have been an integral part of the Canadian federal system since the passage of the Constitution Act, 1867. Initially they reflected a fundamental imbalance between the federal division of legislative powers and fiscal resources. Ottawa's power to raise monies by "any Mode or System of Taxation" gave the national government access to revenues well in excess of its expenditure obligations under the legislative division of powers. The provincial governments, on the other hand, had access to less revenue than their expenditure obligations required. Thus Sections 118 and 119 of the Constitution Act provided for federal subsidies to the provincial governments, subsidies which were constantly being renegotiated and which served as a permanent source of contention between the two levels of government.[62] The "subsidy question" was of particular importance in the Maritimes where the search for "better terms" played a major role in the Nova Scotia Repeal Movement of 1886–87 and the Maritime Rights movement of the 1920s, both discussed in Chapter Four.

The provincial subsidies were intended to correct the fiscal imbalance in the federal system rather than to redistribute wealth from the "have" to the "have-not" regions of Canada, though the latter aspect came into play when the subsidies assumed much greater importance in the Maritime provinces than elsewhere in the country. Redistribution per se came more to the fore in an array of conditional grant programs (*see Glossary*) launched by the federal government in the 1950s and early 1960s.

Conditional grant programs are discussed in some detail in Chapter Seven. Suffice it here to say that they involved shared-cost programs in which Ottawa picked up half the cost of provincially administered programs provided that minimum national standards were observed. Through such programs Ottawa made a very substantial contribution to provincial programs in health care, post-secondary education, and social assistance. Conditional grant programs enabled "have-not" provinces to supply a level of social services roughly equivalent to that provided by the "have" provinces *in those areas covered by conditional grants*. There was, then, some significant redistributive effect; basic social services were provided at a roughly equivalent level to all Canadians regardless of where they happened to live. The redistributive effect was blunted, however, by the fact that the provinces received *matching* grants. By spending more, the wealthier provinces were thereby able to receive more from Ottawa. They were also able to use the federal funds to free up previously committed provincial funds, and thus launch new program initiatives.[63]

The emergence of unconditional equalization payments which were specifically directed toward the have-not provinces rather than toward all provinces began with the 1940 *Report of the Royal Commission on Dominion–Provincial Relations*. In its report, the Rowell–Sirois Commission recognized that the regional structure of the Canadian economy, with its concentration of corporate head offices in Montreal and Toronto, gave Ontario and Quebec disproportionate access to corporate taxes. The Commission therefore recommended a system of National Adjustment Grants paid by the national government so as "to enable each province (including its municipalities) without resort to heavier taxation than the Canadian average to provide adequate social, educational and developmental services."[64] Although the Commission's recommendation was not implemented at that time, the *principle* of equalization endured. The governments of Canada began to move toward a system of fiscal transfers that would ensure that citizens of similar economic status would have equal access to government services and face equal tax loads no matter where they happened to live. This principle is now constitutionally entrenched in Section 36 of the Constitution Act, 1982.

Section 36: Equalization

Section 36 of the 1982 Constitution Act captures the national commitment to equalization that began with the 1940 Rowell–Sirois recommendations:

36 (1) Without altering the legislative authority of Parliament or of the provincial legislatures, or the rights of any of them with respect to the exercise of their legislative authority, Parliament and the legislatures, together with the government of Canada and the provincial governments, are committed to (a) promoting equal opportunity for the well-being of Canadians; (b) fur-thering economic development to reduce disparity in opportunities; and (c) providing essential public services of reasonable quality to all Canadians.

36 (2) Parliament and the government of Canada are committed to the principle of making equalization payments to ensure that provincial governments have sufficient revenues to provide reasonably comparable levels of public services at reasonably comparable levels of taxation.

The principle of equalization was first put into practice through the Federal–Provincial Tax Sharing Arrangements, 1957–62. Provincial governments were provided with unconditional grants from the national treasury designed to bring their yield from individual income taxes, corporate income taxes, and succession duties up to the average per capita yield for the two wealthiest provinces, British Columbia and Ontario.[65] Equalization payments in that first year totalled $139 million. In the 1962–67 fiscal agreement the equalization formula was extended to include provincial revenues from natural resources, and the British Columbia/Ontario average was replaced by the national average. In 1967 the formula was expanded to include sixteen provincial revenue sources, and in the Federal–Provincial Fiscal Arrangements and Established Programs Financing Act of 1977 this was further expanded to include twenty-nine revenue sources, or virtually all the revenue sources available to provincial governments. At that time the formula was also amended to include only 50 percent of the revenue accruing to provincial governments from non-renewable natural resources, a modification to which we shall return shortly.

Table 5.2 provides one snapshot of how equalization payments are distributed across the provinces. There you will note that Quebec receives the largest total payment, whereas the largest per capita payments are received by Prince Edward Island and Newfoundland. In this snapshot, 91.6 percent of the equalization payments went to the five eastern provinces, with Manitoba being the only western province to qualify.[66] As can be seen from the table, the equalization payments to the smaller Atlantic provinces are, on a per capita basis, very substantial. Table 5.2 also records specific purpose transfers from Ottawa to the provincial governments, transfers that cover the federal contribution to medicare, hospital care, advanced education, and social assistance. Again on a per capita basis, these payments are not equal across the ten provinces. Those provinces which qualify for equalization payments also receive higher per capita specific purpose transfers. When both types of transfers are combined, the per capita payments range from $1,034 in Prince Edward Island and $870 in Newfoundland to only $265 in Alberta and $259 in Ontario. The northern territories constitute a special case in that there are no provincial governments in the North, and thus the total transfers from the federal government are much greater than in the case of the provinces.

The application of the equalization formula is a complex undertaking. For each province, the per capita revenue yield is calculated for each of the twenty-nine revenue sources. If, across the twenty-nine sources, the provincial yield is less than the average yield of Ontario, Quebec, Manitoba, Saskatchewan, and British Columbia, the federal government makes up the difference. If the provincial yield is more than this average, no equalization payments are made. The point to be stressed is that equalization payments are made from the federal treasury. The equalization formula does *not* take money from the richer *provincial governments* and redistribute it to the poorer ones. Provincial revenues per se are not redistributed; they are used only in the calculation of equalization payments to be made *by Ottawa* to the have-not provincial governments. Thus the "burden" of equalization is carried by all Canadian taxpayers, including those in the have-not provinces.

One of the reasons for equalization payments is that the constitution gives provincial governments primary access to revenues derived from natural resources. These revenues are not evenly dispersed across the provinces. In the 1970s the concentration of oil reserves in Alberta and to a much lesser extent Saskatchewan severely disrupted the equalization formula. When the price of oil escalated after 1973, and the Alberta government imposed higher royalties, the revenues accruing to Alberta grew enormously. When this increase was fed into the equalization formula, the national treasury faced a significant leap in equalization payments. Yet Ottawa had no access to the oil revenues which were genera-

TABLE 5.2
Fiscal Transfers from the Federal Government to Provincial Governments (1978)

	Total $ (000)			Per Capita $ (1981 Population)			
	Equalization Payments	Specific Purpose Transfers[1]	Total Transfers	Equalization Payments	Specific Purpose Transfers	Total Transfers	Transfers as a % of Total Provincial Revenues[2]
Nfld.	262,851	203,452	493,675	463	358	870	47.9
P.E.I.	62,767	58,100	126,694	512	474	1,034	56.6
N.S.	365,456	244,642	638,321	431	289	753	46.1
N.B.	265,233	229,410	520,642	381	329	748	46.8
Que.	1,226,720	1,734,821	3,126,178	191	269	486	22.1
Ont.	—	1,979,898	2,232,127	—	230	259	22.7
Man.	213,462	318,178	566,945	208	310	552	34.4
Sask.	-12,972[3]	288,956	316,297	-13	298	327	20.9
Alta.	—	489,069	592,519	—	219	265	13.2
B.C.	—	673,339	738,743	—	245	269	18.7
Yuk./N.W.T.	—	24,470	249,575	—	355	3,623	63.5
Canada	$2,383,517	$6,243,835	$9,602,716	$98	$256	$394	24.0

[1] Specific purpose transfers include federal contributions toward hospital care and medicare, advanced education and social assistance.

[2] These percentages are based on 1977 rather than on 1978 data.

[3] Saskatchewan was in a state of transition between a "have" and a "have-not" status, and this state resulted in a bookkeeping negative equalization payment. In fact, the equalization formula does not impose a negative tax on the wealthier provinces.

[4] Equalization payments constituted 71% of all general purpose transfers from the federal government to the provinces. Thus the total transfers column also entails other general purpose transfers such as statutory subsidies, tax revenue guarantee payments, and federal corporate income tax rebates for privately owned utility companies.

Source: Statistics Canada, *Canada Year Book 1980–81*, pp. 829–32.

"This year, in the spirit of national equalization, Reggie and I feel we should spend our vacation in the have-not provinces . . ."

Len Norris, *23rd Annual*. Originally published in *The Vancouver Sun*, January 25, 1974

ting the increased equalization payments. Alberta's revenues were driving equalization payments upward, but it was not those revenues which were being redistributed.

A number of important consequences flowed from the resulting fiscal crisis. The Alberta government diverted a substantial portion of its oil revenues into the Alberta Heritage Saving and Trust Fund. This portion was not included in the equalization formula, and thus reduced the equalization strain on the federal treasury. The formula itself was amended so that no province could receive equalization payments if its per capita income was above the national average. This amendment preempted equalization payments to Ontario which, under the old rules, would have qualified as a have-not province from 1977 to 1982. As noted above, the formula was changed so as to include only 50 percent of non-renewable natural resource revenues in the calculation of payments. The federal government also moved to keep Canadian oil prices below world levels, which further reduced the equalization strain on the national treasury. Finally, in 1980, Ottawa introduced the National Energy Program, which was designed in part to give the national government access to oil revenues, and thus to enable Ottawa to finance the increased equalization payments that the increase in oil prices had brought about.

The redistribution of resource revenues poses a very thorny problem for the Canadian political system. If revenues went primarily to individuals or to corporations, as is the case with oil revenues in the United States, redistribution would be relatively easy, as the national government would have access to such revenues through personal and corporate income taxes. However, to the extent that revenues go to provincial governments in the form of royalties, they are not accessible to Ottawa through personal or corporate taxes even though Ottawa is still faced with the bill for equalization. This leads in turn to attempts by the national government to capture some share of resource revenues, attempts that were incorporated in the controversial National Energy Program. It is in this narrow sense that equalization can promote federal raids on provincial treasuries. More generally, equalization does not entail any expropriation or redistribution of provincial government revenues.

Equalization payments alter the dynamics of individual mobility by reducing the costs of staying in relatively depressed regions. They both reduce the tax load and improve the quality of public services in the have-not provinces. Equalization payments have also altered the dynamics of federalism in the have-not provinces. In conjunction with other federal subsidies, they have transformed the Maritime provinces into virtual client states of the federal government.[67] The extreme case is Prince Edward Island, where nearly 60 percent of the provincial budget comes from federal transfer payments of one kind or another, and where the provincial treasury has become little more than an agent for the distribution of federal funds.[68] Somewhat ironically, equalization payments may also contribute to intergovernmental conflict between the have-not provinces and Ottawa. Thorburn maintains that they have enabled the have-not provinces to strengthen their bureaucracies, and thus to challenge the federal government across a broader front: "in short, the improved financial capacity of the provinces may well have served to accentuate the rivalries between provinces, and between federal and provincial authorities, because it has made possible a level of provincial intervention that could not have occurred without such improved financial capacity."[69] In a crude sense, equalization payments enable the have-not provinces to bite the federal hand that feeds them.

REDISTRIBUTIVE EFFECTS OF FEDERAL PROGRAMS

Equalization payments can rightly be seen as the centrepiece of federal efforts to redistribute wealth across the provincial communities of Canada. There are, however, a host of other federal programs with significant redistributive effects.

In 1961 Parliament passed the Agricultural Rehabilitation and Development Act which was designed to address rural poverty. The Act provided for joint federal–provincial funding of rural development projects, and the coordination of federal and provincial programs in the policy field. In 1965 the terms of the Act were expanded by the passage of the Agricultural and Rural Development Act (ARDA), followed by the creation of the Fund for Rural Economic Development in 1966. More recently, ARDA has been expanded to include development programs in tourism and fisheries. While these legislative initiatives were not designed to redirect economic activity from one region to another, they were designed to promote economic development in rural as opposed to urban Canada.

In 1962 Ottawa established the Atlantic Development Board to coordinate the developmental activities of federal departments and the four provincial governments in the region. As a response to developmental problems in a specific region, the Development Board has enjoyed considerable success. A much less fruitful exercise occurred in 1973 when representatives of the federal government, led by Prime Minister Trudeau, met in Calgary with the four western premiers at the Western Economic Opportunities Conference (WEOC). The primary result of WEOC was not greater federal–provincial cooperation but rather the banding together of the four western provincial governments for almost a decade of intense intergovernmental conflict with Ottawa.

The major federal initiative came with the creation of the Department of Regional Economic Expansion (DREE) in 1969. DREE's mandate was to ensure that economic growth was widely dispersed across Canada, and that employment and income prospects in slow-growth regions were brought up to the national average.[70] Building on the precedents of the Area Development Agency (1963) and the Area Development Incentives Act (1965), DREE was designed to give Ottawa a direct and high-profile role in regional economic development, a role well beyond the provision of equalization payments which were spent solely at the discretion of provincial governments. In 1982 DREE was merged with the Department of Industry, Trade and Commerce to form DRIE, the Department of Regional Industrial Expansion. With the completion of the merger by the end of 1982, DREE grants had become DRIE grants.[71]

Table 5.3 presents the regional distribution of DREE/DRIE grants given out during 1982. Overall, the grants totalled $370,495,000, or $15.22 for every man, woman, and child in Canada. As in the case of equalization payments, Quebec received more grants in total than did any other province, whereas the highest per capita expenditures were made in the Atlantic provinces. With 12.0 percent of the national population, the Atlantic region received 34.6 percent of the DREE expenditures. It should also be noted that all provinces received grants, though the per capita expenditures in the wealthier provinces were minimal. Finally, it should be noted that Table 5.3 does not include expenditures under the Prairie Farm Rehabilitation Administration, which was transferred to the Department of Agriculture during the 1982 fiscal year. PFRA payments that year totalled $45,181,000, which amounts to 12.2 percent of the DREE payments and 35.2 percent of the DREE grants received by the four Atlantic provinces.

While no other federal program has had the scope of DREE/DRIE, redistributive

TABLE 5.3

Regional Distribution of DREE Grants, 1982

	1982 DREE Expenditures* ($000)	Per Capita Expenditures (1981 population)	% Total DREE Expenditures
Nfld.	29,960	$ 52.78	8.1
P.E.I.	19,734	161.09	5.3
N.S.	38,173	45.04	10.3
N.B.	40,451	58.09	10.9
Que.	127,198	19.76	34.3
Ont.	28,992	3.36	7.8
Man.	32,396	31.57	8.7
Sask.	23,452	24.22	6.3
Alta.	11,602	5.18	3.1
B.C.	14,692	5.35	4.0
N.W.T.	1,305	28.53	0.4
Yukon	2,540	109.71	0.7
Canada	$370,495	$ 15.22	100.0

*Includes planning and administration, subsidiary agreements, industrial incentives, and budgetary commitments to other programs. Excludes head office, western regional office, Prairie Farm Rehabilitation Administration, Atlantic regional office, and Atlantic Development Council.

Source: Department of Regional Economic Expansion and Department of Industry, Trade and Commerce, *Annual Reports, 1982–83* (Ottawa: Ministry of Supply and Services, 1984).

elements have been embedded in other programs. The drilling incentives in the National Energy Program, for example, were designed to shift drilling activity onto federal crown lands in the Canadian North and off the east coast of the Atlantic provinces, much to the outrage of the Alberta government. Provincial governments also have programs designed to redistribute economic activity within their provincial boundaries in order to alleviate intraprovincial pockets of poverty and depressed economic activity.

All such programs are designed to influence the locational decisions of private firms. The starting assumption is that market-determined locational decisions may not be optimal from a social or political perspective. Thus an array of public incentives are brought into play to affect locational decisions. These can include tax breaks, the public provision of infrastructure support such as roads and railways, subsidized land, and preferential government services. Unfortunately, their impact on regional economic development is very difficult to assess. In some cases, grants go to firms that might have located in the region anyway. In other cases new firms may not survive, or may displace existing firms in the region.

New firms may discourage additional investment by driving up the costs of wages and services. Finally, Bryan argues that "firms that need to be 'bribed' to invest in an area may be less likely than other firms to reinvest, and therefore the long-term benefits of subsidized investments may be small."[72] Thus while public expenditures may be clearly redistributive, flowing from the national treasury to disadvantaged regions within the country, or from the provincial treasury to disadvantaged regions within the province, it is less clear that such expenditures significantly alter the regional distribution of investment and employment opportunities.

Other federal programs may have redistributive effects even though they have not been designed with any redistributive intent. If the problem that the program is designed to address is more prevalent in one region than another, or if the clientele of a particular program is disproportionately located in one region rather than another, some regional redistribution will occur. For example, if the birth-rate in one region is higher than in others, as it was in Quebec prior to the Quiet Revolution, then a universal program such as Family Allowances will benefit that region more than others. Figure 5.4 illustrates how beneficiaries of the Canada Assistance Plan are not evenly dispersed across the country, with some modest regional redistribution being the consequence. A program to benefit unemployed youths could be of greater benefit to Newfoundland and New Brunswick, where the May 1984 youth unemployment rates were 38.4 percent and 25.6 percent respectively, than it would be to Manitoba and Saskatchewan, where the rates were 12.5 percent and 15.3 percent respectively.[73] The point, then, is that federal programs with no regionally redistributive intent can have redistributive effects if program recipients are not randomly distributed across the country.

In this connection it should be noted that government spending on goods and services can also have a significant impact on the regional distribution of economic activity. In the 1982–83 fiscal year the federal government's Department of Supply and Services spent $4,347 million on supply contracts. Of that total, 47.4 percent went to Ontario vendors, 29.1 percent to Quebec vendors, 14.7 percent to vendors based in western Canada, and 7.4 percent to those based in Atlantic Canada.[74] In that same year, the Department spent $2,178 million on science and engineering procurement service contracting, of which 53.8 percent was captured by Ontario vendors, 31.7 percent by those in Quebec, 9.8 percent by those in the West, and 4.7 percent by those in Atlantic Canada. To the extent that such expenditures are regionally mobile (many may not be), the federal government has at its disposal a significant lever for the regional redistribution of economic activity. The same line of argument applies to the location of military bases, research centres, mints, the head offices of crown corporations, and, in the rare instance, the location of government departments.[75] As Bakvis points out in a more general sense, it is rarely the case that the effects of *any* government policy or development program are distributed evenly across geographical space.[76]

FIGURE 5.4

Beneficiaries of Canada Assistance Plan (% total population)

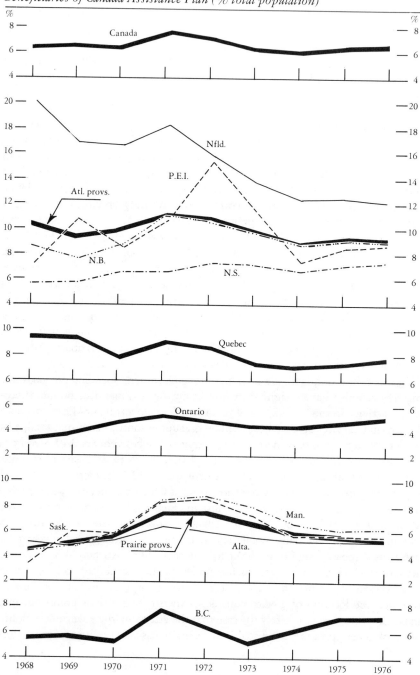

Source: Chart 2.G.-2, Catalogue 86–201, Statistics Canada. In Nydia McCool, *Canadian Facts and Figures* (Edmonton: Hurtig, 1982), p. 27

While expenditure patterns often provide unequal regional benefits, and while specific programs exist to encourage the regional dispersion of economic activity, the net effect on the regional distribution of wealth and employment opportunities is difficult to determine. It is not clear, in other words, whether the *distributional* objectives of public policy are being met and, if they are, at what cost to the *growth* objectives of public policy, assuming that some tension between the two is inevitable.[77] What does seem clear is that the effective management of regional economic development is dependent upon extensive intergovernmental coordination and cooperation. This is not easily achieved given the zero-sum character of locational decisions, where the gain of any one province is the loss of its provincial competitors. It also seems clear that Atlantic Canada is the net beneficiary not only from equalization payments but also, due to disproportionately high rates of usage, from universalistic programs such as unemployment insurance and the Canada Assistance Plan. With respect to DREE, Smiley concluded that "... all that can be said with complete assurance is that the Atlantic provinces have, by any appropriate criteria, gained from DREE activities and these activities appear to have been important in reducing the net out-migration of people from Atlantic Canada to negligible proportions."[78] Such regional benefits have been possible because the region's population is relatively small, and thus substantive redistributive benefits can be provided with a relatively light redistributive burden being imposed on the larger and wealthier regions.

PROVINCE-BUILDING AND REDISTRIBUTIVE POLITICS

Within the context of the national economy, it is of little concern if individuals in depressed regions "go down the road" to seek employment in other regions. Indeed, such mobility is a useful form of adjustment to changing economic conditions. It may alleviate unemployment in depressed regions, raise wages for those left behind, and reduce the costs of social assistance. From the perspective of provincial governments, however, out-migration is a matter of considerable concern. In part, the concern stems from the fact that it is the young and the best educated who are most likely to migrate, leaving behind an impoverished pool of human resources.[79] Out-migration can further depress the local economy by decreasing the size of local markets, and can erode the local tax base to the point where the quality of public services will deteriorate.[80] Thus while out-migration may not be damaging to the national economy, it is resisted by provincial governments who seek to convince voters that their sons and daughters will be able to live and work within their home province no matter what career they may wish to pursue.

Provincial governments seek to ward off out-migration by province-building strategies designed to strengthen the provincial economy. Provincial businesses are shored up through tax breaks, infrastructure support, and preferential purchasing and contracting policies of the provincial government. Extensive efforts are made to attract investment from outside the province and the country, efforts that may entail a "beggar-thy-neighbour" policy of luring investors away from neighbouring provinces. Economic strength alone, however, is not sufficient to prevent out-migration if that strength rests on a capital-intensive rather than labour-intensive base, and if the provincial economy lacks sufficient economic diversification. In the latter case, out-migration can still be forced upon those who choose to pursue careers falling beyond the parameters of the provincial economy. In western Canada, economic diversification has been the primary focus of province-building strategies given the somewhat narrow natural resource base of the regional economy, the concentration of labour-intensive industries in central Canada, and the historical lure of a more complex labour market outside the region.

Province-building strategies can have a somewhat contradictory effect in that *provincial* economic strength may weaken the *national* economy. As Thorburn explains, the understandable effort by provincial governments to curtail out-migration

has counteracted the natural adjustment process by which movements of people and capital would take place in response to variation in wages, job opportunities, production costs, and so forth. The result was the creation of ten provincial economies rather than one Canadian economy.[81]

This suggests in turn that economic management can be a very complex task in a federal state when one level of government tries to ensure a healthy and vital national economy while the second level tries to ensure healthy provincial economies even to the extent of inhibiting the mobility of capital and labour within the national economic community. The management task is not only complex from the standpoint of intergovernmental relations; it is also complex for the federal government alone when it tries to ensure both national economic growth and an equitable regional distribution of economic activity.

In conclusion, it is useful to return to an earlier point. Within the Canadian political system, greater emphasis appears to be placed on the distribution of income and wealth across regions than across individuals. This is particularly true in provincial political systems where the position of the province in the national scheme of things is of much greater importance than the internal distribution of income within the province. In this respect, our perspective on redistributive politics may be unduly narrowed by the regional and intergovernmental dimensions of Canadian political life.

The Redistributive Horizon

The discussion in this chapter has focused on redistributive politics across individuals and across regions. However, these are only two ways in which one could slice the redistributive pie. In the years ahead redistributive politics may come to focus on different concerns, though it is unlikely that those discussed above will disappear from the political agenda. Gender politics can be expected to move increasingly to the fore, with the political debate shifting more to the distribution of income and employment opportunities between men and women rather than across regions or social classes.[82] As the demographic structure of the Canadian population continues to change, as a larger aged population imposes a heavier fiscal load on a shrinking labour force, redistributive conflict across the generations can be expected to intensify. Over the long run Canadians will have to confront international inequities in the distribution of wealth which dwarf those across class, regional, gender, or age groupings within Canada, and which pose a far greater threat to world peace.

The intensity of redistributive politics in the years ahead will depend a great deal upon the state of the economy. Under conditions of economic growth, such as those which prevailed when the Canadian welfare state was put into place, redistributive politics can be relatively non-conflictual. Take, for example, an economic pie divided among three groups differing in their wealth. As long as the pie grows, modest redistribution can take place in a reasonably painless fashion. If the yearly growth is divided up so that each group gets some, but the least advantaged group gets more than its proportionate share, then redistribution takes place at the same time that everyone moves ahead. If we are faced with a static rather than an expanding pie, then redistribution can only take place if some group loses not only in relative terms but also in absolute terms. Under such conditions, redistributive politics are more conflictual as groups will fight harder to preserve what they have than they will to protect their share of growth. If the pie *decreases* in size, the situation deteriorates even further. If I am to hold my own, much less move ahead, you will have to lose.

During the prosperity of past decades, when upward social mobility appeared to be the norm, it seemed possible that a more equal society could be achieved by "levelling up," by increasing the income and opportunities of those at the bottom of the heap. As economist John Kenneth Galbraith has pointed out, however, it may well be that greater equality can only be achieved by levelling down, not up. If so, we can expect redistributive politics to be more conflictual in the future than they have been in the past.

Suggested Readings

1 Dan Butler and Bruce Macnaughton, "More of Less for Whom? Debating Directions for the Public Sector," in Michael S. Whittington and Glen Williams, eds., *Canadian Politics in the 1980s*, 2nd ed. (Toronto: Methuen, 1984), pp. 1–32.

2 John Allan Fry, ed., *Economy, Class and Social Reality* (Toronto: Butterworths, 1979).

3 For an overview of redistributive issues, see Ingrid Bryan, *Economic Policies in Canada* (Toronto: Butterworths, 1982), Chapters 9 (income redistribution across people) and 10 (income redistribution across regions).

4 For an overview of the class structure of the Canadian society, see Dennis Forcese, *The Canadian Class Structure*, 2nd ed. (Toronto: McGraw-Hill Ryerson, 1980).

5 W. Irwin Gillespie, *The Redistribution of Income in Canada* (Ottawa: The Carleton Library, Gage Publishing, 1980).

6 For an interesting set of readings drawing from both Canadian sources and the classics of sociology, see John Harp and John R. Hofley, eds., *Structured Inequality in Canada* (Scarborough: Prentice-Hall, 1980).

7 Douglas McCready and Conrad Winn, "Redistributive Policy," in Conrad Winn and John McMenemy, *Political Parties in Canada* (Toronto: McGraw-Hill Ryerson, 1976), pp. 206–27.

8 For students considering term papers dealing with any aspect of poverty in Canada, the National Council of Welfare has published an extensive collection of papers dealing with virtually every aspect of the issue. For information, write to the National Council of Welfare, Brooke Claxton Building, Ottawa K1A 0K9.

9 Norman Penner, *The Canadian Left: A Critical Analysis* (Scarborough: Prentice-Hall, 1977).

10 David P. Ross, *The Canadian Fact Book on Poverty, 1983* (Ottawa: Canadian Council on Social Development, 1983).

Study Questions

1 How would you characterize the pattern of social mobility within your own family tree? What has been the role played by societal and generational mobility, as opposed to the individual mobility discussed in this chapter?

2 If you were asked to conduct an attitudinal survey and were told that you could allocate five questions to the measurement of respondents' social class, which five would you ask? How would you justify the questions that you included and the potential questions that you chose to exclude?

3 To what extent do the redistributive aspects of class politics and gender politics overlap? In what ways are they quite different phenomena?

4 What arguments might you develop to support an *increase* in federal subsidies to "have-not" provinces? What arguments might you develop to support a *decrease* in such subsidies?

CHAPTER SIX

Canadian–American Relations

Perhaps the most striking thing about Canada is that it is not part of the United States. Somehow more than half of North America has escaped being engulfed by its immensely more powerful neighbor although that neighbor has expanded fairly continuously in North America and elsewhere from 1776 to the present day.[1]

Canadian–American relations have been symbolized by "the world's longest *undefended* border," a border which brings to mind a poem by one of America's foremost poets, Robert Frost. The narrator of "Mending Wall," who is helping his neighbour repair the stone wall separating their properties, questions the very need for such a wall. The neighbour, however, insists that "good fences make good neighbours," and against this insistence Frost's narrator makes no headway:

Before I built a wall I'd ask to know
What I was walling in or walling out,
And to whom I was like to give offence.
Something there is that doesn't love a wall,
That wants it down. I could say 'Elves' to him,
But it's not elves exactly, and I'd rather
He said it for himself. I see him there
Bringing a stone grasped firmly by the top
In each hand, like an old-stone savage armed.
He moves in darkness as it seems to me,
Not of woods only and the shade of trees.
He will not go behind his father's saying,
And he likes having thought of it so well
He says again, 'Good fences make good neighbours.'[2]

In "Mending Wall," Frost has captured the essence of a fundamental tension in the Canadian–American relationship. The walls between the two countries are cumbersome in many respects and continually under attack by the forces of a continental economy, technological innovations such as cable and satellite delivery of television signals, and a continental approach to military defence. And yet *as a consequence*, the building of "good fences" in order to maintain some independent existence from the United States has been a major preoccupation of Canadian public policy. Maintaining those fences in a continental environment has proven to be a daunting and ongoing task.

Canadians, and English Canadians in particular, have not been sheltered from the American society by differences in language, race, or religion. Even the physical features that cross the continent have done more to separate Canadians from one another than from Americans. The international border has been breached by countless corporations, trade unions, service clubs, professional societies, sports leagues, and cultural organizations. With three out of four Canadians living within 150 kilometres of the border and a majority living father south than the forty-ninth parallel, the United States is readily accessible. Canadians and Americans cross the border each year by the millions to visit friends, vacation, and pursue business interests. Kinship ties, fostered by extensive migration between the two countries, span the international border as readily as they do provincial borders within Canada. And yet *because* the border is so permeable, its defence has taken on great importance within the Canadian political system. Given the lack of cultural, linguistic, geographical, religious, or racial defences, political defences have come to the fore.

In focusing upon political boundary maintenance, there is a danger that Canadian–American relations will be painted in overly conflictual hues. Thus it should be stressed that the political preoccupation with "good fences" does not arise because the relationship is predominantly ill-spirited or conflictual. It is precisely because the relationship has generally been so harmonious that boundary maintenance presents such a difficult challenge. It should also be stressed that boundary maintenance is more complex than simply building fences. It may take the form of active cooperation in order to ward off more damaging alternatives. In the Canadian–American case, boundary maintenance is concerned with controlling rather than preventing American access to the Canadian society, with regulating access so as to maximize Canadian gains and minimize Canadian losses across the countless interchanges which take place between the two countries.

If Americans were not so much like Canadians, if there were not such a broad range of common values and interests, boundary maintenance would be far easier. It is precisely because the two countries are good neighbours that the maintenance of good fences is such a problematic and interesting aspect of Canadian public policy.

Historical Backdrop

Over the past two hundred years the United States has had a great impact on Canada while Canada has had a much more modest, though not insignificant, impact on the United States. This asymmetry reflects the basic demographic fact underlying Canadian–American relations—Americans outnumber Canadians ten to one.

The American War of Independence in 1776 helped lay the foundations for the Canadian society. Of the approximately 100,000 United Empire Loyalists who fled the American revolution, over 40,000 came north. More than thirty thousand settled in Nova Scotia, tripling the colony's population and spilling into New Brunswick, which was consequently established as a separate colony in 1784. Others formed the bedrock of what is now Ontario, and led to the Constitutional Act of 1791 which divided what had been the single territory of Quebec into Upper and Lower Canada. In what is now Quebec, "the influx of Anglophone loyalists, pushed by expropriation or drawn by good farmland, changed Quebec once and for all from a homogeneous French-Canadian society to one with a prosperous and vocal English minority."[3] It is in this sense, then, that historian A.R.M. Lower has described Canada as a "by-product" of the American revolution.[4]

The United Empire Loyalists—anti-American Americans—helped put in place the cornerstone of Canadian nationalism. As Careless explains, they

represented a declaration of independence against the United States, a determination to live apart from that country in North America. As a result, they helped to create not only a new province [Ontario], but a new nation.[5]

By rejecting Britain, the Americans allowed Canadians to carve out a distinctive niche on the North American continent through their *attachment* to things British, and in particular through their attachment to parliamentary institutions.

The American Revolution raised fears of military conquest that were to remain with Canadians until Confederation. In 1776 John Adams, who was to become the second president of the United States, declared that "the Unanimous Voice of the Continent is Canada must be ours; Quebec must be taken."[6] In 1775 American forces had in fact captured Montreal and, over the winter, had besieged Quebec until that garrison was relieved by the British fleet in the spring of 1776. Even with the subsequent withdrawal of American forces, the fear persisted that the Americans would not rest until the British had been expelled from the continent. The invitation in Article IV of the American Articles of Confederation that Canada "join us in Congress and complete the American Union" was seen by Canadians more as a threat than as an act of generosity.

Thirty-seven years after the American Revolution, Canadians again found themselves at war with the United States. Although Britain and the United States were the principal players in the War of 1812, some of the fighting took place on Canadian soil as Americans invaded the Niagara Peninsula and burned the city of York (now Toronto), for which Washington was burnt in retaliation by the British. At the start of the conflict, former president Thomas Jefferson declared that "the annexation of Canada this year as far as the neighbourhood of Quebec will only be a mere matter of marching, and this will give us experience for the assault on Halifax next, and the final expulsion of England from the American continent."[7] As events turned out, it was not merely a matter of marching, and the American forces were repelled. The war nonetheless left a strong mark on Canada. Despite the Rush–Bagot Convention of 1817 which demilitarized the Great Lakes, subsequent years saw the construction of the Rideau canal and an impressive string of military fortifications including Kingston's Fort Henry, the Quebec Citadel and its companion forts on the south shore at Levis, and the Halifax Citadel. More importantly, the invading American forces had destroyed not only homes, barns, and crops but also any lingering sense that the United Empire Loyalists were exiled Americans rather than British subjects and, in a nascent sense, Canadians.

The military threat from the United States remained dormant until the aftermath of the American Civil War when, as we discussed in Chapter Two, it reappeared to play a significant role in Confederation. After 1867 the military threat subsided and then disappeared, to be replaced by new forms of American expansionism. The most immediate threat came in the largely unoccupied Canadian West as Americans spread westward and then, as free land disappeared, northward. The more general threat came from the American assertion of a "manifest destiny" which appeared to preclude sharing the continent with an independent Canada. In 1871 the *Globe* warned its readers that "we are divided only by an imaginary border ... from a people ... [who] have before now proved themselves aggressive—a people who believe in 'manifest destiny', 'universal sovereignty', and other ideas not very reassuring to their neighbours."[8] French Canadian assessments were even harsher. Olivar Asselin declared that "the amiable Nation of Pirates which stole Texas, Cuba, Porto Rico and the Philippines cannot be depended upon to act justly towards a weaker nation,"[9] while Henri Bourassa maintained that the United States was "waiting to gobble us up."[10]

Manifest Destiny

The phrase "manifest destiny" was coined in 1845 by John L. O'Sullivan, an American journalist and diplomat. Writing in the US Magazine and Democratic Review, O'Sullivan described America's "manifest destiny to overspread the continent allotted by providence for the free development of our yearly multiplying millions."[11] The theme came to be applied with special force to the northern half of the continent:

- In 1867, the same year in which he acquired Alaska for the United States, Secretary of State W.H. Seward declared that "nature designs that this whole continent, not merely these thirty-six states, shall be, sooner or later, within the magic circle of the American Union."
- In 1889 James G. Blaine, U.S. Secretary of State, said Canada was like "an apple on a tree just beyond reach. We may strive to grasp it, but the bough recedes from our hold just in proportion to our effort to catch it. Yet let it alone, and in due time it will fall into our hands."
- Champ Clark, Speaker of the U.S. House of Representatives, declared in 1911 that "We are preparing to annex Canada ... I hope to see the day when the American flag will float on every square foot of British North American possessions clear to the North Pole."

Such American aspirations did not end with Speaker Clark. In 1952 Representative Timothy Sheehan of Illinois proposed in the House of Representatives that the United States buy Canada from Great Britain! However, despite the American belief in a manifest destiny, the 10-to-1 American edge in population, and the far greater economic and military power of the United States, Canadians ended up with more than half of the continent, albeit the colder part.

As the twentieth century unfolded, Canadian fears of absorption were replaced by anxieties over the growing American presence *within* Canada. Whereas in the past Britain had served as a counterweight to American influence in Canada, that role was weakened as Britain's position in the international order declined, as Canada shed its colonial ties, and as the English Canadian community diversified and drew away from its British roots. British investment in Canada was supplanted by American investment, trade with the United States far surpassed trade with Britain, and American cultural patterns began to prevail over those from the United Kingdom. In short, by the end of the Second World War the North Atlantic triangle formed by the United States, Britain, and Canada had been transformed. From the Canadian perspective at least, the Canadian–American side of the triangle was now dominant. The relationship between Canada and Great Britain had not only declined in relative importance, but had become increasingly irrelevant to the Canadian–American relationship. To an extent unknown in the past, Canada now faced the United States one-on-one.

This new *continental* relationship was highlighted in a speech to the Canadian Parliament by President John F. Kennedy on May 17, 1962:

Geography has made us neighbours. History has made us partners. And necessity has made us allies. Those whom nature hath so joined together let no man put asunder.

If anything, however, history made the two countries antagonists rather than friends. As James Eayrs wrote in response to Kennedy's speech, "if they are friends today, it is in spite of history, not because of it."[12]

The American Presence in Canada

In 1891, when Canadians were grappling with proposals for greater free trade between Canada and the United States, Goldwin Smith wrote what has become a classic statement of support for continental integration:

Let any one scan the economical map of the North American continent with its adjacent waters, mark its northern zone abounding in minerals, in bituminous coal, in lumber, in fish, as well as in special farm products, brought in the north to hardier perfection, all of which the southern people have need: let him then look to its southern regions, the natural products of which as well as the manufactures produced in its wealthy centres of industry are needed by the people of the northern zone: he will see that the continent is an economic whole, and that to run a Customs line athwart it and try to sever its members from each other is to wage a desperate war against nature.[13]

Smith's description of continentalism as a "force of nature" has become common currency in discussions of Canadian–American relations. Holmes, for example, argues that "the threat of continentalization comes not from governments but from forces beyond the control of governments."[14] Eayrs writes that the border between Canada and the United States is political rather than geographic, that "what nature joined together, Canadians have sought to sunder."[15] From wherever they spring, the pressures of continentalism are a fact of Canadian life. Whether they should be embraced or resisted depends in large part on how one assesses the economic underpinnings of continental interdependence.

THE EXTENT OF ECONOMIC INTERDEPENDENCE

In the early decades after Confederation, Britain was Canada's most important trading partner and source of the non-resident investment needed to build the Canadian economy. At the turn of the century British investment in Canada surpassed that from the United States by a margin of nearly six to one. However, with the First World War came an acceleration of American foreign investment, particularly in Canada, coupled with a parallel decline in British foreign investment. By 1926, American investment in Canada surpassed British investment. By the early 1960s American investment accounted for more than 80 percent of all foreign investment in Canada, and by the early 1980s it surpassed British foreign investment in Canada by a margin of more than nine to one.

The decline in British investment reflected a general deterioration in the place of Britain and the British Empire in the international order. As a consequence of this decline and of the continental pull of the United States, Canada's economic, cultural, and strategic focus shifted to the United States. That shift, and the altered international balance between Britain and the United States which lay behind it, had an important impact on English Canadian nationalism. In its formative stages, English Canadian nationalism had enthusiastically embraced imperial themes, drawing its confidence and expansionist thrust from Canada's tie to the British Empire.[16] Thus, Smith argues, "as the Empire faded away in the fifties and sixties and as Britain turned inward to agonize over her own domestic problems, English Canada lost one— perhaps the most profound—of her spiritual props."[17]

The extent of foreign ownership in Canada far surpasses that in any comparable industrialized country. Figure 6.1, which provides but one of many possible snapshots, illustrates both the extent of foreign ownership and the highly variable nature of that ownership across sectors of the economy. Foreign investment has been most prevalent in the manufacturing and energy sectors, and least prevalent in textiles, transportation, communications, and banking. Overall, foreign investors control approximately a third of the assets of the leading five hundred economic enterprises in Canada and, among non-financial corporations, capture approximately 40 percent of Canadian sales and profits.[18] In the Canadian case, foreign investment is primarily American investment; of all foreign investment in Canada, about 80 percent originates in the United States, with 9 percent coming from Great Britain and 11 percent from all other countries combined.[19]

American investment in Canada reflects the continental mobility of capital which also sees extensive Canadian investment in the United States. Canadian investment abroad has been growing rapidly in recent years. In 1982, for example, Canadians invested forty cents abroad for every dollar invested in Canada, with total Canadian foreign investment tripling between 1977 and 1982 to a total of $65 billion.[20] Approximately half of all Canadian foreign investment flows into the United States, where Canada has traditionally been one of the largest sources of foreign investment. In a proportional sense, however, Canadian direct investment in the American economy, which is approximately 0.45 percent of the total assets of non-financial institutions,[21] is minute compared to American investment in Canada.

The extent of American investment in Canada both reflects and reinforces the flow of trade between the two countries. Canada and the United States are each other's largest trading partners, with a sizeable proportion of the trade taking place within corporate entities spanning the border. In 1981, for example, the United States accounted for approximately 66 percent of Canada's exports and about 69 percent of Canada's imports; with the latter constituting about 20 percent of all American exports.[22] The total volume of trade now exceeds $100 billion a year.

In proportionate terms, foreign trade is more important to the Canadian than to the American economy. Canada exports approximately 25 percent of its Gross

FIGURE 6.1

Foreign-Owned Assets as a Percentage of Total Assets in Canada, 1978

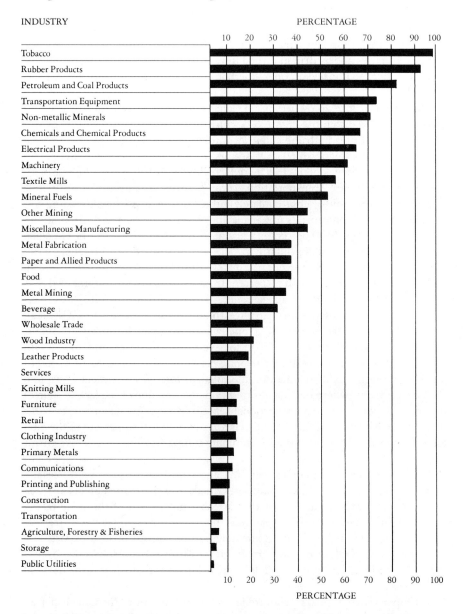

INDUSTRY   PERCENTAGE

Source: Nydia McCool, *Canadian Facts and Figures* (Edmonton: Hurtig, 1982), p. 96.

National Product, compared to approximately 13 percent for Japan and 12 percent for the United States. This heavy reliance on trade means that the Canadian
economy is very dependent upon the condition of foreign markets in general, and
the condition of American markets in particular. If the American economy and
therefore the demand for Canadian imports softens, the impact on Canada can be
severe, as we witnessed with the decline in the American demand for Canadian
lumber in the early 1980s. Hence the expression, "when the American economy
catches cold, the Canadian economy catches pneumonia."

One of the chronic problems in Canadian–American trade has arisen from the
imbalance between natural resources and semi-processed goods, on the one hand,
and manufactured products on the other. While the former have constituted the
bulk of Canadian exports to the United States, the latter constitute the great bulk
of Canadian imports. This imbalance was addressed by the Canada-United States
Automotive Products Trade Agreement of 1965, or Auto Pact. Prior to the Auto
Pact, the Canadian automobile industry was ailing from short production lines,
inefficient plants, competition from Japanese and European compacts, and a
heavy reliance on imported American parts. The Auto Pact, which created a
qualified free trade arrangement for automobiles and automobile parts, addressed
these problems by opening up the American market to Canadian plants and
thereby allowing longer production lines, more specialization and greater effi-
ciency. The Pact greatly increased Canadian–American vehicle trade (the larger
volume of trade in automotive parts was less affected). In the first five years
Canadian vehicle imports from the United States increased from 3 percent to 40
percent of the domestic markets while exports to the United States increased
from 7 percent to 60 percent of the total Canadian output.[23]

Over that initial period, Canada received greater benefits from the Auto Pact
than did the United States. Then, from 1971 to 1980 the balance shifted as the
United States accumulated a trade surplus of $10.4 billion.[24] The accumulating
American surplus sparked Canadian demands that the Auto Pact be renegotiated
but, before any renegotiations took place, the Pact rebounded to Canada's advantage. In 1982 Canada sold $2.85 billion more automobiles and parts to the United
States than the United States sold to Canada, and in 1983 the surplus reached
$3.29 billion.[25]

Not surprisingly, the terms and consequences of the Pact form an ongoing
irritant in the Canadian–American relationship as each side understandably seeks
to maximize national benefits, sheltering its own labour force in the face of
growing competition from Japan and Europe, and ensure that the other side lives
up to the letter and spirit of the agreement. As Drummond points out, any easy
reconciliation of conflicting national interests is ruled out because the Pact is a
classic example of a "beggar-my-neighbour" solution to unemployment; "Canadian output and employment can only rise at the expense of American."[26]

Outside the automobile sector, Canadian–American trade is increasingly unencumbered by tariffs. Both countries are signatories to the General Agreement on Tariffs and Trade (GATT) and, as a consequence, have seen bilateral tariffs fall as part of a general reduction in tariffs among western industrialized countries. (There remains a multitude of non-tariff barriers to trade including quotas, technical standards, valuation and dumping procedures, and government procurement practices, some of which are of increasing concern as barriers to trade *within* Canada.)[27] When the Tokyo round of GATT tariff reductions are completed in 1987, approximately 80 percent of Canadian–American trade will be tariff free. With the remaining tariffs having been cut by approximately 40 percent, Canada and the United States will in effect constitute a free trade zone, at least as far as tariff barriers are concerned. This development is significant indeed when one considers the historical role played by tariffs in Canadian–American economic relations.

In 1879 the Government of Canada erected a 30 percent tariff wall between Canada and the United States to encourage the industrialization of the Canadian economy and, not incidentally, to increase federal revenues. Tariffs, the construction of a transcontinental railway system, and the settlement of the prairie west formed the interlocking pillars of Sir John A. Macdonald's National Policy. The tariff wall, it was hoped, would build an east–west axis for the Canadian economy to counteract the north–south pull of continental forces, an axis which would sustain the transcontinental railway system then being put in place. In introducing the tariff legislation, the Minister of Finance declared that "the time has arrived when we are to decide whether we will simply be hewers of wood and drawers of water...." Through the National Policy, the choice was made; an industrialized economy was to be developed behind the protective wall of the tariff.

The tariff wall was designed to raise the price of American imports to the point where goods manufactured in Canada would be competitive. As a barrier to goods rather than to capital, it was *not* designed to keep out American investment. The tariff actually encouraged foreign investment as American firms wishing to sell to the Canadian market found it more profitable to establish branch plants in Canada, and thus enjoy the protection of the tariff wall, than to try to export goods to Canada from American plants. (American investment was also promoted by proximity, by profitability, by the desire for a secure source of raw materials, and by the basic similarity of the two countries which reduced the anxieties attendant upon investing outside one's own country.) Thus the National Policy laid the foundations for an American-dominated branch-plant economy and, as a consequence, for the extensive intrusion of American labour unions into Canada. The former outcome was by no means inadvertent; Canadian governments and private organizations actively courted American branch plants not only through the tariff but also through vigorous promotional activities in the United States.[28] The goal was a healthy economy *in Canada* rather than a healthy *Canadian* economy. Who owned Canada's industrial plant was not to become a concern until well into the twentieth century.

The branch plant has become an important symbol in political debates over the American presence in Canada. Donald Creighton, for example, writes that "since the Second World War, while Canadians have been steadily selling their birthright in order to live in affluence, Canada has taken on more and more of the characteristics of a branch-plant economy and a branch-plant *state of mind*" [my emphasis].[29] For others, the branch plant symbolizes a fruitful continental relationship that should be embraced.

THE CASE FOR CONTINENTALISM

There is no question that Canada is entangled in a continental economy. For some people, that entanglement is inevitable; continentalism is seen as a force of nature lying beyond the control of Canadian public policy, or one that could only be resisted at an economic price that Canadians would be unwilling to pay. In more positive terms, one could argue that Canadians have benefited from continental interdependence through a higher standard of living and through exposure to a rich and vibrant American society. By extension, if continental interdependence has been not only inevitable but good, further integration is to be encouraged rather than feared. In moderate form, then, continentalism entails support for the freer mobility of trade, capital, and labour across the Canadian–American border. In more extreme form, it embraces the absorption of Canada into a larger continental, and necessarily American, scheme of things.

The case for continentalism rests upon the assertion that Canada's relatively high standard of living—relative to countries other than the United States—stems from its location on the North American continent. Canadian prosperity, in other words, has been continental rather than national; Canada has prospered because the larger and richer society to the south has prospered. This assertion is buttressed by a number of more specific economic arguments:

• The elimination of tariffs between Canada and the United States would promote more efficient domestic industries as Canadian firms specialized in the face of increased import competition. This argument reflects a virtual consensus among economists that by promoting specialization, free trade increases the international community's pool of wealth.

• Free trade between Canada and the United States would open up the much larger American market to Canadian firms and would thereby encourage longer production lines, lower per unit costs, and a generally more efficient Canadian manufacturing industry. As a consequence, Canadian products would be more competitive on world markets.

• Free trade would lower Canadian consumer prices through cheaper imports and by eliminating protected industries and the higher prices that protection brings. Tariffs, it is argued, hurt everyone a little (by increasing the cost of consumer goods) while benefiting a few (those who own protected industries) a lot. However, tariffs also create jobs. While the number of jobs protected by existing tariffs has been placed as low as 40,000 (approximately one manufacturing job in 45),[30] protected jobs are heavily concentrated in specific industries and localities. For example, tariffs are estimated to protect about 6,000 Canadian jobs in the textile industry,[31] at an annual cost to the average Canadian household of $101.[32] In the case of the textile industry, tariff protection and other non-tariff barriers to free trade, primarily quotas, have been imposed in the face of Asian rather than American competition. Thus the employment impact of continental free trade is difficult to estimate.

• In a world of large trading blocs, among which is the United States, Canada risks being isolated and consequently damaged in inter-bloc competition. Given this prospect, Canada might be better off entering the international arena as a continental trading ally of the United States. By standing together behind the walls of "Fortress America," Canadians and Americans might better withstand "unfair" economic competition from outside the continent. As Holmes puts it, "our dilemma is whether to float freer in a world of shifting balances or in self-defence to cast our lot more closely with our overwhelming partner so that we together can be more ruthless to others."[33]

• At the margins, more extensive continental integration could enhance Canadian industrialization by eliminating discriminatory American tariffs which tend to increase as the degree of Canadian processing increases.

• Free trade might correct, again at the margins, a long-standing regional irritant. The employment benefits of tariff protection have tended to flow more toward central Canada, where protected industries have been concentrated, than toward the regional periphery. Free trade would not turn the Canadian West into the continent's industrial heartland, nor would it remove the problems that agricultural producers have on the international market. It would, however, dampen the political conflict that arises from a national tariff policy that is seen, correctly or not, to be discriminatory in its regional effects.

Underlying the economic argument for continentalism is the fear that protection cripples the Canadian pursuit of excellence. While providing shelter, walls may shut out the best the world has to offer. To the degree that Canadian industrialists, writers, television producers, film makers, or academics are sheltered, their craft will not be honed by international competition. There is, then, a sense of optimism among continentalists, a belief that Canadians should *and can* compete with the best of the continent and the best of the world.

The first panel of Table 6.1 shows that, by a margin of about two to one, Canadians feel that Canada would be better off rather than worse off with free

TABLE 6.1

Public Opinion Toward American Investment and Free Trade

The Gallup organization has tracked Canadian public opinion toward American investment through ten surveys conducted from 1964 through 1982. Throughout, the question
was the following: "Do you think there is enough now or would you like to see more U.S.
capital invested in this country?" The national results were very stable until the latest
survey in 1982.

	Enough now	More	Don't know
1982	56%	36%	8%
1981	67	21	12
1980	64	20	17
1978	69	23	9
1977	69	20	12
1975	71	16	13
1972	67	22	11
1970	62	24	16
1967	60	24	16
1964	46	33	21

The Gallup organization has also tracked Canadian public opinion toward free trade.
Here the question read as follows: "Do you think Canada would be better off, or worse
off, if U.S. goods were allowed in here without tariff or customs charges and Canadian
goods were allowed in the U.S. free?"

| | Canada would be: | | |
	Better off	Worse off	Can't say
1983	54%	29%	17%
1968	56	27	17
1963	50	32	18
1953	54	28	18

Source: *The Gallup Report*, June 16, 1983.

trade. The panel also shows that opinion on this matter has been remarkably
stable over the past thirty years. The second panel of Table 6.1 shows similar
stability, at least over the 1970s, in public opinion toward American investment
in Canada. Here we find, however, that there is much less public support for
more American investment than there is for free trade. Taken together, the data
in the two panels suggest that public support for free trade may be conditional on
free trade not eroding Canadian control of the Canadian economy.

Table 6.2 provides a snapshot of public opinion on a related set of economic

TABLE 6.2

Canadian–American Economic Relations, May 1982

	Canada	West	Ont.	Que.	Atlan.
1 "Considering economic relations between Canada and the United States, which do you think would be best for Canada:					
• closer economic ties	37%	33%	34%	43%	42%
• less close economic ties	21%	21%	29%	15%	12%
• or about the same as we have now?"	38%	42%	34%	36%	43%
2 "Is it your opinion that investment by U.S. business firms in Canada is:					
• very beneficial to our country	18%	14%	18%	22%	22%
• somewhat beneficial	48%	49%	41%	53%	55%
• somewhat harmful	23%	26%	26%	17%	19%
• or very harmful?"	5%	4%	8%	3%	1%
3 "Do you think that the Canadian government should encourage or discourage additional investment from the United States?"					
• encourage	45%	36%	37%	63%	53%
• discourage	36%	42%	47%	19%	23%
• neither	10%	10%	8%	11%	19%
Number of respondents	1964	623	504	599	238

Source: Canada West Foundation, *Opinion Update*, Report No. 13, July 14, 1982.

issues. A close inspection of the table reveals a divided public with substantial support evident for all of the possible policy options. The table also shows a rather pronounced regional split in public opinion, with support for American investment and closer economic ties being substantially higher in Quebec and Atlantic Canada than in Ontario and the West. Interestingly, *no* significant differences are to be found between Ontario and western Canadian respondents despite historical conflict between the two regions over the National Policy.

In summary, the case for greater continental integration enjoys substantial public support. There has been a long-standing Canadian interest in freer trade running from the Reciprocity Agreement in 1854 and the Liberal Reciprocity initiatives in the elections of 1891 and 1911 (discussed in Chapter Eight) to the Auto Pact and Ottawa's 1983 announcement that Canada will downplay the search for new markets in Europe and Asia, and will instead push for greater sectoral free trade with the United States. It is a case, however, that has been strongly contested by Canadian economic nationalists, to whom we now turn.

ECONOMIC NATIONALISM

Traditional Canadian beliefs regarding American investment have included the following: that Canada has benefited from such investment, that any attempt to repatriate the Canadian economy would lower the Canadian standard of living, and that an economic price was to be paid for Canada's political independence, for the trappings of the Queen and parliamentary institutions.

These were the tenets that economic nationalists confronted in a virtual flood of studies[34] and publications beginning in the mid-sixties. The forerunner was George Grant's *Lament for a Nation* (1965), in which Grant not only mourned the end of Canada as a sovereign nation, but elevated anti-Americanism to a conservative virtue in the face of an advancing continental and indeed global technological culture. In the early 1970s nationalists advanced the argument that foreign investment not only threatened Canada's political sovereignty and the survival of a distinctive national identity, *but that it harmed the Canadian economy*. Book after book hammered away at the belief that foreign investment was beneficial. Works such as D.W. Carr's *Recovering Canada's Nationhood* (1971), James Laxer's *The Energy Poker Game* (1970), Kari Levitt's *The Silent Surrender* (1970), Ian Lumsden's *Close the 49th Parallel Etc.* (1970), W.H. Pope's *The Elephant and the Mouse* (1971), Abraham Rotstein's *The Precarious Homestead* (1973), Rotstein and Gary Lax's *Independence: The Canadian Challenge* (1972), Philippe Sykes's *Sellout: The Giveaway of Canada's Resources* (1973), and John W. Warnock's *Partner to Behemoth* (1970) contributed to the nationalist case. It is interesting to note that this nationalist outpouring, largely written by English Canadian academics, coincided with the Quiet Revolution in Quebec. "Maîtres chez nous," the slogan of the Quiet Revolution, seems equally fitting for the economic nationalists of English Canada.

Who is to Blame?

While nationalists lament the American domination of the Canadian economy, they place the blame squarely on Canadian rather than American shoulders:

• *Donald Creighton (historian): "Canadians, themselves, half converted to the belief that economic development is the only sure road to happiness, have grown accustomed to selling out their birthright for a quick buck."*

• *Lester Pearson (while Leader of the Official Opposition in 1960): "The dependence of Canada on the United States market for trade and on U.S. capital for development is an increasing threat to our independence.... But, if we lose our national purpose and identity, it will be by our own default, not by the design of anybody else."*

• *Mel Hurtig (publisher): "We are not*

victims of rape so much as witnesses to our own economic prostitution."

• *Myrna Kostash (author and journalist) describes Canada as "... a nation whoring on the sidelines of the world's biggest dollar bonanza while plotting all the time a cultural get-away that will astound the Pharisees and renew the hope of the exploited everywhere."*

• *The late W.L. Morton (historian) argued that the present degree of American investment "... is solely the work and fault of Canadians, particularly of provinces and regions competing for foreign investment in any guise and at any cost. These Canadian har-*

lots, having sold their bodies, usually at a cheaper price than they could have got, will find they have also sold their souls."

• *George Bain* (The Globe and Mail): *"If there is one thing that worries Canadians more than economic domination, it is that someone, sometime, will try to do something about it."*

• *Minutes after endorsing a United Auto Workers resolution calling for Canadian content restrictions on foreign cars, the town council of Tilbury, Ontario, voted to buy a Japanese-made tractor because the dealer knocked $4,500 off the regular price.*

The argument that American investment hurts rather than helps the Canadian economy rests on a number of assertions which, like those supporting the continentalist case, can be presented but not authoritatively assessed within the confines of this text:

• While American investment provides some new capital, for the most part it is financed through retained branch plant earnings or through loans from Canadian financial institutions. At the same time, over 80 percent of the dividends from the leading five hundred firms in Canada are paid to firms and individuals outside Canada.[35] When dividends are combined with management fees, royalties, and other payments made by branch plants to parent firms, there is a capital exodus from Canada approaching $8 billion per year.
• Canada's branch-plant economy inhibits research and development (R and D). Branch plants leave most R and D to the more extensive resources of the parent firm, restricting their own work to adapting parent products to Canadian conditions. The research that is done is largely carried out by governments rather than by the private sector. Overall, Canada spends a much smaller proportion of its Gross National Product on R and D than do its international competitors, and, as a consequence, lies closer to the handle than to the cutting edge of technological change.
• Although branch plants export employment opportunities from the United States to Canada, they can also destabilize the Canadian economy. When American economic conditions deteriorate, multinational corporations may experience

intense political and union pressure to recapture such opportunities for American workers by shutting down Canadian branch plants, stepping up production in the United States, and replacing branch plant products with American imports.

• The branch plant economy limits Canada's export capacity. Because of the "miniature replica" effect—too many firms, too short production lines, and too high per unit costs—branch plants are poor competitors in American or international markets.[36] Parent firms may also prefer that all sales beyond North America be handled by the parent firm, to maximize either profits or the foreign marketing resources of the parent firm. While some Canadian subsidiaries have established an export market through "world product mandating" in which the Canadian subsidiary is mandated by the parent firm to develop, manufacture, and market specific products for the world market, they remain an exception rather than the rule.

• Branch plants may provide unfair competition for Canadian firms. They have the financial support of the parent firm, which may be prepared to carry Canadian losses over the short term in order to establish a niche in the Canadian market; they have less trouble securing loans from Canadian banks given the backing of the parent firm; and they benefit from free "spill-over" advertising directed to the American market. My children, for example, had been well primed for McDonald's "Chicken McNuggets" by American advertising appearing on cable television.

• American legislation such as anti-trust laws and the United States Trading with the Enemy Act, which apply to American residents outside the United States, may curtail the commercial activities of Canadian subsidiaries even though no Canadian laws are being contravened. In the past, the intrusion of "extraterritoriality" has prevented the sale of Canadian flour and locomotives to Cuba, the sale of medical drugs to the American Quakers (who were planning to send Canadian drugs to North Vietnam after their purchase of such drugs in the United States was blocked by the American government), and the sale of miniature submarines to the Soviet Union.[37] In terms of boundary maintenance, the issue here is just where the legal boundary should lie.

• Branch plants make it difficult for Canadians to invest in their own economy while at the same time encouraging Canadian investment in the United States. The problem arises because in many cases it is possible to buy common shares only in the parent firm, and not in the Canadian subsidiary.

• The branch plant economy opens up the possibility of an American firm importing goods from its Canadian subsidiary at an artificially low price, and exporting goods to the same subsidiary at an artificially high price. The result of such "transfer pricing" would be poor profit performance by the Canadian subsidiary and consequently a low tax yield for Canadian governments, and an inflated profit performance for the parent firm with a consequently higher tax yield for American governments. The same result could stem from inflated management or royalty fees being levied by the parent firm, or by a reluctance on the part of the subsidiary to buy from Canadian suppliers.

Economic nationalists reject the argument that free trade with the United States would benefit the Canadian economy. While Canadian firms would have access to the American market, American firms with their longer production lines and lower per unit costs would gain access to the Canadian market. In the exchange, Canadian-owned firms could be swamped while American subsidiaries would be unlikely to enter the American market. As Peter Newman argues,

It is Alice in Wonderland economics to expect branch plants in Canada to compete with their U.S. parent companies on their home ground. Indeed, the reverse phenomenon is more likely: free trade will encourage the dismantling of Canadian branch plants ...[38]

To the extent that branch plants came to Canada because of the tariff, the introduction of free trade could lead to a substantial labour force migration to the United States. Many of the managerial and production tasks now handled in Canada could be handled by the parent firm, leaving only a residual Canadian sales force such as would be required to handle a regional market in the United States.

Of particular concern to economic nationalists is the fear that foreign ownership dilutes Canada's *political* control over its economy. From the nationalist perspective, the economy is an instrument for the attainment of not only individual consumptive goals but also collective social goals. Economic policy can be used to redistribute income among individuals or across regions, to promote employment, or to create nationally distinct social institutions and public services. However, to the extent that the Canadian economy is integrated into a continental scheme of things, the ability of Canadian governments to direct the economy toward social ends is weakened. It is in this sense, Levitt argues, that continentalism "... is fundamentally destructive of Canadian unity because it rejects the maintenance of a national community as an end in itself."[39]

The fears of economic nationalists on this count were crystallized in an often quoted passage by George Ball, the Undersecretary of State for Presidents Lyndon Johnson and John Kennedy. Canada, Ball believed, was fighting a "rearguard action against the inevitable":

Sooner or later, commercial imperatives will bring about free movement of all goods back and forth across our long border; and when that occurs, or even before it does, it will become unmistakably clear that countries with economies so inextricably entwined must also have free movement of the other vital factors of production—capital, services and labor. The result will inevitably be substantial economic integration, which will require for its full realization a progressively expanding area of common political decision.[40]

"First you must file notice of intent."

Macpherson's Editorial Cartoons, Toronto Star, 1972.

It is the "expanding area of common political decision" that poses the threat.

In the almost twenty years that have passed since Ball's prediction, there has in fact been little if any movement toward an expanding area of common political decision. Indeed, the intervening years have witnessed an overall decline in direct foreign investment including takeovers, new businesses, and retained earnings by foreign subsidiaries.[41] Foreign ownership of the Canadian economy has steadily declined. In 1962, 42.7 percent of all Canadian industry (excluding financial institutions) was foreign owned, a percentage that dropped to 37 percent by 1971 and 26 percent by 1981. Foreign ownership in the manufacturing sector alone dropped from 57 percent in 1962 to 41 percent in 1981.[42] The intervening years have also witnessed significant attempts to assert greater political control over the economy. Here the symbolic centrepiece has been FIRA, the Foreign Investment Review Agency.

FIRA's creation had been recommended in the 1972 Gray Report (*Foreign Direct Investment in Canada*) as an essential response to expanding foreign ownership of the Canadian economy. The agency was put into place in 1974 in response to growing nationalist pressure that such ownership be curtailed and growing political pressure on the Liberal minority government by the federal New Democrats. The intent of FIRA was to screen rather than to block foreign investment, to ensure that takeovers and, after 1975, new investment, were of "significant benefit" to Canada. As the Minister of Finance explained to a New York audience when FIRA was introduced, "it's not a dam, it's a filter."[43] Whether FIRA has served as an effective gatekeeper has been a matter of considerable debate. While some have claimed that the only firm likely to be denied entry by FIRA would be Murder Incorporated, FIRA's regulations have forced foreign investors at least to address the issue of Canadian benefit. They have also generated a good deal of red tape, a good deal of confusion as to what is and what is not of "significant benefit" to Canada, and delays of up to two years in the approval of investment proposals.

FIRA was not unique to Canada as most countries, including the United States, impose analogous if less formalized restrictions on foreign investment.[44] For Canadian nationalists it nevertheless served as an important symbol of Canadian political control over the Canadian economy. For those with a more continentalist orientation, it served as an equally important symbol of misguided nationalism and excessive state intervention in the economy. In the early 1980s, as the Canadian economy worsened and unemployment rose, FIRA's nationalist mandate was subordinated to the overarching goal of maintaining a healthy economy. The welcome mat was thrown out to any foreign investment that might generate jobs. In the face of growing unemployment, the fear was not that foreign investors would flood into Canada, but that they might not come at all.[45] After the 1984 election of the new Conservative government, FIRA was renamed Investment Canada. While the agency continues to review major investment proposals of national economic significance, its primary mandate now is to attract rather than to screen foreign investment. Whereas FIRA required evidence that new investment would generate significant benefit for Canada, the operating assumption of Investment Canada appears to be that foreign investment is beneficial unless evidence to the contrary is produced.

A second important nationalist initiative of the last decade came with the creation of Petro-Canada in 1974 and the introduction of the National Energy Program in 1980. Petro-Canada, a Crown corporation, has become a major presence in all aspects of the oil industry from service stations to exploration in the Arctic and off the east coast. The NEP was introduced to increase Canadian ownership of the oil industry from approximately 10 per cent in 1980 to 50 percent in 1990, to protect Canadians from rapidly rising world oil prices, and to promote energy self-sufficiency. While FIRA had sought to regulate foreign investment, the NEP constituted a more dramatic assertion of Canadian sovereignty in an important sector of the economy. The NEP was introduced at a time when the new Reagan administration in the United States was attempting to reduce state intervention in the economy. As a consequence it ruffled ideological feathers in the United States and contributed to a general deterioration in Canadian–American relations.[46] American oil interests were upset at the NEP "back-in" provisions which allowed Petro-Canada to acquire up to 25 percent ownership in frontier and offshore oil leases held by multinational corporations. These provisions were seen as confiscatory, and were attacked because they were a post facto change in the rules of the game governing foreign investment in Canada. The companies argued that if they came into Canada under one set of rules, the rules should not be changed once the investment was in place. The NEP was also criticized within Canada, in part for parallel ideological reasons and, more vociferously, by western Canadians as a federal raid on provincial resource revenues.

In drawing this discussion to a close, note should be made of the association between economic nationalism and the political left. Just as the case for continentalism is, in essence, a case for a laissez-faire economic order in which the flow of capital, resources, and labour would be unimpaired by political constraints, the case for economic nationalism is a case for harnessing the economy to broader national and social goals. The association was central to Grant's argument in *Lament for a Nation*:

After 1940, nationalism [in Canada] had to go hand in hand with some measure of socialism. Only nationalism could provide the political incentive for planning; only planning could restrain the victory of continentalism.[47]

Or again, later in the same work:

No small country can depend for its existence on the loyalty of its capitalists. International interests may require the sacrifice of the lesser loyalty of patriotism. Only in dominant nations is the loyalty of capitalists ensured.[48]

At the extreme, then, economic nationalism can be seen as a means of creating a more socialist economic order.[49] In its more moderate forms, economic nationalism prompts extensive government intervention in the economy in order to regulate foreign investment and ensure that it serves the national interest. Thus the debate over economic nationalism becomes entangled in a broader ideological debate over the appropriate role of the state in the economy, and in a broader political debate over how and by whom the national interest is to be defined. (See Chapter Four).

The tension between continentalism and economic nationalism will be an enduring theme in Canadian political life. There is no final solution; the tension is one that has to be managed rather than resolved. The important political debate will thus centre on matters of degree rather than on polar alternatives. Should there be somewhat more or somewhat less foreign investment? Should investment controls be somewhat more or somewhat less rigorous? Should there be freer, but not free, trade? When, in 1968, Prime Minister Trudeau was asked if he was worried about the influx of American capital, he replied: "Well, I am not worried in the sense that I don't worry over something which is somewhat inevitable, and I think the problem of economic domination is somewhat inevitable ... these are the facts of life, and they don't worry me." While economic nationalists will continue to debate the inevitability of domination, and the extent to which domination can and should be resisted, there is little doubt that extensive foreign investment will remain an economic and political fact of Canadian life.

CULTURAL NATIONALISM

In the nineteenth century, Canada's nascent culture was shielded from American influence by the primitive state of communications technology. The political barrier between the two countries served as a reasonably effective cultural barrier as the main cultural influences on Canadian life flowed from Great Britain, not the United States. However, with the introduction of mass-circulation magazines, wire services, motion pictures, records, radio, and television, the greater proximity of the United States was brought to bear on cultural barriers that were increasingly permeable. Cultural influences flowed from south to north (but *not* from north to south) through a multitude of channels. The airwaves in particular, which were at first envisaged as "highways of national cultural integration" in Canada, became "agents of denationalization by serving as roadways for foreign, largely American, cultural values."[50]

The response to American influence in the cultural realm was patterned after that in the economic realm. Barriers were erected to shelter the Canadian culture and, more specifically, Canadian cultural artisans including authors, publishers, film and television producers, recording artists, and directors of dance and theatre. The intent was to restrict the American cultural presence and, in so doing, to create a protected domestic market for the producers of Canadian cultural artifacts. (In this case there was no anticipation that American artisans would leap the "tariff wall" and relocate in Canada, as American manufacturing firms had done to establish Canadian branch plants.) For example, Canadian content regulations for radio and television broadcasts have created a protected market for Canadians, a market from which "unfair" foreign competition has been legislatively excluded, a market in which the cultural tastes of individual Canadians are denied full expression. It was hoped, then, that a healthy Canadian cultural "industry" would flourish behind the protective wall of cultural tariffs.

". . . To comply with government regulations this picture will be displayed for 7 minutes and 32 seconds to bring our Canadian content to the required 60 percent. Please do not adjust your set. To comply with . . ."

Len Norris, *19th Annual.* Originally published in *The Vancouver Sun*, February 14, 1970

For Canadian nationalists, the cultural threat from the United States has been no less important than the economic threat, as the following quote from John Holmes illustrates:

We are in danger of becoming a zombie nation, our physical structure intact but our souls and minds gone abroad. Having gloriously resisted with our loyal muskets the Yankee invader on the slopes of Quebec and Queenston, Canada may well be conquered by American television.[51]

While it can be argued that foreign investment brings in its wake employment and economic growth, the benefits of the American mass culture are more elusive and contentious. As a consequence, nationalists have contested the American presence on the cultural front with greater moral conviction than they have possessed on the economic front.

In a series of Royal Commissions conducted during the 1950s and early 1960s, two principal themes of Canadian cultural nationalism were established: "... that Canada's capacity for meaningful nationhood is somehow being thwarted and undermined by the proximity and potency of the cultural output of the United States," and that state intervention was essential "to create and support a counter-vailing cultural force to the unrelenting flow of Americana across the border."[52] Such intervention took two basic forms. The first entailed regulations restricting the influx of American culture into Canada, regulations facilitated by the 1932 Supreme Court decision on the *Radio Case* giving jurisdiction over the airwaves to the national government. Examples here would include the 1968 establishment of the Canadian Radio-Television Commission and the Canadian content regulations that the CRTC (now the Canadian Radio-television and Telecommunications Commission) spawned, the elimination of tax deductions for firms advertising in the Canadian edition of *Time* (now defunct as a consequence) and on American border television stations transmitting into Canada, and immigration restrictions which require artistic companies and universities seeking to hire outside Canada to first demonstrate that no suitable Canadian candidates are available. The second entailed public support for Canadian cultural artisans. Examples here would include the 1957 creation of the Canada Council, public funding for the CBC, and current requirements that cable television firms plough some of their revenue back into the production of Canadian programming.

Policies to shelter Canadian culture face serious technological constraints. For decades, Canadians living in major metropolitan centres close to the American border have been able to pick up American radio and television stations. Now, for a modest fee, most Canadians have access to unimpaired American programming through cable television. While the content of cable television can be regulated to a degree by restricting the number of channels carrying American programming, recent advances in cable capacity and satellite delivery threaten the survival of any form of Canadian content regulation. In the future as in the past, technological innovation is likely progressively to erode cultural barriers between Canada and the United States.

During the late 1960s and early 1970s, Canadian universities provided a major battleground for cultural nationalists. Faced with rapid enrolment growth and a limited production of Canadian PhDs, universities had little choice but to hire abroad. As a consequence, universities came to be characterized by a high proportion of non-Canadian faculty members (mostly Americans) and an even higher proportion who had received their graduate training outside Canada. This raised fears about the Canadian content of university education, and about the capacity of universities to help build or at the very least transmit a distinctive national culture.[53] In more recent years the concern has diminished, though not evapo-

WOT'S IN IT
FOR ME ?

CANADIAN ECONOMIC ELITE

GIVE

FIGHT U.S. TAKE-OVER

Macpherson's Editorial Cartoons, Toronto Star, 1972

rated, as Canadians have come to make up a larger and larger proportion of university faculties, as more Canadian PhDs have come on the market,[54] and as many of the landed immigrants who staffed Canadian universities in the past have taken out Canadian citizenship. Whereas in 1969–70 only 57 percent of faculty positions were held by Canadian citizens, this had increased to 77 percent by 1980.[55]

In concluding this discussion, it should be stressed that American cultural influences flow entirely from private sources. The American *government* has not been involved except when its help has been enlisted by private American interests affected by Canadian regulations. Here Henry Luce of *Time Magazine* and border television broadcasters provide two prominent examples. It should also be stressed that restrictions on the inflow of American culture necessarily restrict the freedom of Canadians to watch, read, and listen to whatever they like. Cultural nationalism thus protects collective values—the survival of a distinctive national culture—through the curtailment of individual freedom much as Quebec language policy protects a collective value—the survival of the French language—through similarly modest restrictions on individual freedom. The limited tolerance of Canadians for such curtailment in turn limits the height of cultural walls between Canada and the United States. Cultural barriers are analogous to economic tariffs; we all pay a modest price while a few—recording artists, film and television producers, and so forth—reap substantial benefits. This creates both a vigorous lobby for cultural nationalism and countervailing consumer pressure for freer trade in cultural artifacts.

It is one of the ironies of Canadian life that more effective cultural barriers exist between the linguistic communities within Canada than between Canada and the United States. While technological change has eroded the cultural barrier between Canada and the United States, it has done little to erode the language barrier within Canada. Even the CBC, with its mandate to foster national unity, operates through linguistically differentiated organizations (Radio Canada is the franco-phone voice) which share little in common. Siegel concludes that "the structural arrangement within CBC encourages the 'two solitudes' of Canada, reinforcing differences in outlook by such creative elements as journalists and entertainment producers rather than bridging them," and that, more generally, "television has played an almost insignificant role in explaining the French and English societies to each other."[56] Thus modern technology may erode cultural differences between Canada and the United States while strengthening cultural differences within Canada. In either case, government intervention has modest leverage at best on the tendency of a common language to unit and different languages to divide.

Border Disputes

John Holmes has written that "the great epic of North America is not the sharing of a continent; we only share a border."[57] It should come as no surprise that sharing a border has given rise to numerous disputes. Given the length of the border, that it crosses the Great Lakes and is crossed in turn by rivers and winds, the potential for environmental conflict alone is staggering. As Arthur Meighen, former leader of the national Conservative party, stated in a 1937 address on Canadian–American relations, "we are not in the same boat but we are pretty much in the same waters." Border disputes, then, are bound to provide a source of ongoing irritation between the two national communities. And yet, perhaps because they are inevitable, border disputes rarely disrupt the broader Canadian–American relationship.

It should also come as no surprise that the national impact of border disputes is asymmetrical. Although 90 percent of Canadians live within 300 kilometres of the border, the American population is broadly dispersed well south of the border region. Thus border disputes such as that over acid rain may potentially touch most Canadians, while *relatively* few Americans are affected. For most Americans, the Canadian–American border and the disputes it generates have about as much relevance to their immediate lives as the border separating Portugal and Spain.

Over the years border disputes have taken a variety of forms, with those relating to water playing a predominant role. Disputes over offshore fisheries have been present since the Convention of 1818 set limits on the right of Americans to fish in British North American waters. With the extension of national control over coastal waters from three miles to twelve miles in 1970, and to two hundred miles in 1977, disputes concerning overlapping fishing claims and the need to manage a diminishing resource were further compounded. On the Pacific coast, for example, the inability of the two countries to reach an agreement on salmon fisheries stems in large part from a dispute on whether or not fish stocks should be conserved. The Canadian government has spent millions on salmon propagation and habitat enhancement, and favours reduced fishing quotas to protect both salmon stocks and the survival of the salmon industry in Canada. According to Stephen Clarkson, "American fishermen have retained a free market approach to fisheries, claiming that an exhaustion of the stocks will automatically reduce the number of vessels in the fishery and so allow the fish population to regenerate itself."[58]

Disagreements over the precise location of the international border still persists. A seven-year dispute over the maritime boundary through the Gulf of Maine was finally taken to the International Court of Justice in the Hague. At issue was fishing access to Georges Bank, an area rich in scallops, cod, and halibut, and upon which some 3,500 Canadian fishing jobs depend. Canada had claimed about a third of Georges Bank, while the United States had claimed it all. On October 12, 1984, the International Court fixed a boundary giving Canada about one-sixth of Georges Bank. By prior agreement between Canada and the United States, the new boundary is binding on both sides and cannot be appealed. Other boundary disputes are still outstanding. There is disagreement, for example, on where to set the maritime boundary in the Arctic's Beaufort Sea, a boundary that could affect national ownership of offshore oil resources associated with the Prudhoe Bay oil field in Alaska. Maritime disputes of a more environmental character have arisen over the passage of American oil tankers among the Arctic Islands and down the Strait of Juan de Fuca between Vancouver Island and the British Columbia mainland.

On the continent, the management of shared river basins has been contentious at times. Hydro-electric development of the Columbia River Basin in Washington State touched off a forty-two-year argument over the potential flooding of the Skagit River Valley, running northward into British Columbia. The dispute was finally settled in 1984 when the Canadian and American governments signed an eighty-year treaty prohibiting the flooding of Canadian land in exchange for a Canadian guarantee of extra electrical power to Seattle. For Manitobans, the planned Garrison Diversion irrigation project to irrigate 1.5 million acres in North Dakota has been a source of conflict since it was first proposed in 1965. The Garrison diversion would introduce water from the Missouri River into Canada's Hudson Bay river basin, and thus transfer foreign fish, micro-organisms, and pollutants that could damage Manitoba's fishing industry. Looking ahead, a growing water shortage in the American southwest is likely to reactivate American interest in massive water-diversion projects to move "unused" Canadian water south across the border. One such project, the 1963 North American Water and Power Alliance, proposed spending $150 billion to send Canadian water south through the Rocky Mountain Trench.

In recent decades environmental border disputes have become more common in the wake of greater environmental degradation and stronger environmental lobbies on both sides of the border. The dominant issues have been cleaning up the Great Lakes and the environmental damage to lakes and rivers affected by acid rain. While Canadian industrial emissions of sulphur dioxide contribute substantially to the acid rain problem in Canada, industries and utility plants in the Ohio Valley states (Indiana, Illinois, Ohio, Pennsylvania) play a comparable role through emissions carried hundreds of miles north by prevailing winds into Canada. Canadian emissions contribute to the acid rain problem in the New England states, and Americans have expressed concern about environmental damage arising from the Inco smelter in Sudbury, and from Canadian thermal-power plants at Poplar River, Saskatchewan, and Atikokan, Ontario. On balance, however, and due in large part to the pattern of prevailing winds, the northward drift of acid rain across the international border appears to exceed the southward drift by a margin of three or four to one.[59]

Editorial, *The Globe and Mail* National
Edition, March 2, 1983, p. 6

Political science

Because his thinking disturbed the order of things, Galileo ran into trouble from the authorities (the Inquisition in his case) and was obliged to state publicly that he had erred in thinking that the planets revolved around the sun. He was placed under permanent house arrest and forbidden to raise the matter again.

More than 370 years later, we have come to regard the episode as one of the sadder ones in the history of
science. There is, today, a widely-held opinion that scientists are engaged in a coldly objective search for truth and that nothing should be done to persuade them to adjust the truth to suit political or theological objectives.

How then does one view the 20th-century schism that cleanly separates Canadian scientists from U.S. scientists on the matter of acid rain? It's not as though they were looking through different microscopes, examining differ-

ent water samples or applying different criteria. Over the past couple of
years they have often worked side by
side in task groups that looked at how
pollutants move with the air currents
from point to point, the impact of their
return to earth in the form of acid rain
and the actions that may be taken to
reduce the emissions (mostly industrial
and mostly sulphuric) that cause the
problem.

The reports of the scientists do
cover a lot of shared ground—agreement that what comes out of chimney
stacks does kill fish, frogs, salamanders
and aquatic plants, that the pollution is
a two-way traffic with no more respect
for national borders than for pond
trout, and that excessive amounts of
acid rain are falling on 52,000 square
kilometres of acid-sensitive waters in
Eastern Canada and 36,000 square kilometres in the Eastern United States.

The assembled findings of the final
report build a compelling case for stern
action, but at the last moment the U.S.
version swerves away from the strong
medicine prescribed in the Canadian
version: reduction of the fall-out of
sulphate in precipitation to 20 kilo-
grams per hectare per year to protect
all but the most sensitive aquatic eco-
systems. The U.S. view takes a much
vaguer line, conceding simply that reduction of present levels of sulphur

deposition "would lead to eventual
recovery of those waters that have
been altered by deposition."

This is a dismal result for the work
that has gone into producing it, and the
evidence suggests rather strongly that
it is largely because of U.S. footdrag-
ging, either from reluctance to
contemplate the expense of reducing
emissions or reluctance to put segments of U.S. industry to the trouble of
cleaning up their act.

The sluggishness of U.S. environmental responses in recent years led
Raymond Robinson, head of Canada's
Federal Environmental Assessment
and Review Office, to give some rein to
his suspicions about the reasons.
Addressing a gathering of scientists in
Washington last October, he bluntly
accused the White House of "blatant
efforts to manipulate acid rain work
groups" as part of an attempt to avoid
a commitment to clean up acid rain
pollution.

Mr. Robinson added that, despite
substantial agreement among the
scientists about causes and ways to
control acid rain, "non-experts are
rewriting the conclusions and unhappy
scientists were reassigned. Some of
them lost their jobs."

Galileo would have wept to think
that this sort of thing was going on
three centuries after his death.

Other forms of border disputes are not uncommon: a rock star is denied entry into Canada for drug-related reasons, a union official is denied entry to the United States because of a criminal record, a tourist is subjected to apparently unnecessary harrassment by customs officials. Yet such incidents, when placed against the millions of uneventful border crossings that occur every month, represent an extremely minor source of irritation.

In 1909 Canada and the United States established the International Joint

Commission (IJC) to deal with border-related issues arising from the Boundary Waters Treaty signed in the same year. Canada and the United States are equally represented on the IJC, which is actually made up of a three-member commission in each capital. The IJC, which is empowered to make recommendations to the respective national governments rather than to *impose* solutions, but which can act as a judicial body if the two governments so decide, has been the principal institutional mechanism for handling border disputes. The IJC, however, has by no means supplanted more conventional diplomatic and political relations between Canada and the United States.

Transnational and Intergovernmental Relations

Canadian–American relations are primarily *transnational* rather than *international* in character, transnational being defined as "contacts, coalitions, and inter-actions across state boundaries that are not controlled by the central foreign policy organs of government."[60] Transnational relations encompass interactions among a vast array of private actors—individuals, corporations, trade unions, sports leagues, and service clubs—which in their sheer volume overwhelm inter-governmental relations. The American penetration of Canada, around which so much of the Canadian–American relationship revolves, has been almost entirely non-governmental in character, which may account for the lack of more acute Canadian concern.[61]

The dominance of transnational interaction is reflected in the lack of any coherent "American policy" in Ottawa or "Canadian policy" in Washington. Even though Canadian–American relations are Canada's most important foreign policy concern, they are simply too vast and involve too many issues and actors to be neatly packaged within a single policy perspective. Thus when Ottawa published a major review of foreign policy options in 1970, Canadian policy toward the United States was only obliquely addressed.[62] Nor is any greater coherence readily apparent in American policy toward Canada. As Keohane and Nye point out:

Neither country has found it possible to list formally, with meaningful consensus, its priorities toward the other in any specific form. It could not be done without simul-taneously applying corresponding priorities to aspects of domestic policy, and conse-quently to constituent groups....[63]

Canada and the United States are more affected by each other's domestic poli-cies than by their respective foreign policies. The American deregulation of natu-ral gas prices, for example, has had a marked impact on Canadian gas exports just as American air pollution standards have an impact upon Canadian problems with acid rain. In a similar fashion, American events entirely within the private domain ripple through Canadian life. The establishment of the United States Football league, for example, affected the ability of the Canadian Football League to attract American imports. On the Canadian side of the fence in particular, Canadian–American relations touch upon so many aspects of Canadian life, and are therefore so entangled with both national and provincial governments, that they can often be seen as an extension of Canadian domestic politics rather than as a form of international relations. This was clearly apparent in the case of the National Energy Program where the pursuit of domestic policy goals had a major impact on Canadian–American relations.

Nonetheless, it is important not to lose sight of the international dimension. While in many respects the two countries have a "special relationship" that falls outside the boundaries of conventional international relations, they also interact with one another as they interact with other states. *Intergovernmental* relations remain important. Indeed, there is no evidence, even in the most embryonic form, of an emerging continental state that would supplant the international relationship. There are no institutions which imply, to use Ball's phrase, "a progressively expanding area of common political decision." As Redekop concludes, "... North American intergration, such as it is, remains a low-level, unco-ordinated, almost haphazard phenomenon...."[64] Here Holmes argues that the rules, commitments, and institutions which govern the bilateral relationship are not intended to bring the two countries closer together. To the contrary, their purpose "... is to regulate forces which, unless a Canadian place is staked out, would inevitably erode our sovereignty and our identity."[65]

Before the first Canadian minister to Washington, Vincent Massey, was appointed in 1926, Canadian affairs were handled by the British embassy. Since then, Canada has maintained a vigorous diplomatic presence in the American capital, a presence recently expanded through a $650,000 lobbying campaign. The use of Congressional lobbyists—paid professionals who keep their finger on the pulse of the American Congress, alerting Canadian officials to both threats and opportunities, and presenting Canadian views to Washington politicians—is a diplomatic response to both the complexity of American government and the impact that congressional legislation can have on Canadian interests. During 1983 alone, for example, sixty-three protectionist bills to restrict Canadian imports came before Congress.[66] The point to be stressed is that intergovernmental contact between the Canadian Department of External Affairs and the American State Department cannot alone sufficiently protect Canadian interests. Increasingly, some direct penetration of the congressional arena is being sought.

Apart from the lobbying efforts of the Canadian embassy, there are over fifty "foreign agents" representing Canadian interests in the United States.[67] This rather melodramatic term for what are generally law firms, public relations agencies, or specialists in governmental affairs comes from the need to register with the U.S. Department of Justice under the Foreign Agents Registration Act.

The agents represent a variety of interests: private firms; industry organizations such as the Canadian Softwood Lumber Committee, the Canadian Manufacturers' Association, and the Independent Petroleum Association of Canada; public interest groups such as the Canadian Coalition on Acid Rain; provincial trade offices in the United States; provincial departments such as Ontario's Ministry of the Environment; and federal agencies such as the National Film Board of Canada. In all cases their tasks are essentially the same: warning clients about potentially harmful congressional legislation—legislation that often arises in response to private American interests and not to policy initiatives from the President or from the State Department—and presenting their client's case within the American legislative process.

This lobbying activity reflects a fact of American political life; the U.S. State Department cannot guarantee congressional support for bilateral deals struck with Canada. The American Senate, unlike the Senate in Canada, must approve any treaties negotiated by the executive branch. Senators can thus use the threat of veto to force modifications in the terms of treaties brought before them. Therefore, if Canadian interests are to be protected, Canadians must be prepared to wade into congressional combat on their own behalf and not rely on the State Department alone to carry the Canadian flag. In a somewhat analogous development, provincial governments are increasingly active participants in Canadian–American relations. They too are unwilling to let External Affairs carry the flags of provincial interest. Thus premiers engage in frequent political sorties to Washington, New York, and the capitals of border states while provincial trade offices in the United States continue to expand in number and scope.

The American embassy in Ottawa, like its Canadian counterpart in Washington, is not involved in the great bulk of Canadian–American transnational interactions. Only rarely do American multinationals seek backing from the United States government in disputes with Canadian governments,[68] the most notable exception occurring when the federal government threatened to remove tax deductions for Canadian firms advertising in the Canadian editions of *Time* and *Reader's Digest*. In recent years American ambassadors have become more prone to publicly criticize Canadian domestic policies, a change in diplomatic style that has also been evident for Canadian ambassadors in the United States.

In many ways Canadian–American relations resemble a vast seamless web. For this reason it is easy for issues and disputes to become entangled with one another. Somewhat paradoxically, this very interdependence of issues traditionally led to a mutual avoidance of "linkage politics"—a situation in which the settlement of one issue is tied to, or is dependent upon, the settlement of other, often substantively unrelated, issues. As Holmes has pointed out, not only have Canadians sensed that "linkage was a game that would inevitably be won by the stronger power," but that "the American government machine was too incoherent to formulate a co-ordinated Canadian policy in which fish or pork would be bargained for gas or relations with Cuba."[69] Clarkson, however, argues that in the 1980s Congress has embraced linkage politics, retaliating in one sector of the bilateral relationship when American interests have been hurt in another.[70] Canada, Clarkson suggests, should also embrace linkage politics in order to knit together a more coherent stance toward the bilateral relationship.

Despite the ten-to-one difference in population and economic power, Canada has not fared badly in the bilateral relationship. Canadians have not won on all issues, but certainly win more frequently than the odds might predict. This success has encouraged a strategy of "quiet diplomacy" through which Canadians protect their "special relationship" with the United States by refraining from public criticism of American world leadership. And yet American activities in the international arena have a direct impact on long-term Canadian interests, including the avoidance of nuclear war. As a consequence, the norms of quiet diplomacy can be strained when Canada is drawn into international disputes in which Canadian and American interests or world views do not coincide.

International Relations and Military Defence

Although Canada is not a major international power, it has been an active international player since the Second World War. Through participation in the United Nations, including its peace-keeping forces and specialized agencies such as the UN World Food program and UNESCO, and through multilateral organizations such as GATT, the North Atlantic Treaty Organization (NATO), the British Commonwealth and the International Emergency Food Reserve, Canada has made important contributions to the international order.

International involvement beyond the North American continent can take many forms, all of which may heighten the sense of belonging to a distinctive national community. It may be as personal as travelling abroad, in wearing the maple leaf on the back of one's jeans, in taking pride that strangers recognize the symbol and are able to distinguish Canadians from Americans. It may come through international hockey competition as Canadian teams challenge and, alas, too often fail to beat, the world's best. It may involve governmental participation in international organizations, participation that provides a valuable counterweight in our bilateral relationship with the United States. As Holmes explains, "Canadian governments, if not always the Canadian people, have recognized that international institutions ... are essential for a country our size to act effectively vis-a-vis a great power."[71] The assertion of Canadian sovereignty in the international arena thus protects Canadian sovereignty in the bilateral relationship with the United States. It is interesting to note, however, that the United States, like Canada, is willing to use international institutions to provide leverage on the bilateral relationship. Here an example is provided by the American GATT challenge to conditions imposed by FIRA on the import activities of American sub-sidiaries.

While international activity may strengthen Canada's continental position, it is also heavily encumbered by the Canadian–American relationship. The two countries share many important characteristics which propel them willy-nilly into the same international camp: both are western, northern, non-socialist, and industrialized states, linked together in a continental trading system. Where they differ dramatically is that the United States is a super-power with a global set of strategic interests, obligations, and entanglements that Canada shares only to a limited degree. Thus in the eyes of other states, Canada may be seen primarily as a supporting actor to the United States, a smaller and weaker younger sibling in the international schoolyard.

Militarily, Canada is firmly and unavoidably in the American camp, for in any nuclear exchange the two countries would be a common continental target. In the Ogdensburg Declaration of June 1940, Canada and the United States declared that the "defence of the two countries constituted a single problem," a declaration backed by the establishment of the Permanent Joint Board of Defence to provide a common forum for the discussion and coordination of continental defence. In 1941 the two countries signed the Hyde Park Agreement which all but wiped out the border as far as defence production was concerned.[73] The 1959 Defence Production Sharing Agreements updated and expanded the Hyde Park Agreement by allowing Canadian firms to compete without handicap for American defence contracts. Given that Canada requires modern weapons of war, that these have become too costly to produce for Canada's use alone, and that success as an international arms dealer may be both economically difficult and morally repugnant, the arrangement with the United States allows Canada to at least share in the economic benefits of defence production. Over the first twenty years of the DPS agreements, American military procurements in Canada totalled $5,195 million while Canadian procurements in the United States totalled $5,535 million.[73]

Canada is, with the United States, a member of NATO, and since 1958 has been a partner with the United States in the North American Air Defence Command (NORAD), rechristened the North American *Aerospace* Defence Command in March 1981. Over the years NORAD's importance has declined with the diminished threat of a Soviet bomber attack. NORAD's atrophy has shifted the focus of Canadian defence strategy from the bilateral Canadian–American relationship, in which the United States was overwhelmingly dominant, to the multilateral forum of NATO.

Canada's military alliance with the United States reflects not only her continental location but also a basic agreement between Canadians and Americans on the desired shape of the international order. Yet even if that agreement did not exist, Canada would still lie across the northern flank of the United States. If Canadians were not prepared to defend that flank, the United States would have no choice but to do so itself. Thus the Canadian military not only defends Canada against potential foreign aggression but also defends Canadian political sovereignty from the United States. In this "defence against help," we encounter what has been termed the *sovereignty paradox*. To protect its sovereignty, Canada must participate in bilateral defence arrangements with the United States, arrangements which in turn restrict Canadian sovereignty given that Canada will be a junior, not equal, partner.[74] Fortunately, the diminished bomber threat and technological advances in satellite surveillance, over-the-horizon radar systems, and airborne warning-and-control systems (AWACS) have all but eliminated the need for an American military presence on Canadian soil. At the same time and for the same reasons, Canadians have even less leverage on American defence policy than they had in the past.

Despite the basic complementarity of national views, conflicts between Canada and the United States over military policy are not uncommon. At times Canada is accused of spending too little on defence or, more specifically, of making an insufficient military contribution to NATO. (In proportionate terms, Canada's contribution to NATO ranks above only Luxembourg and Iceland.) Here it is useful to note that the gulf between Canadian and American defence expenditures is immense. In early 1984, for example, President Ronald Reagan asked Congress to approve $313.4 billion in defence spending, an increase of $48.1 billion from the previous year. The *increase alone* was approximately six times the *entire* Canadian defence budget! In rough terms, American military expenditures are forty times those of Canada.

In the late 1950s and early 1960s disagreement arose between the two countries and within Canada over the acquisition of nuclear weapons for Canadian interceptor aircraft and anti-aircraft missiles (the Bomarc) based in Canada and with Canadian forces in Europe. Conservative Prime Minister John Diefenbaker came to symbolize nationalist resistance to American military policy, a resistance that extended to Canada's delay in putting her forces on alert during the 1962 Cuban missile crisis. The nuclear weapons issue played a significant role in the 1963 general election, in which the pro-warhead Liberals defeated the Conservatives to form a minority government. The warheads were subsequently installed, though they remained under American control. In the early 1970s the warheads were withdrawn, leaving the Canadian forces without nuclear weapons of any sort.

American military intervention abroad often evokes public and, more rarely, government criticism in Canada. American involvement in the Vietnam war received a generally negative press in Canada, though official opposition to the war was both muted and, if expressed, resented in the United States. When Prime Minister Pearson criticized the American bombing of North Vietnam in a 1965 speech at Temple University, President Johnson bluntly rebuked Pearson, saying "you peed on my carpet."[75] More recently, the American invasion of the Caribbean island of Grenada in late October 1983, was widely criticized in Canada.

Incidents like the Grenada invasion demonstrate some significant national differences in perceptions of the communist threat and in preferred strategies for coping with that threat. In comparison with the United States, Canada has attached less importance to the global threat of communism and has generally opposed military intervention as a response to communist threats in the Third World. Such incidents also provide the Canadian government with the opportunity to put some distance between Canada and the United States on the international stage without undermining the broader strategic principles of American foreign policies.

During 1983 and 1984 there was considerable protest in Canada over the testing of the Cruise missile guidance system in northern Alberta. To some, the Cruise testing implicated Canada in the international arms race and impaired the prospects for arms reduction, a nuclear freeze, and world peace. For others, the testing was seen as a modest contribution to a strengthened nuclear deterrent, and therefore to nuclear stability and world peace. Perhaps more importantly, it was also seen as a necessary fulfillment of Canadian alliance commitments under NATO. In an open letter to Canadians published in newspapers across the country on May 10, 1983, Prime Minister Trudeau stressed the alliance commitment:

It is hardly fair to rely on the Americans to protect the West, but to refuse to lend them a hand when the going gets rough. In that sense, the anti-Americanism of some Canadians verges on hypocrisy. They're eager to take refuge under the American umbrella, but don't want to help hold it.

In the fall of 1983, Prime Minister Trudeau launched a peace initiative to improve international dialogue on matters of arms control and tension reduction. To the extent that the United States has contributed to the collapse of constructive dialogue, the peace initiative could have been seen as critical of the United States. Any Canadian–American conflict, however, was primarily over the appropriate means to common ends rather than over those ends per se.

The question remains as to just how much independence Canada enjoys on the international stage. A firm answer would require a situation in which Canada and the United States had clearly conflicting international interests, and in which Canada's pursuit of her own interests would be actively opposed by the United States. To date such conflicts have not emerged. Given that both countries share so much in common, they are unlikely to emerge in the years to come.

Modelling the Relationship

Canada's history has been intimately tied to the two great English-speaking countries of the world, and two of the world's great imperial states. When British influence waned in Canada and around the world during the twentieth century, that of the United States waxed. It is not surprising, then, that Canada's colonial past has been used to model Canada's relationship with the United States.

It was Harold Innis, Canada's most famous economic historian, who first described Canada's progression from a British colony through a brief period of national independence, bounded by the two world wars, to a new colonial relationship with the United States. Historian Donald Creighton has written that as Canada was growing apart from Great Britain, her "... links with the United States became so numerous and so powerful that they threatened to convert the nation into a political vassal, an economic tributory, and a cultural colony of the American Empire."[76] Walter Gordon, then President of the Privy Council, developed the colonial theme in a 1967 interview:

During the last fifty years we have freed ourselves of traces of colonial status insofar as Britain is concerned. But having achieved our independence from Britain, we seem to have slipped, almost without knowing it, into a semi-dependent position in relation to the United States.[77]

The colonial model, it should be stressed, is meant to be more than descriptive; it also embodies a sense of anger and despair. To quote again from Gordon's 1967 interview, "... it is sadly ironic that in a world torn asunder by countries who are demanding and winning their independence, our free, independent and highly developed country should be haunted by the spectre of a colonial or semi-colonial future."[78]

The colonial model probably understates Canada's political independence. There can be an important difference between the political freedom to make choices and the fact that in most situations the range of choice is restricted by our continental relationship with the United States. The colonial model fails to recognize the lack of continental political institutions while directing insufficient attention to nongovernmental relations. It may also understate the common values that work to integrate the Canadian and American societies, and which lead many Canadians to embrace the continental relationship. To the extent that a colonial relationship does exist, it has been largely self-imposed. As Redekop points out, "... if the Canadian–American relationship constitutes colonialism, it must surely be the strangest colonial relationship extant."[79]

Redekop goes on to offer a comprehensive survey of concepts that have been used to model the Canadian–American relationship including domination, dependency, partnership, interdependence, hegemony, continentalism, satellite, client state, neo-colonialism, and "continental subsystemic dominance," his own preference. Canada has also been described as an American hinterland, a term that suggests interesting parallels between Canadian–American relations and regionalism within Canada. Clearly, then, the relationship can be modelled in many different ways, each of which directs our attention to different aspects of the relationship, and each of which distorts the reality of the relationship in different ways. Perhaps the most ubiquitous term, at least in American usage, has been "neighbours." Here it is worth citing at length a passage by James Eayrs that has retained its relevance through the years:

If the Canadian–American relationship is to flourish to the mutual benefit of its partners, it will be because statesmen of both countries resist the temptation ... of believing their politics to be neighbourly rather than international. They must realize that the two nations of North America are of the states-system, not beyond and above it, and shape their policies accordingly. President Johnson, with the best intentions in the world, observed ... that "Canada is such a close neighbor and such a good neighbor that we always have plenty of problems there. They are kind of like problems in the hometown." They are kind of not like that at all. They are the problems not of neighbours but of friendly foreign powers.[80]

Canadian Nationalism and the United States

One of the best summaries of the Canadian–American relationship came in a speech to the House of Commons (February 4, 1963) by Robert Thompson, leader of the Social Credit Party. "The Americans," Thompson declared, "are our best friends whether we like it or not." Of course, if there was any choice in the matter, most Canadians would choose the United States.[81] It is ironic, then, that no country poses a greater threat to Canada's survival as a distinct and independent national community. It is because the United States is Canada's best friend that it is also Canada's "worst enemy."

Nationalism has two components that are generally accepted as both core and universal elements: ingroup loyalty, or patriotism, and outgroup hostility toward other nationalities. Hans Kohn, in what has become a classic work on nationalism, stressed the "doublefaced" nature of nationalism: "intranationally, it leads to a lively sympathy with all fellow members within the nationality; internationally, it finds expression in indifference to or distrust and hate of fellow men outside the national orbit."[82] Although this conceptualization is not without its limitations,[83] it does identify the important role played by anti-Americanism in Canadian nationalism.

Survival vis-à-vis the United States has been a central theme of English Canadian nationalism,[84] just as *la survivance* has been a central theme of French Canadian nationalism. Not surprisingly, that quest for survival has often found expression in anti-Americanism. What is perhaps more surprising is that there is no American counterpart to the anti-Americanism one finds in Canada, no "anti-Canadianism" that can be tapped by political actors. For their part Canadians are aggravated by the American indifference to things Canadian, by the too-ready

"I do hope Americans don't think of us as ugly Canadians . . . stuffy, dull, slow, mundane, colorless, bland, self-righteous hypocrites . . . but not ugly."

Len Norris, *The Vancouver Sun*

assumption that Canadians and Americans are essentially the same under their different national skins. Northrop Frye links this reaction to Canadian fears about annexation, arguing that what is resented

> . . . is not annexation itself, but the feeling that Canada would disappear into a larger entity without having anything of any real distinctiveness to contribute to that entity: that, in short, if the United States did annex Canada it would notice nothing except an increase in its natural resources.[85]

To be disliked is one thing; to be ignored is something else entirely.

As Canada's only neighbour, the United States necessarily becomes the mirror in which Canadians see themselves. As a consequence, Canadian nationalism waxes and wanes in response to conditions in the United States as much as in response to conditions in Canada. In the past, the strength of Canadian nationalism was sapped by the national comparison. When Canadians looked at their own country they saw a poorer, colder, less developed, and less vibrant United States. They saw themselves as Americans with overshoes and colds, a country whose national symbol was not the soaring eagle but rather a large rodent noted for its ability to run for cover. Canadian nationalism seemed an irrational emotion that flew in the face of the factual comparison. It was not coincidental, then, that Canadian nationalism bloomed during the 1960s when the American society was experiencing deep distress. Looking south at racial conflict, a spiraling crime rate, deteriorating cities, student unrest, and the horror of the Viet Nam war, and drawing upon radical American critiques of the American society, Canadians could objectively and somewhat smugly conclude that it was better to live in Canada than in the United States.

With a little help from our friends . . .

The annual strawberry festival with which Portage La Prairie, Manitoba, reinforces its claim to be the "Strawberry Capital of Canada" will be held in June—just far enough ahead of the season that organizers will be relying on strawberries imported from the United States.

Meanwhile, the Nova Scotia Government's $300,000 television special to promote tourism will be counting on footage shot in Bermuda to give it that summery look.

Will this rampant nationalism never subside? The Globe and Mail, *April 10, 1984, p. 6.*

Canada looked good and Canadian nationalism was strong because things looked so much worse in the United States. As Canadian Senator John Nicol somewhat unkindly observed, just as Americans "... have seen their sense of destiny falter, we have picked up the torch of plastic nationalism and are dashing off at a dead run."[86] This dependency means, however, that any improvement in American conditions can have a corrosive impact on Canadian nationalism. The price of a healthy America is self-doubt among Canadians as to the worth of an independent country on the northern tier of the continent. To the extent that Canadian nationalism feeds off blemishes on the American society, Canadians may become too tolerant of blemishes on their own society and remain too unaware of the excellence Canada has attained. It is here that Canada suffers from having but a single point of national comparison, and that being perhaps the wealthiest and most powerful country in the world. As Margaret Atwood points out:

One of Canada's problems is that it's always comparing itself to the wrong thing. If you stand beside a giant, of course you tend to feel a little stunted.[87]

An ironic feature of Canadian nationalism comes from the patriotic pride Canadians take in the very *weakness* of their nationalism. The more fervent

"Your problem of course is that you're too nationalistic . . ."

Roy Peterson, *The Vancouver Sun*

displays of American nationalism, such as one encounters during halftime shows in college football games, are often demeaned by Canadians who refuse to sing their own national anthem in public. Moving beyond the American comparison per se, John Meisel has discussed the absence of a vigorous and active nationalism in Canada, "an absence, incidentally, which in the eyes of many who have else-where experienced the parochialism and inhumanity of chauvinism, bestows on Canada one of its most attractive characteristics."[88] While this point is well taken, the question remains whether Canadian nationalism is sufficiently strong to counterbalance the centrifugal forces inherent in a regionally diverse national community.

The United States has been the source of new and at times disruptive political ideas since the arrival of the United Empire Loyalists. Prior to the 1837 rebellions, radical reformers in both Upper Canada—the Clear Grits—and Lower Canada—the supporters of Louis-Joseph Papineau—drew much of their political inspiration from the United States, just as the later agrarian radical reformers in the Canadian West drew upon American populist thought. As Mallory points out, "Canada has been nourished by the same stream of constitutional ideas, and in many respects, the same constitutional atmosphere, as the United States."[89] At the same time, there has been a countervailing reluctance to imitate American political institutions. Wise and Brown argue that "the real puzzle in the history of Canadian ideas about the United States is why the bulk of Canadians, standing on the very threshold of liberty, were so little susceptible to American institutions, a seeming contradiction of nature, environment, and proximity."[90] It was a contradiction, they argue, with an unfortunate impact on Canada:

the urgent necessity for a small people, in the overwhelming presence of a supremely confident neighbour, to insist not merely upon their separateness and distinctiveness, but even upon their intrinsic political and moral superiority, had a paralytic effect upon the Canadian mind and upon the quality of Canadian thought. The rigidities established by the compulsion to maintain identity narrowed the range of political debate, channeled political thought along familiar paths, and discouraged the venturesome, the daring, and the rash. There is an imprecision and superficiality, a lack of progression and proliferation, about Canadian thought with respect to the United States that mirrors the general state of Canadian political thought in this era.[91]

Although one would have to be cautious in projecting this assessment of late nineteenth-century Canada onto the contemporary political scene, one might argue that we have not been sufficiently attentive to the American experience in coping with political conflict in a vast, transcontinental society more like Canada than any other in the world.[92]

Canadian–American relations have often intensified regional and intergovernmental conflict in Canada. The tariffs of Macdonald's National Policy that were designed to promote industrial development soon became an enduring symbol of regional discontent and exacerbated provincialism and regional conflict:

The alleged "unfairness" of the tariff has always served as a potent argument for spokesmen, mainly provincial politicians, from the non-manufacturing regions of Canada when they have been seeking measures to promote their own self-interest. The resulting rampant regionalism has been antithetical to Confederation....[93]

The strong central government needed to counter American economic control clashes with provincial governments' search for American investment. Thus, as Wilson points out, any attempt by Ottawa to restrict or influence the location of foreign investment is likely to embroil the national government in a two-front conflict with Washington and the provincial governments.[94] Canadian–American trade relations may also impair national policies designed to enhance regional development as special subsidies or tax breaks to lure firms to regional locations in which they might not otherwise invest may incite contravailing duties on Canadian exports to the United States.

Canadian–American relations are also entangled with the relationship between the English- and French-speaking communities. Lacking an effective language barrier with the United States, English Canadian nationalists have sought to erect economic and cultural barriers. Such endeavours, because they necessitate a relatively strong and activist national government, have been viewed with suspicion by the Government of Quebec. Although English Canadian attempts to fend off assimilationist pressures from the United States parallel French Canadian attempts to fend off assimilationist pressures from English-speaking North America, the two goals have at times come into conflict. When English Canadian nationalists promote a Canadian identity that obscures the French fact, such as occurred with John Diefenbaker's vision of "one Canada," they intensify the assimilationist threat to French Canada. Thus, while both Quebec and Ottawa have tried to build effective cultural walls, they have done so along quite different borders. On the more positive side, French Canada makes a valuable contribution to English Canadian nationalism as it is Canada's bilingual and bicultural character that more than anything else sets it apart from the United States. The question that arises is what English Canada has to offer French Canada in return. As Kari Levitt wrote in 1970, why should French Canadians

... remain within Confederation when the dominant English-Canadian majority appear to put such a low value on Canada's national independence? What is being offered? To wander hand-in-hand, biculturally and bilingually, into the gravitational orbit of the American empire?[95]

The catch is that a more vibrant Canadian nationality could itself pose a threat to French Canada if it does not fully embrace French Canadian culture and tradition.

Canada's relationship to the United States also has an impact on redistributive politics. American television, movies, magazines, and books are used by Canadians in making sense out of the world around them. Thus if the American culture deemphasizes class politics, if it promotes a social vision in which people succeed or fail primarily on the strength of their own efforts, and if it promotes a mythology that anyone can become a millionaire or president, such values will be absorbed into the Canadian political culture and will reduce the salience of class politics. Emigration to the United States also provides a safety valve for Canada. Those who are dissatisfied with their position or prospects have an easier alternative than class-based politics; they can pack up and move. Between 1881 and 1891, when the Canadian economy was badly depressed, over one million people (out of a total population of less than five million) left Canada for the United States.[96]

When conditions improved between 1897 and the outbreak of the First World War, over one million people emigrated from the United States to Canada, including many who had earlier left Canada for the United States.

It is an open question as to what impact ideological swings in the United States have on Canadian political life. Clearly, many issues that rise to the top of the American political agenda tend to appear on the Canadian agenda as well, though perhaps not at the same place or with the same intensity. The American debate over neoconservatism (*see Glossary*), for example, has had an impact upon Canadian political life even though the ideological debate has been by no means identical in the two countries. Other American issues, such as the prolonged and acrimonious debate over prayer in school, have not crossed the border to any significant extent. At times, ideological change in Washington will have a more direct impact on the Canadian–American relationship. The drift of the American administration to the ideological right during the early 1980s sharpened American attacks on Canadian interventionalist policies such as the National Energy Program, policies that were found offensive not only to American economic interests but also to American ideological convictions.

In summary, Canadian–American relations are not only of intrinsic importance. They are also entangled with the other major strands of Canadian political life. Moreover, while conflict between Canada and the United States will wax and wane over time, and will shift in focus from one set of issues to another, it will never disappear. Nor will the debate within Canada between nationalist and continentalist options disappear. Canada's location on the North American continent ensures continued American penetration, and continued Canadian efforts both to embrace and resist that penetration.

Here it is useful to refer to a characterization of Canada advanced by Mason Wade. Writing in 1964, Wade asserted that "Canada has always been a willed nation, existing despite the conscious and unconscious forces which have sought to absorb it into its much more populous and powerful neighbour."[97] The notion of a "willed nation" seems particularly powerful even if it is by no means unique to the Canadian case. It points to the importance of nationalism in Canadian life, for it is by the strength of nationalism that we can measure the will of Canadians to resist a continental future. It also suggests that if the strength of Canadian nationalism is unduly sapped by regional conflict, if a national vision cannot be found that embraces the bilingual and bicultural realities of Canadian life, if political institutions fail to articulate a national interest that is truly national, then Canada's continued independence on the North American continent may be imperiled.

Suggested Readings

1 Charles F. Doran, *Forgotten Partnership: U.S.–Canada Relations Today* (Baltimore: Johns Hopkins University Press, 1984).

2 Terence J. Fay, "Canadian Studies on the American Relationship, 1945–1980," *The American Review of Canadian Studies* XIII, 3 (Autumn 1983), pp. 179–200. The appendix to this article contains a bibliography of 326 articles, books, and professional papers, grouped by historical period.

3 For an excellent overview of Canadian–American relations, see John W. Holmes, *Life with Uncle: The Canadian–American Relationship* (Toronto: University of Toronto Press, 1981); for a more extended treatment, see Graeme S. Mount and Edelgard Mahant, *An Introduction to Canadian–American Relations* (Toronto: Methuen, 1984).

4 For an analysis of the Auto Pact, see James F. Keeley, "Cast in Concrete for All Time? The Negotiation of the Auto Pact," *Canadian Journal of Political Science* XVI: 2 (June 1983), pp. 281–98.

5 For a classic and still insightful look at the American economic presence in Canada, see Kari Levitt, *Silent Surrender: The Multinational Corporation in Canada* (Toronto: Macmillan, 1970). For a more contemporary discussion of many of the same themes, see David Leyton-Brown, "Canada and Multinational Enterprises," in Norman Hillmer and Garth Stevenson, eds., *A Foremost Nation: Canadian Foreign Policy and a Changing World* (Toronto: McClelland and Stewart, 1977), pp. 63–84.

6 Although now twenty years old, George Grant's *Lament for a Nation: The Defeat of Canadian Nationalism* (Toronto: McClelland and Stewart, 1965) still provides a provocative ideological analysis of the Canadian–American relationship.

7 For an insightful look at the economic realities confronting Canada as the twentieth century draws to a close, see Glen Williams, *Not for Export: Toward a Political Economy of Canada's Arrested Industrialization* (Toronto: McClelland and Stewart, 1983).

8 Donald Barry, "The Politics of 'Exceptionalism': Canada and the United States as a Distinctive International Relationship," *Dalhousie Review* 60: 1 (Spring 1980), pp. 114–37.

Study Questions

1 In the early 1980s Francis Fox, at that time the federal minister responsible for Canadian communication policy, warned that by 1985 the spread of U.S. television channels through satellite delivery could make Canada "an occupied land, culturally." To what extent has this come to pass? To what extent can and should the Government of Canada impose controls on satellite reception by Canadian citizens? What risks do we run if such controls are not or cannot be imposed?

2 Where do you stand on the question of "free trade"? What are the *political* arguments

that you would amass in defence of your position, and what are the *political* counter-arguments that you might expect?

3 To what extent, if any, might you expect residents of your own province to have a different perspective on Canadian–American relations than that held by the residents of other provinces? How would you explain such differences, should they exist?

CHAPTER SEVEN

Intergovernmental Relations and the Canadian Federal State

One of the most important features of the Canadian political system is the *concentration* of power within cabinets, both in Ottawa and in the provinces. As a consequence of the conventions of responsible government and the party discipline that those conventions foster, cabinets dominate not only the executive arm of government but also the legislative process. (See Appendix B for an expanded discussion of executive dominance.) Of equal importance is the federal *dispersion* of power among eleven national and provincial governments. The product of these two characteristics is a unique pattern of intergovernmental relations that sets Canadian federal politics apart from the experience of other federal states.

For many readers the term "intergovernmental relations" may conjure up images of federal–provincial conflict. Indeed, it is difficult to pick up a newspaper without encountering disputes between Ottawa and the provinces. Federal–provincial conflict is so pervasive it seems to flow into virtually every crack and crevice of the political system. Unfortunately, its very pervasiveness obscures the fact that Canadian governments collaborate more than they fight, that a web of programs, agreements, committees, and conferences draws the governments together in a common cooperative enterprise. For example, despite the poor tone of federal–provincial relations in Alberta during the early 1980s, 124 federal–provincial programs and agreements were in effect as of March 31, 1982. These ranged from major programs such as the Alberta Health Care Insurance Program and major agreements such as the Canada/Alberta Memorandum of Agreement Relating to Energy Pricing and Taxation to ones with a much lower profile such as the Fort Chipewyan Water Pipeline Agreement, the Comprehensive Turkey Marketing Program, and the Record of Performance for Swine.[1] No matter where Canadians might live, many of the government services that they receive are the product of intergovernmental collaboration. Your university or college, for instance, draws financial support from both levels of government, though Ottawa's support is less direct and hence less visible than that coming from your provincial government.

In large part, the scale of contemporary intergovernmental relations reflects the growth of government that was discussed in Chapter Five. As the "night-watch state," in which government was responsible for little more than the protection of borders and the maintenance of public order, gave way to the welfare state and extensive government intervention in the economy, the sphere of government expanded further and further. As Rose points out, the growth of government was a general phenomenon that was in no way restricted to Canada or to federal political systems:

Government is big in itself, big in its claims upon society's resources and big in its impact upon society. By every conventional measure, government looms large in the life of every Western nation today; governments differ from nation to nation only in their degree of bigness.[2]

In federal states such as Canada, however, the growth of government takes on added dimensions because it is seldom even across the various levels of government, and because it has such a marked impact on intergovernmental relations.

In the Canadian case, governmental growth has been most pronounced in subnational governments. From 1950 to 1977 spending by the federal government rose from 11.5 percent of the Gross National Product to 16.1 percent while provincial government spending rose from 5.7 percent to 12.4 percent and municipal government spending from 4.9 percent to 8.9 percent.[3] As Figure 7.1 illustrates governmental growth has been accompanied by an increase in intergovernmental contact and interaction. That increase in turn has resulted in "... a large network of cooperative federal–provincial programs, most of which operate unobtrusively and cooperatively and together form a network of government which enables the country to function through the maze of elaborate jurisdictional overlaps that have emerged as government activities have expanded in recent years."[4] Those overlaps, however, have also increased intergovernmental conflict.

In almost a parody of the old western cliché "this town ain't big enough for both of us," governments within federal states interact more and thus collide more as they grow. Intergovernmental friction also stems from a number of additional sources. In some fields, such as agriculture, the constitution has given *concurrent jurisdiction* to both levels of government while in other fields, such as transportation and consumer protection, both levels of government are legislatively active. Thus intergovernmental conflict can arise if the two levels of government pursue different legislative intentions or regulatory procedures within the same policy domain. In policy areas not explicitly addressed in the formal constitutional division of powers, such as regulatory control over cable television, inter-

FIGURE 7.1

Growth of Government and Governmental Conflict/Interaction

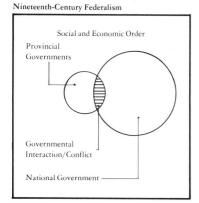

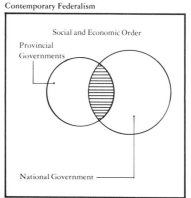

governmental conflict can arise as the federal and provincial governments jockey for constitutional control. As will be discussed in greater detail below, the national government may use its spending powers to invade provincial areas of jurisdiction. We also find that the actions of one level of government, even when taken exclusively within its own domain, can have a major impact on programs at the other level. National policies to regulate foreign investment, for example, can affect substantially the development plans of provincial governments and their ability to raise capital from the private sector. Conversely, provincial budgets may reinforce or counteract the fiscal policies of the national government, and thus affect Ottawa's management of the national economy. All of these entanglements necessitate governmental interaction and provide fertile soil for intergovernmental conflict.

Although extensive intergovernmental relations are characteristic of all modern federal states, the nature of those relations can vary considerably. In Canada, they have taken on a higher public profile and a more acrimonious tone than has been the case elsewhere.[5] To understand why, we must place intergovernmental relations against the broader backdrop of a volatile federal system.

Evolution of the Canadian Federal State

Confederation created a highly centralized federal system in which the principal legislative responsibilities of the day were assigned to the national government, and in which the powers of reservation and disallowance placed Ottawa in a quasi-imperial relationship with the provinces. If we imagine a continuum of hypothetical federal systems anchored at one end by highly centralized federal systems and at the other by very decentralized systems in which provincial or state governments would be preeminent, the Constitution Act of 1867 lodged Canada at the centralized end. However, the *evolution* of Canadian federalism has been characterized neither by entrenchment at the centralized end of the continuum nor by a steady progression toward the decentralized end. Instead, the federal system has oscillated across this continuum. Within the bounds of a constitutional division of powers largely untouched by formal amendment, Canadians have experienced a variety of quite different federal arrangements.

CENTRALIZING FACTORS

In the early years after Confederation, the centralized federal system put into place by the Constitution Act was reinforced by a massive migration of political talent to Ottawa. With the exception of Ontario's Oliver Mowat, who went on to become the province's premier, all the politicians voting for Confederation opted for elected or appointed *national* office.[6] For the political movers and shakers, the action was in Ottawa and not in the provinces. The new provincial governments were all but denuded of political talent and, as a consequence, were not in a position to challenge Ottawa's dominance. It was not long, however, before the provincial governments, led by Premier Mowat, began to develop as political centres of gravity and to emerge as increasingly effective counterweights to Ottawa. Federal–provincial conflicts emerged over language and education issues in Ontario and Manitoba, over the search for "better terms" in the Maritimes, and over boundary extensions for Ontario and Quebec. Nevertheless, the scope of intergovernmental conflict was contained by the small size and limited scope of the governments of the day. Given that neither level of government penetrated very extensively into the lives of citizens, there was little need for governmental interaction with respect to programs and services, and thus little opportunity for intergovernmental conflict. Both the federal and provincial governments were just beginning to occupy their own legislative domains, much less encroach upon the domain of the other level of government.

As the nineteenth century drew to a close, Ottawa's stature within the federal system was eroded by Canada's sluggish economic growth. Caught in the midst of a prolonged world-wide depression, the national government failed to deliver on the economic promise of Confederation. The West remained largely unsettled, and Canadians by the tens of thousands emigrated to seek their fortunes in the United States. Relief finally came in the mid-1890s. Coincident with the victory of Sir Wilfrid Laurier and the national Liberal party in the election of 1896 came a lifting of the depression, the depletion of free land in the American West, and a spectacular increase in immigration to the "last, best West." The consequence was an unprecedented economic boom which spurred the agricultural settlement of the West and the industrialization of central Canada. Both the national and provincial governments shone in the reflected light of the economic boom. In terms of federal politics, the Laurier years were "... characterized by a more constructive and harmonious pattern of relations between the federal and provincial governments than prevailed in the previous decades or was ever established again."[7]

The First World War brought English Canadians together in a collective national endeavour and, not coincidentally, ushered in a sustained period of national dominance within the federal system. (The quite different response of French Canadians to the war is discussed in the next chapter.) The war experience and the economic growth it generated, the concentration of political power in Ottawa under the terms of the War Measures Act (*see Glossary*), and the recognition of Canadian independence that came with the 1926 Balfour Declaration and the 1931 Statute of Westminster all contributed to the growth of both Canadian nationalism and the national government.

During the 1930s, provincial and local governments buckled under the massive economic and social dislocation of the Great Depression. Only the national government appeared to have the fiscal and administrative resources to provide bandaids, if not solutions. Yet Ottawa's response was limited by an ideological disinclination to intervene, and by a series of decisions by the Judicial Committee of the Privy Council which narrowly defined Parliament's jurisdictional domain. In short, the federal system was not up to the admittedly extraordinary demands of the day. As a consequence, a major overhaul of the federal system was recommended by the Rowell–Sirois Royal Commission on Dominion–Provincial Relations. In its 1940 report the Commission called for a restructured federal system in which the national government would have a greater role in social policy and economic management, and in which federal–provincial fiscal arrangements would be reformed to provide a more uniform national tax structure and greater federal assistance to the provinces.

Although the distraction of the Second World War preempted any formal governmental response to the Rowell–Sirois recommendations, the war effort itself and the national economic recovery that it engendered moved the Canadian federal system along the path outlined by the Commission. As a general rule federal systems tend to centralize during times of military crisis,[8] and Canada was no exception. Provincial government opposition to increased centralization was quickly quelled as federal politicians campaigned provincially in Ontario and Quebec to defeat what they depicted as opponents of the nation's war effort. Just as the new national government had done in 1867, Ottawa attracted "the best and the brightest" to Ottawa to staff the huge bureaucratic machine that regulated, and regulated surprisingly well, virtually every aspect of Canadian life during the war years. At the war's end, Stevenson writes,

the federal government appeared to stand at the height of its power and prestige in relation to the provincial governments. Canada had operated in wartime practically as a unitary state, and the provincial governments had been reduced to insignificance.[9]

During the war years, Stevenson argues, Canadians had come to expect a predominant federal role in social legislation and economic management, a role that the enlarged federal bureaucracy was ready and eager to play in postwar Canada.

Between 1945 and 1960 the federal government greatly expanded its legislative reach, encroaching into provincial fields of jurisdiction. It did so principally through its spending power which allowed Ottawa to spend, and thus indirectly to legislate, in provincial fields of jurisdiction. As Smiley explains, "according to the constitutional doctrine that came to prevail, the central government might legally spend revenues as it chose, even on matters within the jurisdiction of the provinces, and could at its discretion fix the circumstances under which a potential recipient ... might receive the federal largesse."[10] Fuelled by tax money from a rapidly growing post-war economy, Ottawa established a series of *conditional grant programs* in the fields of health care, advanced education, and social welfare.

Conditional grant programs shared a number of characteristics, the most important being that they fell within the jurisdictional domain of the provinces. Program delivery was thus left to the provinces. Federal participation was largely confined to financial support, with Ottawa matching provincial expenditures in return for the imposition of national standards such as universal accessibility. Conditional grant programs, and the national standards that they embodied, enjoyed broad public support in the post-war Canadian society. Although the provinces could choose not to participate, as Quebec did in some cases, the political and financial costs of so doing were high. Federal funds were generally welcomed, at least outside Quebec, as the provincial governments faced growing fiscal pressures from post-war electorates demanding enhanced programs in education, health care, and the social services. Caught between rising demand and limited fiscal resources—only Ottawa had the power to raise money "by any Mode or System of Taxation"—the provincial governments had little option but to accept conditional grants from the federal government.

Conditional grant programs were by no means cost-free to the provinces. They distorted provincial spending priorities by forcing provincial governments to give highest priority to those programs where matching federal funds were available. Provincial governments raised concerns about the long-term cost of the programs, the long-term commitment of the federal government to its share of the cost, and the inflexibility that conditional grant programs imposed on provincial budgets and spending priorities. There was also growing provincial resistance, led by Quebec, to the federal intrusion onto provincial constitutional turf that the programs represented. It is also worth noting that the programs significantly altered the nature of federal–provincial relations by requiring extensive intergovernmental collaboration and coordination.[11] The name given to this new pattern of intergovernmental relations was "cooperative federalism," a term that belied the fact that cooperation was largely a one-way street, and that the government that paid the piper called the tune.

To observers at the end of the 1950s, Ottawa's dominance in the Canadian federal system was an established fact. Bora Laskin, who was later to become Chief Justice of the Canadian Supreme Court, wrote in 1960 that "never since Confederation have the ideas so cherished by Macdonald for a strong and powerful central government subordinating the provincial legislatures like so many larger municipal institutions, been so close to realization as they have been in the past ten years."[12] Also writing of the 1950s, Corry painted a similar scene:

The most [a province] can hope to hold is its freedom for minor adventure, for embroidering its own particular patterns in harmony with the national design, for playing variant melodies within the general theme ... it is everywhere limited in the distance it can go by having become part of a larger, although not necessarily a better, scheme of things.[13]

And yet by the early 1960s the federal government was in retreat across a broad front in the face of resurgent provincial governments. What had appeared to be evolutionary movement toward an Ottawa-centred federal system had not only been stopped but suddenly reversed. What, then, had changed in order to produce such a dramatic realignment of the Canadian federal system?

DECENTRALIZING FACTORS

Even during the heyday of the Macdonald governments, the provincial governments had begun to resist what they saw as an excessively centralized federal system. The principal resistance came from the two central Canadian provinces, with Liberal-dominated Ontario being by far the most militant.[14] While in the early decades after Confederation the provincial governments were unable to muster political and bureaucratic resources comparable to those possessed by Ottawa, their command over such resources would only increase with the passage of time. In this respect they were greatly assisted by a series of judicial interpretations of Canadian federalism which significantly augmented the powers of the provincial governments and eroded those of the federal government.

Until 1949 the umpire for the Canadian federal system was the Judicial Committee of the Privy Council, a circumstance that reflected not only Canada's colonial past but also that the 1867 Constitution Act was an act of the British rather than of the Canadian Parliament. Thus its adjudication ultimately rested in British rather than Canadian judicial hands. In the majority of cases in which the Judicial Committee was asked to adjudicate the federal division of powers, the Canadian governments themselves were not the protagonists and intergovernmental conflict per se was not the source of the litigation. Most cases were

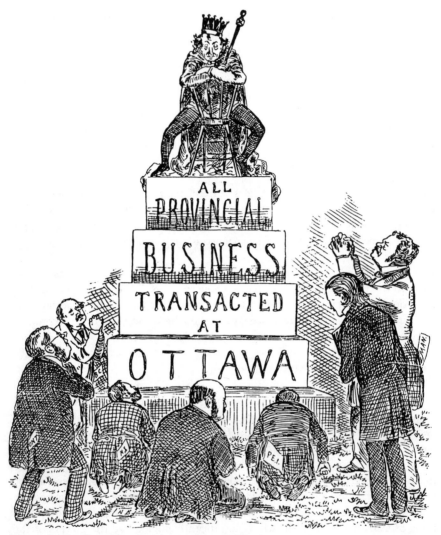

"Centralization;" or, "Provincial autonomy abolished." Is this what Sir John is aiming at?

In J.W. Bengough, *A Caricature History of Canadian Politics*, Vol. 2 (Toronto: Grip Printing and Publishing, 1886), p. 273.

brought forward by private interests trying to stem the growth of government, federal or provincial.[15] Canadian governments were nonetheless greatly affected by a series of Judicial Committee decisions over sixty years which eroded the constitutional position of the national government. Without formally altering sections 91 and 92 of the Constitution Act the Committee expanded provincial powers, curtailed those of the national government, largely transferred residual powers to the provinces (at least in peacetime), reduced the strength of the trade and commerce clause, and cut down federal attempts to regulate natural resource trade with the United States. The Peace, Order, and Good Government clause was restricted to the enumerated headings of Section 91, to emergency situations, and to matters of national concern or having a "national dimension."[16] During the Depression a "judicial massacre" struck down Prime Minister R.B. Bennett's attempt to impose a Canadian version of President Franklin Roosevelt's New Deal.[17]

The long-term impact of the Judicial Committee on the evolution of Canadian federalism is a matter of considerable debate. On the one hand, Smiley describes a consensus among English-speaking scholars that the Committee's decisions were "nothing short of calamitous" in their erosion of the national government's constitutional position.[18] Fletcher concurs, arguing that the Committee established a legal framework which "… operated as a centrifugal force in the federation, dividing jurisdiction and thwarting attempts to centralize control in important areas of economic and social concern."[19] Cairns, on the other hand, argues that while the Committee's decisions unquestionably affected the nature of Canadian federalism and did depart from the 1867 formula, they were not out of line with other changes which were also promoting a more decentralized federalism.[20]

The legislative domain of the provinces had become increasingly important with changes in the Canadian society. Whereas in the 1860s many of the matters assigned to the provinces were in fact left to the private sector, by the 1950s they had become not only primary concerns of government but also insatiable consumers of public funds and programs. Education, hospitals, highways, and social services all fell within the provincial bailiwick, and as a consequence provincial governments grew in both absolute and relative terms as they engaged these new and costly responsibilities. As they grew, provincial governments began to attract a degree of bureaucratic expertise comparable to that traditionally recruited by Ottawa. While this bureaucratic expertise was not to reach full flower in the wealthier provinces until the 1960s and in the poorer provinces until the 1970s, its impact was beginning to be felt by the late 1950s when a reversal in Canada's post-war economic prosperity undercut public support for an expansive national government. The failure of national policies to provide what were seen as adequate levels of material welfare "… projected the provincial administrations into a more active role in economic affairs than they had heretofore assumed."[21] It was a role that the provincial governments were unwilling to surrender as the Canadian economy roller-coasted its way through the next twenty-five years. Finally, it should be noted that the federal powers of reservation and disallowance had fallen into disuse. The latter had last been used in 1943, and by the late 1950s both had become constitutional dead letters.

This stew of change in the federal system was brought to a boil by the onset of the Quiet Revolution in Quebec. Before 1960, Quebec had not challenged the fundamental character of the confederation agreement. Quebec governments had concentrated on protecting those powers assigned to the provinces and in warding off incursions by the national government. After 1960, a number of interdependent changes were sought including Ottawa's withdrawal from provincial areas of jurisdiction, the expansion of provincial jurisdiction to provide more autonomous control over cultural and social policy, the conversion of conditional grants to unconditional grants in order to provide greater fiscal autonomy for provincial governments, higher equalization payments, more formalized intergovernmental relations analogous to those between sovereign states, and the right to participate in international relations on matters falling within provincial jurisdiction. At the very least such changes entailed a fundamental restructuring of the federal system. To many observers both inside and outside Quebec, their realization implied a degree of political autonomy indistinguishable from independence.

Taken alone, the Quebec demands were a major shock to the federal system. The shock then spread as other provincial governments used Quebec as the pointman for their own assault on the federal status quo. In a 1977 speech to the Alberta Progressive Conservative party, Premier Peter Lougheed drew an explicit parallel between the Alberta and Quebec positions on confederation:

Just as Albertans want more control over their destiny—primarily for economic reasons—Quebecers, I sense, want also more control over their destiny, essentially for cultural and linguistic reasons. Hence, just as Albertans want more government decisions made in Edmonton than in Ottawa, I think Quebecers, for different reasons, but somewhat similar motives, want more government decisions made in Quebec City, and fewer in Ottawa.[22]

To be sure, no other provincial government went as far as Quebec, or came close to endorsing the extremes of independence or sovereignty association. There was also considerable variability among the English Canadian provinces, with Ontario and the Maritime provinces being more supportive of a strong national economic union refereed by a strong national government than were provincial governments in the West and Newfoundland. Nevertheless, Quebec's pursuit of expanded provincial jurisdiction, the rollback of federal incursions, and greater fiscal autonomy had broad governmental support outside Quebec. Across the board, provincial governments became more sensitive to jurisdictional issues, more alert to federal encroachments onto their constitutional turf, than they had been during the 1950s.

To the extent that there was a broadly shared provincial constitutional strategy, it contained the following elements: (1) the rollback of federal intrusions into provincial fields of jurisdiction while retaining the federal funds that had accompanied such intrusions (2) the erection of more watertight barriers around provincial fields of jurisdiction (3) the creation of more permeable barriers around federal fields of jurisdiction in order to facilitate greater provincial input into federal policy-making, particularly with respect to economic management (4) more formalized intergovernmental relations and (5) expanded provincial jurisdiction in selected fields. In the West, the search for a greater *national* role for provincial governments was intensified when the elections of 1963, 1965, 1972, 1974, and 1980 produced national governments with meagre elected representation from the West.

FEDERALISM IN THE 1980s

For a time Ottawa's response to the provinces was one of accommodation. "Opting-out" provisions initiated in 1964 allowed provinces to withdraw from joint federal–provincial programs without incurring any financial penalty if analogous provincial programs were established. While in theory any province could opt out, the hope that only Quebec would do so turned out to be the case. (With respect to the Canada Pension Plan, Quebec exercised its constitutional prerogative under Section 94A of the Constitution Act and did not opt in, establishing instead its own separate but fully compatible Quebec Pension Plan.) Fiscal ground rules were changed as conditional grants gave way to unconditional grants. Although federal funding of shared-cost programs continued under the terms of the Federal–Provincial Fiscal Arrangements and Established Programs Financing Act of 1977, the provinces were not obligated to spend the federal funds in any specific way nor was the level of federal funding tied to the level of provincial expenditure. In an extended round of constitutional discussions during the 1970s, Ottawa appeared willing to discuss the devolution of some federal powers to the provinces. Thus despite Pierre Trudeau's image in parts of the country as an unrelenting centralist, his first eleven years in office were marked by an appreciable *decentralization* of the Canadian political system, a trend clearly at odds with that in other western countries.[23]

Figure 7.2 illustrates the dramatic changes that have occurred in the fiscal balance of the Canadian federal system. The Second World War sharply reversed the position of the two orders of government as federal wartime expenditures climbed to over 70 percent of all government expenditures in Canada. Since the end of the war Ottawa's dominance has been progressively eroded. By the mid-1960s combined provincial and local government expenditures surpassed those of the national government, and from that point onward the fiscal gap steadily widened. It must be stressed, however, that fiscal transfers from Ottawa to the provincial governments are counted as provincial, not federal, expenditures in Figure 7.2. As the 1984 Canada Health Act demonstrated, such provincial expenditures are not without some element of federal control. The federal expenditures

FIGURE 7.2

Changes in the Fiscal Balance of the Canadian Federal System

Distribution of government revenue *after* intergovernmental transfers have been
subtracted from the revenues of the paying governments and added to the revenues of the
receiving governments.

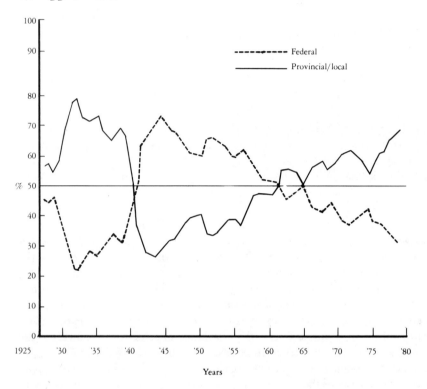

Source: Richard Bastien, *Federalism and Decentralization: Where Do We Stand?* (Ottawa: Minister of Supply
and Services, 1981), p. 36.

are also made by one government, whereas the provincial and local expenditures
are spread over ten provincial and a multitude of local governments. Thus the
figure may somewhat overstate the degree to which the fiscal centre of gravity in
the Canadian federal state has shifted to local and provincial governments.

When the Trudeau Liberals returned to power in 1980, the accommodative
stance disappeared as Ottawa began to reassert the presence of the national
government within the federal system. Cooperative federalism was devalued and
Ottawa became increasingly resistant to provincial encroachments upon its own
domain. Federal–provincial conferences, which had provided a highly publicized

Andy Donato, *Toronto Sun*

In a 1982 news conference, Prime Minister Trudeau declared the death of cooperative federalism: "the old type of federalism where we give money to the provinces, where they kick us in the teeth because they didn't get enough . . . is finished." (Cited in Sheilagh M. Dunn, *The Year in Review 1982: Intergovernmental Relations in Canada* (Kingston: Institute of Intergovernmental Relations, Queen's University, 1982), p. 6.)

stage for provincial attacks on the national government, were deemphasized as Ottawa tried to recapture the power of unilateral action. (Federal–provincial constitutional conferences were an exception.) Extensive media campaigns were launched to explain what the Government of Canada was doing for, rather than to, Canadians, and to strengthen the bond between individual Canadians and their national government.

Ottawa also began to pull back from shared-cost programs, which were consuming a large part of the federal budget and contributing to a growing national debt. The government was accountable to Parliament for funds spent on such programs even though it had little control over how those funds were spent by the provinces. Of particular importance was the matter of political credit or "visibility." If Ottawa, for example, was to continue to pick up half the cost of advanced education, federal politicians wanted taxpayers to realize that advanced education was not being provided exclusively by the provincial governments. Ottawa did not want to be seen as the government that taxed heavily and did little in return for "the average Canadian," while the provincial governments enjoyed the envious position of supplying popular programs invisibly financed in large part by federal transfer payments.

In short, it was "no more Mr. Nice Guy," as a reassertive national government and unrelentingly assertive provincial governments met in the wake of the 1980 Quebec referendum to hammer out a new constitutional framework for the Canadian federal state.

The Constitution Act, 1982

The seventeen months following the Quebec referendum witnessed intensive constitutional negotiations between the federal and provincial governments, and extensive constitutional discussions across the land. While the leading actors throughout were the federal and provincial governments, important supporting roles were played by the courts, the Conservative and New Democratic opposition parties in the House of Commons, the British Parliament, public opinion polls, journalists, academics, innumerable private Canadians participating in countless public debates, and a plethora of special interest groups among which women and native peoples were the most active. Yet despite all the activity little progress was made until November 1981 when Ottawa and nine of the ten provincial governments, *excluding Quebec*, signed a Constitutional Accord. Five months later, on April 17, 1982, the Constitution Act was proclaimed. After a prolonged, tortuous, and at times bitter process Canadians had a new constitution, or what ex-Senator Eugene Forsey has more accurately described as the old constitution "with knobs on." Let us look first at the knobs.

CONSTITUTIONAL CHANGE

The Constitution Act of 1982 embodies a number of important constitutional changes. First, the Canadian constitution has been patriated; no longer will the assent of the British Parliament be needed for constitutional amendment. Patriation required the adoption of a formal mechanism of constitutional amendment, and this has been built into Part V, Sections 38 through 49, of the Constitution Act. The basic amendment procedure is defined in Section 38(1):

An amendment to the Constitution of Canada may be made by proclamation issued by the Governor General under the Great Seal of Canada where so authorized by (a) resolutions of the Senate and House of Commons; and (b) resolutions of the legislative assemblies of at least two-thirds of the provinces that have, in the aggregate, according to the then latest general census, at least fifty per cent of the population of all the provinces.

However, any amendment "that derogates from the legislative powers, the proprietary rights or any other rights or privileges of the legislature or government of a province" requires the consent of each province affected. Any amendment to the amending formula itself, to the office of the Queen, Governor General, or Lieutenant-Governor, to the composition of the Supreme Court, to the right of a province to have at least the same number of MPs as it has Senators, and to most language guarantees would require the *unanimous* consent of Parliament and all ten provinces. Finally, the Senate has been granted only a suspensive veto on constitutional amendments. Under Section 47(1), an amendment can proceed without the need for Senate approval if, after the passage of 180 days from approval by the House of Commons, the House again adopts a resolution in support of the amendment.

The long-term significance of the amending formula remains to be seen. As a general rule, formal procedures of constitutional amendment are rarely used in federal states. (The tortuous efforts to pass the Equal Rights Amendment in the United States illustrates the very cumbersome nature of formal methods of constitutional amendment.) Other means such as judicial reinterpretation in the United States and ad hoc federal–provincial agreements in Canada's past provide more flexible means of keeping some rough congruence between constitutional rules and political realities. To the extent that formal amendment procedures inhibit more informal means of constitutional amendment, the significance of the amending procedure may come less from the constitutional flexibility that it engenders than from the flexibility it impairs.

The change of the greatest potential importance came with the Charter of Rights and Freedoms. Prior to 1982, Canadian constitutional documents primarily addressed the structure of Canadian governments and the division of powers among governments. The Constitution Act of 1982 expands the reach of the written constitution to embrace the relationship between *citizens* and governments. This is not to suggest that Canadians lacked rights and freedoms in the past, for they did not, or that such rights and freedoms were devoid of protection in the past, for they were not. However, the Charter enumerates those rights and freedoms, entrenches them within the written constitution, and transfers the power to determine the practical limits to their application from a political process that is federally divided to a judicial process which is not.[24] For the first time, the courts have been placed in a position where they can judge acts of either Parliament or the provincial legislatures to be unconstitutional on grounds other than contravening the federal division of powers.

There are a number of important caveats on the extent to which the Charter might restrict Canadian governments. Section 1 states that the Charter "guarantees the rights and freedoms set out in it *subject only to such reasonable limits prescribed by law as can be demonstrably justified in a free and democratic society*" [emphasis added]. How this clause will be interpreted over the long run remains to be seen, though the Supreme Court's ruling on the conflict between Bill 101 and the Charter, discussed in Chapter Three, suggests that "reasonable limits" will not be broadly interpreted. Legislation can also be exempted from the Charter for a renewable five-year period through the use of a "notwithstanding" clause. As Section 33 reads, "Parliament or the legislature of a province may expressly declare in an Act of Parliament or of the legislature, as the case may be, that the Act or a provision thereof shall operate notwithstanding a provision included in section 2 or section 7 to 15 of this Charter." These sections include the fundamental freedoms of conscience, religion, thought, expression, peaceful assembly, and association; legal rights; and the equality rights set forth in Section 15. They do *not* include basic democratic rights, mobility rights, language rights, minority language educational rights, and gender equality (Section 28 reads "notwithstanding anything in this Charter, the rights and freedoms referred to in it are guaranteed equally to male and female persons"), all of which have been placed beyond Section 33. This override clause provides a constitutional mechanism of non-compliance with Supreme Court decisions, a mechanism that is available to both levels of government.[25] In May 1982, only weeks after the Constitution Act was proclaimed, the Quebec National Assembly passed Bill 62, which applied the notwithstanding provision to *all* Quebec legislation passed up to that point in time. All Quebec legislation passed since then has incorporated the notwithstanding clause. Quebec's own Charter protections, it should be stressed, still apply. At issue is *which* Charter should be used to protect individual rights in Quebec, not whether such rights should be protected. To this point, the notwithstanding provision has not been used by other provincial legislative assemblies or by Parliament.

The Supreme Court of Canada

The Supreme Court of Canada was created in 1875. In order to diminish French Canadian fears that the Court would pose a threat to provincial rights and powers, the Supreme Court Act guaranteed Quebec representation on the Court. At the same time Parliament rejected a proposal that at least one of the judges come from British Columbia "because of the feeling on both sides of the House that the representative principle was not of the same importance to the other provinces as it was to Quebec."[26] The composition of the contemporary Supreme Court, which now encompasses nine justices including three from Quebec, is entrenched in Section 41.(d) of the Constitution Act and can only be changed with the unanimous consent of Parliament and the ten provincial legislative assemblies.

The Supreme Court Act did not abolish the right of appeal to the Judicial Committee of the Privy Council, and thus the Court became only a link in the chain of appeal rather than the final arbiter. Only in 1949 was the right of appeal to the JCPC abolished and the Court made supreme in fact as well as in name. The 1949 change opened the door for the Court's more active participation in Canadian political life.

The Supreme Court provides an interesting combination of the rule of law and the principle of representation. In theory the rule of law is incompatible with the more political notion of representation. Nevertheless, while it is expected that the decisions of the Court will be guided by law, its structure, like that of other central government institutions, is based on representational principles. Thus the six non-Quebec justices are selected so as to ensure Atlantic and western Canadian "representation."

An important structural feature of the Supreme Court is that appointments are made by the national government alone.

That the Supreme Court is a creature of the national government has some important consequences. As Mallory explains, "the Supreme Court of Canada—like that of the United States—is capable of playing a role of a 'nationalizing' institution, which interprets and imposes the sense of the whole community even when the consensus is openly rejected by part of the community."[27] At the same time, provincial governments have been wary of that very nationalizing potential. There has been a corresponding reluctance to have federal–provincial disputes settled in a judicial arena where the umpires have been appointed by one of the parties in the dispute. While to date the Supreme Court has not been overly centralist in its

interpretation of constitutional disputes, provincial fears on that account have not evaporated.[28]

Historically, the Court's role in the Canadian political process was limited not only by the right of appeal to the JCPC but also by the general subordination of Canadian courts to legislative assemblies. Apart from interpretations of the federal division of powers, the doctrine of parliamentary supremacy limited the Court's ability to strike out in different directions from those established by Parliament or the provincial legislative assemblies. Now, with the Charter in place, the Court may have the constitutional authority and the political legitimacy to play a more central role in Canadian political life.

It will be the Supreme Court that will decide in practice just what the Charter will mean, and this alone will propel the Court into the political arena. The Charter provides an important political resource for groups who feel that their interests are not being adequately taken into account by Parliament or provincial legislatures, or for groups who have lost in the legislative arena. We can expect, then, the greater pursuit of political ends through judicial means and within a judicial arena that is national in design and intent.[29] The impact of the Charter on Canadian federalism remains to be seen, though there are some interesting straws in the wind. As we saw in Chapter Three, the Quebec government has argued that the Court's ruling on the conflict between Bill 101 and the Charter has altered the nature of Canadian federalism by giving supremacy to a national document— the Charter—in a provincial field of jurisdiction—education. Hence even though the Constitution Act of 1982 did not address the federal division of powers directly, the implementation of the Charter may nonetheless have significant effects. In part those effects will depend upon whether the Charter has a greater impact on provincial legislation than on legislation passed by Parliament. If the thrust of Charter interpretations turns out to be one that strikes down provincial departures from the national standards embodied in the Charter, then the Charter could tilt the federal balance by having a nationalizing effect on Canadian political life.[30]

Equality Rights

It is likely that the Charter's most wide-   *ranging impact on Canadian life will* come from the equality provisions set forth in Section 15:

15.(1) Every individual is equal before and under the law and has the right to equal protection and equal benefit of the law without discrimination and, in particular, without discrimination based on race, national or ethnic origin, colour, religion, sex, age or mental or physical disability.

15.(2) Subsection (1) does not preclude any law, program or activity that has as its object the amelioration of conditions of disadvantaged individuals or groups including those that are disadvantaged because of race, national or ethnic origin, colour, religion, sex, age or mental or physical disability.

Section 15(2) thus gives constitutional sanction to what are termed "affirmative action programs." For example, a program designed to increase the employment of aboriginal persons within the federal government could not be overturned because it violated the equal rights provisions of Section 15(1) by discriminating against those of non-aboriginal descent.

Section 35 of the Constitution Act defines the aboriginal peoples of Canada as including the Indian, Inuit, and Métis peoples, and states that "the existing aboriginal and treaty rights of the aboriginal peoples of Canada are hereby recognized and affirmed." However, as neither these rights nor the constituent groups are defined in the Constitution Act, the practical significance of this provision remains to be determined. Section 37 called for a First Ministers' conference within one year of proclamation, the agenda of which was to include matters affecting the aboriginal peoples of Canada. That meeting and a subsequent meeting were held in March 1983, and March 1984, the outcome of which was a constitutional amendment providing for further meetings in the years ahead.

Three additional sections of the Constitution Act should be noted here. Section 36 builds in a constitutional commitment to equalization payments, discussed in Chapter Five. It is unlikely that this section will have any immediate impact on public policy, for the principles that it enshrines are not new to the Canadian political community. Section 6 guarantees mobility rights including the right of every citizen of Canada to enter, remain in, and leave Canada, and the right of every citizen to take up residence in and pursue a livelihood in any province of his or her choice. Section 6(4), however, states that these latter provisions "do not preclude any law, program or activity that has as its object the amelioration in a province of conditions of individuals in that province who are socially or economically disadvantaged if the rate of employment in that province is below the rate of employment in Canada." Thus provincial legislation designed to give employment preference to residents of a particular province could be struck down by the courts if passed in Ontario, but not if passed in Newfoundland. Finally, Section

At the November 1981 Constitutional Conference, Quebec was the odd man out as the other nine provinces joined Ottawa in signing the accord that was to lead to the Constitution Act, 1982. In this photo Prime Minister Trudeau confers with Finance Minister Allan MacEachen as Premier Lévesque looks on.

Canapress Photo Service

92A, which amends the 1867 division of powers, shores up provincial ownership of and control over non-renewable natural resources, forestry resources, and electrical energy.

CONSTITUTIONAL CONTINUITY

The 1982 Constitution Act has undeniably altered Canada's constitutional underpinnings. Some of the "knobs" referred to by Senator Forsey are very big knobs indeed. However, the outstanding *federal* characteristic of the Constitution Act lies in its continuity with the past. Apart from the Section 92(A) amendments, there was no formal amendment to the federal–provincial division of powers even though that division was an ongoing source of intergovernmental friction throughout most of the 1960s and 1970s. The Act's impact on the division of powers, such as what may be entailed in the Charter's erosion of provincial jurisdiction over education and the likelihood that the Charter may impinge more on provincial than on federal legislation, has been more subtle and indirect. Nothing has been done to secure the place of Quebec within the national political community even though the Government of Canada pledged itself to a "renewed federalism" during the campaign to defeat the 1980 sovereignty-association referendum. If anything, the constitutional enterprise weakened the position of Quebec, as it demonstrated that the constitution could be amended without Quebec's consent. Not coincidentally, the Government of Quebec has refused any formal recognition or acceptance of the new constitutional arrangements. This refusal, along with the ongoing constitutional talks with Canada's aboriginal peoples, represents a major "loose end" from a constitutional process that began in the late 1960s.

The Constitution Act did not address the institutional constraints on regional representation discussed in Chapter Four. Although both the amending formula and the Section 92(A) amendments closely match the stance adopted by the western premiers in the constitutional negotiations, the larger issues of Senate reform and electoral reform were not addressed. By making any future constitutional amendment the prerogative of governments and not the people, by *not* appealing to popular sovereignty, the Act did nothing to strengthen the identification of individual Canadians with the constitutional apparatus of the federal state. As Whitaker has argued,

a functioning federal state must strike some stable balance between regional, provincial or subcultural identities, and an identity *qua* citizens with their national state. The recognition of the principle of the sovereignty of the people is a way of encouraging such attachment over more limited identities.[31]

Over the long run the Charter and a more activist Supreme Court may strengthen the bond between individual Canadians and national institutions. In the short run, however, the Constitution Act did not address the major structural problems that had launched the search for a new constitution in the first place.

Reaction to the Constitution Act has been nicely captured by the title of one of the first major studies of the Act, *And No One Cheered*. In that volume, Alan Cairns makes the following observation:

What was in happier days described as the "living Canadian constitution" still lives, modified in some ways, but still essentially much as before. Its survival is due at least as much to the difficulties of change and the profound disagreement about the desirable direction of change as to any massive support by elites or masses for the particulars of the existing constitutional system. It survives because no other constitutional option enjoys enough first choice support to replace it. It survives because in competition with its rivals it alone possesses the supreme advantage of existence, and its continuation does not spell chaos for the private and public interests whose affairs it regulates and channels.[32]

What, then, does the future hold? Again we quote from Professor Cairns:

In French–English relations, Quebec–Ottawa relations, and federal–provincial relations more generally, there is no resting place, no end to tensions and frustrations. There are no constitutional utopias. We have to be satisfied with the stumbling efforts of imperfect men to keep our problems at bay. From that perspective a restrained half cheer may be suggested as the appropriate response to the new Canadian constitution. It is the only constitution we have.[33]

Intergovernmental Relations

Intergovernmental relations in Canada have encountered few constitutional constraints. The only intergovernmental mechanism built into the 1867 Constitution Act was the Lieutenant-Governor, who "... was originally envisaged as being a federal officer entrusted with the responsibility of communicating the views of the national government to provincial authorities and, if necessary, making certain that the provincial governments did not step too far off the path deemed correct for them by the national government."[34] It was assumed that the national and provincial governments would operate within their own constitutional domains and would rarely come into contact. Federal–provincial interaction would mainly occur through informal party mechanisms. *Governmental* interaction was not institutionally accommodated apart from whatever national intervention in provincial affairs might occur through the Lieutenant-Governor, and through Ottawa's powers of disallowance and reservation. As a consequence the very complex intergovernmental infrastructure that we have today evolved independently of the formal constitution, though its constitutional informality in no way negates its importance. In Canada, as in other federal states, intergovernmental relations are central to the operation of modern government.

THE EVOLUTION OF INTERGOVERNMENTAL RELATIONS

The early years saw little need for extensive or formalized intergovernmental relations. The governments of the day were largely inactive even within their own legislative domains, and encroachments upon each other's turf were rare. The initial conference of "first ministers"—the Prime Minister of Canada and the provincial premiers—was not held until 1906 when Wilfrid Laurier met with the premiers in Ottawa. Subsequent Dominion–Provincial Conferences, as they were then called, were held in 1910, 1918, and 1927. The conferences were characterized by a short agenda, poor staff work, and the dominance of the national government. The major topic of discussion was that perennial bugbear of Canadian federalism, fiscal transfers. The initial Premiers' Conference was held in 1887, followed by meetings in 1902, 1910, 1913, and 1926. The 1887 conference, which was a meeting of predominantly Liberal premiers called to orchestrate a partisan attack on the Conservative government in Ottawa,[35] set the tone for the meetings to follow. Then as now, the premiers dealt less with the coordination of provincial programs and administrative practices than with complaints against the national government.[36]

The near collapse of provincial governments during the Depression increased the tempo of federal–provincial, though not interprovincial, interaction. The first ministers met four times during the 1930s and began to consider greater institutionalization of federal–provincial relations. Speaking at the 1935 Dominion–Provincial Conference, Prime Minister Mackenzie King stated that "cooperation between the Dominion and the provinces is too vital a matter to be left entirely for intermittent conferences and to correspondence between governments."[37] King's stand was endorsed by the Rowell–Sirois Royal Commission which recommended that a permanent intergovernmental relations secretariat be established. However, the outbreak of the Second World War preempted any such action. The War Measures Act sliced away federal–provincial entanglements, enabling Ottawa to act as if Canada were a unitary rather than a federal state. Moreover, after the initial electoral confrontations between Ottawa and the provincial governments of Quebec and Ontario, the war itself pushed federal–provincial issues from the nation's political agenda and reduced the public's tolerance for intergovernmental conflict.

By 1945 eighteen federal–provincial committees had been established to orchestrate Ottawa's wartime involvement in provincial fields of jurisdiction. This network formed the nucleus of what was to become a huge intergovernmental infrastructure. By the mid-fifties, when cooperative federalism was coming into full flower, more than sixty federal–provincial committees were in place, including a Coordinating Agency on Disease of the Beaver. The most important was the Continuing Committee on Fiscal and Economic Matters, a committee of senior finance officials which Smiley has described as a major breakthrough in the institutionalization of federal–provincial fiscal relations.[38] By 1968 the number of federal–provincial committees, boards, and agencies had risen to 190.[39] In 1972 there were more than 400,[40] and by 1975 the total reached almost 800.[41] With the growth in this infrastructure came an increase in the number of federal–provincial conferences, with the first ministers alone meeting nearly twice a year during the 1970s.

This was the heyday of what Donald Smiley has termed "executive federalism," a time when intergovernmental affairs overshadowed what seemed to be the more prosaic activities of the federal and provincial governments operating within their own jurisdictional domains. The importance of executive federalism stemmed not only from the frequency with which first ministers, ministers, and senior officials interacted, but also from the fact that such interaction played a critical role in shaping the multitude of programs and services which the governments of Canada provided for the Canadian people. Its importance was further reinforced

The Annual Premiers' Conference, held in August 1984 at Charlottetown, Prince Edward Island. Pictured from left to right: Hon. Grant Devine, Saskatchewan; Hon. John Buchanan, Nova Scotia; Hon. Richard Hatfield, New Brunswick; Hon. James Lee, Prince Edward Island; Hon. Howard Pawley, Manitoba; Hon. William Davis, Ontario; Hon. Brian Peckford, Newfoundland; Hon. Peter Lougheed, Alberta; Hon. Bill Bennett, British Columbia; Hon. René Lévesque, Quebec.

George Wotton/Island Information Service

by the Canadian pattern of executive dominance vis-à-vis legislative assemblies, be they provincial or national. Thus the participants in executive federalism could be confident that whatever agreements they hammered out would be endorsed by their respective legislative assembly.

Extensive as they may be, federal–provincial relations encompass only part of the intergovernmental activity that takes place. They coexist with, and to a degree engender, an imposing network of interprovincial relations. Federal–provincial conferences themselves and the interprovincial meetings held in preparation for such conferences provide provincial officials with the opportunity to discuss common interests and to promote interprovincial cooperation, often through the vehicle of federal–provincial programs. Interprovincial conferences quite apart from those linked to federal–provincial conferences are also commonplace. To provide but one example at the minsiterial level, the Council of Ministers of Education brings the provincial education ministers together on an annual basis. The Premiers' Conference, initiated as an annual affair in 1960 by Quebec's Premier Jean Lesage, brings together the ten premiers and approximately 150 aides, federal observers, spouses, and children for three days of socializing, informal discussions, and rhetorical broadsides at the federal government. The Council of Maritime Premiers brings together the premiers of New Brunswick, Nova Scotia, and Prince Edward Island while the annual Western Premiers' Conference brings together the four western premiers.

There is also extensive interaction between provincial governments and the local governments falling under their jurisdiction. However, at the present time there is little direct interaction between Ottawa and local governments, a situation unlike that in the United States where the large cities are vigorous congressional lobbyists and where federal progams frequently bypass the state governments to provide direct federal aid to local governments. Although Ottawa established a Ministry of State for Urban Affairs in the early 1970s, the experiment was quickly abandoned.

Table 7.1 provides some indication of the sheer volume of contemporary inter-governmental relations. While the Alberta case may not be typical of all Canadian provinces, the fact that most federal–provincial conferences are multilateral—involving all or most of the provincial governments—suggests that it is not abnormal. Table 7.1 shows that from 1975 to 1978 federal–provincial conferences occurred *every second working day.* During the early 1980s, conferences were still occurring at a rate of more than one a week.

The extensive Canadian network of intergovernmental relations attests to the fact that most matters of public policy have an intergovernmental dimension. For example, when legislation was first introduced in 1983 to transfer responsibility for national security matters from the RCMP to a new civilian agency, it ran afoul of provincial governments who charged that the proposed legislation would encroach upon the provincial responsibility for the administration of justice. We need only wait for the definitive Canadian spy novel in which lawyers from eleven governments lead the reader in an exciting chase through the Constitution Act in order to determine whether the foreign agent is a matter of federal or provincial jurisdiction.

INSTITUTIONALIZATION

In a detailed study of the evolution of Canadian intergovernmental relations, Timothy Woolstencroft notes that during the 1950s and early 1960s, when co-operative federalism was in its prime and federal–provincial interaction centred upon shared-cost programs, "a community of interest, cutting across jurisdictional borders, developed among officials which facilitated harmony and cordial rela-tions between the two levels of government."[42] By the late 1960s this community of interest, knit together by federal and provincial program officials who shared similar educational backgrounds, professional norms, and program commitments, came under growing suspicion. Provincial politicians in particular became con-cerned that bureaucrats were not sufficiently sensitive to jurisdictional issues and that their commitment to program objectives might lead to the surrender of provincial jurisdiction in exchange for federal funds.[43] Thus both governments began to create new central agencies through which they could exercise greater *political* control over the conduct of federal–provincial relations. These central agencies were established to protect the jurisdictional domain of their govern-ment from intrusions by other governments and from jurisdictional compromises

TABLE 7.1
Intergovernmental Relations: The Case of Alberta

Since 1974, the Alberta Department of Federal and Intergovernmental Affairs has maintained a detailed record of the province's participation in federal–provincial and interprovincial conferences. While this record may not reflect that of other provincial governments, it does illustrate the scope of intergovernmental relations in the Canadian federal system.

	1974	1975	1976	1977	1978	1979	1980	1981
Frequency of Federal–Provincial Meetings and Conferences								
• Bilateral (Alberta and federal governments only)	12	27	26	44	19	15	12	26
• Regional (Alberta, one or more of the other western provinces, and the federal government)	4	7	7	17	9	13	9	3
• Multilateral (all or most of the provinces and the federal government)	55	119	105	83	109	47	41	55
Total	71	153	138	144	137	75	62	84
Frequency by Level of Participation								
• First Ministerial	4	4	3	1	3	6	3	2
• Ministerial	27	76	49	47	52	31	32	47
• Deputy Ministerial	40	73	86	96	82	38	27	35
Total	71	153	138	144	137	75	62	84
Frequency of Interprovincial Meetings and Conferences	35	32	52	60	72	43	58	89

Source: Annual Reports of the Alberta Department of Federal and Intergovernmental Affairs.

which might be entertained by program specialists within their own bureaucratic apparatus. They were also a response to the growing scope of intergovernmental relations, to the organizational demands imposed by the constant round of federal–provincial meetings, and to the need for greater intergovernmental expertise in order to protect oneself in, and extract maximum advantage from, the intergovernmental arena.

In Ottawa the first steps toward institutionalization were taken by creating separate federal–provincial divisions within the line departments such as Health and Welfare, Transport, and Agriculture. Here the cornerstone was laid by the 1954 establishment of a federal–provincial relations division in the Department of Finance. In 1968 a special Federal–Provincial Affairs division of the Privy Council Office was established to deal with federal–provincial relations, and by 1975 this had evolved into the Federal–Provincial Relations Office. In 1977 a Federal–Provincial Relations portfolio was established in the federal cabinet, but this was discontinued after the 1980 election. The FPRO now operates under the umbrella of the Prime Minister's Office, and reports to the prime minister through the Secretary to the Cabinet for Federal–Provincial Relations. Quite apart from FPRO there is an Intergovernmental Conference Secretariat in Ottawa staffed by officials seconded from the federal and provincial governments. The secretariat provides liaison for the steady stream of federal–provincial conferences, many of which are held in Ottawa's old Union Station, which has been renovated as the National Conference Centre.

Given that federal–provincial relations touch most activities of the national government, the conduct of federal–provincial relations can be centralized to only a limited degree. While FPRO deals with high-profile issues that have important symbolic or constitutional components—it spearheaded, for instance, Ottawa's counterattack on the Quebec independence movement—the line departments must also maintain a capacity for extensive federal–provincial liaison and policy interaction. With a staff of approximately sixty officials, FPRO cannot *direct* the conduct of federal–provincial relations across the massive federal bureaucracy. At the provincial level, where federal–provincial relations have also been institutionalized, the central control of intergovernmental relations has been more complete.

The provincial trend-setter was Quebec, which established a *Ministère des Affaires federal-provinciales* in 1961. As the Quebec government expanded its international contacts the mandate of the new ministry was also expanded, its name being changed in 1967 to the *Ministère des Affaires intergouvernementales*. The *Ministère* was divided into two sections covering international and Canadian affairs. In 1984 the two sections were elevated to independent departments, *Affaires internationales* (discussed below) and *Affaires canadiennes*. The latter department maintains offices in Edmonton, Moncton, and Toronto, and contains a special branch to handle liaison with francophone communities outside Quebec.

Other provinces soon followed the Quebec example, with the larger provinces going faster and further than the smaller ones. Ontario created a Federal–Provincial and Intergovernmental Affairs Secretariat in 1965. The Secretariat was upgraded to a ministry in 1978 and, until 1981, also had responsibility for municipal affairs. In 1971 the Alberta government created the Department of Federal and Intergovernmental Affairs, while in 1973 Newfoundland created an intergovernmental affairs secretariat attached to the premier's office. Saskatchewan created an Office of Intergovernmental Affairs within the Executive Council Office in 1977, and upgraded it to a ministry in 1978. British Columbia created an Office of Intergovernmental Affairs attached to the premier's office in 1976, upgrading it to a full ministry in 1979. The British Columbia ministry maintains offices in Toronto and Ottawa, as does Alberta's FIGA. While intergovernmental affairs are still handled out of the premier's office in some provinces, the trend has been toward greater institutionalization with independent ministries.[44] Bucking this trend was Grant Devine's Conservative government in Saskatchewan, which in 1982 closed its Department of Intergovernmental Affairs and transferred the department's responsibility back to the premier's office.

There has been considerable controversy among Canadian political scientists as to the impact of institutionalization. Donald Smiley, one of Canada's foremost federal scholars, has argued that institutionalization has intensified intergovernmental conflict by shifting federal–provincial relations from line departments to more politicized central agencies where the symbolic, jurisdictional, and electoral stakes are considerably higher. Of particular concern to Smiley is the intergovernmental specialist whose "single-minded devotion to the power of his jurisdiction" makes the specialist an agent of jurisdictional aggrandizement rather than a conflict conciliator.[45] Woolstencroft, on the other hand, argues that Smiley overstates the impact of and damage from intergovernmental relations specialists. He maintains that their dominance over program officials is far from complete, that when they do influence policy they are not always single-minded province-builders and that, in any event, more profound forces than the specialists underlie intergovernmental conflict.[46]

Whether it is for better or for worse, or whether it is simply an inevitable response to environmental change in the scope of intergovernmental relations, institutionalization has created what Thorburn describes as "a large and efficient machine" in each province to ward off intrusions from other governments, and "to sustain a status quo situation of watchful defence of individual provincial interests."[47] In this setting, Woolstencroft describes the intergovernmental relations specialists as "the sentinels of the federal principle."[48]

THE INTERNATIONAL DIMENSION

In recent years provincial governments have become increasingly active internationally. There are now over 40 provincial offices abroad in addition to the 140 staffed by the Department of External Affairs. Most of the missions represent the governments of Quebec, Ontario, Alberta, and British Columbia. The government of Alberta, for example, has offices in New York, Houston, Los Angeles, London, Hong Kong, and Tokyo. Such offices are used to attract foreign investment and tourism, to search for new markets, and to provide political intelligence on both foreign governments and the international activities of the Canadian government.

Although there is no question that provincial governments are pursuing legitimate interests through their posts abroad,[49] there is some concern about the duplication of, and even conflict with, the representation of Canadian interests by the Department of External Affairs. In their frequent forays abroad to promote trade and foreign investment, the provincial premiers may send out signals somewhat at odds with those emanating from Ottawa. Programs such as Alberta's $7 million international aid program, which provides matching grants to Canadian non-governmental aid organizations rather than government-to-government grants, may be at odds with federal programs. In 1983, for example, the Alberta program cut off aid to Nicaragua at the same time that the Canadian International Development Agency was expanding Canadian aid.[50] Thus one can imagine situations in which people both outside and inside the country may be confused as to who is speaking for Canada.

This problem is of most concern in the case of Quebec where provincial governments have made a major effort to stake out an international presence for the province. Quebec's *Affaires internationales* maintains posts in Abidjan, Atlanta, Boston, Brussels, Buenos Aires, Caracas, Chicago, Dallas, Dusseldorf, Hong Kong, Lafayette, Lisbon, London, Los Angeles, Mexico City, Milan, New York, Paris, Port-au-Prince, Rome, Tokyo, and Washington. These posts are staffed by over three hundred men and women at a yearly cost of $15.8 million.[51] Internally, the department contains seven branches covering France, Europe, Asia, the United States, South America, cultural and educational affairs, and economic affairs.

THE FIRST MINISTERS' CONFERENCE

The intergovernmental centrepiece in Canada has been the First Ministers' Conference, which brings together the prime minister and the ten premiers. The importance of the FMC comes from the parliamentary concentration of power in the hands of the political executive and the further concentration of that power in the hands of the respective first ministers. If consensus reigns, the FMC can be a very powerful policy instrument as the participants can ensure the cooperation of both their cabinet colleagues and legislative assemblies. The First Ministers can shuffle jurisdictional responsibilities without formal constitutional amendment as long as all the participants agree. The existence of a consensus is essential for there is no decision-making rule apart from unanimous consent. If one of the participants disagrees with the rest, no mechanism exists through which the majority will can be imposed.[52] Decisions are binding only to the extent that participants wish to be bound and only to the extent that they are legislatively enacted. The FMC has no constitutional or legal foundation; it is not a government but rather a meeting of governments. When the first ministers do not agree, as will likely be the case when serious matters are on the agenda, the FMC can become little more than a means of dodging responsibility, of pointing the finger of blame at the other level of government. It is political theatre, not government.

Here it is useful to point out two important features of the FMC. The first is that the participants must play several conflicting roles. The prime minister is not only the conference chairman but also one of the active players, representing his government and his party. In one sense he articulates the *national interest*, as opposed to the more narrow *provincial* interests articulated by the premiers, though in another sense the national interest is expected to emerge from the joint deliberations of all eleven first ministers. For their part, the premiers are expected to represent their province while at the same time compromising that interest in order to reach an intergovernmental consensus. The second and related feature is that the most productive sessions tend to be those held in private, frequently over dinner and drinks, and away from the television cameras and the glare of publicity. *Negotiation and compromise* are difficult in a public arena where the forceful defence of one's governmental interests is likely to be of greater electoral value.

It should not be surprising that intergovernmental consensus, either between the federal and provincial governments or among the provincial governments themselves, is difficult to achieve at First Ministers' Conferences. Few of the issues that confront contemporary governments are easily resolved, and the participants at the FMC represent a wide variety of regional, governmental, and partisan interests. Neither should it be surprising that the FMC has come in for a good deal of critical comment. Premier Lévesque and Prime Minister Trudeau both assailed the 1982 First Ministers' Conference on the economy, Lévesque calling it a "dialogue of the deaf" and Trudeau accusing the premiers of using the conference "... to make ten speeches on television blaming the federal government for all the evils of the nation."[53] Political scientist Garth Stevenson concludes that "despite all the advance preparation, expense and ballyhoo, the record of First Ministers' Conferences in reaching agreements or solving problems is exceedingly poor."[54] The FMC, Stevenson charges, resembles "a meeting of a medieval king with his feudal barons more than it does the government of a modern state."[55]

There is some concern that the symbolic output of the FMC may damage the fabric of Canadian federal politics. More often than not, the FMC has been a showcase for conflict and disunity, particularly in the public sessions. Related to this is a fear that the FMC may erode the legitimacy and authority of national

Roy Peterson, *The World According to Roy Peterson* (Vancouver: Douglas and McIntyre, 1979), p. 41.

parliamentary institutions. This general argument was advanced by Prime Minister Trudeau in a 1981 address:

Executive federalism is characterized by the idea that the role of Parliament in governing the country should diminish while premiers should acquire more influence over national public policy. In effect, this theory means that Canada's national government would be a council of first ministers....[56]

The FMC and executive federalism more generally undercut the importance of cabinet ministers, MPs, and Senators as channels of regional representation in the national political system, their role being preempted by provincial premiers and governments. Of equal importance, executive federalism undercuts the role of the parliamentary opposition. The opposition parties are not represented around the conference table. If they attend it is as observers only, and any agreements that might result are subjected to the most perfunctory parliamentary scrutiny. The federal–provincial bargaining process, already convoluted and complex, would become even more so if Parliament or the provincial legislative assemblies were allowed to tinker with intergovernmental agreements.

For example, in the year following the introduction of the 1980 federal budget, Ottawa and the Alberta government were locked in a protracted dispute about energy pricing. When an energy pact was finally negotiated between the energy ministers, and ultimately between Premier Lougheed and Prime Minister Trudeau, it was beyond the power of Parliament to modify. The provincial legislature in Alberta was similarly excluded, as were the federal and provincial cabinets. The intergovernmental negotiations had been so difficult that they were likely to unravel if exposed to legislative revision. An even more important example comes from the negotiations leading up to the 1982 Constitution Act. Although the last round of negotiations began with a parliamentary resolution, the real breakthrough came in the November 1981 Constitutional Accord signed by the prime minister and nine of the ten premiers. As far as Parliament and the provincial legislatures were concerned, the Accord was a fait accompli that was fine-tuned through bilateral, long-distance telephone negotiations between the federal and provincial governments.[57]

Although the FMC may be a flawed institution, there is little doubt that it will continue to play an important role in Canadian federal politics. Provincial governments will continue to have an important stake in national economic management, and will demand a stage upon which provincial opinions can be heard. For its part, the national government will continue to need to bring the provincial governments onside if it is to pursue effectively its management of both the economy and social programs. While unilateral action is not ruled out, its effectiveness is circumscribed by the importance of provincial governments in the economy and in the administration of basic national programs. Thus some institutional forum in which the governments of Canada can be brought together is essential.

Factors Affecting Canadian Intergovernmental Relations

Intergovernmental relations in Canada, at least as they are perceived by the person on the street, often take on a very acrimonious tone. Indeed, it can be argued that the pervasiveness of "Ottawa-bashing" and "province-baiting" sours public life. Federal–provincial conflict may also squeeze more important issues off the nation's political agenda. This is not to imply, however, that the tone of intergovernmental relations is in some way aberrant, that it distorts the true nature of Canadian political life or that it is the fault of particular personalities. While personality clashes are not without consequence, they contribute to rather than explain the tone of intergovernmental conflict. The more important roots are to be found deep within the institutional fabric of the Canadian state.

Some of these roots have already been discussed in Chapter Four. An impotent Senate, party cohesion within the House, the secrecy that envelops both cabinet and caucus, and an electoral system that distorts the regional composition of parliamentary parties all impair the representation of regional interests *within* the national government. As a consequence regional interests at times may find their primary expression through provincial governments; they are represented *to* rather than *within* national institutions. Regional and intergovernmental conflict thus blend into and reinforce one another; regional conflict within national institutions becomes supplanted by conflict between powerful governments and their supporting bureaucracies.

Another root can be traced to the concentration of political power that occurs in parliamentary systems. In 1972, Richard Simeon introduced the notion of federal–provincial *diplomacy*.[58] The term is an insightful one acknowledging that federal–provincial relations have taken on many of the trappings of international relations: the importance attached to the symbols of sovereignty; a stress on the formal equality of all actors regardless of the size of the province or the level of government; the conduct of federal–provincial "summit meetings" in an atmosphere laden with pomp and ceremony; the treatment of governments as unitary actors rather than as complex packages of conflicting bureaucratic, partisan, and personal interests; and the use of diplomatic "listening posts" on one another's turf. This diplomatic mode of intergovernmental relations and the broader phenomenon of executive federalism of which it is a part is made possible by the parliamentary concentration of power. Agreements reached by first ministers are assured of governmental and legislative support. This means, though, that the role of the House of Commons and provincial legislatures in federal–provincial relations is reduced to little more than a discussion of actions that have already been taken and the rubber-stamping of deals that have already been made. Given the scope of intergovernmental relations, this can mean a substantial neutering of the national and provincial legislatures.

The limited number of provincial governments also facilitates a diplomatic mode of interaction. With only eleven participants at federal–provincial conferences, everyone gets a chance to be seen and be heard, to know one another, and to garner maximum media coverage from conference events. The norm of formal equality can be maintained, whereas in the United States fifty states and the enormous gulf between the positions of President and Governor preclude anything analogous to the Canadian FMC. An implication of the role played by numbers is that the creation of new provinces in the North would seriously disrupt the intergovernmental status quo. The additional northern premiers, some of whom would represent populations equivalent to those found in small southern Canadian towns, would erode the diplomatic fiction of provincial equality, reduce the attention paid to any given premier and, as a result, enhance the stature of the Prime Minister.

There is no question that intergovernmental conflict is at times exploited and exacerbated in election campaigns. Ottawa-bashing is employed by provincial governments who prefer to campaign against a distant national government rather than against provincial opponents. (Because it is easier to campaign against the national government when it is of an opposing partisan stripe, provincial governments may offer only lukewarm campaign support for the national wing of their party.) While the opportunities are less frequent, national parties have also featured intergovernmental conflict in their campaigns, with the government party presenting itself as the one party able to stand up against avaricious and fractious provincial governments, and the opposition parties pledging that they will return a spirit of harmony and cooperation to intergovernmental relations. Thus to a modest degree intergovernmental conflict can be seen as a campaign artifact. The more important roots, however, draw their nourishment from institutional features of the Canadian federal state.

The Canadian Federal Community

In the confederation agreement we came to the collective decision that Canadians would be served by a federal system, that the powers of the state would be divided among the national and provincial governments. The latter in turn have delegated some of their powers to local governments, giving Canadians a three-tiered political system. Over time, this decision has resulted in an extensive network of intergovernmental relations, the federal–provincial component of which has been the focus of this chapter. As governments at all levels expanded in size and extended their regulatory reach further into the economy and society, this network became not only more complex but also more vital to the provision of government programs and services. To borrow an analogy used by the American political scientist Karl Deutsch, intergovernmental relations can be seen as the nervous system of the modern federal state. Just as the nervous system of an athlete coordinates the various parts of his or her body to produce fluid motion, intergovernmental relations coordinate the governments of the federal state. And, to extend the analogy further, just as the athlete occasionally stumbles or performs below potential, intergovernmental relations also fail us from time to time.

While a great deal of the interaction between governments occurs in a cooperative and productive atmosphere, some intergovernmental friction and conflict is inescapable. Both national and provincial governments have become large, complex, and ponderous entities, and the task of coordination is inherently difficult. The federal system represents a precarious balance of fiscal resources, jurisdictional responsibilities and citizen demands and ongoing economic and social stress. Maintaining this balance in the face of changing economic and social conditions requires no small degree of political skill. Friction is generated by competition among political elites,[59] by conflicting partisan interests, by conflicting bureaucratic ambitions, and by substantive disagreements over the direction of public policy. Such friction is the price we pay for the size and complexity of modern government, and for the adoption of a federal system. While the system can always be fine-tuned and lubricated, intergovernmental friction will never entirely disappear.

Intergovernmental conflict becomes a more serious matter when it serves as an outlet for major cleavages within the Canadian society. Conflict between Ottawa and the government of Quebec, for example, may go well beyond the intrinsic problems of governmental coordination to a fundamental debate over the place of Quebec within the Canadian political community. At issue is which government best speaks for Quebec when the two governments pursue quite different political visions. Conflict between Ottawa and the western provinces may go beyond the intergovernmental friction inherent in any modern federal state to regional dissatisfaction with the representational character of national political institutions. Intergovernmental conflict in the energy sector may reflect opposing views on Canada's economic relationship with the United States, and the competing interests of energy-producing and energy-consuming provinces. Intergovernmental conflict over medicare engages basic redistributive principles as did conflict between Newfoundland and Ottawa over the ownership and control of offshore resources. Not infrequently, then, intergovernmental relations provide the stage upon which we act out the dominant themes in Canadian political life.

It is at this point that intergovernmental conflict becomes more than the inevitable price of federalism. Intergovernmental conflict can seriously disrupt the provision of government services and programs. As Thorburn observes, "... our economy has become balkanized and our politics confrontational, leading us to dissipate our top decision-making resources on struggles of allocation between regions, provinces, industries and so on instead of building a consensus around an agreed-upon program of development."[60] Both Thorburn and Stevenson argue that intergovernmental conflict weakens Canada's international trading position, with Stevenson going on to argue that it distorts the Canadian political agenda: "... a lessening of the Canadian obsession with provincial interests and jurisdictional controversies might direct our attention to more significant issues, such as the unequal distribution of wealth, power and opportunity across the population."[61] There is a danger that our political imagination has become too blinkered, too narrowly confined to the intergovernmental arena. By restricting our gaze to visions of which government should do what, we may ignore important ideological questions concerning the role of the state in the Canadian society and economy, the maintenance or dismemberment of the post-war welfare state, and the nature of our economic relationship with the United States.

Given the general importance of intergovernmental relations and their more specific entanglement with the basic cleavages of Canadian political life, it is not surprising that the call for reform is frequently heard. Suggestions for reform include replacing the Senate with a provincially appointed upper house, redistributing legislative powers so as to provide a more watertight compartmentalization and thereby reduce the need for intergovernmental relations, passing a constitutional amendment that would require annual meetings of the First Ministers, and creating an elected Senate to strengthen the political authority of the national government. Richard Simeon, one of Canada's foremost experts on intergovernmental relations, has recommended the establishment of a permanent intergovernmental forum, a Council of Federation that would not have legislative powers and would not serve as a revised Senate, but which would enhance coordination and cooperation among governments. At the same time, however, Simeon argues that

to rely almost entirely on the intergovernmental mechanism to reconcile centre and periphery, French and English, is to place an intolerable burden on this fragile structure. Thus, while strengthening this mechanism, we must at the same time look elsewhere: and in particular to political parties.[62]

Just as we cannot untangle the "big" issues of Canadian political life from intergovernmental relations, we should not expect an intergovernmental solution to those issues.

Suggested Readings

1. For an insightful collection of essays on the 1982 Constitution Act, see Keith Banting and Richard Simeon, eds., *And No One Cheered: Federalism, Democracy and The Constitution Act* (Toronto: Methuen, 1983). For a lively account of the process leading up to the Constitution Act, see Robert Sheppard and Michael Valpy, *The National Deal: The Fight for a Canadian Constitution* (Toronto: Fleet Books, 1982).

2. For a conceptual discussion of Canadian federalism, see Edwin R. Black, *Divided Loyalties: Canadian Concepts of Federalism* (Montreal: McGill-Queen's University Press, 1975).

3. For a discussion of fiscal transfers in the Canadian federal system, see Dan Butler and Bruce D. Macnaughton, "More of Less for Whom? Debating Directions for the Public Sector," in Michael S. Whittington and Glen Williams, eds., *Canadian Politics in the 1980s*, 2nd ed. (Toronto: Methuen, 1984), pp. 1–32.

4. Alan C. Cairns, "The Governments and Societies of Canadian Federalism," *Canadian Journal of Political Science*, Vol. 10, 1977, pp. 695–726.

5. For a discussion of the impact of intergovernmental relations on legislative authority, see John Meisel, "New Challenges to Parliament: Arguing Over Wine Lists on the

Titanic?", *Journal of Canadian Studies*, Vol. 14, 1979, p. 23; and Donald V. Smiley, "Federalism and the Legislative Process in Canada," in William A.W. Neilson and James C. MacPherson, eds., *The Legislative Process in Canada: The Need for Reform* (Montreal: Institute for Research on Public Policy, 1978), p. 73.

6 Larry Pratt, "The State and Province-Building: Alberta's Development Strategy," in Leo Panitch, ed., *The Canadian State: Political Economy and Political Power* (Toronto: University of Toronto Press, 1977), pp. 133–62. For an examination of province-building in Ontario and Quebec, see the special issue of the *Journal of Canadian Studies*, Vol. 18, No. 1 (Spring 1983).

7 Roy Romanow, John Whyte, and Howard Leeson, *Canada ... Notwithstanding: The Making of the Constitution 1976–1982* (Toronto: Methuen, 1984).

8 Donald V. Smiley, *Canada in Question: Federalism in the Eighties*, 3rd ed. (Toronto: McGraw-Hill Ryerson, 1980).

9 Garth Stevenson, "Federalism and Intergovernmental Relations," in Michael S. Whittington and Glen Williams, eds., *Canadian Politics in the 1980s*, 2nd ed. (Toronto: Methuen, 1984), pp. 371–90.

10 H.G. Thorburn, *Planning and the Economy: Building Federal–Provincial Consensus* (Toronto: James Lorimer, 1984).

11 Timothy B. Woolstencroft, *Organizing Intergovernmental Relations* (Kingston: Institute for Intergovernmental Relations, Queen's University, 1982).

Study Questions

1 Over the course of this term, what federal–provincial conference activity has been reported in the press? What meetings have been held, and who attended—were the participants first ministers, cabinet ministers, or deputy ministers? What coverage were the meetings given in the press, what issues did they deal with, and with what result?

2 This chapter has suggested that the growth of government has been a major factor in the growth of intergovernmental relations, and in the increase in intergovernmental conflict. To what extent do you think this relationship might work in reverse? If the growth of government is brought to a halt or if the size of government is actually decreased, should we expect any corresponding change in intergovernmental relations? What factors might promote or inhibit such change?

3 Make a note of all government programs and services to which you and your family have had access over the past few years. Try to be as inclusive as possible, keeping in mind local services and programs such as Medicare and Youth Allowances. What proportion of these programs and services have been provided by the federal government? By your provincial government? By your local government? What proportion have involved more than one level of government?

4 How does your own province handle federal–provincial relations? Is there a provincial ministry charged with this responsibility, or are they handled through the

premier's office? If there is a ministry or department, does your library have its annual report? Can you document the scope of your province's involvement in federal–provincial interaction?

5 Carefully read through the *Constitution Act, 1982.* What are the sections of the Act which strike you as most important? Which are likely to have the greatest impact on your own life in the years ahead?

CHAPTER EIGHT

The Canadian Party System

Political parties play a starring role in democratic politics. Much if not most of what we think of as "politics" entails political parties, their leaders, and the competition among parties and leaders in federal and provincial election campaigns. Yet while there is little dispute as to the centrality of the party role, there is considerable disagreement as to the nature of that role. At the heart of the disagreement lie conflicting expectations about the policy role parties should play in democratic elections.

Elections provide one instrument through which citizens can convey their policy preferences to governments. Admittedly, the ballot is a very simple if not crude instrument, allowing voters only to print a single "X" on a piece of paper. Because of this, elections can convey policy preferences only if there are reasonably clear policy differences among the parties competing on the ballot. Only then can elections provide a "policy mandate." As a consequence, parties which differ only as Tweedledum and Tweedledee are often seen to rob elections of their meaning. More importantly, they are seen to rob citizens of the opportunity to direct their governments, to use the electoral process to deliver not only a judgment on the past performance of government but also a mandate for the future.

The normative vision of electoral politics underlying this stance is largely discounted by political scientists who see parties primarily as *brokerage* organizations, bound together by the pursuit of office rather than by any consistent or even distinctive set of ideas, policies, or principles. As Clarke et al. explain,

Rather than dividing the electorate among themselves along clear and stable lines of social cleavage, [brokerage parties] constantly compete for the same policy space and the same votes.... They organize around leaders rather than around political principles and ideologies, and expect the leader to work out the multitude of compromises required....[1]

"Of course our party recognizes the fundamental nature of the crisis we find our nation facing. . . . We have to get elected again."

Len Norris, *27th Annual.* Originally published in *The Vancouver Sun*, March 15, 1978

From a brokerage perspective, elections are seen primarily as an instrument through which voters can cast a retrospective judgment on the past performance of governments, and through which they can choose *representatives but not policies* for the future. Election campaigns feature the clash of leaders, not ideologies, and are fought on the plains of policy consensus rather than from the heights of competing principles.

Brokerage parties and the electoral competition among such parties can provide important means of bridging cleavages within the political order. As Van Loon and Whittington explain, the brokerage party "... must aggregate a wide range of interests into a voting coalition, and in so doing it performs an integrative function for the political system as a whole."[2] However, although the Canadian parties have generally tried to build electoral coalitions spanning the linguistic, regional, and class cleavages within the Canadian society, their success in so doing has been less than complete. As vehicles for national political integration, both the party system and its constituent elements have at times encountered considerable difficulty. Brokerage aspirations have not ensured brokerage results.

The Evolution of the Canadian Party System

Although they are in part shaped by a series of specific election outcomes, party systems reflect and respond to a broad spectrum of influences which transcend elections and go to the very roots of society.[3]

Only a handful of Canada's thirty-three general elections have had a major impact on Canadian political life. Only twelve elections resulted in a change in government,[4] and in some of these instances the change represented little more than a minor ripple in the established pattern of Canadian politics. Between June 1979 and February 1980, for example, the government changed hands twice, but the nine-month Conservative government headed by Joe Clark can best be seen as a temporary deviation from Liberal rule. As Figure 8.1 illustrates, Canada's political history has been marked by long periods of one-party dominance rather than by any regular alternation in party control of the national government.

National political life has been dominated by two parties. The first to emerge was the Conservative Party—it did not become the *Progressive* Conservative party until 1942—which began to take shape around 1854 as the Liberal–Conservative legislative coalition in the Province of Canada. Led by John A. Macdonald and George-Etienne Cartier, the Conservatives brought together the business interests of Montreal and Toronto and the hierarchy of the Catholic Church in Quebec. In the 1867 general election, a post-mortem on Confederation fought out among a wide array of candidates in four separate provincial campaigns, the loosely-knit Conservatives won 60 percent of the seats and Macdonald became Canada's first prime minister. Although they lost in 1874, the Conservatives were returned to power in 1878 where they remained through the election of 1891, the last fought by Macdonald. Shortly after its victory in 1891, the party's strength began to unravel with the death of Macdonald, a series of short-lived and generally ineffectual leaders, and the erosion of the party's electoral base in Quebec. The stage was set for the first sustained period of Liberal rule.

Under the uncertain leadership of Alexander Mackenzie, the Liberals had first come to power in 1874 when the Pacific Scandal (*see Glossary*) led to the defeat of Macdonald's Conservative government. The Liberal base was found among agrarian populist reformers from Ontario, the "Clear Grits." The Liberal coalition also included anti-clerical francophones from Quebec, anti-confederates from Quebec, New Brunswick, and Nova Scotia, and, more generally, those who supported provincial rights and opposed the centralist and nation-building thrust of the Macdonald Conservatives. It was a "disparate and ineffectual alliance,"[5] easily routed by the Conservatives in 1878. Only after their defeat did the Liberals begin to pull together as a truly national party, and only under the direction of a new leader, Quebec's Wilfrid Laurier, did they emerge as a serious threat to the dominant Conservatives.

FIGURE 8.1

Party Forming National Government, 1867–1984

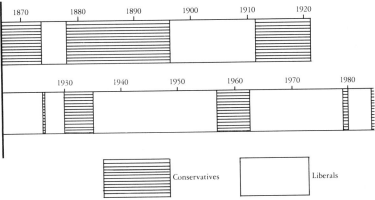

Conservatives

Liberals

The Liberal rise to national power came with a reversal of the two parties' fortunes in Quebec. In the 1884 general election the Liberals, whose association with anti-clerical elements in Quebec brought down the political wrath of the Catholic church, won only sixteen Quebec seats compared to forty-nine for the Conservatives. In 1887, following the hanging of Riel, the Liberals captured thirty-two Quebec seats to the Conservatives' thirty-three. In the 1891 election, with Wilfrid Laurier at the helm, the Liberals won thirty-seven Quebec seats compared to twenty-eight for the Conservatives, the first in a string of Liberal majorities in Quebec that was not to be broken until 1958. In 1896 the Laurier Liberals came to power, winning forty-nine of the sixty-five Quebec seats in the process.

The Liberals were to remain in power until 1911, during which time their earlier support for provincial rights gave way to the enthusiastic leadership of nation-building activities in the Canadian West. In 1911 they went down to defeat in an election that featured debate over the proposed introduction of greater free trade with the United States (discussed below) and, as war clouds gathered in Europe, over Canada's participation in the naval defence of the British Empire. The new Conservative government was led by Robert Laird Borden, who was to steer Canada's passage through the First World War.

The elections of 1917 and 1921 were of critical importance in the evolution of the national party system. The 1917 election was fought on the single issue of military conscription, which was strongly opposed in Quebec and by the Liberals, and was generally supported elsewhere in Canada and by the Conservatives. The election had at least three major consequences. The Liberals were all but purged in western Canada, winning only two of the regon's fifty-six seats. Second, Quebec was turned into a Conservative wasteland, with the party winning only three of Quebec's sixty-five seats, down from twenty-seven in 1911. In combination, the election results in the West and Quebec meant that the two national parties were no longer national in terms of electoral support and representation in the House. Third, the election blurred existing party lines as both the Conservatives and a significant number of pro-conscription Liberals ran under the banner of the Union Government. This was to set the stage for a new political movement that held non-partisanship as one of its leading principles.

At Last, Women Get the Vote!

Since the late 1800s, suffragettes in Britain, the United States, and Canada had been campaigning for the extension of the voting franchise to women. They were not successful, however, until the First World War.

The war years fundamentally changed the place of women within the Canadian economy and society. The domestic war effort, coupled with the manpower demands of the military, produced a dramatic surge in female participation in the labour force which threw their exclusion from the franchise into greater and greater question. The war years were also marked by widespread interest in social reform. Through their leadership of reform organizations such as the Women's Christian Temperance Union, women were able to place the extension of the franchise near the top of the reform agenda. If the war was being fought to protect democracy, women argued, then surely women were entitled to the vote at home.

The specific impetus for the extension of the franchise came from the Wartime Elections Act, a notorious piece of legislation which inflated support for conscription in the 1917 election. Among other things, the Act enfranchised the close female relatives of men on active overseas service on the assump-

tion that such women would endorse conscription. The rationale for extending the vote was that servicemen, who were predominantly English Canadians

Nellie McClung was born in Chatsworth, Ontario, in 1873 and moved to Manitoba when she was seven. Trained as a teacher, McClung became a leader in the Women's Suffrage Movement. In 1921 she was elected to the Alberta Legislature, becoming the first woman in the British Empire to be elected to a Legislative Assembly.

Public Archives of Canada/C27674

Women's political organizations have a long history in Canada. The above photo shows an 1898 meeting of the National Council of Women with the Governor General of Canada, Lord Aberdeen.

Public Archives of Canada/PA28033

rather than French Canadians, would have trouble finding the time to vote. Their female relatives could thus vote in their place. In fact, however, servicemen were given twenty-seven days and every opportunity in which to vote. Few if any were disenfranchised.

In 1921 the federal franchise was extended to all women on the same terms as it was applied to men.

The events set in motion by the 1917 election, including the crippling of both the Conservatives and the Liberals as national organizations, led to a fundamental transformation of the Canadian party system in 1921. The incumbent Conservatives, having discarded the wartime umbrella of the Union Government, failed to win a seat in Quebec or on the prairies. Overall, they captured only 50 seats, down from 153 Union Government seats in 1917. The Liberals formed Canada's first minority government with 116 seats, including every seat in Quebec but only 5 in the West. The most dramatic transformation came with the emergence of the Progressive Party of Canada, which swept out of the prairie West to capture sixty-four seats including thirty-seven of the thirty-nine prairie seats, twenty-four seats in Ontario, three in British Columbia and one in New Brunswick.

Although the Progressive Party drew its core support from agrarian unrest in western Canada and rural Ontario, the new party also encompassed a more widespread interest in social reform that was a direct product of the war years. The Progressives' non-partisan approach to politics appealed to those who had supported the wartime Union Government. The Progressive Party also provided a vehicle through which western Canadians could register their growing regional discontent with the partisan and parliamentary organization of Canadian political life, discontent that transcended agrarian concerns alone. Yet despite these numerous, albeit overlapping, sources of support, the Progressives faded quickly. In 1925 they won only twenty-four seats, twenty-two of which came from the prairie provinces. In 1926 the Progressives won only twenty seats, eighteen from the prairies, and in 1930 only twelve, of which eleven were on the prairies and nine in Alberta alone. In less than a decade the Progressives had been driven back to an Alberta enclave and almost from the political stage.

As Figure 8.2 illustrates, the Conservative and Liberal parties rebounded quickly after the debacle of 1921. By 1930, when together they won 94 percent of the votes cast and 93 percent of the seats, it appeared that the 1921 election had been but a temporary deviation from an enduring pattern of two-party dominance. That pattern, however, was conclusively broken in the 1935 election, fought in the middle of the Great Depression. Voters turned out the Conservative government, which had come into power in 1930 just as the Depression was descending, and returned the Liberals to power. At the same time they elected thirty-two candidates from a variety of third parties, two of which were to leave a permanent mark on the Canadian party system.

In 1935, the Co-operative Commonwealth Federation, a left-of-centre party that brought together the remnants of the Progressive Party, agrarian organizations from western Canada, elements of the nascent labour movement, and central Canadian left-wing intellectuals grouped under the banner of the League for Social Reconstruction, captured 8.8 percent of the popular vote and seven seats in the House of Commons. Over the next five general elections the CCF averaged 11.9 percent of the popular vote and over nineteen seats in the House, and in 1944 was to form the provincial government in Saskatchewan. The Social Credit party also ran candidates for the first time in 1935. Although the party captured only 4.1 percent of the popular vote, the greater regional concentration of that vote gave the Social Credit party three more seats than the CCF. Across the next five general elections the Social Credit party averaged 4.2 percent of the popular vote and over thirteen seats in the House.[6] The other significant entry in the 1935 election, the Reconstruction Party, was essentially a splinter group of Conservatives running under the leadership of H.H. Stevens, the Minister of Trade and Commerce in R.B. Bennett's Conservative government. Although Reconstruction candidates captured 8.7 percent of the popular vote, only Stevens was elected. Shortly after the election the Reconstruction party vanished without a trace.

The 1921 and 1935 elections not only marked the end of an uncomplicated

FIGURE 8.2

*Percentage of Seats and Popular Vote Won by the Conservative and Liberal
Parties Combined*

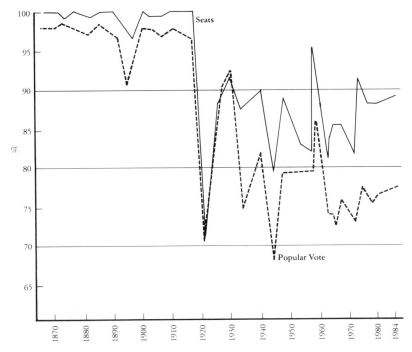

two-party system but also established a Liberal dominance of national politics that
was to stretch through to 1984. Reelected in 1935, the Liberals remained in office
until defeated by John Diefenbaker in 1957, and then returned to power in 1963.
From 1963 to 1984 (apart from the brief Conservative interlude of 1979–80) they
dominated the federal scene. During the sixty-three years from 1921 to 1984 a
quip by Jack Pickersgill, Liberal cabinet minister and party stalwart, took on the
appearance of an iron law: "living under a Conservative government is like
having a childhood disease—everyone has to experience it once, but never wants
to do it again."[7]

The major departure from Liberal dominance came with the "Diefenbaker
interlude" from 1957 to 1963. A prairie populist with a dramatic platform style,
John Diefenbaker fundamentally transformed the Conservative party by shifting
its centre of gravity westward. The Conservatives had earlier sought western
Canadian support when they enticed John Bracken, the Progressive premier of
Manitoba, to lead the national party in 1942. Part of that enticement had been the
change in the party's name to the *Progressive* Conservative Party of Canada. As

Table 8.1 shows, however, neither Bracken's leadership nor the change in name greatly improved the party's position in the West. When Bracken was replaced in 1948 by the Conservative premier of Ontario, George Drew, little improvement in the West could be expected and none was forthcoming.

John Diefenbaker was chosen as the Conservative leader in 1956 after Drew resigned for reasons of health. In the 1957 campaign Diefenbaker led his party to a minority government with strong support in Atlantic Canada (twenty-one seats, up from five in 1953) and Ontario (sixty-one seats, up from thirty-three in 1953), and more modest gains in the West and Quebec. Then in 1958 the Conservatives rolled up the largest majority ever recorded in a federal election,[8] taking 208 of the 265 seats in the House including 70 of 75 seats in western Canada and 50 of the 75 seats in Quebec. The Liberals won only forty-nine seats and were shut out in six provinces, CCF seats were cut from twenty-five to eight, and no Social Credit candidates were elected. Although Diefenbaker himself was closely associated with the West, Conservative candidates did well across the country, collecting 55 percent of the popular vote in Atlantic Canada, 50 percent in Quebec, 56 percent in Ontario, and 54 percent across the West.

Despite the 1958 landslide, the Conservatives retained only a minority government after the 1962 election, and in 1963 lost power to the Liberals under the leadership of Lester Pearson. The 1958 Conservative gains in Quebec quickly evaporated; thirty-six of the fifty seats won in 1958 were lost in 1962, with another six being lost in 1963. Ontario support also faded, with the Conservative seat total falling from sixty-seven in 1958 to thirty-five in 1962 and twenty-seven in 1963. What did *not* evaporate was the Conservative resurgence in western Canada. As Table 8.1 demonstrates, Diefenbaker not only led the West, and particularly the prairie West, into the Conservative camp but kept it there during the early sixties. Although regional support for the Conservatives fell off in 1968, it quickly rebounded. Thus Diefenbaker's transformation of the Canadian West from a Conservative wasteland to the Conservative heartland was a lasting gift to the party he had led.

The Diefenbaker years touched off a number of other important changes in the party system. The Conservative rout of the CCF led to that party's collapse and, in 1961, to its reincarnation as the New Democratic Party. The NDP brought together what was left of the CCF's agrarian support in western Canada with the political interests of the Canadian Labour Congress. The new party also reached out more effectively than its predecessor to white-collar, urban constituencies, though, like the CCF's, its support all but stopped at the Quebec–Ontario border. Since its first campaign in 1962 the NDP has been a major player in Canadian national politics, though not a contender for national office.

The 1962 election also marked the rebirth of Social Credit, this time in Quebec under the leadership of Réal Caouette.[9] Although restricted almost exclusively to Quebec, the "Créditistes" had a significant impact on the politics of the time,

TABLE 8.1

Conservative Support in Western Canada

	% of Popular Vote			Western Canadian Seats	
	All 4 provs.	Prairies only	B.C. only	#	%
1940	21.2%	17.7%	30.5%	7	9.9
1945	23.5	20.7	30.0	10	14.1
1949	20.8	17.6	27.9	7	9.9
1953	16.0	17.0	14.1	9	12.9
1957	30.0	28.6	32.6	21	30.4
1958	53.9	56.2	49.4	65	92.9
1962	38.8	44.9	27.3	48	68.6
1963	38.8	47.0	23.4	45	64.3
1965	36.0	45.3	19.2	45	64.3
1968	33.0	40.8	19.4	25	36.8
1972	42.1	47.5	33.0	42	61.8
1974	47.2	50.6	41.9	49	72.1
1979	49.6	53.0	44.4	57	74.0
1980	46.8	50.6	41.5	49	63.6
1984*	52.1	55.8	46.6	58	75.3

*Preliminary, unofficial returns.

winning twenty-six federal seats in 1962, twenty in 1963, and nine in 1965. They survived as a political force in Quebec even during the Liberal hegemony of the Trudeau years, winning fourteen seats in 1968, fifteen in 1972, eleven in 1974, and six in 1979 before being driven from the political stage in 1980.

In many respects, the most dramatic transformation of the party system to date came with the 1984 federal election, in which the Conservative party, led by Brian Mulroney, captured 211 of the 282 seats in the House of Commons. The Conservative sweep occurred across the country, with Tory candidates taking twenty-five of the thirty-two seats in Atlantic Canada, fifty-eight of seventy-five in Quebec, sixty-seven of ninety-five in Ontario, fifty-eight of seventy-seven in the West, and all three in the North. After more than two decades in which neither the Conservatives nor the Liberals had been able to maintain a truly *national* base, the country again had a national government enjoying strong electoral support across the land. In Quebec, the magnitude of the electoral change was staggering. Led for the first time by a Quebec leader, the Conservatives increased their share of the Quebec popular vote from 12.6 percent in 1980 to 50.3 percent in 1984.[10] Conversely, the Liberal share of the Quebec popular vote fell from 68.2 percent in 1980 to only 35.4 percent in 1984. Fifty-eight Tory candidates were elected in 1984, compared to a single candidate in 1980. One of the most important constants in Canadian political life—the Liberal fortress of Quebec—had been shattered. The Liberal party has *never* done worse in a federal election. Even in the 1958 Diefenbaker rout, the Liberals retained forty-nine seats and almost 34 percent of the vote. The party that had come to be known as "the government party" was now out of office not only in Ottawa but also across the ten provinces.[11] The NDP was much more successful in withstanding the Tory tide, actually gaining eight seats in Ontario to help offset the nine NDP seats lost in the West.

Table 8.2 presents the 1984 results for the other parties in the 1984 campaign. The Rhinoceros Party placed fourth, with 84 percent of its votes coming from Quebec, where Rhino candidates came within 2,000 votes of beating the Parti Nationaliste. Indeed, in most constituencies where both PN and Rhino candidates were on the ballot, Rhino candidates received more votes. The PN had been established in 1983 in order to carry the independence flag in federal elections. In June 1984, the PN had been endorsed by the Parti Québécois, but over the summer a majority of PQ ministers gave public approval to the Conservative revival in Quebec. In the West the Confederation of Regions Western Party failed to make an appreciable impact with its call for a restructured federal system. The Green party, composed of a rough coalition of environmentalists, managed to field sixty candidates in its first Canadian campaign but received only about one vote in every five hundred cast.

Whether the realignment of the Quebec electorate will persist in forthcoming federal elections is difficult to predict. It is clear, however, that the face of Canadian electoral politics was dramatically altered in 1984. At the margins of that change, voters are now confronted with a considerable smorgasbord of electoral choices, though to date most of the dishes have been left all but untouched. More importantly, the Conservative party has been reestablished in Quebec while the Liberal party's now traditional weakness in western Canada has been further exacerbated. The NDP, while no closer to power, is closer than it has ever been to forming the official opposition.

Electoral Patterns in the Canadian Party System

At this point it is useful to step back from the details of the Canadian party system, and to look at the general patterns which tie that detail together.

MAJOR PARTY DOMINANCE

The national dominance of the Conservative and Liberal parties has already been noted in Figure 8.2. While that dominance was shaken in 1921 and substantially

TABLE 8.2

*1984 National Election Results**

Party	Number of Candidates	Candidates Elected	Number of Votes	% Total Popular Vote	Average Vote per Candidate
Progressive Conservative	282	211	6,191,589	50.0	21,956
Liberal	282	40	3,474,556	28.1	12,321
New Democratic	282	30	2,323,268	18.8	8,239
Rhinoceros	89		101,306	.8	1,138
Parti Nationaliste	75		86,728	.7	1,156
Confederation of Regions Western Party	55		65,552	.5	1,192
Independents	84	1	59,404	.5	707**
Green Party	60		26,737	.2	446
Libertarian	72		23,357	.2	324
Social Credit	51		16,493	.1	323
Communist	52		8,258	.1	159
Party for a Commonwealth of Canada	65		7,874	.1	121
Total	1,449	282	12,385,122	100.0	8,547

*Preliminary, unofficial returns.

**The independent vote total has been inflated by a single constituency result. In the Ontario riding of York North, Tony Roman ran as an independent against the incumbent Conservative MP, John Gamble. In the campaign, a good number of Conservatives worked for Roman, who had tried but failed to capture the Conservative nomination from Gamble. In the election, Roman captured the riding with 30,933 votes, or 2,462 more votes than received by *all* of the other 83 independent candidates *combined*. If the York North constituency is not included, independent candidates averaged only 343 votes each.

reduced from 1935 onward, the two major parties continue to capture the support of three Canadian voters in four. Figure 8.3 shows that among "third parties" the dominance of the NDP is equally apparent, that with the disappearance of the Créditistes it is as complete as the Conservative and Liberal dominance of the total national party system. Other parties continue to exist, and indeed may even be increasing in number. Yet the party *system* is no more complex, as these other parties are in the electoral arena but not in the game.

PROVINCIAL VARIATIONS ON THE NATIONAL THEME

One of the most important features of the Canadian party system is that the

FIGURE 8.3

Distribution of the Third-Party Popular Vote

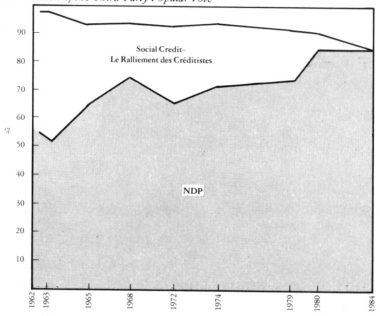

national cast of party actors is not faithfully replicated across the ten provincial party systems.

In Atlantic Canada, the Liberal and Conservative parties have dominated both federal and provincial elections. In federal elections they have been even more dominant in the region than they have been nationally. In the nine general elections held between 1962 and 1984, Liberal and Conservative candidates captured 76 percent of the national popular vote while capturing 88 percent across the four Atlantic provinces. Across those same nine elections, Liberal and Conservative candidates won 286 of the 291 Atlantic seats (98 percent), losing just 4 seats to the New Democrats and one to an independent. In provincial elections held between 1960 and 1981, the two major parties were even more dominant. In Prince Edward Island and New Brunswick their candidates captured 100 percent of the seats with 98 percent of the popular vote; in Newfoundland and Nova Scotia they captured 97 percent of the seats with 94 percent and 89 percent of the vote respectively.[12] Thus where Atlantic Canada departs from the national pattern is in the relative weakness of third-party support.

The national party system is best replicated in Ontario, where provincial politics have also been dominated by the Conservatives, Liberals, and New Democrats. However, although the party players are the same, their relative strength differs across the federal and provincial arenas. While the Conservatives have formed the provincial government since 1943, the Liberals have enjoyed a slight edge federally, winning 400 seats in the nine elections held between 1962 and 1984 compared to 331 Ontario seats won by the Conservatives. The NDP has enjoyed greater provincial than federal success within Ontario, although it remains competitive at both levels.

In Quebec we find strong provincial parties that do not have a federal counterpart. The Union Nationale, which controlled the Quebec provincial government for twenty-four years between 1936 and 1970, did not run federal candidates. The Parti Québécois has not run federal candidates, though in 1984 it did endorse the Parti Nationaliste. Conversely, the federal Conservative party has not had a provincial counterpart in Quebec since 1936. Thus federal and provincial campaigns in Quebec are fought between quite different political parties.

The relationship between the federal and provincial party systems in western Canada defies any simple regional description. The most "deviant" province has been British Columbia, where since 1952 provincial elections have been fought between the Social Credit and the CCF/NDP, with the provincial Liberal and Conservative parties being all but moribund. Yet on the federal scene the Liberals and Conservatives have been both active and successful. Only the New Democrats have been competitive at both levels while the Social Credit party, in power provincially for all but three years since 1952, has not been active federally since 1965, when three Socred MPs were elected.

Alberta provincial politics have been dominated in turn by the Liberals (1905–1921), the United Farmers of Alberta (1921–1935), the Social Credit party (1935–1971) and, since 1971, the Progressive Conservatives. Opposition parties of whatever stripe have been chronically weak, with government control of over 90 percent of the legislative seats being the rule rather than the exception. In the early 1980s both the federal and provincial Conservatives faced weak NDP and Liberal opponents. Since Social Credit's defeat in 1971 and its subsequent departure from the provincial stage, Alberta has deviated from the national pattern more in terms of the relative strength of the party players than in the players themselves.[13]

Saskatchewan voters elected North America's first socialist government in 1944 when the CCF broke the Liberals' virtual monopoly in the provincial arena. The CCF remained in power until 1964 when the Liberals returned to power. The Liberals were then defeated by the New Democrats in 1971, who were defeated in turn by Grant Devine's Conservatives in 1982. Both federal and provincial politics in the mid-1980s feature strong competition between the Conservatives and New Democrats, with the Liberals trailing a distant third.

Historically, Manitoba presented a different picture again. In the midst of the Depression the provincial Liberals and Progressives merged to form the nucleus of a non-partisan and initially all-party administration which was to govern Manitoba until 1958. Over time, the government became more Liberal and less non-partisan as first the CCF left in 1942 and then Conservatives left in 1952. In the 1958 provincial election the Conservatives came to power, and were to remain in power until 1969 when they were defeated by the New Democrats. The Conservatives returned to power in 1977 and then lost again to the New Democrats in 1982. Thus in both the provincial and federal arenas, contemporary Manitoba politics are characterized by vigorous two-party competition between the Conservatives and New Democrats, with the Liberals trailing the field. The Liberal weakness is now common to all three prairie provinces, as is the provincial strength of the Conservatives. The principal difference across the three provincial party systems comes from the New Democrats, whose electoral strength declines as one moves westward across the prairies.

The Canadian party system is not only asymmetrical across the ten provinces. In many cases it is also asymmetrical *within* provinces in that the cast of parties competing for provincial office differs considerably from the cast competing for federal seats in the province. Here the best illustrations are provided by Quebec and British Columbia.[14] This latter asymmetry is reflected in the growing organizational independence of federal and provincial parties sharing the same party label. Thus Van Loon and Whittington conclude that "... while the Canadian political system can be described as federal, its political parties are at best only confederal."[15]

PARTY TENURE

The Canadian political system is marked by the longevity of its governments. As Figure 8.1 has shown, it is an unusual federal election in which the government changes hands. This stability is further demonstrated by Figure 8.4, which plots the proportion of the popular vote received by the Conservative and Liberal parties. Figure 8.4 shows sustained periods of dominance rather than regular oscillation in party fortunes.

The partisan stability at the federal level is surpassed by even more steadfast support of provincial governments, many of which have enjoyed quite remarkable tenures. The Ontario government has been in Conservative hands since 1943, a period of more than forty years. The Social Credit party was in power in Alberta from 1935 to 1971, and in British Columbia from 1952 to the present with the exception of a brief NDP interregnum from 1972 to 1975. Joey Smallwood's Liberal party controlled the government of Newfoundland from 1949 to 1971.

To illustrate the lengthy tenure of Canadian governments, it is useful to draw upon an American comparison. During the time that Pierre Trudeau was prime minister of Canada, Americans experienced five different presidential administrations: those of Lyndon Johnson, Richard Nixon, Gerald Ford, Jimmy Carter, and Ronald Reagan. Each administration, with the possible exception of Ford's, is

FIGURE 8.4

Percentage of the Popular Vote in General Elections, 1878–1984

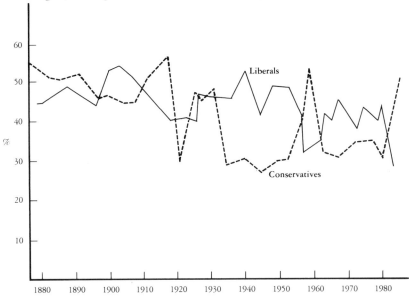

commonly seen as a unique and distinctive episode in American political life. In Canada, the tempo of change is much slower as voters retain incumbent governments and as leaders enjoy terms of office whose length is virtually unknown in the United States.

ELECTORAL "DISTORTIONS"

In the general election of 1984 over twelve million votes were cast to determine the occupants of 282 seats in the House of Commons. It is the *electoral system* which translates votes into seats and thereby determines the partisan composition of the government. That system is based on single-member constituencies, the winner in each constituency being the candidate receiving a *plurality* of the votes cast. Thus to win in what is called a "first-past-the-post" system one needs only more votes than any other candidate, and *not a majority* of the votes cast. Given that the three major parties run candidates in every riding, pluralities that are well short of majorities are common. The party winner of the election is determined by aggregating the results of the 282 constituency contests, the party having the most seats winning the right to form the next national government.[16] While party leaders play a critical role in the national campaign, they do not run as national candidates but rather seek election as MPs in specific constituencies.

The simple plurality electoral system is only one of many possible mechanisms that could be used to translate votes into seats. Many countries use systems of *proportional representation* designed to ensure that a party's share of seats is roughly proportionate to its share of the popular vote. This feature is not characteristic of the electoral translation that takes place in Canada. The Canadian system tends to overreward the party capturing a plurality of the national vote. In Figure 8.5 we can see that the winning party in national elections consistently receives a much higher percentage of the seats in the House of Commons than its percentage of the popular vote. Indeed, since 1921 the winning party has received a majority of the popular vote on only three occasions. On four occasions—1957, 1962, 1972, and 1979—minority governments were formed by parties receiving less than 40 percent of the popular vote. This tendency of the electoral system to overreward the leading party is often seen as a positive distortion, one that increases the probability of stable majority government despite the lack of a majority preference among Canadian voters.

There is an important caveat to note here. Although it is generally true that the party winning a plurality of the national popular vote also receives a plurality of seats in the House of Commons, this is not always the case. In 1979, for example, the Liberals received 39.8 percent of the popular vote compared to only 35.6 percent for the Conservatives, yet the Conservatives won 136 seats compared to only 114 for the Liberals. Thus it is not the number of votes alone that counts but also the distribution of those votes across the 282 federal constituencies. In 1979 Liberal candidates ran up huge wins in Quebec, outpolling the Conservatives by a margin of over five to one. Yet in a sense such massive majorities are wasted in that a party is no farther ahead winning a constituency by 20,000 votes than it is winning by a single vote. While the Conservative share of the 1979 national popular vote was depressed by the massive Liberal victories in Quebec, Conservative candidates won seats in the much closer Ontario contests.

If winning parties tend to be overcompensated, other parties are disadvantaged by the simple plurality electoral system. In general terms, the parties that finish in second and third place receive a smaller proportion of seats than their share of the popular vote. Here again, however, the electoral effects depend upon the distribution of the vote. Parties with a broadly dispersed popular vote tend to fare more poorly than do parties whose vote is regionally concentrated. In the abstract, one can see that a party could win 10 percent or 20 percent of the vote in every constituency across the land without winning a single seat. The NDP, which runs candidates in every federal constituency no matter what the odds are of success, received 17 percent of the votes cast by Canadians between 1962 and 1984 but won only 8.8 percent of the seats in the House of Commons. Conversely, the Social Credit party received only 4.3 percent of the votes cast in the six general elections held between 1935 and 1957 and yet, because that vote was concentrated in Alberta, managed to capture 5.5 percent of the seats.

FIGURE 8.5

Percentage of Seats and Popular Vote Received by Winning Party in General Elections, 1867–1984

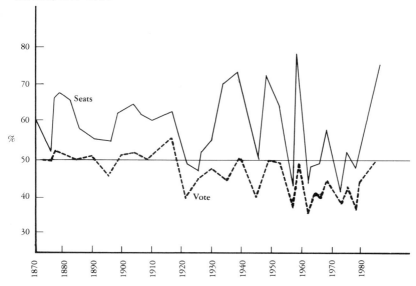

In most elections, the majority of people vote for *losing* parties and candidates. In the eight elections held between 1962 and 1980, 59.2 percent of Canadians voted for losing parties. In the West, the losers averaged 67.3 percent of the electorate compared to 57.2 percent in Ontario, 55.7 percent in Atlantic Canada and 55.1 percent in Quebec. (The high average in the West may not only have reflected western alienation but may also have been a contributing factor.) To take but one provincial example, in the twelve consecutive elections won by the Ontario Conservatives between 1943 and 1981, the party averaged only 43.3 percent of the popular vote. Here it is interesting to speculate whether the relative proportion of winners and losers is related to citizen support for and satisfaction with government, whether a system like the American presidential system which produces more winners than losers might also generate higher levels of citizen support and satisfaction. The fact that more people usually vote against rather than for the winning party should also make us wary of election assessments that begin with statements like "Newfoundlanders renew government's mandate" or "Canadians vote for change." What most people want is not what they get.

As Figure 8.5 has illustrated, minority governments in which the government party holds less than 50 percent of the seats are not uncommon; five of the last nine national governments have been minority governments. They are the consequence, but not the only possible consequence, of a multi-party system. In other countries with multi-party systems, coalition governments in which legislators from two or more parties hold cabinet portfolios are common. In Canada, however, coalition governments have not emerged at the federal level[17] and have been rare in provincial politics.[18] Minority governments behave in essentially the same manner as majority governments, though they may be more cautious and can expect a shorter life. All cabinet ministers come from the party with the plurality of seats.

The greatest concern with the Canadian electoral system stems from the fact that the regional composition of parliamentary parties often fails to reflect the regional composition of their popular vote. The party system may consequently exacerbate rather than moderate cleavages within the electorate, driving the country apart rather than pulling it together. This problem was first addressed in a landmark article by Alan Cairns,[19] and can be illustrated by a brief look at party fortunes during the Trudeau years.

The Trudeau years started well for the Liberal party in western Canada. After a severe drought under the leadership of Lester Pearson, the Liberals rebounded in 1968 to win twenty-seven seats and 37 percent of the popular vote across the region. In the ensuing four elections Liberal fortunes waned again as the party's share of the regional popular vote fell to 28 percent in 1972, rose slightly to 30 percent in 1974, and then fell to only 23 percent in 1979 and 1980. In terms of western seats the party did much worse; 30.7 percent of the regional popular vote across the five Trudeau elections yielded only 14.5 percent of the seats. In the 1980 election 23 percent of the regional popular vote yielded only two seats, or less than 3 percent of the regional total. As a consequence the essential two-way flow of communications between citizens and the government was twice disrupted; there were insufficient Liberal MPs from the West to carry regional input into the national government, and insufficient numbers of elected spokespeople to enable the government to communicate with the West. Western Canadians perceived the national government almost exclusively through the understandably jaundiced eyes of opposition MPs. In this respect, then, the electoral system contributed to western alienation.

The Conservatives faced a similar problem in Quebec. Although the Trudeau years were not fruitful ones for the Conservatives in Quebec, they did average 16.6 percent of the vote across the five elections. Yet this vote yielded only 3.2 percent of the Quebec seats, including just a single seat in 1980. If the Conservatives had won seats in proportion to their share of the popular vote, there is little question that the party would have been more sensitive to the concerns of Quebec and that the Liberals would not have been able to claim that they alone were the party of national unity. More Conservative seats would probably have produced more Conservative votes, just as a more proportionate share of western seats would have enhanced the Liberals' appeal in the West.

Such regional distortions weakened the national parties as vehicles of political integration. In observing the House of Commons in the late 1970s and early 1980s, it was easy to forget that there were Liberals by the hundreds of thousands in the West just as there were Conservatives by the hundreds of thousands in Quebec. In response to this situation, interest developed within the political science community in finding an electoral system that would generate parliamentary contingents which more faithfully reflected the party shares of the regional popular vote.[20] Given the national character of the government elected in 1984, and given the Conservatives' strength across the country, such interest will probably subside.

Organizational Characteristics of Canadian Political Parties

Both the Conservatives and Liberal parties find their roots in the organizational imperatives of parliamentary government. The conventions of responsible government required that a group of MPs coalesce under the leadership of a single individual—the prime minister—and that the group assume collective responsibility for the conduct of government. The adversarial format of the House of Commons forced a similar coalescence among those left out of the government coalition, as power on both sides of the House is wielded more effectively by groups than by individuals. While there is nothing to say that this legislative orchestration of MPs need produce party organizations that are stable over time, such evolution has invariably occurred across western political systems. In the decades after Confederation, the parliamentary caucuses—the MPs and Senators—*were* the national parties; they chose the party leaders and organized legislative activity in Ottawa. The "extra-parliamentary" parties consisted of little more than a loose assortment of financial backers, fund raisers, backroom advisors, and journalistic supporters unbound by any formal organizational structure. Away from Parliament Hill, the national parties were phantom organizations which came briefly to life during election campaigns and then quickly faded away. While partisanship was often pervasive and intense in local communities across Canada, there was no organizational infrastructure through which the local parts were knit into a coherent national whole.

As time progressed, the extra-parliamentary wings of the two parties came to acquire greater organizational coherence and stability. In 1919 in the case of the Liberals and 1927 in the case of the Conservatives the selection of the national party leader passed from the exclusive control of the parliamentary caucus to a national leadership convention in which MPs and Senators formed a small, albeit very influential, minority. The national parties began to acquire an organizational presence that continued between election campaigns. In 1932, for example, the National Liberal Federation was formed to provide some organizational coherence to the national party independent of that provided by the parliamentary caucus or by provincial Liberal parties. Constituency organizations became more stable, more formal in their organizational structure, and more extensive in their membership. If we consider only those individuals who occupy a formal executive position somewhere within the extra-parliamentary organizations of the three major federal parties, be it at the constituency, provincial, or national level, we are looking at close to 10,000 men and women. Thus, while the primary role of extra-parliamentary parties is still that of providing campaign support for the legislative parties, they have become significant political actors in their own right. This is particularly true for opposition parties.

Most of the third parties that have played upon the Canadian political stage have originated outside Parliament or the provincial legislative assemblies. Parties such as the CCF and the NDP, the Parti Québécois, the Alberta and British Columbia Social Credit parties, and the Quebec Créditistes emerged from strains in the broader social fabric and were at least initially characterized by relatively strong extra-parliamentary organizations. Even so, there have been no ready Canadian equivalents for some of the mass parties that have existed in western Europe, parties with formal memberships running into the millions and which provide a wide array of not only political but also recreational, educational, and social activities for their members. With the exception of small ideological organizations like the Communist Party, Canadian parties are first and foremost electoral organizations. Their memberships swell when election campaigns or leadership conventions are to be held, and shrink as such activity winds down. Relatively few members are required to keep the national, provincial, and constituency organizations ticking over until their services are called upon again for electoral combat, and thus we find that less than 5 percent of Canadian adults are active party members.[21]

On average, about 75 percent of Canadians vote in federal elections, a turnout that is relatively modest by international standards.[22] Other more visible and more demanding forms of political participation[23] are engaged in much less frequently. The 1979 Election Study found that with respect to federal politics 43 percent of the respondents said that they often read about politics in the newspapers, 25 percent that they often discussed politics with friends, 8 percent that they often tried to convince friends to vote as they did, 4 percent that they often attended political meetings or rallies, 3 percent that they actively campaigned on behalf of candidates, and 3 percent that they often tried to contact public officials or politicians.[24] (Findings at the provincial level were essentially identical.) In a parallel study of the 1974 campaign the same authors note that "the range of participation is wide—from the mere act of voting, which only 5 percent to 10 percent report *never* doing in federal and provincial elections respectively, to working in a campaign, which only 17 percent report *ever* doing at either level."[25] Overall, high rates of political participation tend to be associated with relatively high levels of income, formal education, and occupational prestige.

Who Is to Blame?

William Mishler argues that more could be done by the political parties to draw citizens into active participation:

"Part of the reason that citizens do not participate more extensively in political parties and campaigns may be that many are unaware of the opportunities that exist. Surveys indicate that greater numbers are willing to contribute both time and money, but have never been contacted by parties and candidates and asked to contribute. In Canada, as in the United States, political parties are poorly organized and highly inefficient in recruiting volunteer political activists."[26]

Mishler nonetheless concludes that "the structure of citizen participation in Canada is surprisingly wide and deep."[27]

Against this participatory backdrop we can sketch in a rough model of Canadian political parties. The apex is formed by the small handful of party members who hold elected *public* office. Such individuals make up a minute percentage of the total party membership, a percentage that is necessarily exaggerated in Figure 8.6. Below them comes a wider but still narrow band of individuals who hold an elected office within national or provincial party organizations, or within local constituency associations. Next comes a broader band of party members who do not at the time hold any formal party position but who attend party meetings, rallies, and conventions, and who participate in election campaigns by knocking on doors, giving or raising money, distributing literature, stuffing envelopes, and answering phones. The level of participation within this band, which embraces less than 10 percent of the electorate, can vary from those for whom politics is a major part of their lives to those who are formal but generally inactive party members.

A larger group than those who are formal party members are the citizens who have a strong partisan identification with one of the parties even though they do not belong formally to it. Such individuals think of themselves as Conservatives, Liberals, or New Democrats. They view political life through distinctly partisan spectacles, cheering on "their team" and suffering with it in defeat. They generally (though not always) vote for their party whenever the opportunity arises. In the 1974 Election Study, 28 percent of the respondents reported a strong federal party identification.[28] Another 40 percent reported a "fairly strong" party identification, and 18 percent reported a party identification that was "not very strong." Only 14 percent reported no partisan attachment whatsoever at the federal level.[29] It is probably among individuals with strong party identifications but without formal party memberships that we find the greatest overlap in the composition of federal and provincial parties sharing a common party label.

Political parties reach much further into the electorate than their limited formal memberships would suggest. Large numbers of Canadians have a very real emo-

FIGURE 8.6

The Party Hierarchy

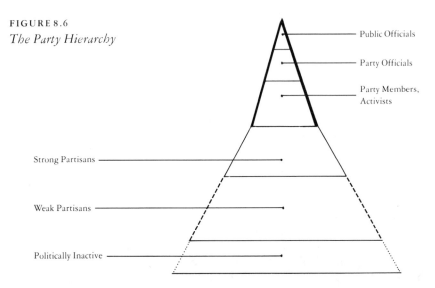

Public Officials

Party Officials

Party Members, Activists

Strong Partisans

Weak Partisans

Politically Inactive

tional stake in the party system even though they are not card-carrying Conservatives, Liberals, or New Democrats. However, as we move "down" through the layers of Figure 8.6, the parties become increasingly wraithlike. As partisanship weakens, so too does the general level of citizen involvement in political life. Thus, toward the bottom of Figure 8.6 we find those individuals who have not only a tenuous connection to the party system but are characterized by low levels of political participation and unstable electoral preferences.

The notion of partisanship is an important one in political science, bridging as it does the formal party organizations with the electoral behaviour of the vast majority of citizens who maintain no formal party ties.[30] Partisan identifications tend to be acquired early in life, to be relatively stable over time, and to have a significant impact on a wide range of political perceptions.[31] Partisanship is not the same as an individual's voting intention, for in any given election many voters, for a multitude of reasons, will abandon "their" party. Party identification is nonetheless the best predictor of voting behaviour. Strong partisans will stick by their party through hell or high water, believing that nothing could be worse than having the other team win. Weaker partisans are more likely to be swayed by the host of short-term factors at work in any election campaign.[32]

Partisanship enables us to make sense out of what can be a very complex and confusing political world. It does so by narrowing the range of political opinion to which we are exposed and to which we attribute some credibility. Partisanship thereby simplifies and, in so doing, invariably distorts a complex reality. This act of simplification is essential given that the great bulk of our time and energy will be quite properly devoted to non-political activities. In short, partisanship provides a chart and compass with which we can sail our own private ship through the turbulent waters of political life.

Like most other private organizations, political parties have an important social dimension. While many people join parties in pursuit of policy objectives, others are drawn into party affairs through friends, relations, and business associates, and for a variety of reasons that are more social than political. Brokerage parties in particular are held together less by a common set of principles than by the social bonds formed through the intense interpersonal relations characteristic of political activity. Political activity, in other words, can be socially rewarding in and of itself, quite apart from its instrumental value.

During his 1984 bid for the leadership of the federal Liberal party, Jean Chrétien was asked why he entered political life. His reply goes to the roots of party politics:

My dad got me the taste of politics as a game, as a sport. In some ways it was a kind of a hobby for him. He had strong convictions but he enjoyed politics as an activity, a social activity.[33]

Political parties differ from other private organizations, however, in that their overriding objective, their raison d'être, is to capture *public office*. Because they seek to do so through the ballot, which is a public rather than a private instrument, parties come under much closer public scrutiny than do most other private organizations. Scrutiny has become particularly intense with respect to the raising and expenditure of party funds.

The financing of political parties in general and of campaign expenditures in particular has been a matter of long-standing public concern. The basic fear has been that elections might be "bought" by those with the financial wherewithal to do so, and the electoral process thus distorted to the advantage of monied interests. Public concern was made more acute by the growing reliance of modern election campaigns on widespread advertising, extensive travel by party leaders, direct mailing appeals, and exhaustive public opinion polls, all of which cost dearly. The major federal legislative response to such concerns came with the 1974 Election Expenses Act, for which legislative counterparts now exist in most provinces.[34] The Act and its subsequent amendments regulate the campaign activities of registered political parties and their candidates. (To be registered through the office of the Chief Electoral Officer, parties must present candidates in at least fifty ridings.) A 1983 amendment—Bill C-169—forbids unregistered parties or other groups from advertising to promote or oppose a particular candidate or party without the permission of a registered party or candidate. If such advertising takes place, its cost must be included under the campaign expenditures of the candidate or party sanctioning the advertising.[35]

The Election Expenses Act imposes campaign spending limits on both national party organizations and local candidates. During the 1984 campaign the limits on national party organizations amounted to approximately forty cents for each voter in each constituency in which the party was running candidates, or approximately $6.5 million for the three major parties running full slates. Individual candidates were allowed to spend up to $1.30 for each of the first 15,000 names on the electoral list in their riding, plus $.65 each for the next 10,000 voters and $.33 for each voter thereafter. In 1984, the average candidate faced an expenditure ceiling of approximately $35,000. The Act controls advertising expenditures by prohibiting party advertising during the first twenty-two days of the campaign. It also requires each broadcast outlet to allocate six and a half hours for party advertising during the last four weeks of the campaign. This time is allocated to the parties by the Canadian Radio and Telecommunications Commission on the basis of the parties' shares of the popular vote during the last election. Finally, the Act requires public disclosure of the total funds raised by the parties and candidates, and the identification of all sources contributing more than $100. Registered parties must file an annual financial statement and a post-election financial statement with the Chief Electoral Officer. The statements reveal how much money was raised during the year, who it was raised from, and how much was spent. In 1983 the nine registered parties raised over $31 million from 233,700 individual and corporate sources making an average donation of $133.

Party Finance

In 1983 the national Progressive Conservative party raised more than $14 million from 117,716 individual and corporate sources. The average donation was approximately $120. The Liberals raised only $7.3 million from 42,338 sources, for an average donation of $172, while the NDP raised $8.6 million from 67,058 sources making an average donation of $128.

Other parties trailed well behind. The Communist Party of Canada raised $977,728 from 596 sources who gave, on average, $1,640 each. The Libertarian party raised $33,994 from 290 sup-

porters and the Social Credit party $54,808 from 467 sources, both receiving an average contribution of $117.

Only two people contributed to the Marxist–Leninist party, donating $2,565. The Rhinoceros party attracted a solitary donation of $100.

The largest corporate donation came from Canadian Pacific Ltd., which gave $51,958 to the Liberals and $51,407 to the Conservatives. The largest single donation came from a Calgary widow who gave $453,365 to the federal NDP.

Chief Electoral Officer, 1983 Annual Report.

The Election Expenses Act also provides three forms of public subsidy. First, the federal government now reimburses the parties for half of the advertising bill charged by private broadcasters. Second, candidates who receive 15 percent or more of the popular vote are entitled to a federal rebate on campaign expenses up to a maximum of approximately forty cents per voter in the candidate's constituency. In aggregate, this can amount to a hefty subsidy. For example, the 1,497 candidates in the 1980 election spent more than $15 million on their campaigns while the four largest parties spent an additional $11.5 million. When the campaign dust had settled, the candidates and parties received reimbursements totalling $11,780,000, or approximately 45 percent of their total expenditures.[36] Third, the Act encourages financial contributions to registered parties by providing tax credits. Seventy-five percent of donations up to $100 can be claimed as a tax credit when the donor computes his or her federal income tax the following year. Donations ranging from $100 to $500 qualify on a sliding scale, with a refund of 55 percent being paid for a donation of $500. Similar tax credits are available in most provinces for contributions to provincial parties.

The Costs of Democracy

The 1984 election was expected to cost Elections Canada approximately $95 million, up from $63 million in 1980 and $64 million in 1979. This amounts to $5.60 a voter in 1984.

The 1984 expenditures covered a variety of costs including the hiring of about 110,000 enumerators at approximately $200 each, $90 each for polling clerks in the country's 68,000 polling stations, salaries for returning officers (approximately $9,000 each) and deputy returning officers, between $5 million and $6 million to mail out cards informing voters where to vote, and an estimated $15–18 million rebate to the registered parties and their candidates to cover the federal contribution to campaign expenditures.

To get some handle on the total price tag, it is useful to consider the per capita cost. Given that federal elections occur about once every three years, the annual cost per voter works out to $1.85, or about the price of a beer or a package of cigarettes. From this perspective, the cost of democracy seems less than onerous. "Electoral machinery shifts into high gear," The Globe and Mail, National Edition, July 10, 1984, p. 5.

Although the Election Expenses Act and similar provincial legislation have opened up party financing to public scrutiny and have broadened the financial base of the parties, they have not reduced the cost of elections. Indeed, by making both public and private funds more readily available, they have enabled the parties to spend more rather than less. Spending limits have generally been set well above anticipated expenditures, and in neither the 1979 nor 1980 election did the major parties reach their limits.

Recently, increased attention has been paid to the gender composition of party organizations. Although women have been active in party organizations for most of this century, their participation was traditionally channelled through separate women's organizations parallel to and yet apart from the mainline party organization. The National Liberal Federation, for example, had three affiliated organizations—the Women's Liberal Federation of Canada (formed in 1928), the Young Liberal Federation, and the Canadian University Liberal Federation—which hived off their constituent groups from the main party.[37] Few women were chosen as major party candidates, except in ridings where a party was given no chance of winning and thus where male candidates were hard to find, and only a minuscule number were elected either to the House of Commons or to provincial legislatures. No Canadian prime minister, national party leader, or premier has been a woman, and no woman has led a provincial party that was a serious contender for provincial office.

In recent years, women have been playing a more active role within the mainline party organizations. In 1973 the WLFC was disbanded and replaced by the Women's Liberal Commission. The WLC is responsible to the women's caucus *within* the national party and is not an affiliated organization. In 1983 Iona Campagnolo was elected president of the Liberal Party of Canada. At the 1983 Conservative and 1984 Liberal leadership conventions women delegates were present in great numbers though there were no female candidates. In the 1984 election women's issues played a major role in the campaigns of all major parties, and more women than ever ran for the House of Commons. The three major parties ran 131 women among their 846 candidates, up from 70 in the 1980 campaign. This still meant, however, that only 15.5 percent of the major party candidates were women even though women constituted a majority of the electorate. The number of women candidates ranged from 65 New Democrats (23 percent) to 43 Liberals (15 percent) and only 23 (8 percent) Conservatives. Of the 282 MPs elected in 1984, 27 (just under 10 percent) were women. In the American election held two months later, 22 (or 5 percent) of the 435 members elected to the House of Representatives were women, as were two of the one hundred U.S. Senators.

Political parties are unlike other private organizations in a number of important ways. They extend more broadly and deeply into the Canadian society, if not through their formal memberships then at least through the partisan identifications held by most members of the electorate. Their financial affairs are subjected to extensive public regulation, and their expenditures are heavily subsidized by the public treasury. Their composition, be it in terms of gender, ethnicity, or regional residence, is seen as a legitimate matter of public concern and inquiry. Because they compete through a public ballot for the control of public office, parties are hybrid organizations, both quasi-private and quasi-public.

Parties, Interest Groups, and Public Opinion Polls

In a Canadian general election some twelve million voters go to the polls. They carry with them multitudinous concerns and interests, policy preferences and principles, inbred prejudices and partisan loyalties. Yet an election makes sense to us only when the twelve million individual voting decisions are aggregated into a *collective* decision. In part, this aggregation is achieved through the electoral system which reduces the individual decisions to 282 constituency decisions, and from the latter extracts a national government. But because elections are so central to democratic political life, we cannot help but look for some meaning in election outcomes beyond the composition of the next government. We cannot help but look for the *policy mandate* lying behind individual voting decisions.

In the mythology of democratic politics, elections provide an opportunity for citizens not only to *choose* their government but also to *instruct* it. In practice, elections rarely provide citizens with a meaningful vehicle through which to convey policy preferences to those who govern. If elections were to provide a policy mandate, there would first have to be meaningful policy differences among the parties with respect to those issues of concern to voters. Policy-oriented elections, however, are the exception rather than the rule in Canada. Engelmann, for one, argues that we have not "... had a truly policy-oriented campaign since 1911, when the Grits stood for reciprocity with the United States and the Tories for support of the imperial navy."[38] To the degree that parties do differ, they are likely to do so across an array of issues, thereby raising a second difficulty in determining the policy mandate of any given election. For example, I may vote for Party A because it supports my views on tax reform even though it does not support my views on Canadian–American relations. If successful, Party A may then interpret its victory as a mandate for its policy on Canadian–American relations but not on tax reform.

Take what may have been some of the policy concerns of a typical voter going into the 1984 federal election. She may have been particularly concerned about her own employment situation and that of her spouse, along with the employment prospects for her children. With the mortgage coming up for renewal, interest rates may have been a concern. She may have seen the election as the opportunity to advance a range of feminist concerns. She may have been concerned about the growing national debt without fully understanding, if anyone could, what should and could be done. She may have had a nagging irritation with policies already in place—bilingualism, the abolition of capital punishment—and a marginal interest in a range of new policy issues including pornography, acid rain, and aboriginal self-government. Behind all of these concerns may have lurked a growing fear of nuclear war and a growing mistrust of those who seek to preserve peace by building weapons of mass destruction. All of these concerns had to be reduced to a single "X" printed on a ballot, to a choice among parties which may not have addressed her concerns or may not have differed in any meaningful way, to an endorsation of a local candidate about whose views on these issues she knows nothing at all.

The authors of *The Absent Mandate* conclude that "the persistent failure of

major political parties to present voters with distinctive, well-defined policy plat-
forms turns the electoral process into more of a spectator sport for those who
enjoy political 'horseraces' than an exercise in informed citizen participation."[39]
Elections, however, do produce a clear policy mandate in one very important
sense. They give to the winner the right to articulate a mandate, to state what the
people meant to say when they elected their government. A new or returning
prime minister has been given the authority to give shape to the election mandate
in words and legislation. Admittedly, we have no way of knowing if the mandate
that emerges corresponds with what the voters were trying to say, but if the two
diverge too markedly the government can be expected to pay the price in the next
election.

While parties may be primarily instruments of governance rather than transmission belts for the flow of policy preferences from the electorate to the government, other transmission belts do exist. There are, for instance, a number of steps
that individuals can take on their own. They can write or phone their MP, their
MLA or the cabinet minister(s) responsible for the policy at issue. They can write
letters to the editor and phone in to radio talk shows. They can write to the
various departments of the federal and provincial governments that may be
involved. There are nonetheless very real limits on the ability of any individual to
move the policy process. What is generally called for is some form of collective
action, and it is here that organized interest groups come into play.

To illustrate the role of organized groups, let us look briefly at the case of
"saving the whales." As an individual I may be very concerned about the fate of
the whales, having watched them off the Pacific coast and listened to stereo
recordings of their songs. There is, however, little direct action that I can take on
their behalf. I could refuse to buy products containing whale components, but only
if I knew what such products were and only if they were for sale in Canada. I
cannot set forth from home to stop foreign whaling fleets, nor can I expect
individual letters sent to the governments of whaling nations to have much effect.
In short, as an individual I would be powerless were it not for the existence of
organized groups such as Greenpeace. Through Greenpeace I can lobby internationally for the protection of whales, sail small boats in front of the whaling fleets,
organize consumer boycotts, and raise concern for whales in newspapers and
magazines around the world. Greenpeace becomes my hired gun in the fight
against the whalers, and yet no more is demanded of me than the thirty seconds it
takes to write a small cheque. This very minimal form of individual participation,
when aggregated across thousands of individuals, provides the foundation for an
effective political organization.

Interest groups, of which Greenpeace is but one example, are private organizations which attempt to influence public officials and through them public policy,
rather than running candidates for office under their own label. While interest
groups may at times try to influence election outcomes by throwing their weight

behind candidates sympathetic to their cause, their primary activity takes place between elections and is directed toward cabinet and the government's bureaucratic arm rather than toward the political parties. Given the strictures of party discipline and the cabinet's dominance of the legislative process, interest groups expend relatively little energy lobbying backbench MPs and MLAs.

Most interest groups are stable organizations representing long-standing group interests within the society. Groups such as the Canadian Medical Association, the Canadian Manufacturers' Association, the Sierra Club, the Canadian Association of University Teachers, the Canadian Broadcasters Association, the Consumers' Association of Canada, the Canadian Federation of Agriculture, and the Canadian Hospital Association will remain in place no matter who wins a given election. These "institutionalized" groups are interested in protecting their access to government, and are thus unlikely to become embroiled in election campaigns that might fragment their membership base and disrupt that access.[40] Because they are as interested in the implementation of public policy as they are in its formulation, contacts with the federal and provincial bureaucracies are carefully nurtured. There are other "issue-oriented" interest groups, however, which may pursue a more active electoral role and which are less concerned with, though not indifferent to, their own organizational survival. At least in theory, their issues are capable of resolution and could potentially be removed from the nation's political agenda. Such issues might include the reinstatement of capital punishment, drought relief for sub-Sahara Africa, and free elections in Nicaragua.

While institutionalized groups generally pursue interests which are negotiable—one can have, for example, somewhat more or somewhat less consumer protection or tariff protection—"single-interest" groups often pursue non-negotiable interests. Right-to-life groups, for instance, will not settle for *fewer* abortions. In general, non-negotiable interests are much more difficult for the political system to handle than are issues for which compromises and tradeoffs can be struck. Here it should also be noted that we cannot assume that all "interests" within the society will find adequate expression through organized groups. Effective organization requires money, leadership skills, and organizational resources, none of which are evenly distributed throughout the population or across the multitude of interests potentially open to political mobilization. Thus interest group politics may extend the political influence of already powerful interests as much as it opens up the political arena to a wider array of competing interests.

While interest groups are important political actors, they are not exclusively or even primarily concerned with political activity. An organization like the Canadian Medical Association engages in a wide range of non-political activities including medical conferences, research support, group life insurance and travel assistance, legal advice, informational seminars, and professional education. As Paul Pross points out, for many groups political activity "... is a minor and unwelcome addition to more general concerns."[41] Individuals may also join interest groups for a variety of non-political reasons including social functions, access to charter airfares, and an interest in publications put out by the groups. Yet at some point interest groups will be involved in the political process, representing interests which their members share in common. This may take place through ongoing contact with federal and provincial bureaucrats, through cabinet presentations, briefs to task forces and royal commissions, letters of concern or support to cabinet ministers, and even media advertisements designed to increase public support for policies in line with the group's interests. Interest groups thus play an essential role in the communication of citizen policy preferences. If I wish to communicate with the government as an academic or as a supporter of whales, the Canadian Association of University Teachers and Greenpeace provide far more effective channels than does the ballot.

Interest groups keep governments informed about the opinion of *specific sectors* of the electorate. If, however, governments want to know the opinion of the public *at large* rather than the specific opinions of cattle ranchers, oil executives, academics, physicians, or manufacturers, they have at their disposal sophisticated public opinion polls which provide a more precise and less biased reading of the public mood than can be obtained through election results or party organizations. Thus polls provide another, albeit passive, instrument through which citizens can communicate their concerns to governments. Polling itself can assume many forms. Governments follow the routine polling by commercial firms, much of which we encounter in the daily press. They also commission a great deal of polling research, often "piggybacking" their questions onto omnibus commercial surveys. In whatever form, polls have become an indispensable tool for keeping governments abreast of the shifting currents of public opinion.

Public opinion polls have been subjected to a great deal of critical commentary. Even if we put aside questions about their accuracy, neutrality, and cost, serious concerns remain. To argue that polls report but do not shape opinion seems less tenable after the experience of the 1984 election campaign.[42] Polls have been accused of having a pernicious impact on campaigning, leading parties and candidates to do little more than echo what the public wants to hear. There is no question, however, that polls provide a powerful means by which governments can dissect the public mood. Thus the ambiguous policy mandate which can be discerned by reading the entrails of election results is supplemented and to a large degree replaced by an ongoing diagnosis of the citizen predispositions carried out through public opinion polls.

Ever Wonder Why No One Interviews You?

In a typical Gallup poll, approximately 1,000 respondents are interviewed. Given an adult Canadian population of some 17,000,000 persons, the odds of any one individual being interviewed are remote. If a Gallup survey was con-

Gable, *Regina Leader Post*. Reprinted in *Calgary Herald*, August 4, 1984

*ducted every month and an entirely dif-
ferent set of respondents used each
time, any given individual could expect
to be interviewed once in every 1,417
years!*

The odds of being picked as a

*respondent in any one survey are
approximately one in 17,000. The odds
of being picked in your lifetime, should
you live to be eighty, are approximately
one in 23.*

Given the role played by interest groups and opinion polls, it is clear that the
parties have been relegated to second place in conveying citizen policy preferences
to governments. Parties nonetheless continue to perform a number of essential
roles. They continue to structure the legislative process, providing reasonably
stable governments and a focused legislative opposition. They continue to recruit
political leaders. Most importantly, it is the parties which enable voters to hold
governments responsible for their actions. As Van Loon and Whittington point
out, "we can vote to 'throw the rascals out' because we can draw a line between
'rascals' and 'non-rascals'; the party labels provide us with this line."[43] Thus the
electoral process enables citizens to cast a retrospective judgment on government
performance. The fact that it does not enable citizens to direct or handcuff the
course of public policy seems of little consequence given that a profusion of
alternative policy instruments exists. If the party system is to be judged, it should
be with respect to its success or failure in holding the country together, in

moderating rather than exacerbating those conflicts which strain the national fabric.

Political Parties and Political Conflict

The preceding chapters have identified five principal axes of Canadian political life, axes which provide a useful framework for assessing Canadian parties and the party system. Chapter Five has already discussed how the party system has shaped, and has been shaped by, redistributive politics. Here we turn to a brief discussion of how the other four axes have shaped and have been shaped by party politics.

LANGUAGE POLITICS

In the early decades after Confederation, Macdonald's Conservative party formed the political bridge between Canada's two linguistic communities. Indeed, the Conservatives' initial dominance of national political life reflected the party's electoral success in both communities, just as the rise to power of the Laurier Liberals reflected the collapse of Macdonald's linguistic coalition. Speaking in 1904, Henri Bourassa described the vision of Canada that underlay the success of both the Macdonald Conservatives and the Laurier Liberals:

We work for the development of a Canadian patriotism which is in our eyes the best guaranty of the existence of the two races and of the mutual respect they owe each other.... The nation that we wish to see develop is the Canadian nation, composed of French Canadians and English Canadians, that is of two elements separated by language and religion ... but united in a feeling of brotherhood, in a common attachment to a common fatherland.[44]

The mutual respect and brotherhood of which Bourassa spoke were to be severely tested and found wanting in the conscription crisis of World War I, a crisis that for the first time excluded one of the linguistic communities from the national government.

Canada had gone into the First World War with a volunteer army and, prior to 1917, Robert Borden's Conservative government steadfastly maintained that conscription would not be introduced. However, by 1917 the unexpected and prolonged carnage of trench warfare had created a desperate manpower shortage. Efforts in the first part of that year to recruit additional volunteers were largely futile. In English Canada the manpower pool was all but exhausted, and in Quebec, where the recruiting drive produced only ninety-two volunteers, an earlier enthusiasm for a short European war had evaporated. As Armstrong explains:

... there could not have been any more striking illustration of the indifference and hostility of French Canada to the Dominion's war effort. The wholehearted enthusiasm of 1914 had turned to bitter mistrust and open opposition by the summer of 1917.[45]

The attempt to recruit French Canadian volunteers turned into a shambles as anglophone recruiters were sent into Quebec urging French Canadians to fight not for Canada but for England and France, an appeal that fell on deaf ears. Finally, the government introduced the Military Service Bill on June 11, 1917. The Bill's introduction was greeted by massive anti-conscription rallies across Quebec, and its proclamation on August 29 met with violence and riots in Montreal.

French Canadian opposition to conscription can be traced in part to the isolation of a small linguistic community, cut off from its European roots for 150 years and isolated further on a predominantly anglophone continent. It also reflected French Canadian anger over the limits placed on Ontario bilingual schools in 1915. Perhaps of greatest importance were the different forms of Canadian nationalism that emerged during the war. While involvement in the British war effort was an expression of Canadian nationalism for most English Canadians, the nationalist horizon of French Canadians stopped at Canadian shores. In the parliamentary debate on the Military Service Bill, "hardly a French Canadian spoke ... who did not insist that his compatriots felt deeply that the only country to which they owed loyalty and service was Canada and that to ask them to rush to the aid of France and England was asking a great deal too much."[46]

Conscription had a profound impact on both the Conservative and Liberal parties. In an attempt to broaden the political base of support for conscription, Borden formed a Union Government in October comprising thirteen Conservative ministers and ten pro-conscription Liberal ministers. The Union Government unquestionably served its purpose in English Canada, but it also isolated Quebec. The cabinet included only two weak French Canadian ministers and, in the December general election, only three Unionist candidates were elected in Quebec. Those Liberals who remained under the leadership of Wilfrid Laurier fought conscription and in so doing further strengthened the Liberal position in Quebec. Figure 8.7 illustrates the wedge that the 1917 election drove between the two major parties in Quebec. At the same time, Laurier's opposition to conscription caused a deep division within the Liberal party itself. Many English Canadian Liberal MPs crossed the floor of the House to support the Union government, and the party's electoral base in English Canada was severely damaged. *The 1917 conscription crisis witnessed the collapse of the party system as a vehicle of political integration across the linguistic divide.*

In the Second World War the conscription crisis was played out again, this time with Mackenzie King as prime minister. King, who had become leader of the Liberal party in 1919, was acutely aware of the damage to both his party and the national fabric caused by the conscription crisis of the First World War. Thus in a

FIGURE 8.7

Party Shares of the Quebec Popular Vote in Federal Elections

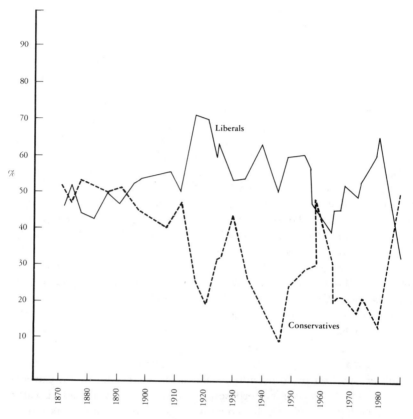

speech to the House of Commons shortly after the Second World War broke out, King promised that Canada's war effort would not entail conscription:

I wish to repeat the undertaking I gave in Parliament on behalf of the Government on March 30th last. The present Government believes that conscription of men for overseas service will not be a necessary or effective step. No such measure will be introduced by the present Administration.[47]

This was the bargain King presented to Quebec in the 1940 general election; Canada would pursue the war at Britain's side but not at the cost of conscription. The Liberals captured sixty-one of Quebec's sixty-five seats in that election, with three seats going to independent Liberals and only one to a Conservative candidate.

As the war dragged on, King's promise proved more and more difficult to keep, and the Liberal government began a series of incremental steps toward conscription. In a rare national plebiscite held in April 1942, King asked voters to release the government from its pledge not to impose conscription. The plebiscite, it should be stressed, was held on the government's pledge and not on conscription per se. The government's policy, King maintained, was "conscription if necessary but not necessarily conscription." The plebiscite quantified the sharp cleavage that existed on conscription: 72 percent of Quebecers voted "no" while 80 percent of those outside Quebec and a national majority overall voted "yes."[48] Conscription was subsequently introduced, but *not* for overseas service. By late 1944, the attrition of Canadian forces overseas and the government's inability to raise sufficient replacements through voluntary enlistment forced King to send conscripted men overseas. After five years of war and despite strenuous opposition from Quebec, conscription had again been imposed.

This time, however, the impact on the party system was less pronounced. In the 1945 general election the Liberals lost only eight Quebec seats while the nationalistic and anti-conscriptionist Bloc Populaire elected ten members. As Figure 8.7 shows, the Conservatives were devastated in Quebec, electing only one member with a meagre 8.4 percent of the vote in their worst showing ever. Although the Liberal government had eventually imposed conscription, Mackenzie King had clearly resisted doing so as long as possible. French Canadians who were nonetheless dissatisfied could hardly throw their support to the Conservatives, who had been much more supportive of conscription than had the Liberals, and to vote en masse for the Bloc Populaire was to risk Quebec's isolation from the national government. Thus the Liberals survived more or less intact in Quebec while the poor showing by the Conservatives was an extension of, rather than a significant change in, the political status quo. Even though the Liberals lost forty-eight seats outside Quebec and the Conservatives gained twenty-six, the Liberals retained both a seven-seat advantage over the Tories outside Quebec and a majority government. The country was not split along linguistic lines as it had been in 1917.

Following the war the Conservatives found themselves trapped within a vicious circle, or what George Perlin has called the "Tory Syndrome," in Quebec.[49] Because so few Conservatives were elected from Quebec, the party's parliamentary caucus lacked sufficient sensitivity to Quebec and French Canadian concerns. Because the party lacked such sensitivity, it tended to come down on the "wrong side" of whatever French–English conflicts arose, further damaging its electoral prospects in Quebec. Because the party did so poorly in Quebec, it could not compete on equal terms with the Liberals in federal elections. Successive national defeats led to self-perpetuating internal attacks on the party's leaders, attacks which undermined the party's credibility as an alternative government and thus further weakened its electoral support.

The syndrome was broken briefly in 1958 when Quebec voters, encouraged by the Union Nationale government, climbed aboard the Diefenbaker bandwagon and elected fifty Conservative MPs. The Quebec MPs, however, felt ill at ease within the predominantly anglophone Tory caucus. Nor were they a particularly able lot, and the performance of Tory cabinet ministers from Quebec left a great deal to be desired. For his part, Diefenbaker was unable to exploit the 1958 Conservative opening in Quebec. As George Grant explains,

the keystone of a Canadian nation is the French fact.... English-speaking Canadians who desire the survival of their nation have to co-operate with those who seek the continuance of Franco-American civilization. The failure of Diefenbaker to act on this maxim was his most tragic mistake.[50]

In 1962 only fourteen Quebec Tories were reelected, and in 1963 only eight.

While the Conservatives were mired in Quebec, the Liberals were making the province their own. In 1948 King retired and was replaced by Louis St. Laurent, the Liberals' second French Canadian leader. St. Laurent was replaced by Lester Pearson in 1957, who was in turn replaced by Pierre Trudeau in 1968. Trudeau was very popular in Quebec, and his leadership came to be identified with the bilingualism policies of the federal government. While those policies were initiated before Trudeau became prime minister and were endorsed by the opposition parties, they along with Trudeau provided a seemingly invincible Liberal fortress in Quebec. (When the Official Languages Act came to a vote, seventeen Conservative MPs, including John Diefenbaker, defied Robert Stanfield and voted against the legislation.) The party's strength in Quebec enabled the Liberals to argue that they alone could form a truly national government spanning the country's two linguistic communities. At a time when English Canadians were nervous about a growing separatist movement in Quebec, the Liberals' argument was a telling one.

During Trudeau's leadership, 47 percent of the Liberal seats *came* from Quebec and 84 percent of Quebec's seats *went* to the Liberal party. The party's near monopoly in Quebec gave it a virtual armlock on national power. In the 1972 general election the Conservatives elected more MPs than the Liberals in eight of the ten provinces, and tied with the Liberals in the ninth. Yet this was not enough to overcome the Liberal edge in Quebec, where the Liberals won fifty-six seats to only two for the Conservatives. Without a breakthrough in Quebec, the most that the Conservatives could hope for was a minority government, and even that eluded Robert Stanfield by two seats in 1972.

The Conservative resurgence in Quebec began with Joe Clark's leadership. Clark devoted more time and effort to Quebec than any Conservative leader had done before, and improved his own grasp of the French language to the point where he could campaign effectively in Quebec. Ironically, though, Clark's efforts bore no fruit whatever in the short run. In the 1979 general election, the Conservative share of the Quebec popular vote fell from 21.2 percent in 1974 to only 13.5 percent. In the 1980 election it fell again to 12.6 percent, and the Conservatives elected only one Quebec MP.[51] Yet Clark's efforts, in combination with the 1979 minority Conservative government and its 1980 defeat, drove home to Conservatives the necessity of a breakthrough in Quebec. The promise of that breakthrough was the major card played by Brian Mulroney in his successful 1983 bid for the leadership of the Conservative party.

Mulroney was the first Tory leader to come from Quebec, and the first central Canadian Conservative leader in twenty-seven years. Fluent in both official languages, he proved to be the standard-bearer so badly needed by the Conservative party in Quebec. In the 1984 campaign Mulroney's appeal coupled with the retirement of Pierre Trudeau, the defeat of Jean Chrétien's bid for the Liberal leadership, and a weariness in Quebec over a decade of confrontation between nationalists and federalists produced the long-awaited breakthrough as Tory candidates captured fifty-eight Quebec seats, a gain of fifty-seven from 1980.

Overall, and with the exception of the conscription crisis in the Second World War, the parties have been more affected by language-related conflict than they have shaped the resolution of such conflict. As Smith points out, the parties per se made at best a modest contribution to resolving the constitutional crisis posed by Quebec in the 1970s and early 1980s; Ottawa's response was a governmental response rather than one emerging from the Liberal party.[52] Prior to the 1984 election there was still some linguistic tension between the Liberal party, with seventy-four of the seventy-five Quebec MPs, and the Conservative party, which continued to house a small minority of MPs opposed to bilingualism. Since the 1984 election that tension has shifted to within the Conservative caucus, where it is less likely to affect competition among the parties. With both the Conservative and Liberal parties now competitive in Quebec, with the constitutional entrenchment of official bilingualism, and with some apparent moderation of language legislation in Quebec, conditions are such that linguistic conflict can be expected to slip down, though not off, the nation's political agenda.

REGIONAL POLITICS

Although the emergence of national political parties has been associated with the decline of territorial conflict in many western countries,[53] this association has been less apparent in Canada. The history of protest parties in western Canada and the contemporary collapse of the Liberal party in the region suggest that the party system has been an imperfect vehicle of national political integration. Whether the parties have contributed to regional conflict or whether they have been impaled upon it is more difficult to determine.

Figure 8.8 traces out the regional composition of the Liberal and Conservative

FIGURE 8.8

Regional Composition of the Party Vote

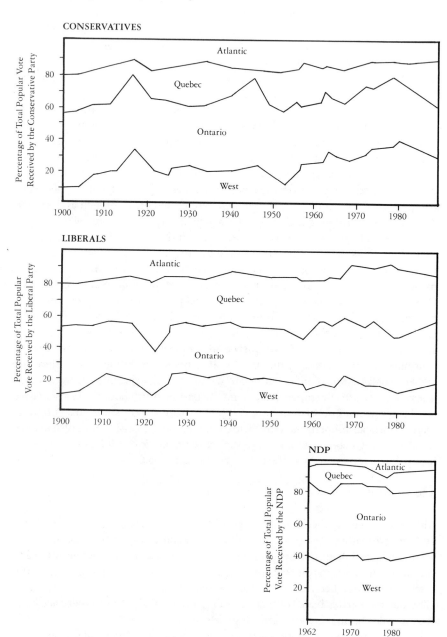

electoral coalitions from the turn of the century, and of the NDP coalition from 1962. As discussed in more detail above, the contribution of Quebec voters varies considerably across the three parties. While traditionally a core component of the Liberal coalition, they have constituted a more erratic component of the Conservative coalition and a negligible part of the NDP coalition.

If we turn to voters from Atlantic Canada, Figure 8.8 shows a modest but generally progressive decline in their contribution to the Conservative and Liberal coalitions. It is not, however, that Atlantic voters are turning away from the two parties, as the figure shows no migration to the NDP, but rather that they constitute a declining share of the national electorate. There is nothing in Figure 8.8 to suggest that the regional interests of Atlantic Canadians have found clear champions or opponents within the national party system. With the exception of very modest NDP support, Rawlyk and Brown's discussion of the region in the 1870s applies with equal force to the subsequent century:

Throughout the region the disintegration of any political movement which did not correspond to the sole Canadian cleavage of Liberal and Conservative signified the complete political integration of the Maritimes into Canada ... there would be no significant attempts to channel regional protest outside the traditional two-party system.[54]

Figure 8.8 shows that all three parties draw a major portion of their vote from Ontario, as we might expect given Ontario's share of the national population. It is nonetheless interesting to note that it is the NDP which draws the largest share of its vote from Ontario. Across the nine elections from 1962 to 1984, 43.0 percent of the total NDP vote compared to 38.1 percent of the Conservative and 36.9 percent of the Liberal vote came from Ontario, a finding that reflects the electoral weakness of the NDP east of the Ontario–Quebec border. It is also interesting to note that Ontario's contribution to the total Conservative vote has declined over time. In the twelve elections held between 1900 and 1945, the Conservatives drew almost 46 percent of their total vote from Ontario. In post-war elections that share fell to just under 40 percent. In 1984 the Tory resurgence in Quebec dropped Ontario's contribution to only 33 percent.

The Diefenbaker elections of 1957 and 1958 initiated a pronounced westward shift in the Conservative party's centre of gravity and an offsetting, though less pronounced, eastward shift for the Liberal party. The modest 1984 Liberal revival in the West suggested by Figure 8.8 is deceptive, for the "revival" is an artifact of the Liberal collapse in Quebec. In the 1984 election, Liberal candidates in the West captured only 16.3 percent of the regional popular vote, *down* from 23.4 percent in 1980. In all four western provinces, the Liberal party finished third. It is thus somewhat ironic that the Liberals emerged from the 1984 election with a party leader representing a Vancouver riding.

Overall, Figure 8.8 suggests a party system that has been reasonably stable in its regional composition, though there are two important qualifications to any such conclusion. The first is that a somewhat more erratic picture emerges if we look at the regional distribution of party *seats* rather than *votes*. The difference can be illustrated by a comparison of the regional composition of the Conservative popular vote, shown in Figure 8.8, and the regional composition of Conservative seats in the House of Commons, shown in Figure 8.9. The latter figure brings Ontario's pre-Diefenbaker dominance of the party into bold relief. The patterns revealed in Figure 8.8 are amplified in Figure 8.9. The Conservatives' historical weakness in Quebec is more dramatic, as are the regional shifts that occurred in 1984 and following the Diefenbaker sweep in 1958.

The second qualification is that Figure 8.8 does not capture the host of protest parties that have arisen in western Canada since 1921. Certainly it can be argued that parties such as the Progressives, the United Farmers of Alberta, the CCF, the Social Credit, and the Western Canada Concept constitute an indictment of the party system's inability to integrate the West into the Canadian political mainstream. As Smith notes, such parties have been carriers of skepticism toward the national community since 1921.[55] It can also be argued that the western penchant for third parties was more than a reflection of western alienation, that it also contributed to alienation by choking off western input into the only parties to form national governments. If western Canadians have elected MPs to protest rather than to govern, then to a degree they have been architects of their own misfortune.

In recent decades idiosyncratic western parties of any significance have all but disappeared from the federal scene.[56] Thus in more contemporary terms, the regional "failure" of the party system boils down to the inability of the Liberal party to win seats in the West while at the same time forming the national government for all but nine months between 1963 and 1984. As David Smith explains, the party

succeeded in becoming identified with the promotion of a dualism as old as Canada and an array of interests rooted in the heartland of the St. Lawrence. In the bargain, it lost the support of a region which under Laurier had become for the world synonymous with Canada and which had acted as one of the two pillars of Canadian liberalism in the first half of the century.[57]

It was nonetheless the exclusion of the West from the national *government* that lay at the root of western alienation. In this sense, the unabated Liberal weakness in the 1984 election is of less consequence given that the Conservatives and not the Liberals won nationally. The West is now very much a part of the government coalition, and thus the stage for regional conflict shifts from parliamentary battles between Liberal governments and their Conservative and NDP opponents to within the parliamentary caucus of the national Conservative party.

FIGURE 8.9

Regional Distribution of Conservative Seats in the House of Commons

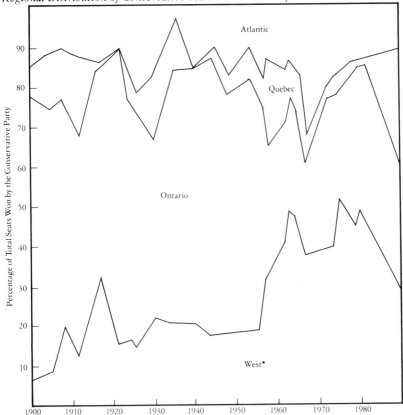

*Including Yukon and Northwest Territories.

CANADIAN–AMERICAN RELATIONS

Canada's economic relationship with the United States played a central role in the 1891 and 1911 general elections, and the military relationship between the two countries played a significant if less central role in 1963. Apart from these instances, Canadian–American relations have played a rather peripheral role in federal elections. In recent campaigns, more attention has been paid to the tone than to the substance of the relationship.

In 1891 Sir John A. Macdonald's Conservative government appeared on the brink of collapse. Macdonald himself was ailing, the country had been unable to shake a prolonged economic depression, and the government was plagued by scandal and the acrimonious Manitoba Schools dispute. The Liberal opposition moved to the attack with a proposal for *unrestricted reciprocity* with the United States,[58] and in so doing handed Macdonald the issue that was to save the Conservative government. Reciprocity, Macdonald argued, would reduce the national government's revenues and necessitate an annual per capita tax of $15 to make up for the loss. More importantly, Macdonald portrayed reciprocity as a threat to Canada's British ties and to the very survival of Canada. He accused the Liberals of "veiled treason which attempts by sordid means and mercenary proffers to lure our people from their allegiance."[59] There was, he concluded, "... a deliberate conspiracy by force, by fraud or by both to force Canada into the American union."[60] This was strong language indeed, and was reinforced by Macdonald's ringing statement that "a British subject I was born, and a British subject I shall die."

The campaign engaged the country's major economic interests. The farming community endorsed reciprocity while transportation, financial, and manufacturing interests opposed it, the latter carrying more weight in the campaign. Of greatest importance, however, were the emotional loyalties brought into play. In Quebec, the Conservative party argued that reciprocity would launch French Canadians down the slippery slope to absorption into American secular materialism. In the Maritimes, the threat to the British connection was emphasized. The *Halifax Morning Herald*, planting the Red Ensign on its masthead for the duration of the campaign, proclaimed that the Canadian people were being brought to a parting of the ways: would they choose to be bound in vassalage to their foreign foes—the Americans—or to continue to prosper as part of the greatest empire the world had ever seen?[61] Under the emotional barrage of Macdonald's campaign, the Liberals and the reciprocity proposal went down to defeat.

In 1911 the Liberals, now in power, once again ventured into the reciprocity thicket. In January 1911, a reciprocity agreement had been reached between Canada and the United States, and had been approved by the American Congress. Prime Minister Wilfrid Laurier, however, decided to go to the people in a general election before seeking Parliament's approval of the agreement. Again the farming community supported reciprocity, and again it was opposed by the major transportation, financial, and manufacturing interests. As in 1891, the economic debate was soon obscured by an emotional debate over the future of Canada. The Conservatives campaigned on "No Truck Nor Trade with the Yankees," a slogan coined in the advertising department of a wholly-owned American subsidiary.[62] Premier McBride of British Columbia summed up the emotional stakes with a simple placard superimposing "Which?" over pictures of the Union Jack and the Stars and Stripes. The Liberals again had the wrong emotional end of the issue, and the reciprocity proposal led to their electoral defeat. Both the 1891 and 1911 campaigns demonstrated that the Canadian–American relationship could engage deeply-felt emotions and national insecurities. Twice burned, the Liberals were never again to inject proposals for free trade into federal campaigns. When

Canadian–American relations entered the 1963 campaign, the focus was upon Canada's military relationship with the United States.

During its term of office, John Diefenbaker's Conservative government had purchased a considerable stock of military hardware that required tactical nuclear warheads to be effective. By early 1963, however, warheads had not yet been acquired and the cabinet, badly split on the issue, vacillated on whether or not to proceed with their acquisition. The government's indecision was openly criticized by the American government and was made a central issue in the 1963 general election campaign by the Liberal opposition. The Liberal leader, Lester Pearson, argued that Canada must acquire nuclear weapons to fulfill its alliance commitment to the United States and NATO. The Conservatives remained divided on the issue, and it is likely that the government's internal disarray hurt it as much at the polls as did Diefenbaker's opposition to nuclear weapons. George Grant argues that Diefenbaker faced the "full power of the Canadian ruling class, the American government and the military," and that in the unequal contest Canadian nationalism was dealt a lethal blow.[63] In any event, the minority Conservative government went down to defeat, to be replaced by a minority Liberal government.

Since 1963, the substance of Canadian–American relations has rarely intruded into federal election campaigns. In their extensive analysis of issue-voting in Canadian elections, the authors of *The Absent Mandate* conclude that debate over important Canadian–American issues in the 1970s "... occurred outside the electoral arena, as did any conflict resolution."[64] To the extent that Canadian–American relations have played a significant role, the focus has been on the tone rather than on the substance of the relationship. Thus in the 1984 campaign the Conservatives called for an improved and friendlier relationship without specifying what an altered relationship might entail.

Among the federal parties, the NDP has staked out the clearest position on Canadian–American relations, a position falling to the nationalist end of the continuum. Historically, the Liberal party has been most closely associated with continentalism, though more recent Liberal governments have been the architects of the nationalist policies embedded within the Foreign Investment Review Agency and the National Energy Program. Under Diefenbaker's leadership the Conservative party fell toward the nationalist end of the continuum, whereas under Mulroney's leadership the party has endorsed closer economic ties with the United States. No party, however, has sought to move Canadian–American relations toward the top of the electoral agenda. Perhaps past experience has shown that the emotions which can be released carry too great a political risk.

INTERGOVERNMENTAL RELATIONS

In the complex world of federal–provincial relations, conflict among governments has often been overlaid with partisan conflict. The first meeting of provincial premiers, held in 1887, was called by the predominantly Liberal premiers to orchestrate a partisan attack on the then Conservative national government. As the Depression descended in 1930, Prime Minister King declared in the House of Commons that his government would not give a nickel in federal relief to provincial governments controlled by Conservative administrations. During the latter part of the Trudeau era, when the Liberals controlled the national government while all ten provincial governments were in non-Liberal hands, intergovernmental conflicts frequently took on a partisan air. Certainly the energy conflicts between the government of Canada on one side and the governments of Alberta and Newfoundland on the other appeared to be sharpened by the partisan conflict between federal Liberals and provincial Conservatives.

Despite such examples, there is a general consensus within the political science literature that partisanship plays at most a very modest role in the bargaining positions and outcomes of federal–provincial negotiations,[65] that it affects the tone more than the substance of intergovernmental relations. This consensus has been pulled together by Donald Smiley, who notes that political parties "… appear to be of diminishing importance in the aggregation and articulation of citizen interests and the conversion of these into public policy."[66] While this diminished importance is a general phenomenon, it has been particularly evident in federal–provincial relations. In First Ministers' Conferences, Smiley argues, cleavages "… are on axes other than partisan ones: between 'have' and 'have-not' provinces; between governments which put an urgent priority on bilingual and bicultural matters and those which do not; between Quebec and other jurisdictions; between the heartland of Ontario and Quebec and the peripheral provinces."[67] The provinces have enduring characteristics including their size, wealth, resource base, and regional location which persist no matter which party forms the provincial government, and which are of primary importance in shaping intergovernmental relations. Partisanship may influence the tone of and strategy employed in such relations, but the substance will be dominated by relatively immutable provincial interests and concerns.

In federal states, political parties have a potentially important role to play in the operation of the federal system. Highly centralized party systems, in which the national parties dominate those in the states or provinces, may centralize the federal system far beyond what we might expect from the constitutional framework by acting as a solvent on the constitutional division of powers.[68] In the Canadian case, however, the party system has if anything reinforced the division of powers. In part, this reinforcement stems from an asymmetrical party system featuring quite different dominant parties at the federal and provincial levels. This very asymmetry precludes political parties serving as effective bridges across the constitutional division of powers and among the governmental actors in executive federalism. It also contributes to the lack of career mobility across the levels of the federal system (see below). The situation which arose after the 1984 election, in which the same party was in power both nationally and in seven of the ten provinces, has not been typical of the Canadian experience.

Career Paths

Relatively few politicians move from provincial to federal politics. Of the MPs elected in 1980, only 11.7 percent had ever run for provincial office, only 6.4 percent had done so successfully, and only 2.8 percent had served in a provincial cabinet before being elected to the House of Commons. No premier has become prime minister of Canada, though a few, including Ontario's George Drew, Nova Scotia's Robert Stanfield and Manitoba's John Bracken, have gone on to lead national parties. Recent prime ministers including Brian Mulroney, John Turner, Pierre Trudeau, and Lester Pearson have had no background whatsoever in provincial legislative politics.

This lack of career mobility stems in part from the asymmetrical party system. Successful Social Credit members in British Columbia or Parti Québécois members in Quebec, for example, have no federal option. In the case of provincial premiers, mobility is impaired by the long and relatively secure tenure enjoyed by many premiers; by the limited turnover among federal party leaders; and by the fact that most premiers enjoy more clout, more opportunity to leave their mark on public life, and even a higher profile in national *politics than do virtually all MPs apart from party*

leaders.

The lack of mobility has important consequences for intergovernmental relations. Most federal MPs, cabinet ministers, and party leaders lack the sensitivity to provincial concerns that might have come from provincial legislative experience. There is a tendency for federal and provincial politicians to see one another as a very different breed of political animal, with MPs seeing their provincial counterparts as those who choose to restrict themselves to the narrow horizons of provincial life while provincial legislators tend to see their federal counterparts as those who have lost touch with, if not abandoned, their provincial roots. Because most provincial cabinet ministers lack federal ambitions, they may be more receptive to the transfer of power from Ottawa to the provinces than they would be if their ultimate goal was to serve with the national government. Greater mobility, such as exists within the United States, could provide a useful lubricant to federal–provincial relations. Instead, as Smiley concludes, "so far as federal–provincial relations are concerned, cabinet ministers deal with one another in the absence of either personal experience or ambition at the other level of government."[69]

The impression should not be left that intergovernmental relations are completely divorced from party politics. The atmosphere within which intergovernmental relations are conducted can be affected by the partisan mix of governments and first ministers. "Ottawa-bashing" can often play an important role in provincial election campaigns as government parties wage electoral combat with the federal government rather than with provincial opponents. Federal–provincial relations can also enter national campaigns, as they did in 1979 and 1980 when Pierre Trudeau offered his leadership as the country's best defence against voracious provincial premiers, and in 1984 when both Brian Mulroney and John Turner pledged that their administrations would bring renewed harmony to federal–provincial relations. Nonetheless, party influences operate primarily at the margins of intergovernmental relations, acting more as a lubricant or grit within intergovernmental machinery that is driven by an array of forces largely removed from the partisan arena.

Political Parties and Political Leadership

Writing in 1975, John Meisel argued that "in the absence of national and nationalizing nonpolitical institutions ... parties and the party system have become important factors in nation building and in the evolution and preservation of national unity."[70] Although the parties have not had an unblemished record as vehicles of national integration, they have generally pursued brokerage strategies designed to knit together the often disparate elements of the Canadian political community. In such strategies party leaders have played a pivotal role. Indeed, one could argue that a campaign focus on leaders and leadership, rather than upon issues and ideology, constitutes the basic feature of Canadian brokerage politics.

One of the outstanding characteristics of Canadian party leaders has been their longevity. Premier Joey Smallwood of Newfoundland was in power for over twenty years, Premier W.A.C. Bennett of British Columbia for twenty years, Premier Ernest Manning of Alberta for twenty-five years, and Premiers William Davis of Ontario and Richard Hatfield of New Brunswick for fourteen years. Federal leaders have served for equally long periods. Macdonald led his Conservative party into Confederation in 1867 and remained at its helm until his death in 1891. Laurier led his party for over thirty years and was prime minister for fifteen of those years. Mackenzie King was leader of the Liberal party for twenty-nine years, and was prime minister for twenty-one. Pierre Trudeau led his party from 1968 to 1984, during which time he was prime minister for all but nine months.

Leaders at both the provincial and federal level have left an indelible mark on the political life of this country. It is difficult to imagine, for example, Newfoundland politics without Joey Smallwood, Quebec politics without Maurice Duplessis and René Lévesque, Saskatchewan politics without Tommy Douglas, Alberta politics without Ernest Manning and Peter Lougheed, or British Columbia politics without W.A.C. Bennett and William Bennett, his son. At the national level, leaders such as Macdonald, Laurier, Diefenbaker, and Trudeau did more than ride the political currents of their times. They shaped their political environment as much as they took shape from it. The 1984 general election provides a more contemporary example of the central role leaders play in the political process. Both the Conservative and Liberal campaigns were built around the national leaders, with emphasis being placed on such qualities as confidence, trust, and competence.

Phrases like "the Macdonald era," "the Trudeau years" and the "Mulroney Conservatives" capture the central role that leaders have played in the life of both their party and nation. Given this importance, the constitutional framework of the Canadian state does not coincide with political reality. Although voters in the 1984 campaign were urged to "vote for John Turner," only the voters in Vancouver Quadra in fact had the opportunity to do so, just as only the voters in Manicouagan had the opportunity to vote directly for Brian Mulroney. Although party leaders tend to dominate both federal and provincial campaigns, the format of the ballot restricts voters to a choice among local candidates. Nor is the public at large involved in the selection of party leaders in the first place. While the national conventions that selected Brian Mulroney in 1983 and John Turner in 1984 were each attended by three to four thousand party members, those in attendance constituted a minuscule proportion of the national electorate. In a somewhat contradictory fashion, the constitutional framework fails to recognize the central role of party leaders while at the same time the parliamentary concentration of power in the hands of the political executive contributes so much to the power leaders wield, and to their ability to shape the political landscape.

Consensus as to the importance of leaders should not imply any consensus on what distinguishes good leadership from bad. Canadians may hold quite contradictory leadership expectations, as Ron Graham illustrates in his 1983 comparison of the public's reaction to Joe Clark and Pierre Trudeau.

For seven years Clark had suffered in comparison with Pierre Trudeau, although most agreed that Clark was a better human being, more sympathetic, more dedicated, more open-minded, perhaps more complex and courageous. But Trudeau was what Canadians really wanted to be—intellectual, suave, worldly, independent, and unpredictable—while Clark was what they feared they were—earnest, nice, competent, unimaginative, honest and rather dull.... Joe Clark wasn't good enough. They wanted to be something greater.[71]

In democratic countries there is a special tension to leadership expectations. Leaders are expected to lead and yet to follow the people, to rise above the narrow views of the electorate while remaining its servant.

Canada has experienced leaders who have been charismatic in character, who have risen above the confines of party politics to capture, if only momentarily, a national vision that touched not only the minds but also the hearts of the electorate. There is little question that René Lévesque accomplished this in Quebec, just as John Diefenbaker and Pierre Trudeau were able to do in the 1958 and 1968 campaigns. Yet it should also be noted that some of Canada's most successful leaders have been marked by a very different political style. For example, although few political commentators described Ontario's Premier Bill Davis as a charismatic leader, his low-keyed search for the middle ground was coupled with daunting electoral success.

Canada's most famous example of successful non-charismatic leadership is provided by William Lyon Mackenzie King. Although often defeated himself at the polls (as a consequence King represented ridings in Ontario, Saskatchewan, and Atlantic Canada), King led his party to victory in 1921, narrowly lost to the Conservatives yet clung to power in 1925, won in 1926, lost in 1930, and then piled up impressive wins for the federal Liberals in 1935, 1940, and 1945. King was cautious in the extreme, arguing that "... in the course of human history far more has been accomplished for the welfare and progress of mankind in preventing bad actions than in doing good ones."[72] As Wearing notes, King was not devoid of principles, but he "... was not one to let his ideals lead him into precipitate action."[73] A poor speaker who lacked both friends and a commanding presence, King has been widely and harshly criticized. F.R. Scott, who was closely associated with the CCF during King's leadership of the Liberal party, summed up King's style in a poem, "W.L.M.K.," written shortly after King's death:

He blunted us.

We had no shape
Because he never took sides,
And no sides
Because he never allowed them to take shape.

He skilfully avoided what was wrong
Without saying what was right,
And never let his on the one hand
Know what his on the other hand was doing....

He seemed to be in the centre
Because we had no centre,
No vision
To pierce the smokescreen of his politics.

Truly he will be remembered
Whenever men honour ingenuity,
Ambiguity, inactivity, and political longevity.[74]

Whitaker describes King's government as "the defender of the people against the big interests and the defender of the big interests against the people."[75]

Nonetheless, King has a legitimate claim to being Canada's most successful prime minister. His party enjoyed significant electoral support across the country, including both the prairie West and Quebec. In the seven national elections in which King was leader, the Liberals won 913 seats compared to only 541 for their Conservative opponents. He reinforced the Liberal base in Quebec, even though he himself was unilingual, while maintaining a solid electoral base in English Canada. He steered the country through the Second World War, during which Canada's impressive military contribution abroad was combined with economic growth and, compared to the First World War, political tranquility at home. His career stands as a monument to political craftsmanship. He may not have lifted the hearts and souls of Canadians, but the party he led commanded their electoral support.

In contemporary electoral politics, the party leader is so central to the campaign, so much the focus of media coverage and campaign advertising, that the party and leader have almost fused into a single entity.[76] The importance of the leader, however, extends well beyond the electoral process. As the late Walter Young noted, the contemporary importance of leadership is a response to the growth of government:

Instead of the vast and faceless bureaucracy, there is a prime minister who speaks for and to the nation. At a time when the engine of the state at both the federal and provincial levels is large and complicated, the existence of a single individual as the functioning head of the apparatus provides credibility and a much needed focus. The need for such a figure increases with the growth of the machine, and the power of such a figure increases accordingly.[77]

Leaders help personify the political system, and thus provide us with handles on a reality which might otherwise be overwhelming in its complexity.

Suggested Readings

1 Ivan Avakumovic, *The Communist Party in Canada: A History* (Toronto: McClelland and Stewart, 1975); and *Socialism in Canada: A Study of the CCF–NDP in Federal and Provincial Politics* (Toronto: McClelland and Stewart, 1978).

2 For informative and highly readable snapshots of the general elections held between 1867 and 1968, see J.M. Beck, *Pendulum of Power: Canada's Federal Elections* (Scarborough: Prentice-Hall, 1968).

3 William Christian and Colin Campbell, *Political Parties and Ideologies in Canada*, 2nd ed. (Toronto: McGraw-Hill Ryerson, 1983).

4 Harold D. Clarke, Jane Jenson, Lawrence LeDuc, and Jon H. Pammett, *Political Choice in Canada* (Toronto: McGraw-Hill Ryerson, 1979); and *Absent Mandate: The Politics of Discontent in Canada* (Toronto: Gage, 1984).

5 Frederick C. Engelmann and Mildred A. Schwartz, *Canadian Political Parties: Origin, Character, Impact* (Scarborough: Prentice-Hall, 1975).

6 Patrick Martin, Alan Gregg, and George Perlin, *Contenders: The Tory Quest for Power* (Scarborough: Prentice-Hall, 1983).

7 Christina McCall-Newman, *Grits: An Intimate Portrait of the Liberal Party* (Toronto: Macmillan, 1982).

8 William Mishler, *Political Participation in Canada* (Toronto: Macmillan, 1979).

9 Paul Pross, ed., *Pressure Group Behavior in Canadian Politics* (Toronto: McGraw-Hill Ryerson, 1975).

10 Jeffrey Simpson, *Discipline of Power: The Conservative Interlude and the Liberal Restoration* (Toronto: Personal Library, 1980).

11 Hugh G. Thorburn, ed., *Party Politics in Canada*, 5th ed. (Scarborough: Prentice-Hall, 1984).

12 Conrad Winn and John McMenemy, *Political Parties in Canada* (Toronto: McGraw-Hill Ryerson, 1976).

13 Walter D. Young, *The Anatomy of a Party: The National CCF, 1932–1961* (Toronto: University of Toronto Press, 1969).

Study Questions

1 To get a grip on the concepts of partisanship and party identification, ask yourself the following questions. Do you find that you have an emotional loyalty to one party rather than another, that you tend to identify with one particular partisan camp? If so, has your identification always been with one party, or has it changed over time? If it has changed, how would you account for the change? Do you identify with the same or different parties in federal and provincial politics? Which level of government commands the strongest partisan loyalties in your case? Can you identify the partisanship of your parents? How evident were partisan affiliations in your environment when you were growing up? Is your own partisanship in line with, or at odds with, that of your parents?

2 Divide a piece of paper into three columns, labelling the first Conservative–Liberal, the second Conservative–NDP, and the third Liberal–NDP. Now jot down, in the appropriate column, those aspects of public policy for which you feel significant party differences exist. How many differences can you identify? Which two parties are the most clearly distinguishable, and which two are the least so?

3 If the national government were to change hands overnight, what difference would you expect the change to make for yourself and people like you? Jot down any significant differences on a piece of paper. Now pose the same question for your

provincial government; what changes would you expect if the government were to change hands? In examining your answers, determine the policy significance of election outcomes for people such as yourself.

CHAPTER NINE

Conclusions

The issues addressed in this text have been perennial features of the Canadian political landscape, and they are unlikely to fade from view in the foreseeable future. At the same time, it is essential to be alert for the emergence of new political cleavages which, over time, could come to rival though not supplant those discussed in the preceding chapters.

Some of these cleavages have already established themselves on the nation's political agenda. The 1984 federal election campaign brought gender politics to the fore. As the demographic structure of the population changes over time, as the proportion of Canadians who are elderly continues to grow and the proportion in the labour force continues to shrink, redistributive conflict across generations may emerge. The continuing quest by aboriginal Canadians for a fundamental redefinition of their relationship with the Canadian state will test the political system's capacity for institutional accommodation and innovation. Social concerns with pornography, racial discrimination, and the handicapped may move up the political agenda. The development of natural resources in the North, coupled with the evolution of new political institutions in the region, promises to provide daunting challenges for the political system. And, as a country that has always been exposed to the international environment, Canada will continue to be buffeted by changes in international trade, by the problems of development in the Third World, and by the continuing threat of international conflict.

Here it is interesting to note the neoconservative current that appears to be flowing through Canada's closest neighbours, the United States and Britain. The central ideological thrust of neoconservatism—the emphasis on a reduced role for government in the economic and social orders—runs counter to the activist state that has been used to address many of the political issues discussed in this text. For example, nationalist attempts to restrict American intrusions into the Cana-

"I say, Roger . . . do we look to the new year in trepidation, or as a challenge to the enduring spirit of man, or simply let the universe unfold however the hell it likes?"

Len Norris, *26th Annual*. Originally published in *The Vancouver Sun*, December 31, 1976

dian economy have relied upon state intervention. The development of Quebec nationalism since the onset of the Quiet Revolution, and the language policies of both the Quebec and federal governments, have entailed an activist state. Province-building can be linked to both regional tensions and intergovernmental conflict, while redistributive debates are still tied to debate over the appropriate size of the state even though to this point the redistributive effects of governmental growth are equivocal. It seems, then, that neoconservatism could have a marked impact on the manner in which Canadians grapple with major political issues.

Given that the political agenda is already so full, that perennial problems refuse to leave while a host of new problems looms on the horizon, it could be easy to slip into a state of apathy or cynicism. We might follow the acerbic advice of Toronto columnist Richard Needham, who sees little hope for the world "until voters are as cynical towards politicians as the politicians are towards them."[1] Yet the fact that there are no perfect or final solutions does not mean that solutions do not exist, or that some solutions are not better than others. Neither the search for perfection nor the rejection of the real world when perfection proves to be elusive, as it always will, are of great value in the political world. As an old aphorism observes, the best is the enemy of the good.

The study of political science offers a modest remedy for the frustration that can arise in trying to come to grips with a complex political reality. Courses in political theory provide a way of strengthening one's conceptual grasp of political issues, of appreciating how a variety of thinkers have grappled with common political problems across the ages. Courses in comparative politics provide an opportunity to examine how other political systems have handled the types of issues that have shaped Canadian political life. Courses in international relations map out the international context of, and constraints upon, Canadian political life. I hope, though, that a wider exposure to the study of political science will not have the same disheartening impact as political exposure seemed to have on the Atlantic Canadian respondents surveyed by Rawlyk and Perlin in 1978. The 1,939 respondents in the survey were asked the following question: "Comparing your opinions when you first began to think about politics and government with your opinions now, would you say you have more confidence or less confidence in the people in politics, and in government generally?" Across the region, only 17 percent had come away with more confidence while 58 percent had less, 10 percent felt there was no difference, and 15 percent did not know.

Political science in general, and perhaps the format of this text in particular, may emphasize the conflictual side of political life. In closing, then, it is appropriate to draw attention to what in many ways has been a remarkable success story. Canada has thus far succeeded, where many other countries have failed, in maintaining a relatively harmonious tension between two linguistic communities. The survival and contemporary vitality of the French fact in Canada provide evidence of political success, just as the dominance of one community would be a mark of political failure. Canadians have succeeded in maintaining a reasonable degree of independence from the United States, which has been no mean feat in itself given the economic and cultural pull exerted by our continental neighbour. Canadian governments have created a reasonably stable framework for the economy so that our citizens have been able to provide for themselves an enviable degree of material security and well-being. Governments have also attempted, and partially succeeded, in smoothing out individual and regional variations in the standard of living.

While enduring lines of cleavage are a fact of Canadian political life, they are not necessarily a mark of system failure. One might, for example, argue that the survival of modestly distinct regional communities and their consequent citizen identifications enriches Canadian life. If regional conflict is the price to be paid for warding off a more homogeneous and monolithic national community, it may well be a price worth paying. In more general terms, we should not expect low levels of political conflict in a society in which political participation is reasonably high and the freedoms of individuals are constitutionally entrenched. Vibrant democratic societies are ones in which sparks fly, in which individuals and groups pursue conflicting interests through common political arenas.

If we measure the Canadian political system against what seems to be the boundless potential of the country, it may be that we have fallen short. If, however, we measure the political system against the many serious problems that it has been forced to confront, there is reason for a considerable degree of satisfaction and even pride. At the very least, our attempts to grapple with enduring political problems have not seriously eroded or infringed upon the rights and freedoms enjoyed by individual Canadians. While we might have done better, we could certainly have done worse.

The Legislative Process

When Canadians think of Parliament, they think first and foremost of the House of Commons. Parliament, however, incorporates not only the House but also the Senate and the Queen as integral if unequal components of the legislative process. Any legislative proposal becomes an Act of Parliament only when it has been passed by both the House and the Senate, and has been given royal assent by the Queen's representative in Canada, the Governor General. The legislative process can thus be seen as a chain in which the House of Commons, the Senate, and the Governor General are the formal links. Figure A provides an expanded, albeit still somewhat simplified illustration of this chain.

Legislative proposals emerge from a complex policy environment which includes departments within the federal bureaucracy, interest groups, task forces and Royal Commissions (*see Glossary*), other governments both domestic and foreign, the parliamentary caucus of the governing party, and party policy resolutions. It is Cabinet which forms the interface between that policy environment and the legislative process. Parliament itself is the recipient rather than the initiator of legislative proposals. Its primary legislative role is to debate *and then ratify* government legislation.

Cabinet ministers have the exclusive right to introduce tax legislation or legislation calling for the expenditure of public funds. Moreover, most legislation of any general application *and with any prospect of being enacted* is introduced to Parliament as a government "bill," the term applied to legislative proposals which have not yet been ratified as "Acts of Parliament." Although "private members' bills" can be introduced by any member of Parliament on any subject, as long as they do not call for the expenditure of public funds, their prospects of being passed are remote.[1] In the words of an old advertising cliché, private members' bills are used to "run an idea up the flagpole and see if anyone salutes."

FIGURE A
The Legislative Process

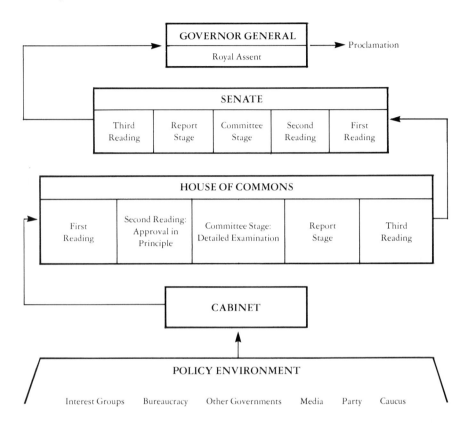

Very rarely does anyone do so, or at least very rarely does the government do so, which is all that really counts.

Both government bills and private members' bills are termed *public bills* in that they are intended to have some general impact on the population. *Private bills* apply only to specified individuals. They are used primarily for the federal incorporation of individuals, companies, and charitable foundations. Private bills are generally introduced in the Senate, where they are given detailed committee examination before being sent to the House for more pro forma consideration, and to the Governor General for royal assent.

Most bills are first introduced in the House, where the minister responsible places the bill on the order paper, and asks "leave to introduce" the legislation. (While there is nothing to prevent legislation being first introduced in the Senate and then being sent to the House, this is rarely done with public bills.) The bill is then "read" for the first time. There is no debate on first reading, which is used solely to alert Parliament to the proposed legislation and to allow for its printing. With the bill's second reading, vigorous debate takes place across the floor of the House on the principles *but not the details* of the legislation. Amendments are not permitted at this stage, which concludes with a resolution to approve the legislation in principle. In virtually all cases, party discipline ensures that government bills will be approved in principle unless the government itself decides to withdraw the legislation.

Once the bill has passed second reading and been approved in principle, it moves to the committee stage for a detailed, clause-by-clause examination. Here a number of paths can be followed. The bill can be sent to the Committee of the Whole, in which case it is examined by the House sitting as a committee with more relaxed rules of procedure. It can also be sent to one of approximately twenty standing committees of the House, or to a special committee formed to consider that particular bill. In most cases the second route is followed.

Prior to 1968, the standing committees played a modest role at best in the legislative process, as most legislation was processed through the Committee of the Whole. From 1968 on, the principal legislative routing has been through the standing committees, which have between ten and fifteen members allocated in proportion to the parties' strength in the House of Commons. The government party has a majority on all committees, and all except the Public Accounts Committee are chaired by a government backbencher. Only the Joint Committee on Regulations and Other Statutory Instruments and the Public Accounts Committee have regular support staff. Party discipline prevails within the committee system just as it prevails on the floor of the House. While the strictures of party discipline may be somewhat looser at the committee stage, the cabinet is no more prepared to see its legislation lost or rewritten in committee than on the floor of the House. Committee latitude is further circumscribed by the fact that the legislation has already been approved in principle.

The committee stage concludes with a report to the full House where committee amendments are considered and new amendments may be proposed. When all amendments have been dealt with, the third reading is held. Debate at this point is brief, and party discipline virtually guarantees the passage of government legislation. Third reading concludes the legislative process in the House, and the bill is then sent to the Senate.

In a formal sense, the appointed Senate has nearly the same legislative powers as the elected House; legislation must be passed by *both* chambers to become law. (The Senate, however, cannot introduce money bills.) In practice, a bill's passage by the House ensures its acceptance by the Senate. Debate in the Senate, which largely takes place in standing committees, focuses primarily on legislative craftsmanship and technicalities rather than on the broader principles embodied in the legislation. The Senate has not rejected a House bill for over forty years, and its amendments "... are almost always clarifying, simplifying, tidying-up amendments, and are almost always accepted by the House of Commons."[2] If there is any consistent pattern to the input of the Senate apart from that of legislative craftmanship, it comes in the form of corporate vigilance. As Jackson and Atkinson point out, "... a small portion of the Senate's membership is actively engaged in challenging, delaying, and amending any government legislation which may be detrimental to major business and financial concerns."[3]

The legislative stages within the Senate are essentially identical to those within the House. Once a bill has passed third reading in the Senate, and any Senate amendments have been approved by the House, it goes to the Queen's representative in Canada, the Governor General, for royal assent. This stage is a true formality as royal assent has never been refused in Canada. (It was last refused in Britain in 1707.) Once a bill has been signed by the Governor General it comes into immediate effect as an Act of Parliament unless the legislation contains a provision for proclamation at a later date.

This, in broad outline and stripped of its many interesting quirks and anomalies, is the national legislative process. The provincial process is similar except that committees tend to have less weight, there is no Senate stage as no province has an upper chamber, and royal assent is given by the Lieutenant-Governor rather than by the Governor General.

The Speech from the Throne

The Throne Speech, which is used to open each new session of Parliament, plays a special role in the legislative process. Written by the Prime Minister and the cabinet, the Throne speech is read by the Governor General to a joint meeting of the Senate and House of Commons held in the Senate Chamber. The Throne Speech does not introduce legislation directly, but rather sets forth the legislative priorities of the government for the forthcoming session of Parliament. While providing few legislative details, the speech does alert both the opposition parties and the public to the government's legislative agenda. The subsequent debate on the Throne Speech enables the opposition parties to set forth their own agenda, and to attack the government for interests neglected or opportunities lost in the Throne Speech.

Throughout the legislative process there is a good deal of tension between the government's desire to move bills quickly through the legislative process and the opposition's desire to maintain adequate opportunity for criticism and delay. This tension, and the procedural complexities that it engenders, are presided over by the Speaker of the House. While the Speaker is nominated by the Prime Minister and comes from the ranks of the governing party, he or she is elected by the

House and is expected to preside over the affairs of the House in a non-partisan manner. Primary control over the flow of legislation through Parliament rests with the government House Leader whose task is to enforce the government's legislative priorities and steer government bills through the legislative process. The opposition parties, however, can have a considerable impact on the flow of legislation, if not on its substance. The ability of the opposition to obstruct the legislative process can at times be bartered for changes in government bills.

As the only institution composed of elected politicians from across the land, the House of Commons provides the symbolic centrepiece for the Canadian political system. Its importance, however, goes well beyond the symbolic. The House provides the pool from which the prime minister draws the cabinet. The daily Question Period when the House is in session brings into focus the clash of parties, principles, and personalities that energizes political life. The House provides the national stage upon which the government can present and defend its policies, and upon which opposition parties can hold it accountable for such policies. The House dramatizes and to an important degree simplifies political life for the electorate, making it easier for citizens to throw bouquets and brickbats, to allocate credit and blame for the conditions of national life. If we adopt David Easton's now-famous definition of politics as the "authoritative allocation of values,"[4] it is the House which provides that authoritative allocation in federal politics.

Suggested Readings

1 For a discussion of the provincial legislative process, see Michael M. Atkinson and Graham White, "The Development of Provincial Legislatures," in Harold D. Clarke, Colin Campbell, F.Q. Quo, and Arthur Goddard, eds., *Parliament, Policy and Representation* (Toronto: Methuen, 1980), pp. 255–75; Allan Kornberg, William Mishler, and Harold D. Clarke, *Representative Democracy in the Canadian Provinces* (Scarborough: Prentice-Hall, 1982), pp. 171–83; and Philip Laundy, "Legislatures," in David Bellamy, Jon H. Pammett, and Donald C. Rowat, eds., *The Provincial Political Systems: Comparative Essays* (Toronto: Methuen, 1976), pp. 280–96.

2 For an overview of the national legislative process, see Michael M. Atkinson, "Parliamentary Government in Canada," in Michael S. Whittington and Glen Williams, eds., *Canadian Politics in the 1980s*, 2nd ed. (Toronto: Methuen, 1984), pp. 331–50. For a more extended discussion, see J.R. Mallory, *The Structure of Canadian Government*, rev. ed. (Toronto: Gage, 1984), Chapters Six and Seven; and Robert J. Jackson and Michael M. Atkinson, *The Canadian Legislative System*, 2nd ed. (Toronto: Macmillan, 1980).

APPENDIX B

The Government of Canada

It is common for people to speak of "the Government of Canada" or "the Government of Saskatchewan" as if it were a simple, unitary actor. We speak, for instance, of "the government" doing this or that, of governments clashing like gladiators in the federal–provincial arena. Thus it is important to note that modern governments are in fact complex and elaborate organizations which embrace a vast number of loosely coordinated and at times competitive components.

The national government encompasses close to five hundred departments and ministries, Crown corporations, regulatory agencies, boards, commissions, and councils. On the provincial side of the ledger the situation is no less complex. In Ontario, for example, there are almost seven hundred semi-independent agencies, boards, and commissions that fall under the purview of the Ontario legislature.[1] In the regulatory field alone there are some 117 federal and 1,253 provincial agencies, boards, commissions, and tribunals, including Atomic Energy of Canada, the British Columbia Grape Marketing Board, the Prince Edward Island Rentalsman, the Nova Scotia Horse Racing Commission, the Ontario Securities Commission, and the ten provincial liquor control boards.[2]

There is, however, a focal point to this picture, a more specific sense in which the term "government" is used. When one talks about the "Government of Canada," or the "Government of British Columbia" the specific reference is to the federal or provincial *cabinet*. The larger governmental apparatus radiates out from and is responsible to the cabinet. To risk what may be a contentious analogy, the cabinet rests at the centre of government like a spider at the centre of an immense and complex web.

If we restrict our gaze to the national government, the executive authority exercised by the cabinet is formally vested in the *Privy Council*, which in turn

"They start messing about with the organization and it will end up in chaos."

Len Norris, *9th Annual*. Originally published in *The Vancouver Sun*, January 21, 1960

consists of all those who are or ever have been in the cabinet and who have thus taken an oath as Privy Councillors.[3] Once admitted into the Privy Council, an individual retains the title "The Honourable" for life. The Council, however, has met in its entirety only three times; when it was first constituted in 1867, when Elizabeth II became Queen of Canada in 1952, and when the Constitution Act was proclaimed in 1982. In practice, the Privy Council's powers are exercised by the cabinet, *a committee of the Privy Council* whose members have seats in Parliament (either in the House or the Senate) and who have been invited into the cabinet by the current prime minister.[4]

It is difficult to overstate the importance of the federal cabinet in the Canadian political system. Cabinet ministers control the executive or administrative side of the federal government; all departments are headed by cabinet ministers who direct and are responsible for their operations. Because the cabinet is drawn from the majority party in the House and is able to rely upon firm party discipline, the cabinet also dominates the legislative process. Thus cabinet serves as a "buckle," tying together the executive and legislative branches of government.

The cabinet exercises what are called *prerogative powers*, or "those powers of the sovereign that have never been formally delegated to any other government organ and which are exercised by the cabinet on behalf of the sovereign."[5] These include the right to introduce money bills, to recommend the dissolution of

Parliament (this being exercised by the prime minister alone), to participate in international affairs, and to grant clemency. The cabinet also exercises *statutory powers* which have been delegated to it by Parliament. In many cases legislation passed by Parliament does not include the detailed rules and administrative details necessary to put it into effect. Parliament delegates the formulation of such subordinate legislation to cabinet or to the particular minister responsible for the Act, restricting itself to providing a "... framework for the rulemaking that will take place in the bureaucracy."[6] When cabinet exercises statutory or prerogative powers it does so through Orders-in-Council or minutes of council which are as legally binding as Acts of Parliament. There are literally thousands of Orders-in-Council and council minutes issued each year.

Cabinet meetings are governed by a number of important conventions. First, ministers are sworn to secrecy by their oath as Privy Councillors. Second, all members of cabinet are collectively responsible for each and every decision reached by cabinet. In public and in tendering its advice to the Crown cabinet speaks with a single voice and individual ministers speak with the authority of the full cabinet behind them. Collective responsibility is made possible by the confidential nature of cabinet meetings; ministers can disagree among themselves while retaining a united front in public. Third, votes are not taken within cabinet. Voting would imply equality among the ministers when in fact they are not at all equal. Some head ministries that are more directly involved in the issue at hand, some may represent regional interests which are more directly at stake, some will be brighter and others more politically astute. Thus decisions are made by consensus, and the consensus is articulated by the prime minister. Ministers who disagree with that consensus must support it in public or resign from cabinet.

In recent decades the size of federal cabinets has increased considerably. At the end of the Second World War, the cabinet contained nineteen ministers. This increased to twenty-seven with Pierre Trudeau's first cabinet in 1968, and to thirty-seven by Trudeau's last cabinet. While John Turner's short-lived cabinet, appointed in June 1984, contained only twenty-nine ministers, the forty-member cabinet appointed by Brian Mulroney in September 1984 was the largest in Canadian history. Along with major portfolios such as National Defence, External Affairs, Finance, and Justice, the Mulroney cabinet included ministers responsible for youth, tourism, small business, fitness and amateur sport, and forestry.

The Size of Provincial Cabinets

Proportionate to the size of their legislative assemblies, provincial cabinets are considerably larger than the federal cabinet. In Nova Scotia, for example, the twenty-three members of the 1983 cabinet accounted for 61 percent of the government caucus and 44 percent of the entire legislative assembly. A federal cabinet of similar proportions would contain 124 members.

In 1983, columnist Don McGillivray (Calgary Herald, November 14, 1983, p. A8) compared the sizes of the federal and provincial cabinets. Alberta's cabinet at that time had thirty members, only six members less than the federal cabinet, while Ontario's had twenty-nine and Quebec's had twenty-seven. Saskatchewan

(twenty-five), New Brunswick (twenty-three) and Nova Scotia (then twenty-one) were not far behind. Prince Edward Island (ten) and Newfoundland (eighteen) held down the low end of the scale.

In total, there were 257 federal and provincial cabinet ministers, an increase from 224 five years before, 200 ten years before, and only 155 twenty years before.

Cabinets have grown in size in part because of the increased scope of modern government, and in part because of the desire of prime ministers to represent a broader array of interests within the cabinet. As a consequence of both the increase in size and the increased complexity of government legislation, a great deal of the cabinet's workload is now handled through an elaborate cabinet committee system. The cabinet committees are backstopped by the Privy Council Office secretariat which provides not only support services but also policy advice. The most important committee is the Committee on Planning and Priorities, chaired by the prime minister. This committee, which contained fifteen members in the 1984 Mulroney government, forms the de facto "inner cabinet."

The Canadian political system is characterized by executive dominance. The cabinet sits astride the legislative process like a jockey astride a horse, controlling the formulation of policy, its ratification by Parliament, and its administration by the federal public service. While in theory cabinet is responsible to Parliament, in fact Parliament has little control over a cabinet backed by a majority in the House. Parliament debates government legislation before passing it, rather than debating to determine whether it should pass.

Executive dominance has also come to characterize internal dynamics within cabinet. Traditionally, the prime minister's relationship with his cabinet colleagues was described by the phrase "primus inter pares," or "first among equals." If that phrase ever fit the reality of the relationship, it certainly does not today. The prime minister's dominance over his cabinet colleagues, both individually and collectively, stems from a number of sources:

• The prime minister decides not only who is appointed to the cabinet but also what portfolio they will hold and how long they will hold it.
• The prime minister alone has the authority to call for the dissolution of Parliament, and thus to cast his cabinet colleagues to the electoral wolves.
• The prime minister has been elected as party leader by a national convention of the extra-parliamentary party, not by his cabinet colleagues or by the parliamentary caucus, and the mantle of leadership can only be removed by that party.

• The prime minister controls much of the government patronage that may be of critical importance to ministers' constituents or to their long-term career plans.

• Because national election campaigns have become so leader-oriented, the prime minister can claim responsibility for the electoral success of his party. Cabinet ministers hold their positions because of the prime minister's electoral appeal, not the other way around.

• It is the prime minister who ultimately articulates the consensus of cabinet, and thus has the final say in the arbitration of policy disputes within cabinet.

The prime minister's mastery is further strengthened by his personal control of the Privy Council Office and the Prime Minister's Office. As noted above, the PCO not only acts as the secretariat to the cabinet but has also come to play a critical role in the governmental policy process. The PMO performs similar functions for the prime minister, providing secretarial support, policy information, and strategic advice. The PCO and the PMO, along with the Federal–Provincial Relations Office, strengthen the prime minister's hand in dealing not only with his cabinet colleagues, individually or as a group, but also with the larger governmental system.

Provincial Comparisons

Executive dominance is even more characteristic of provincial legislatures than it is of the House of Commons.[7] Within the Canadian political science literature there is "... a rather firm consensus that all provinces have been characterized by a debilitating subservience of the legislature to the executive."[8] A number of factors may account for this subservience, including the shorter length of provincial sessions, the proportionately larger size of provincial cabinets, less firmly entrenched parliamentary norms, and less developed legislative committee systems.

With respect to his cabinet colleagues, the premier's position is very similar to that of the prime minister. His role in *provincial election campaigns equals that of the prime minister in federal campaigns. The premier exercises the same control over cabinet appointments and dissolution, and he has the same control over central agencies, the organization of cabinet committees, and executive staff resources. Just as the prime minister can enhance his standing within the government and the country through international travel and participation in world affairs, so can the premier enhance his own standing through travel and high-profile participation in federal–provincial diplomacy. In short, as Kornberg et al. conclude, "... he is the boss, and the other ministers, although colleagues, are his agents."[9]*

While the prime minister is not on an equal plane with his cabinet colleagues, this should not imply that he can run roughshod over their views. A successful prime minister leads rather than imposing his will, or at least imposes his will only in carefully limited areas of concern and expertise. The prime minister must try to maintain unity within cabinet and within caucus, and in this endeavour a dictatorial style is of little use. Still, in a cabinet of forty ministers, the prime minister stands apart. Preoccupied with their own portfolios, ministers are not in a position to challenge the preeminence of the prime minister even should they wish to do so.

APPENDIX C

Constitution Act, 1982

Part I
Canadian Charter of Rights and Freedoms

Whereas Canada is founded upon principles that recognize the supremacy of God and the rule of law:

GUARANTEE OF RIGHTS AND FREEDOMS

Rights and freedoms in Canada

1. *The Canadian Charter of Rights and Freedoms* guarantees the rights and freedoms set out in it subject only to such reasonable limits prescribed by law as can be demonstrably justified in a free and democratic society.

FUNDAMENTAL FREEDOMS

Fundamental freedoms

2. Everyone has the following fundamental freedoms:
(*a*) freedom of conscience and religion;
(*b*) freedom of thought, belief, opinion and expression, including freedom of the press and other media of communication;
(*c*) freedom of peaceful assembly; and
(*d*) freedom of association.

DEMOCRATIC RIGHTS

Democratic rights of citizens

3. Every citizen of Canada has the right to vote in an election of members of the House of Commons or of a legislative assembly and to be qualified for membership therein.

Maximum duration of legislative bodies

4. (1) No House of Commons and no legislative assembly shall continue for longer than five years from the date fixed for the return of the writs at a general election of its members.

Continuation in special circumstances

(2) In time of real or apprehended war, invasion or insurrection, a House of Commons may be continued by Parliament and a legislative assembly may be continued by the legislature beyond five years if such continuation is not opposed by the votes of more than one-third of the members of the House of Commons or the legislative assembly, as the case may be.

Annual sitting of legislative bodies

5. There shall be a sitting of Parliament and of each legislature at least once every twelve months.

MOBILITY RIGHTS

Mobility of citizens

6. (1) Every citizen of Canada has the right to enter, remain in and leave Canada.

Rights to move and gain livelihood

(2) Every citizen of Canada and every person who has the status of a permanent resident of Canada has the right
(*a*) to move to and take up residence in any province; and
(*b*) to pursue the gaining of a livelihood in any province.

Limitation

(3) The rights specified in subsection (2) are subject to
(*a*) any laws or practices of general application in force in a province other than those that discriminate among persons primarily on the basis of province of present or previous residence; and
(*b*) any laws providing for reasonable residency requirements as a qualification for the receipt of publicly provided social services.

Affirmative

(4) Subsections (2) and (3) do not preclude any law, pro-

action
programs

gram or activity that has as its object the amelioration in a province of conditions of individuals in that province who are socially or economically disadvantaged if the rate of employment in that province is below the rate of employment in Canada.

LEGAL RIGHTS

Life, liberty
and security
of person

7. Everyone has the right to life, liberty and security of the person and the right not to be deprived thereof except in accordance with the principles of fundamental justice.

Search or
seizure

8. Everyone has the right to be secure against unreasonable search or seizure.

Detention or
imprisonment

9. Everyone has the right not to be arbitrarily detained or imprisoned.

Arrest or
detention

10. Everyone has the right on arrest or detention
(*a*) to be informed promptly of the reasons therefor;
(*b*) to retain and instruct counsel without delay and to be informed of that right; and
(*c*) to have the validity of the detention determined by way of *habeas corpus* and to be released if the detention is not lawful.

Proceedings in
criminal and
penal matters

11. Any person charged with an offence has the right
(*a*) to be informed without unreasonable delay of the specific offence;
(*b*) to be tried within a reasonable time;
(*c*) not to be compelled to be a witness in proceedings against that person in respect of the offence;
(*d*) to be presumed innocent until proven guilty according to law in a fair and public hearing by an independent and impartial tribunal;
(*e*) not to be denied reasonable bail without just cause;
(*f*) except in the case of an offence under military law tried before a military tribunal, to the benefit of trial by jury where the maximum punishment for the offence is imprisonment for five years or a more severe punishment;
(*g*) not to be found guilty on account of any act or omission unless, at the time of the act or omission, it constituted an offence under Canadian or international law or was criminal

according to the general principles of law recognized by the community of nations;

(*h*) if finally acquitted of the offence, not to be tried for it again and, if finally found guilty and punished for the offence, not to be tried or punished for it again; and

(*i*) if found guilty of the offence and if the punishment for the offence has been varied between the time of commission and the time of sentencing, to the benefit of the lesser punishment.

Treatment or punishment

12. Everyone has the right not to be subjected to any cruel and unusual treatment or punishment.

Self-incrimination

13. A witness who testifies in any proceedings has the right not to have any incriminating evidence so given used to incriminate that witness in any other proceedings, except in a prosecution for perjury or for the giving of contradictory evidence.

Interpreter

14. A party or witness in any proceedings who does not understand or speak the language in which the proceedings are conducted or who is deaf has the right to the assistance of an interpreter.

EQUALITY RIGHTS

Equality before and under law and equal protection and benefit of law

15. (1) Every individual is equal before and under the law and has the right to the equal protection and equal benefit of the law without discrimination and, in particular, without discrimination based on race, national or ethnic origin, colour, religion, sex, age or mental or physical disability.

Affirmative action programs

(2) Subsection (1) does not preclude any law, program or activity that has as its object the amelioration of conditions of disadvantaged individuals or groups including those that are disadvantaged because of race, national or ethnic origin, colour, religion, sex, age or mental or physical disability.

OFFICIAL LANGUAGES OF CANADA

Official languages of Canada

16. (1) English and French are the official languages of Canada and have equality of status and equal rights and privileges as to their use in all institutions of the Parliament and government of Canada.

Official
languages of
New Brunswick

(2) English and French are the official languages of New Brunswick and have equality of status and equal rights and privileges as to their use in all institutions of the legislature and government of New Brunswick.

Advancement
of status and
use

(3) Nothing in this Charter limits the authority of Parliament or a legislature to advance the equality of status or use of English and French.

Proceedings of
Parliament

17. (1) Everyone has the right to use English or French in any debates and other proceedings of Parliament.

Proceedings of
New Brunswick
legislature

(2) Everyone has the right to use English or French in any debates and other proceedings of the legislature of New Brunswick.

Parliamentary
status and
records

18. (1) The statutes, records and journals of Parliament shall be printed and published in English and French and both language versions are equally authoritative.

New Brunswick
statutes and
records

(2) The statutes, records and journals of the legislature of New Brunswick shall be printed and published in English and French and both language versions are equally authoritative.

Proceedings in
courts
established by
Parliament

19. (1) Either English or French may be used by any person in, or in any pleading in or process issuing from, any court established by Parliament.

(2) Either English or French may be used by any person in, or in any pleading in or process issuing from, any court of New Brunswick.

Communications
by public
with federal
institutions

20. (1) Any member of the public in Canada has the right to communicate with, and to receive available services from, any head or central office of an institution of the Parliament or government of Canada in English or French, and has the same right with respect to any other office of any such institution where

(a) there is a significant demand for communications with and services from that office in such language; or

(b) due to the nature of the office, it is reasonable that communications with and services from that office be available in both English and French.

Communications
by public with
New Brunswick
institutions

(2) Any member of the public in New Brunswick has the right to communicate with, and to receive available services from, any office of an institution of the legislature or government of New Brunswick in English or French.

Continuation
of
existing
constitutional
provisions

21. Nothing in sections 16 to 20 abrogates or derogates from any right, privilege or obligation with respect to the English and French languages, or either of them, that exists or is continued by virtue of any other provision of the Constitution of Canada.

Rights and
privileges
preserved

22. Nothing in sections 16 to 20 abrogates or derogates from any legal or customary right or privilege acquired or enjoyed either before or after the coming into force of this Charter with respect to any language that is not English or French.

MINORITY LANGUAGE EDUCATIONAL RIGHTS

Language of
instruction

23. (1) Citizens of Canada
(a) whose first language learned and still understood is that of the English or French linguistic minority population of the province in which they reside; or
(b) who have received their primary school instruction in Canada in English or French and reside in a province where the language in which they received that instruction is the language of the English or French linguistic minority population of the province,
have the right to have their children receive primary and secondary school instruction in that language in that province.

Continuity of
language
instruction

(2) Citizens of Canada of whom any child has received or is receiving primary or secondary school instruction in English or French in Canada, have the right to have all their children receive primary and secondary school instruction in the same language.

Application
where numbers
warrant

(3) The right of citizens of Canada under subsections (1) and (2) to have their children receive primary and secondary school instruction in the language of the English or French linguistic minority population of a province
(a) applies wherever in the province the number of children

of citizens who have such a right is sufficient to warrant the provision to them out of public funds of minority language instruction; and

(*b*) includes, where the number of those children so warrants, the right to have them receive that instruction in minority language educational facilities provided out of public funds.

ENFORCEMENT

Enforcement of guaranteed rights and freedoms

24. (1) Anyone whose rights or freedoms, as guaranteed by this Charter, have been infringed or denied may apply to a court of competent jurisdiction to obtain such remedy as the court considers appropriate and just in the circumstances.

Exclusion of evidence bringing administration of justice into disrepute

(2) Where, in proceedings under subsection (1), a court concludes that evidence was obtained in a manner that infringed or denied any rights or freedoms guaranteed by this Charter, the evidence shall be excluded if it is established that, having regard to all the circumstances, the admission of it in the proceedings would bring the administration of justice into disrepute.

GENERAL

Aboriginal rights and freedoms not affected by Charter

25. The guarantee in this Charter of certain rights and freedoms shall not be construed so as to abrogate or derogate from any aboriginal, treaty or other rights or freedoms that pertain to the aboriginal peoples of Canada including

(*a*) any rights or freedoms that have been recognized by the Royal Proclamation of October 7, 1763, and

(*b*) any rights or freedoms that may be acquired by the aboriginal peoples of Canada by way of land claims settlement.

Other rights and freedoms not affected by Charter

26. The guarantee in this Charter of certain rights and freedoms shall not be construed as denying the existence of any other rights or freedoms that exist in Canada.

Multicultural heritage

27. This Charter shall be interpreted in a manner consistent with the preservation and enhancement of the multicultural heritage of Canadians.

Rights
guaranteed
equally to
both sexes

28. Notwithstanding anything in this Charter, the rights and freedoms referred to in it are guaranteed equally to male and female persons.

Rights
respecting
certain schools

29. Nothing in this Charter abrogates or derogates from any rights or privileges guaranteed by or under the Constitution of Canada in respect of denominational, separate or dissentient schools.

Application to
territories and
territorial
authorities

30. A reference in this Charter to a province or to the legislative assembly or legislature of a province shall be deemed to include a reference to the Yukon Territory and the Northwest Territories, or to the appropriate legislative authority thereof, as the case may be.

Legislative
powers not
extended

31. Nothing in this Charter extends the legislative powers of any body or authority.

APPLICATION OF CHARTER

Application of
Charter

32. (1) This Charter applies
(a) to the Parliament and government of Canada in respect of all matters within the authority of Parliament including all matters relating to the Yukon Territory and Northwest Territories; and
(b) to the legislature and government of each province in respect of all matters within the authority of the legislature of each province.

Exception

(2) Notwithstanding subsection (1), section 15 shall not have effect until three years after this section comes into force.

Exception
where express
declaration

33. (1) Parliament or the legislature of a province may expressly declare in an Act of Parliament or of the legislature, as the case may be, that the Act or a provision thereof shall operate notwithstanding a provision included in section 2 or sections 7 to 15 of this Charter.

Operation of
exception

(2) An Act or a provision of an Act in respect of which a declaration made under this section is in effect shall have such

operation as it would have but for the provision of this Charter referred to in the declaration.

Five year limitation

(3) A declaration made under subsection (1) shall cease to have effect five years after it comes into force or on such earlier date as may be specified in the declaration.

Re-enactment

(4) Parliament or a legislature of a province may re-enact a declaration made under subsection (1).

Five year limitation

(5) Subsection (3) applies in respect of a re-enactment made under subsection (4).

CITATION

Citation

34. This Part may be cited as the *Canadian Charter of Rights and Freedoms*.

Part II
Rights of the Aboriginal Peoples of Canada

Recognition of existing aboriginal and treaty rights

35. (1) The existing aboriginal and treaty rights of the aboriginal peoples of Canada are hereby recognized and affirmed.

Definition of "aboriginal peoples of Canada"

(2) In this Act, "aboriginal peoples of Canada" includes the Indian, Inuit and Métis people of Canada.

Part III
Equalization and Regional Disparities

Commitment to promote equal opportunities

36. (1) Without altering the legislative authority of Parliament or of the provincial legislatures, or the rights of any of them with respect to the exercise of their legislative authority, Parliament and the legislatures, together with the government of Canada and the provincial governments, are committed to

(a) promoting equal opportunities for the well-being of Canadians;

(*b*) furthering economic development to reduce disparity in opportunities; and

(*c*) providing essential public services of reasonable quality to all Canadians.

Commitment respecting public services

(2) Parliament and the government of Canada are committed to the principle of making equalization payments to ensure that provincial governments have sufficient revenues to provide reasonably comparable levels of public services at reasonably comparable levels of taxation.

Part IV
Constitutional Conference

Constitutional conference

37. (1) A constitutional conference composed of the Prime Minister of Canada and the first ministers of the provinces shall be convened by the Prime Minister of Canada within one year after this Part comes into force.

Participation of aboriginal peoples

(2) The conference convened under subsection (1) shall have included in its agenda an item respecting constitutional matters that directly affect the aboriginal peoples of Canada, including the identification and definition of the rights of those peoples to be included in the Constitution of Canada, and the Prime Minister of Canada shall invite representatives of those peoples to participate in the discussions on that item.

Participation of territories

(3) The Prime Minister of Canada shall invite elected representatives of the governments of the Yukon Territory and the Northwest Territories to participate in the discussions on any item on the agenda of the conference convened under subsection (1) that, in the opinion of the Prime Minister, directly affects the Yukon Territory and the Northwest Territories.

Part V
Procedure for Amending Constitution of Canada

General procedure for amending Constitution

38. (1) An amendment to the Constitution of Canada may be made by proclamation issued by the Governor General under the Great Seal of Canada where so authorized by

(*a*) resolutions of the Senate and House of Commons; and

of Canada

(*b*) resolutions of the legislative assemblies of at least two-thirds of the provinces that have, in the aggregate, according to the then latest general census, at least fifty per cent of the population of all the provinces.

Majority of members

(2) An amendment made under subsection (1) that derogates from the legislative powers, the proprietary rights or any other rights or privileges of the legislature or government of a province shall require a resolution supported by a majority of the members of each of the Senate, the House of Commons and the legislative assemblies required under subsection (1).

Expression of dissent

(3) An amendment referred to in subsection (2) shall not have effect in a province the legislative assembly of which has expressed its dissent thereto by resolution supported by a majority of its members prior to the issue of the proclamation to which the amendment relates unless that legislative assembly, subsequently, by resolution supported by a majority of its members, revokes its dissent and authorizes the amendment.

Revocation of dissent

(4) A resolution of dissent made for the purposes of subsection (3) may be revoked at any time before or after the issue of the proclamation to which it relates.

Restriction on proclamation

39. (1) A proclamation shall not be issued under subsection 38(1) before the expiration of one year from the adoption of the resolution initiating the amendment procedure thereunder, unless the legislative assembly of each province has previously adopted a resolution of assent or dissent.

Idem

(2) A proclamation shall not be issued under subsection 38(1) after the expiration of three years from the adoption of the resolution initiating the amendment procedure thereunder.

Compensation

40. Where an amendment is made under subsection 38(1) that transfers provincial legislative powers relating to education or other cultural matters from provincial legislatures to Parliament, Canada shall provide reasonable compensation to any province to which the amendment does not apply.

Amendment by unanimous consent

41. An amendment to the Constitution of Canada in relation to the following matters may be made by proclamation issued by the Governor General under the Great Seal of Can-

ada only where authorized by resolutions of the Senate and House of Commons and of the legislative assembly of each province:

(*a*) the office of the Queen, the Governor General and the Lieutenant Governor of a province;

(*b*) the right of a province to a number of members in the House of Commons not less than the number of Senators by which the province is entitled to be represented at the time this Part comes into force;

(*c*) subject to section 43, the use of the English or the French language;

(*d*) the composition of the Supreme Court of Canada; and

(*e*) an amendment to this Part.

Amendment by general procedure

42. (1) An amendment to the Constitution of Canada in relation to the following matters may be made only in accordance with subsection 38(1):

(*a*) the principle of proportionate representation of the provinces in the Houses of Commons prescribed by the Constitution of Canada;

(*b*) the powers of the Senate and the method of selecting Senators;

(*c*) the number of members by which a province is entitled to be represented in the Senate and the residence qualifications of Senators;

(*d*) subject to paragraph 41(*d*), the Supreme Court of Canada;

(*e*) the extension of existing provinces into the territories; and

(*f*) notwithstanding any other law or practice, the establishment of new provinces.

Exception

(2) Subsections 38(2) and (4) do not apply in respect of amendments in relations to matters referred to in subsection (1).

Amendment of provisions relating to some but not all provinces

43. An amendment to the Constitution of Canada in relation to any provision that applies to one or more, but not all, provinces, including

(*a*) any alteration to boundaries between provinces, and

(*b*) any amendment to any provision that relates to the use of the English or the French language within a province, may be made by proclamation issued by the Governor General under the Great Seal of Canada only where so authorized by resolutions of the Senate and House of Commons and of the legislative assembly of each province to which the amendment applies.

Amendments
by Parliament

44. Subject to sections 41 and 42, Parliament may exclusively make laws amending the Constitution of Canada in relation to the executive government of Canada or the Senate and House of Commons.

Amendments
by provincial
legislatures

45. Subject to section 41, the legislature of each province may exclusively make laws amending the constitution of the province.

Initiation of
amendment
procedures

46. (1) The procedures for amendment under sections 38, 41, 42 and 43 may be initiated either by the Senate or the House of Commons or by the legislative assembly of a province.

Revocation of
authorization

(2) A resolution of assent made for the purposes of this Part may be revoked at any time before the issue of a proclamation authorized by it.

Amendments
without Senate
resolution

47. (1) An amendment to the Constitution of Canada made by proclamation under section 38, 41, 42 or 43 may be made without a resolution of the Senate authorizing the issue of the proclamation if, within one hundred and eighty days after the adoption by the House of Commons of a resolution authorizing its issue, the Senate has not adopted such a resolution and if, at any time after the expiration of that period, the House of Commons again adopts the resolution.

Computation
of period

(2) Any period when Parliament is prorogued or dissolved shall not be counted in computing the one hundred and eighty day period referred to in subsection (1).

Advice to issue
proclamation

48. The Queen's Privy Council for Canada shall advise the Governor General to issue a proclamation under this Part forthwith on the adoption of the resolutions required for an amendment made by proclamation under this Part.

Constitutional
conference

49. A constitutional conference composed of the Prime Minister of Canada and the first ministers of the provinces shall be convened by the Prime Minister of Canada within fifteen years after this Part comes into force to review the provisions of this Part.

Part VI
Amendment to the Constitution Act, 1867

Amendment to
*Constitution
Act, 1867*

50. The *Constitution Act, 1867* (formerly named the *British North America Act, 1867*) is amended by adding thereto, immediately after section 92 thereof, the following heading and section:

"NON-RENEWABLE NATURAL RESOURCES, FORESTRY RESOURCES AND ELECTRICAL ENERGY

Laws respecting
non-renewable
natural
resources,
forestry
resources and
electrical
energy

92A. (1) In each province, the legislature may exclusively make laws in relation to

(*a*) exploration for non-renewable natural resources in the province;

(*b*) development, conservation and management of non-renewable natural resources and forestry resources in the province, including laws in relation to the rate of primary production therefrom; and

(*c*) development, conservation and management of sites and facilities in the province for the generation and production of electrical energy.

Export from
provinces of
resources

(2) In each province, the legislature may make laws in relation to the export from the province to another part of Canada of the primary production from non-renewable natural resources and forestry resources in the province and the production from facilities in the province for the generation of electrical energy, but such laws may not authorize or provide for discrimination in prices or in supplies exported to another part of Canada.

Authority of
Parliament

(3) Nothing in subsection (2) derogates from the authority of Parliament to enact laws in relation to the matters referred to in that subsection and, where such a law of Parliament and

a law of a province conflict, the law of Parliament prevails to the extent of the conflict.

Taxation of resources

(4) In each province, the legislature may make laws in relation to the raising of money by any mode or system of taxation in respect of

(*a*) non-renewable natural resources and forestry resources in the province and the primary production therefrom, and

(*b*) sites and facilities in the province for the generation of electrical energy and the production therefrom,

whether or not such production is exported in whole or in part from the province, but such laws may not authorize or provide for taxation that differentiates between production exported to another part of Canada and production not exported from the province.

"Primary production"

(5) The expression "primary production" has the meaning assigned by the Sixth Schedule.

Existing powers or rights

(6) Nothing in subsections (1) to (5) derogates from any powers or rights that a legislature or government of a province had immediately before the coming into force of this section."

Idem

51. The said Act is further amended by adding thereto the following Schedule:

"The Sixth Schedule
PRIMARY PRODUCTION FROM NON-RENEWABLE NATURAL RESOURCES AND FORESTRY RESOURCES

1. For the purposes of section 92A of this Act,

(*a*) production from a non-renewable natural resource is primary production therefrom if

(i) it is in the form in which it exists upon its recovery or severance from its natural state, or

(ii) it is a product resulting from processing or refining the resource, and is not a manufactured product or a product resulting from refining crude oil, refining upgraded heavy crude oil, refining gases or liquids derived from coal or refining a synthetic equivalent of crude oil; and (*b*) production from a forestry resource is primary production therefrom if it consists of sawlogs, poles, lumber, wood chips, sawdust or any other primary wood product, or wood pulp, and is not a product manufactured from wood."

Part VII
General

Primacy of
Constitution
of Canada

52. (1) The Constitution of Canada is the supreme law of Canada, and any law that is inconsistent with the provisions of the Constitution is, to the extent of the inconsistency, of no force or effect.

Constitution
of Canada

(2) The Constitution of Canada includes
(*a*) the *Canada Act, 1982*, including this Act;
(*b*) the Acts and orders referred to in the schedule, and
(*c*) any amendments to any Act or order referred to in paragraph (*a*) or (*b*).

Amendments to
Constitution of
Canada

(3) Amendments to the Constitution of Canada shall be made only in accordance with the authority contained in the Constitution of Canada.

Repeals and
new names

53. (1) The enactments referred to in Column I of the schedule are hereby repealed or amended to the extent indicated in Column II thereof and, unless repealed, shall continue as law in Canada under the names set out in Column III thereof.

Consequential
amendments

(2) Every enactment, except the *Canada Act, 1982*, that refers to an enactment referred to in the schedule by the name in Column I thereof is hereby amended by substituting for that name the corresponding name in Column III thereof, and any British North America Act not referred to in the schedule may be cited as the *Constitution Act* followed by the year and number, if any, of its enactment.

Repeal and
consequential
amendments

54. Part IV is repealed on the day that is one year after this Part comes into force and this section may be repealed and this Act renumbered, consequential upon the repeal of Part IV and this section, by proclamation issued by the Governor General under the Great Seal of Canada.

French version
of Constitution
of Canada

55. A French version of the portions of the Constitution of Canada referred to in the schedule shall be prepared by the Minister of Justice of Canada as expeditiously as possible and, when any portion thereof sufficient to warrant action being taken has been so prepared, it shall be put forward for enactment by proclamation issued by the Governor General under the Great Seal of Canada pursuant to the procedure then applicable to an amendment of the same provisions of the Constitution of Canada.

English and
French versions
of certain
constitutional
texts

56. Where any portion of the Constitution of Canada has been or is enacted in English and French or where a French version of any portion of the Constitution is enacted pursuant to section 55, the English and French versions of that portion of the Constitution are equally authoritative.

English and
French versions
of this Act

57. The English and French versions of this Act are equally authoritative.

58. Subject to section 59, this Act shall come into force on a day to be fixed by proclamation issued by the Queen or the Governor General under the Great Seal of Canada.

Commence-
ment of
paragraph
23(1)(*a*)

59. (1) Paragraph 23(1)(*a*) shall come into force in respect of Quebec on a day to be fixed by proclamation issued by the Queen or the Governor General under the Great Seal of Canada.

Authorization
of Quebec

(2) A proclamation under subsection (1) shall be issued only where authorized by the legislative assembly or government of Quebec.

Repeal of
this section

(3) This section may be repealed on the day paragraph 23(1)(*a*) comes into force in respect of Quebec and this Act amended and renumbered, consequential upon the repeal of this section, by proclamation issued by the Queen or the Governor General under the Great Seal of Canada.

Short title
and citations

60. This Act may be cited as the *Constitution Act, 1982*, and the Constitution Acts 1867 to 1975 (No. 2) and this Act may be cited together as the *Constitution Acts, 1867 to 1982*.

Excerpts from the Constitution Act, 1867

The federal division of powers is set forth in a number of sections of the Constitution Act, 1867. The most general treatment is contained in Sections 91 and 92, while subsequent sections deal in more detail with particular powers.

VI. Distribution of Legislative Powers

POWERS OF PARLIAMENT

91. It shall be lawful for the Queen, by and with the advice and consent of the Senate and House of Commons, to make laws for the peace, order, and good government of Canada, in relation to all matters not coming within the classes of subjects by this Act assigned exclusively to the Legislatures of the Provinces; and for greater certainty, but not so as to restrict the generality of the foregoing terms of this section, it is hereby declared that (notwithstanding anything in this Act) the exclusive Legislative Authority of the Parliament of Canada extends to all matters coming within the classes of subjects next hereinafter enumerated, that is to say:—

1. The amendment from time to time of the Constitution of Canada, except as regards matters coming within the classes of subjects by this Act assigned exclusively to the Legislatures of the Provinces, or as regards rights or privileges by this or any other Constitutional Act granted or secured to the Legislature or the Government of a Province, or to any class of persons with respect to schools or as regards the use of the English or the French language or as regards the requirements that there shall be a session of the Parliament of Canada at least once each year, and that no House of Commons shall continue for more than five years from the day of the return of the Writs for choosing the House: provided, however,

that a House of Commons may in time of real or apprehended war, invasion or insurrection be continued by the Parliament of Canada if such continuation is not opposed by the votes of more than one-third of the members of such House.(39)

1A. The Public Debt and Property.(40)

2. The regulation of Trade and Commerce.

2A. Unemployment insurance.(41)

3. The raising of money by any mode or system of Taxation.

4. The borrowing of money on the public credit.

5. Postal service.

6. The Census and Statistics.

7. Militia, Military and Naval Service, and Defence.

8. The fixing of and providing for the salaries and allowances of civil and other officers of the Government of Canada.

9. Beacons, Buoys, Lighthouses, and Sable Island.

10. Navigation and Shipping.

11. Quarantine and the establishment and maintenance of Marine Hospitals.

12. Sea Coast and Inland Fisheries.

13. Ferries between a Province and any British or Foreign country or between two Provinces.

14. Currency and Coinage.

15. Banking, incorporation of banks, and the issue of paper money.

16. Savings Banks.

17. Weights and Measures.

18. Bills of Exchange and Promissory Notes.

19. Interest.

20. Legal tender.

21. Bankruptcy and Insolvency.

22. Patents of Invention and Discovery.

23. Copyrights.

24. Indians and lands reserved for the Indians.

25. Naturalization and Aliens.

26. Marriage and Divorce.

27. The Criminal Law, except the Constitution of Courts of Criminal Jurisdiction, but including the Procedure in Criminal Matters.

28. The establishment, maintenance, and management of Penitentiaries.

29. Such classes of subjects as are expressly excepted in the enumeration of the classes of subjects by this Act assigned exclusively to the Legislatures of the Provinces:

And any matter coming within any of the classes of subjects enumerated in this section shall not be deemed to come within the class of matters of a local or private nature comprised in the enumeration of the classes of subjects by this Act assigned exclusively to the Legislatures of the Provinces.(42)

EXCLUSIVE POWERS OF PROVINCIAL LEGISLATURES

92. In each Province the Legislature may exclusively make laws in relation to matters coming within the classes of subjects next hereinafter enumerated, that is to say,

1. The amendment from time to time, notwithstanding anything in this Act, of the Constitution of the Province, except as regards the Office of Lieutenant-Governor.

2. Direct Taxation within the Province in order to the raising of a Revenue for Provincial purposes.

3. The borrowing of money on the sole credit of the Province.

4. The establishment and tenure of Provincial offices and the appointment and payment of Provincial officers.

5. The management and sale of the Public Lands belonging to the Province, and of the timber and wood thereon.

6. The establishment, maintenance, and management of public and reformatory prisons in and for the Province.

7. The establishment, maintenance, and management of hospitals, asylums, charities, and eleemosynary institutions in and for the Province, other than marine hospitals.

8. Municipal institutions in the Province.

9. Shop, saloon, tavern, auctioneer, and other licenses, in order to the raising of a revenue for Provincial, local, or municipal purposes.

10. Local works and undertakings other than such as are of the following classes,—

    a. Lines of steam or other ships, railways, canals, telegraphs, and other works and undertakings connecting the Province with any other or others of the Provinces, or extending beyond the limits of the Province;

    b. Lines of steam ships between the Province and any British or Foreign country;

    c. Such works as, although wholly situate within the Province, are before or after their execution declared by the Parliament of Canada to be for the general advantage of Canada or for the advantage of two or more of the Provinces.

11. The incorporation of companies with Provincial objects.

12. The solemnization of marriage in the Province.

13. Property and civil rights in the Province.

14. The administration of justice in the Province, including the constitution, maintenance, and organization of Provincial Courts, both of civil and of criminal jurisdiction, and including procedure in civil matters in those Courts.

15. The imposition of punishment by fine, penalty, or imprisonment for enforcing any law of the Province made in relation to any matter coming within any of the classes of subjects enumerated in this section.

16. Generally all matters of a merely local or private nature in the Province.

EDUCATION

93. In and for each Province the Legislature may exclusively make laws in relation to education, subject and according to the following provisions:—

1. Nothing in any such law shall prejudicially affect any right or privilege with respect to denominational schools which any class of persons have by law in the Province at the Union.

2. All the powers, privileges, and duties at the Union by law conferred and imposed in Upper Canada on the separate schools and school trustees of the Queen's Roman Catholic subjects shall be and the same are hereby extended to the dissentient schools of the Queen's Protestant and Roman Catholic subjects in Quebec.

3. Where in any Province a system of separate or dissentient schools exists by law at the Union or is thereafter established by the Legislature of the Province, an appeal shall lie to the Governor-General in Council from any Act or Decision of any Provincial authority affecting any right or privilege of the Protestant or Roman Catholic minority of the Queen's subjects in relation to education.

4. In case any such Provincial law as from time to time seems to the Governor-General in Council requisite for the due execution of the provisions of this section is not made, or in case any decision of the Governor-General in Council on any appeal under this section is not duly executed by the proper Provincial authority in that behalf, then and in every such case, and as far only as the circumstances of each case require, the Parliament of Canada may make remedial laws for the due execution of the provisions of this section and of any decision of the Governor-General in Council under this section.(43)

·   ·   ·

OLD AGE PENSIONS

94A. The Parliament of Canada may make laws in relation to old age pensions and supplementary benefits, including survivors' and disability benefits irrespective of age, but no such law shall affect the operation of any law present or future of a provincial legislature in relation to any such matter.(44)

AGRICULTURE AND IMMIGRATION

95. In each Province the Legislature may make laws in relation to Agriculture in

the Province, and to Immigration into the Province; and it is hereby declared that the Parliament of Canada may from time to time make laws in relation to Agriculture in all or any of the Provinces, and to Immigration into all or any of the Provinces; and any law of the Legislature of a Province relative to Agriculture or to Immigration shall have effect in and for the Province as long and as far only as it is not repugnant to any Act of the Parliament of Canada.

. . .

VIII. Revenues; Debts; Assets; Taxation

. . .

109. All lands, mines, minerals, and royalties belonging to the several provinces of Canada, Nova Scotia and New Brunswick at the Union, and all sums then due or payable for such lands, mines, minerals, or royalties, shall belong to the several Provinces of Ontario, Quebec, Nova Scotia and New Brunswick in which the same are situate or arise, subject to any trusts existing in respect thereof, and to any interest other than of the Province in the same.(48)

. . .

Writing a Term Paper

Instructors vary considerably in what they expect from student term papers. The following notes are therefore intended to provide guidelines which can be adapted to fit the requirements of your course and instructor.

1. PAY ATTENTION TO THE SPECIFIC ASSIGNMENT

All term paper assignments are *not* the same. The nature of the assignment will differ across departments within your university, and across courses and instructors within departments. Therefore it is essential to pay close attention to the *specific* assignment. Do not assume that a paper format that has worked well for you in the past will necessarily work this time around.

2. GET AN EARLY START

The sooner you start on the paper assignment, the more likely you are to find research material. Library resources will invariably be strained toward the end of the term. If you give yourself enough lead time, useful material is likely to emerge from newspaper and magazine articles, from other courses, from conversations with friends, and from random thoughts and observations that you might have.

3. SOURCES

There are a number of leads that can be pursued in trying to locate research material for your paper. Use the suggested readings in this and other recent texts, and work backward from the footnotes. Use the card catalogue in your library. Use the *Canadian Periodicals Index*, and go through the recent and as yet unindexed issues of journals such as the *Canadian Journal of Political Science*, *Canadian Public Policy*, and the *Journal of Canadian Studies*. Keep a close eye on newspapers, and on magazines such as *Macleans*, *Saturday Night*, and *Canadian Forum*. When you find one useful source, plunder its footnotes and bibliography for other leads.

4. DO NOT REINVENT THE WHEEL

Your paper should draw upon the existing social science literature, as a term paper in an introductory course can carry only a limited amount of original research. What counts is your ability to apply existing knowledge and theories to the particular subject under examination in your paper.

5. CREATE A MEMORY BANK

Set up a file folder or large envelope for each assignment you face during the term. Then, whenever you have a thought or insight into the assignment, whenever you encounter a possible source of research material, jot it down on a piece of paper and file it away in the folder or envelope. Whenever you encounter something that might be useful, be it in a text, journal article or newspaper, take notes (including the source of the information) and file them away. All the relevant material for each assignment will then be gathered together in one place, ready to be dumped out on your desk when the writing begins. Less material will be lost from a paper memory than from a mental one.

6. RESPECT DEADLINES AND PAGE LIMITS

Take deadlines seriously, and frame your assignment within the page limits set by your instructor. After all, in the "real world" projects have to be done on time and within specified limits. If you are asked for a fifteen-page synopsis by Friday, your employer will not expect a thirty-page synopsis by the following Thursday.

7. WRITE *AT LEAST* TWO DRAFTS

Do not expect to produce a good paper on the first draft. Allow enough time that you can write a rough draft and let it sit for a few days. Then go through the draft as dispassionately as possible, pretending, if you like, that someone else wrote it. Rewrite the sections that are rough, add in new material, and correct problems of style, substance, and interpretation. Remember that rewriting in the early stages often entails substantial reorganization of the material, not merely correcting spelling and grammatical errors. Writing is a cognitive process, a way of thinking about your material and discovering what you want to say. Thus do not be surprised if your paper changes considerably from one draft to the next.

8. A RESEARCH PAPER IS NOT AN ESSAY

A research paper must do more than present your own viewpoint. It should explore a particular theme or question through a marshalling of the available evidence. While it is acceptable to be argumentative, you should not stray beyond the bounds of the existing evidence. The argument should be derived from the evidence, or at least supported by it, rather than an expression of one's own beliefs.

THE THEMATIC STRUCTURE

A good paper pursues an explicit theme or thesis. This should be laid out as early as possible, perhaps in the introductory paragraph. The main body of the paper should then develop this thesis or theme, and the concluding paragraph should link back to the introductory paragraph. There is, then, a circular structure to the paper: you state what it is you intend to do, you go out and do it, and then you conclude by summarizing what you did, answering the questions posed in your introductory paragraph.

10. PAY ATTENTION TO STYLE AND ORGANIZATION

In the famous words of Marshall McLuhan, "the medium is the message." How you communicate your ideas will have a critical impact on their reception. Do not expect your instructor to sift through awkward sentences, indifferent organization and a sloppy style searching for intellectual gold. Good ideas poorly presented are indistinguishable from poor ideas poorly presented.

11. DO NOT RUSH TO THE ATTACK

It is relatively easy and at times satisfying to attack, to condemn and deplore. However, while a moralistic stance *may* enrich a paper, your primary task is to *understand* the phenomenon, event, or personality under investigation. Why did something happen? What were the alternatives? Why were some options pursued and others avoided? Once you understand the complexities of the issue, then and only then are you in a position to render some judgment.

12. AVOID LOADED WORDS

Be careful in your use of words like genocide, lie, murder, deceive, catastrophic, and disaster. Strong words in a research paper are analogous to swear words in more common discourse; if overused, they lose their impact. If you call something a disaster, be sure that you really mean a *disaster* and not merely an unfortunate or unpleasant event. Readers are more impressed by firm but *reasonable* statements supported by evidence than by fervently held beliefs expressed in highly charged language.

13. DO NOT PLAGIARIZE

To plagiarize means to pass off the words *or ideas* of others as your own. In many schools, plagiarism can lead to automatic failure and even expulsion. If you use the words of other writers, enclose them within quotation marks and provide their source in a footnote. If you paraphrase other writers, you must still indicate the source of the material. There is no problem in using the work of other people, and indeed this is what much of the research enterprise is all about—building upon an existing body of knowledge and insights. However, where the work of others is used, *it must be acknowledged*.

14. PARAGRAPHING

A good paragraph has its own internal structure and coherency. It explores a single theme or issue, and the break between paragraphs is used to signify a shift in analysis or emphasis. (A good check on the coherence of a paragraph is to read the first and last sentences; they should make sense together and should contain the essence of the paragraph.) Be wary of very long paragraphs—I once received a paper with a paragraph that stretched over five and a half pages! Paragraphs of over a page in length suggest an indifference on the part of the writer to organization.

15. SUBHEADINGS

Subheadings can be used to impose an organizational structure upon your paper. They break up the paper into more easily digested chunks, and convey the impression that you have paid attention to the structural form and coherency of your argument. It is essential, however, to provide some transition between the sections of your paper. Subheadings emphasize points of transition; they do not provide a substitute for transitions in the body of your text.

16. DO NOT ASSUME SHARED KNOWLEDGE

Students are often unsure whether to include information that they feel will be "obvious" to the marker. Often when I have criticized students for failing to include certain information, they have replied "I just assumed you knew that." The problem is that it is difficult for a marker to assume that the writer indeed knows information that is not contained in the paper. You may well assume that I know that John A. Macdonald was the leader of the Conservative party, but I have less grounds for assuming that you know. Therefore it pays to err on the side of including what you may assume to be shared or common knowledge. Write less for your instructor than for some other, impartial audience that is not privy to what has gone on in your course.

17. AVOID LONG QUOTES

Excessively long quotes suggest an overreliance on the work of others, and a reluctance on the writer's part to come to grips with the ideas behind the quote. Your job, after all, goes well beyond *presenting* the works of others. When quotes of more than one sentence in length are used, they should be set off from the main body of the paragraph and they should be introduced. Phrases like "As Smith has observed ..." and "Jones elaborates upon this point at some length" can be useful in introducing long quotes.

18. AVOID TERMINOLOGICAL CONFUSION

A good argument can be obscured by terminological confusion. Be careful, for example, not to confuse Parliament with the Government of Canada, or French Canadians with the Québécois, or Nova Scotia with the Government of Nova Scotia. Be sure to define the key terms and concepts in your paper. In doing so, do not rely on an English language dictionary. A dictionary of political science or an encyclopedia of the social sciences provides a much better source.

19. FOOTNOTES

Footnotes provide the linkage between your text and the research material that you have employed. Whatever footnote style you adopt—and some institutions specify a particular format—apply it consistently. Footnotes are not peripheral to a good research paper; they are an intrinsic part of it and should not be passed over lightly. It should be possible for a reader to reconstruct the paper from the footnotes, and thus to verify your findings.

20. BIBLIOGRAPHY

A bibliography should be included to acknowledge the sources that you consulted, and in particular those sources that have been of general use but to which specific reference has not been made either in the text or in the footnotes. Do not pad your bibliography by throwing in material that you have *not* looked at.

21. END WITH AN EMPHATIC CONCLUSION

Avoid a paper that fizzles out at the end, that creates the impression that you ran out of things to say and just stopped. The conclusion should not simply review the main points in the paper. It should tie the paper together, looping back to the introduction in order to demonstrate that you have done what you set out to do. Admittedly, a conclusion is often not easy to write, but it is the conclusion that pulls the research enterprise together and answers the question, "so what?"

22. HAND-WRITTEN PAPERS

Most universities and colleges have regulations which state that students are not to be penalized for hand-written papers. The fact remains, however, that poor handwriting will lessen the impact of your paper. If the reader has to struggle through, word by word and sentence by sentence, there is a good chance that at the end of the paper he or she will have little appreciation of the paper's broader theme and argument. Poor handwriting *will* hurt you, no matter how hard the marker tries to keep to the spirit of institutional regulations.

23. PROOFREAD

Always proofread your paper and, better still, have a friend do it also. Pay particular attention to grammar and spelling, and to the agreement between subjects and verbs. A paper that has not been proofread suggests sloppiness and indifference on the part of the author. A careful proofreading ensures that your paper is as good as it can be, that the marker will not be distracted from your argument and ideas by a progression of typos, spelling mistakes, and grammatical errors.

24. GOOD LUCK!

Glossary

Asbestos Strike. In 1949 a prolonged strike by Quebec asbestos miners in Asbestos and Thetford Mines provided a highly publicized stage for a confrontation between Quebec trade unions and reform-minded intelectuals (including P.E. Trudeau) on the one side and the Union Nationale provincial government on the other. Retrospectively, the Asbestos strike is seen as one of the first signs of the Quiet Revolution.

"Better Terms." Regional discontent in the Maritimes has been associated with the search for "better terms." The reference is to adjustments in the financial terms under which the Maritime provinces entered Confederation rather than to other constitutional parameters such as the federal division of powers.

Canada West Foundation. The Canada West Foundation was established in 1973 as a non-profit and non-partisan organization to pursue two objectives: (1) to conduct economic, social, and political research on western Canadian concerns, and (2) to conduct informational and educational programs encouraging an appreciation of the Canadian heritage, and of the role played by the West in Canada. Based in Calgary, the Foundation is supported by governments, corporations, and individuals in western Canada.

Conditional Grant Programs. Conditional grant programs came into use in the 1950s and early 1960s. Through such programs Ottawa provided matching funds to the provinces for health care, advanced education, and social assistance programs administered by the provincial governments. Although such programs fell within provincial jurisdiction, the federal government was able to impose national standards as a condition for the receipt of federal funding. In this sense conditional grant programs represented the fiscal intrusion of the national government into provincial fields of jurisdiction.

Co-operative Commonwealth Federation. The Co-operative Commonwealth Federation (Farmer, Labour, Socialist) was formed at a 1932 Calgary meeting of delegates from farm, labour, and socialist organizations in the West, and to a lesser extent from labour organizations and left-of-centre intellectuals in the East. The CCF's platform, set forth in the 1933 Regina Manifesto, was emphatically socialistic, calling for the public ownership of banks and trust companies, insurance companies, utilities and "all other industries and services essential to social planning."

Crown Lands. All land in Canada which is not privately owned by individuals or corporations belongs to the Crown. Thus the term "Crown land" refers to land owned by the Government of Canada or by one of the ten provincial governments.

Disallowance. Under the terms of the Constitution Act, 1867, the federal government can "disallow" provincial legislation, or prevent it from coming into effect, up to one year after its passage. Disallowance can occur even if the legislation falls wholly within the province's jurisdictional domain. Last used in 1943, disallowance has now become a constitutional dead letter.

Equalization Payments. Equalization payments are unconditional grants from the national government to those provinces whose yield from provincial tax sources is less than the average yield of all provinces. They are designed to ensure that Canadians, no matter where they live, will have access to approximately the same level of public services provided at roughly the same level of taxation.

Great Depression. The 1929 collapse of the American stock market signalled the onset of a prolonged economic depression that lasted until the start of the Second World War and afflicted all industrialized countries. Per capita income in Canada fell by 50 percent, export prices fell to a fraction of 1929 prices, and the number of unemployed rose from 107,000 in 1929 to 646,000 at the height of the Depression in 1933. In western Canada the Depression's impact was intensified by ruinous agricultural markets, drought, and crop infestation.

Judicial Committee of the Privy Council. Under the terms of Great Britain's Colonial Laws Validity Act, the Judicial Committee of the Privy Council served as Canada's court of final appeal. Canadian court decisions, including those of the Supreme Court, could thus be appealed to the JCPC in London. This right of appeal was finally abolished in 1949 by the Supreme Court Act which established the Supreme Court of Canada as the court of final appeal.

National Policy. The National Policy is most closely associated with the protective tariffs adopted by the Government of Canada in 1878, tariffs designed to protect an infant Canadian manufacturing base and to encourage foreign investment. The tariffs were also designed to raise public funds for the construction of a transcontinental railway system, and to ensure sufficient east–west trade on that railway system. More generally, the National Policy is associated with the industrialization of central Canada and the agricultural settlement of the West.

Neoconservatism. Neoconservatism encompasses a number of beliefs which arose in reaction to the post-war growth of government. These include the belief that the size of government should be reduced, that government regulation of the economy should be reduced, and that the private market should be restored as the primary vehicle for the distribution of wealth and economic opportunity.

North-West Rebellion, 1885. In the spring of 1885 several hundred Métis from settlements along the South Saskatchewan River, led by Louis Riel, took up arms against the Canadian government. The rebellion ended at Batoche, Saskatchewan, where the Métis and a small number of Indians faced roughly one thousand recently mobilized Canadian troops. Approximately one hundred men lost their lives, and Riel was subsequently executed.

October Crisis. The 1970 October Crisis was touched off by the kidnapping of James Cross, the British trade commissioner in Montreal, by a cell of the *Front de liberation québécois* (FLQ). The crisis escalated with the kidnapping of Pierre Laporte, Quebec's Minister of Labour, the imposition of the War Measures Act by the federal government, and the murder of Laporte. The crisis ended with the release of Cross in early December.

Pacific Scandal. The financial entanglements of John A. Macdonald and his Conservative party with the backers of the proposed Canadian Pacific Railway came to light in the Pacific Scandal of 1873–74. The scandal led to the Conservatives' defeat in the 1874 general election.

Paramountcy. Section 95 of the Constitution Act, 1867, gives Parliament and the provincial legislatures concurrent powers with respect to agriculture and immigration. However, should provincial and federal legislation conflict, Parliament is held to be paramount and the federal law to prevail: "any law of the Legislature of a Province relative to Agriculture or to Immigration shall have effect ... as long and as far only as it is not repugnant to any Act of the Parliament of Canada."

Remedial Legislation. Section 93.3 of the Constitution Act, 1867, gives Parliament the power to pass remedial legislation should a province make laws "affecting any Right or Privilege of the Protestant or Roman Catholic Minority of the Queen's Subjects in relation to Education." In this narrow sense, Parliament is permitted to legislate within a provincial field of jurisdiction.

Residual Powers. At the time that a constitution is written there will inevitably be powers that are not enumerated and responsibilities for which the constitution writers cannot be aware. For example, the allocation of powers in Sections 91 and 92 of the Constitution Act does not cover such contemporary concerns as cable television and nuclear wastes. Federal constitutions thus contain a provision which assigns residual powers, or the power to deal with unforeseen eventualities, to one level of government or the other. In the Canadian case, residual powers are covered in part by the Peace, Order and Good Government clause of Section 91.

Royal Commissions. Royal Commissions are appointed by the Government of Canada or by provincial governments to investigate specific problems or policy issues. They are not legislative bodies; their responsibility is to make appropriate recommendations for government action. Although in most cases Royal Commissions have quite restricted mandates, at times their scope can be very extensive, as the Royal Commission on the Economic Union and Development Prospects for Canada illustrates.

Social Gospel. The movement for social reform which arose within Protestant churches during the early part of this century came to be known as the Social Gospel. Its proponents argued that individuals trapped by destitution could not be expected to live virtuous lives, and thus that social reform was a necessary precondition for saving souls. The Social Gospel was a particularly active force in western Canada, where it was closely associated with the agrarian revolt of the early 1920s.

War Measures Act. The War Measures Act gives the federal cabinet virtually unlimited powers in times of war or invasion, and in times of "real or apprehended insurrection." It served as a fundamental instrument of government during the First and Second World Wars, and was invoked in a more limited form during the 1970 October Crisis. The Act allows the national government to put aside temporarily the federal division of powers and permits widespread restrictions on individual freedoms.

Winnipeg General Strike, 1919. Canada's only general strike began in Winnipeg in May 1919, with a strike in the metal and building trades over wages and union recognition. The Winnipeg Trades and Labour Council then called for a general strike in support of the metal and building trades. The city was all but paralyzed in a six-week strike. The strike climaxed with, and was brought to a close by, a clash between parading strikers and police on "Bloody Sunday," June 21, in which two people were killed and scores injured.

Notes

CHAPTER ONE

1 *Minority Report*, 1956. Cited in Jonathon Green, *The Book of Political Quotes* (New York: McGraw-Hill, 1982), p. 213.
2 In a 1979 survey of 840 students attending ten Ontario universities, respondents were given a list of thirty occupations and, for each, were asked if they contributed a great deal to the general good of society, whether they contributed more good than harm, or more harm than good. Overall, politicians ranked twenty-fourth, coming ahead of corporate executives, bank presidents, oil company presidents, public relations experts, advertising executives, and bill collectors, but behind military generals, plumbers, musicians, actors, sports stars, lawyers, union leaders, and even professors! Only 4 percent of the students felt that politicians contributed a great deal to the general good of society; another 4 percent felt that they contributed more good than harm while 92 percent felt they contributed more harm than good. *Saturday Night*, October 1979, pp. 35–40.
3 Speech to the Confederation Dinner, Toronto, October 27, 1982.

CHAPTER TWO

1 Donald Creighton, *The Passionate Observer: Selected Writings* (Toronto: McClelland and Stewart, 1980), p. 19.
2 *Ibid.*, p. 51.
3 For example, see W.L. Morton, *The Critical Years: The Union of British North America 1857–1873* (Toronto: McClelland and Stewart, 1964).
4 Cited in Sheila McLeod Arnopoulos and Dominique Clift, *The English Fact in Quebec* (Montreal, McGill-Queen's University Press, 1980), pp. 56–57.
5 J.M.S. Careless, *Canada: A Story of Challenge*, rev. ed. (Toronto, Macmillan, 1963), p. 198.
6 *The Toronto Globe*, December 27, 1861.
7 Garth Stevenson, *Unfulfilled Union: Canadian Federalism and National Unity* (Toronto: Macmillan, 1979), p. 30.
8 R.W. Winks, *Canada and the United States: The Civil War Years* (Baltimore, 1960), pp. 210–11 and 220–29.

9 Cited in John Murray Gibbon, *Canadian Mosaic* (Toronto: McClelland and Stewart, 1938).

10 William H. Riker, *Federalism: Origin, Operation, Significance* (Boston: Little, Brown, 1964), pp. 12–13.

11 Stevenson, *Unfulfilled Union*, pp. 31–32.

12 S.F. Wise and Robert Craig Brown, *Canada Views the United States: Nineteenth-Century Political Attitudes* (Toronto: Macmillan, 1967), p. 94.

13 Careless, *Canada: A Story of Challenge*, rev. ed., p. 202.

14 John Bartlet Brebner, *North Atlantic Triangle* (Toronto: McClelland and Stewart, 1966), p. 158.

15 G.A. Rawlyk and Doug Brown, "The Historical Framework of the Maritimes and Confederation," in G.A. Rawlyk, ed., *The Atlantic Provinces and the Problems of Confederation* (St. John's: Breakwater, 1979), pp. 7–8.

16 A.I. Silver, *The French-Canadian Idea of Confederation, 1864–1900* (Toronto: University of Toronto Press, 1982), pp. 47–48.

17 W.T. Easterbrook and Hugh G.J. Aitken, *Canadian Economic History* (Toronto: Macmillan, 1967), p. 376.

18 Eric Nicol and Peter Whalley, *100 Years of What?* (Toronto: Ryerson, 1966), p. 10.

19 Pierre Berton, *The National Dream: The Great Railway, 1871–1881* (Toronto: McClelland and Stewart, 1970).

20 Jean-Charles Bonenfant, "Quebec and Confederation: Then and Now," in Dale C. Thomson, ed., *Quebec Society and Politics: Views from the Inside* (Toronto: McClelland and Stewart, 1973), p. 55.

21 Cited in J. Bartlet Brebner, *Canada: A Modern History* (Ann Arbor: University of Michigan Press, 1960), p. 277.

22 Nicol and Whalley, *100 Years of What?*, p. 6.

23 Cited in Brebner, *Canada: A Modern History*, p. 281.

24 John A. Munro, ed., *The Wit and Wisdom of John Diefenbaker* (Edmonton: Hurtig, 1982), p. 30.

25 Municipal governments and the territorial governments in northern Canada are creatures of the provincial and federal governments respectively. Exercising only delegated powers, they are not components of the federal system per se.

26 Silver, *The French-Canadian Idea of Confederation*, p. 34.

27 *Ibid.*, p. 220.

28 R.M. Punnett, *British Government and Politics*, 4th ed. (London: Heinemann, 1980), p. 173.

29 An important exception here is in the event of war, invasion, or apprehended insurrection, when the War Measures Act gives the national government virtually unlimited power. The War Measures Act was employed during both World Wars, and in the October Crisis (*see Glossary*) of 1970 when British Trade Commissioner James Cross and Pierre Laporte, Quebec's Minister of Labour, were kidnapped by the FLQ.

30 Thomas A. Hockin, "Adversary Politics and Some Functions of the Canadian House of Commons," in Richard Schultz, Orest M. Kruhlak, and John C. Terry, eds., *The Canadian Political Process*, 3rd ed. (Toronto: Holt, Rinehart and Winston, 1979), p. 315.

31 Allan Kornberg, William Mishler, and Harold D. Clarke, *Representative Democracy in the Canadian Provinces* (Scarborough: Prentice-Hall, 1982), p. 175.

32 Colin Campbell, *Canadian Political Facts, 1945 to 1976* (Toronto: Methuen, 1977), pp. 69–70.

33 Kornberg, Mishler, and Clarke, *Representative Democracy in the Canadian Provinces*, p. 175.

34 Campbell, *Canadian Political Facts*, p. 32.

35 The concept comes from Seymour Martin Lipset, *The First New Nation* (New York: Basic Books, 1963), p. 7.

36 Cited in Robert A. MacKay, *The Unreformed Senate of Canada* (Toronto: McClelland and Stewart, 1963), p. 35.

37 Donald V. Smiley, *The Canadian Political Nationality* (Toronto: Methuen, 1967), pp. 4–5.

38 K.C. Wheare, *Federal Government* (London: Oxford University Press, 1953), p. 19.

39 Silver, *The French-Canadian Idea of Confederation*, p. 218.

40 *Ibid.*, p. 35.

41 *Ibid.*, pp. 48–49.

42 For an example of this line of thought see Ralph Heintzman, "The Spirit of Confederation: Professor Creighton, Biculturalism, and the Use of History," *Canadian Historical Review*, September 1971, pp. 245–75.

43 Donald Creighton, "John A. Macdonald, Confederation, and the Canadian West," in Donald Swainson, ed., *Historical Essays on the Prairie Provinces* (Toronto: McClelland and Stewart, 1970), p. 62.

44 Government of Quebec, *Quebec–Canada: A New Deal* (Editeur officiel du Québec, 1979), p. 9.

45 Stevenson, *Unfulfilled Union*, p. 47.

CHAPTER THREE

1 René Lévesque, *An Option for Quebec* (Toronto: McClelland and Stewart, 1968), p. 14.

2 The capture of Quebec by British forces was one of many military campaigns during prolonged hostilities between Britain and France. Hostilities were brought to a close by the Treaty of Paris, which ceded New France to Great Britain. The treaty also contained guarantees for the freedom of religious worship in the ceded territory.

3 Richard Joy, *Languages in Conflict* (Toronto: Macmillan, 1972), p. 86.

4 Between 1966 and 1976, 52.6 percent of the immigrants who settled in Canada were anglophones, only 6.7 percent were francophones, and 40.7 percent were neither. Rejean Lachapelle and Jacques Henripin, *The Demolinguistic Situation in Canada* (Montreal: Institute for Research on Public Policy, 1982), p. 233.

5 Joy, *Languages in Conflict*, p. 58.

6 *Ibid.*, p. 123.

7 *Ibid.*, p. 69.

8 *Ibid.*, p. 51.

9 Daniel Kubat and David Thornton, *A Statistical Profile of Canadian Society* (Toronto: McGraw-Hill Ryerson, 1974), p. 38.

10 *The Globe and Mail*, National Edition, November 17, 1983, p. 8.

11 Lachapelle and Henripin, *The Demolinguistic Situation in Canada*, p. 196.

12 Government of Quebec, *Quebec–Canada: A New Deal* (Editeur officiel du Québec, 1979), p. 30.

13 Lévesque, *An Option for Quebec*, p. 93.

14 *The Globe and Mail*, National Edition, October 18, 1983, p. 8.

15 *The Globe and Mail*, National Edition, October 20, 1983, p. 8.

16 The changing ethnic and racial composition of the Canadian population is addressed in *Equality Now*, The Report of the Special Committee on Visible Minorities in Canadian Society, Bob Daudlin, MP, Chairman (Ottawa: Queen's Printer, March 1984).

17 Lachapelle and Henripin, *The Demolinguistic Situation in Canada*, p. 310.

18 *Ibid.*, p. 174.

19 Donald V. Smiley, "Reflections on Cultural Nationhood and Political Community in Canada," in R. Kenneth Carty and W. Peter Wards, eds., *Entering the Eighties: Canada in Crisis* (Toronto: Oxford University Press, 1980), p. 33.

20 Lévesque, *An Option for Quebec*, p. 14.

21 Herbert F. Quinn, *The Union Nationale: A Study in Quebec Nationalism* (Toronto: University of Toronto Press, 1963), p. 105.

22 Cited in C. Nish, *Quebec in the Duplessis Era* (Toronto: Copp Clark, 1970), p. 36.

23 Kenneth McRoberts and Dale Posgate, *Quebec: Social Change and Political Crisis*, rev. ed. (Toronto: McClelland and Stewart, 1980), p. 74.

24 For a fascinating discussion of Union Nationale patronage and the electoral manipulation with which it was associated, see Quinn, *The Union Nationale*, Chapter 7.

25 Dominique Clift, *Quebec Nationalism in Crisis* (Kingston: McGill-Queen's University Press, 1982), p. 15.

26 McRoberts and Posgate, *Quebec*, p. 94.

27 Both trade union and intellectual discontent had been brewing since the early 1950s, with the latter finding expression in the small but politically influential magazine *Cité libre*, to which Pierre Trudeau was a frequent contributor.

28 Report by the Quebec Assembly of Bishops to the Pope. *The Globe and Mail*, National Edition, November 28, 1983.

29 For a discussion of this point see Albert Breton, "The Economics of Nationalism," *Journal of Political Economy*, August 1964, p. 385.

30 For a discussion of the new middle class and the consequent restructuring of class politics in Quebec, see Herbert Guidon, "The Modernization of Quebec and the Legitimacy of the Canadian State," in D. Glenday, H. Guidon, and A. Turowetz, eds., *Modernization and the Canadian State* (Toronto: Macmillan, 1978). See also Henry Milner, *Politics in the New Quebec* (Toronto: McClelland and Stewart, 1977).

31 Cited in Lévesque, *An Option for Quebec*, p. 9.

32 Sheila McLeod Arnopoulous and Dominique Clift, *The English Fact in Quebec* (Montreal: McGill-Queen's University Press, 1980), p. 61.

33 J.R. Mallory, *The Structure of Canadian Government* (Toronto: Macmillan, 1971), p. 397.

34 For a discussion, see André Bernard, *What Does Quebec Want?* (Toronto: James Lorimer, 1978).

35 John Meisel, *Working Papers on Canadian Politics* (Montreal: McGill-Queen's University Press, 1973), p. 205.

36 The most influential American analogy was drawn by Pierre Vallières in *White Niggers of America*, trans. Joan Pinkham (Toronto: McClelland and Stewart, 1971).

37 For an English-language expansion of this theme, see Sheilagh Hodgins Milner and Henry Milner, *The Decolonization of Quebec* (Toronto: McClelland and Stewart, 1973).

38 Lévesque, *An Option for Quebec*, p. 26. Writing in *Le Devoir* (September 19, 1967), Lévesque argued that Quebec's independence "would allow our two majorities to extricate themselves from an archaic federal framework in which our two very distinct 'personalities' paralyze each other by dint of pretending to have a third personality common to both."

39 See Ron Haggart and Aubrey E. Golden, *Rumors of War* (Toronto: New Press, 1971); and Denis Smith, *Bleeding Hearts — Bleeding Country: Canada and the Quebec Crisis* (Edmonton: Hurtig, 1971).

40 For a discussion of this point see Pierre Vallières, *Choose!*, trans. Penelope Williams (Toronto: New Press, 1972).

41 See Maurice Pinard and Richard Hamilton, "The Parti Québécois Comes to Power: the 1976 Election," *Canadian Journal of Political Science* 11 (December 1978), pp. 739–75.

42 Government of Quebec, *Quebec–Canada*, p. 109.

43 As Louis Balthazar points out, "paradoxically, people had to be brought to vote for Canada in the name of Quebec." "Quebec at the Hour of Choice," in R. Kenneth Carty and W. Peter Ward, eds., *Entering the Eighties: Canada in Crisis* (Toronto: Oxford University Press, 1980), p. 73.

44 *The Globe and Mail*, National Edition, May 20, 1983, p. 8.

45 McRoberts and Posgate, *Quebec*, p. 107.

46 In 1973, some 31,000 Quebec francophones made up 12.4 percent of the English-language school population. William D. Coleman, "From Bill 22 to Bill 101: The Politics of Language under the Parti Québécois," *Canadian Journal of Political Science*, XIV:3 (September 1981), p. 467.

47 *Ibid.*, p. 468.

48 *Ibid.*, p. 459.

49 Bill 101 abolished English as an official language of the legislature and courts, but this provision was overturned by the Supreme Court of Canada in 1979.

50 *The Globe and Mail*, National Edition, October 26, 1983, p. 10.

51 *The Globe and Mail*, National Edition, November 4, 1983, p. 8.

52 *The Globe and Mail*, National Edition, March 18, 1983, p. 2.

53 *The Globe and Mail*, National Edition, July 27, 1984, p. 2.

54 *Ibid.*

55 See Pierre Fournier, *The Quebec Establishment: The Ruling Class and the State* (Montreal: Black Rose, 1976).

56 Cited in Raymond Reid, *The Canadian Style* (Toronto: Fitzhenry and Whiteside, 1973), p. 93.

57 J.W. Dafoe, *Laurier: A Study in Canadian Politics* (Toronto: McClelland and Stewart, 1922, reprinted 1963), p. 26.

58 *Ibid.*, p. 26.

59 In the general election of 1882, the Conservatives captured fifty-one seats in Quebec with 52.3 percent of the popular vote. In 1887, two years after Riel's execution, they won only thirty-three seats after a very modest erosion of their popular vote to 49.6 percent. In the 1891 general election, the Conservative vote marginally increased to 50.8 percent while the number of Conservative seats fell to twenty-eight. The major drop occurred in 1896 when the party won only sixteen seats with 45.8 percent of the vote. Thus Riel's execution does not appear to have had a dramatic impact on voting patterns within Quebec.

60 A second example is provided by Ontario during the early years of the First World War, when conflict over the educational rights of Franco-Ontarians intensified French Canadian opposition to conscription.

61 At the time of writing, these funds total approximately $200 million a year, with more than half of the total allocated to Quebec.

62 Christina McCall-Newman, *Grits: An Intimate Portrait of the Liberal Party* (Toronto: Macmillan, 1982), p. 62.

63 Richard Gwyn, *The Northern Magus* (Toronto: McClelland and Stewart, 1980), p. 220.

64 *Ibid.*, p. 236.

65 McCall-Newman, *Grits*, p. 79.

66 Cited in Mason Wade, *The French Canadians, 1860–1967*, Volume II (Toronto: Macmillan, 1968), pp. 618–19.

67 Dalton Camp, *Points of Departure* (Toronto: McClelland and Stewart, 1979).

68 An exception to this rule was an article by Donald Creighton, one of Canada's foremost historians, published in *Maclean's* (June 27, 1977). Creighton lashed out at what he termed the politics of blackmail, intimidation, and coercion wielded by Quebec. He called for an end to the "politics of appeasement," and for an extremely tough stand in any independence negotiations with Quebec.

69 W.A. Matheson, *The Prime Minister and the Cabinet* (Toronto: Methuen, 1976), p. 22. Matheson uses consociationalism as a conceptual framework in this insightful look at cabinet government in Canada. For a more extended conceptual treatment, see K.D. McRae, ed., *Consociational Democracy: Political Accommodation in Segmented Societies* (Toronto: McClelland and Stewart, 1974).

70 Lachapelle and Henripin, *The Demolinguistic Situation in Canada*, pp. 32 and 39.

71 Gwyn, *The Northern Magus*, p. 223.

72 This decline is in part attributable to the disappearance of French-language entrance and exit requirements in most English Canadian universities. Gwyn, *The Northern Magus*, p. 230.

73 Gwyn, *The Northern Magus*, p. 225.

74 Patrick Martin, Allan Gregg, and George Perlin, *Contenders: The Tory Quest for Power* (Scarborough: Prentice-Hall, 1983), p. 120.

75 *Toronto Star*, June 5, 1983, p. F3.

76 *The Calgary Herald*, September 29, 1983, pp. A1-2.

77 Smiley, "Reflections on Cultural Nationhood," p. 29.

78 W.L. Morton, "Confederation, 1870–1896: The End of the Macdonaldian Constitution and the Return to Duality," in Bruce Hodgins and Robert Page, eds., *Canadian History Since 1867: Essays and Interpretations* (Georgetown: Irwin-Dorsey, 1972), pp. 195–200.

79 Government of Quebec, *Quebec-Canada*, p. 43.

CHAPTER FOUR

1 Task Force on National Unity, *A Future Together* (Hull: Supply and Services Canada, 1979), p. 29.

2 For an expansion of this contrast, see Roger Gibbins, *Regionalism: Territorial Politics in Canada and the United States* (Toronto: Butterworths, 1982).

3 June, 1936. Cited in Warner Troyer, *The Sound and the Fury* (Toronto: John Wiley and Sons, 1980), p. 11.

4 See Robert W. Jackman, "Political Parties, Voting and National Integration: The Canadian Case," in Richard Schultz, Orest M. Kruhlak, and John C. Terry, eds., *The Canadian Political Process*, 3rd ed. (Toronto: Holt, Rinehart and Winston, 1979), pp. 130–44; and Richard Johnston, "Federal and Provincial Voting: Contemporary Patterns and Historical Evolution," in David J. Elkins and Richard Simeon, eds., *Small Worlds: Provinces and Parties in Canadian Political Life* (Toronto: Methuen, 1980), pp. 131–78.

5 See Seymour Martin Lipset and Stein Rokkan, "Cleavage Structures, Party Systems, and Voter Alignments: An Introduction," in Lipset and Rokkan, eds., *Party Systems and Voter Alignments: Cross-National Perspectives* (New York: The Free Press, 1967), pp. 1–64; and Herman Bakvis, *Federalism and The Organization of Political Life: Canada in Comparative Perspective* (Kingston: Institute of Intergovernmental Relations, Queen's University, 1981), pp. 40–48.

6 For an expansion of this discussion see Roger Gibbins, *Prairie Politics and Society: Regionalism in Decline* (Toronto: Butterworths, 1980).

7 The years since the 1981 census have likely seen a *decline* in the West's share of the national population. Between July 1, 1983 and July 1, 1984, for example, Alberta's population is estimated to have dropped by some 5,000 persons.

8 Statistics Canada figures, cited in the *Calgary Herald*, November 12, 1984, p. A1.

9 Ernest R. Forbes, *The Maritime Rights Movement, 1919-1927: A Study in Canadian Regionalism* (Montreal: McGill-Queen's University Press, 1979), p. 2.

10 *Ibid.*

11 G.A. Rawlyk and Doug Brown, "The Historical Framework of the Maritimes and Confederation," in G.A. Rawlyk, ed., *The Atlantic Provinces and the Problems of Confederation* (St. John's: Breakwater, 1979), p. 14.

12 Forbes, *The Maritime Rights Movement*, p. 8.

13 Rawlyk and Brown, "The Historical Framework of the Maritimes and Confederation," p. 18.

14 *Ibid.*

15 Forbes, *The Maritime Rights Movement*, pp. 20–21.

16 *Ibid.*, p. 18.

17 *Ibid.*, p. 35.

18 *Ibid.*, p. 37.

19 Rawlyk and Brown, "The Historical Framework of the Maritimes and Confederation," p. 26.

20 When Alberta and Saskatchewan were created in 1905, the ownership of natural resources was

retained by the federal government. Ownership was not transferred to the western provinces until 1931.

21 Raymond Reid, *The Canadian Style* (Toronto: Fitzhenry and Whiteside, 1973), p. 105.

22 Terry Campbell and G.A. Rawlyk, "The Historical Framework of Newfoundland and Confederation," in G.A. Rawlyk, ed., *The Atlantic Provinces and the Problems of Confederation* (St. John's: Breakwater, 1979), p. 70.

23 It must be recognized that Newfoundland was playing for much larger stakes. The huge Hibernia oil field has been proven out by test wells, whereas it is still not clear whether or not the Nova Scotia gas fields will be of a sufficient size to be commercially viable. Alberta, moreover, is presently sitting on a vast surplus of natural gas which further impairs the commercial viability of the Nova Scotia resource.

24 Rawlyk and Brown, "The Historical Framework of the Maritimes and Confederation," p. 31.

25 *Ibid.*, p. 42.

26 See Anthony Careless, *Initiative and Response: The Adaptation of Canadian Federalism to Regional Economic Development* (Montreal: McGill-Queen's University Press, 1977).

27 Cited in Frank H. Underhill, *In Search of Canadian Liberalism* (Toronto: Macmillan, 1960), p. 55.

28 Vernon C. Fowke, *The National Policy and the Wheat Economy* (Toronto: University of Toronto Press, 1957), p. 282.

29 Kenneth H. Norrie, "Some Comments on Prairie Economic Alienation," in J. Peter Meekison, ed., *Canadian Federalism: Myth or Reality*, 3rd ed. (Toronto: Methuen, 1977), p. 325.

30 For an expanded discussion of western alienation, see Gibbins, *Prairie Politics and Society*, Chapter Five.

31 J.R. Mallory, *Social Credit and the Federal Power in Canada* (Toronto: University of Toronto Press, 1953), p. 39.

32 See W.L. Morton, *The Progressive Party of Canada* (Toronto: University of Toronto Press, 1950).

33 Stanley C. Roberts, "Canadian Federalism and the Constitution: What is at Stake in the West," Alan B. Plaunt Memorial Lecture, Carleton University, April 6, 1979, p. 2. For empirical data on the relationship between western alienation and antipathy to Quebec, see Roger Gibbins, "Models of Nationalism: A Case Study of Political Ideologies in the Canadian West," *Canadian Journal of Political Science*, June 1977, pp. 341–73.

34 Denis Smith, "Liberals and Conservatives on the Prairies, 1917–1968," in David P. Gagan, ed., *Prairie Perspectives* (Toronto: Holt, Rinehart and Winston, 1970), p. 41.

35 W.L. Morton, "The Bias of Prairie Politics," *Transactions of the Royal Society of Canada*, Series III, Vol. XLIX, June 1955, Section II, p. 66.

36 For an elaboration of this point, see Roger Gibbins, "Constitutional Politics and the West," in Keith Banting and Richard Simeon, eds., *And No One Cheered: Federalism, Democracy and the Constitution Act* (Toronto: Methuen, 1983), pp. 119–32.

37 For a discussion see Ralph Matthews, *The Creation of Regional Dependency* (Toronto: University of Toronto Press, 1983), and Paul Phillips, *Regional Disparities*, rev. ed. (Toronto: James Lorimer, 1982).

38 For an interesting look at the negative impact of reform within the Liberal party on the regional sensitivities, see David E. Smith, *The Regional Decline of a National Party: Liberals on the Prairies* (Toronto: University of Toronto Press, 1981), Chapter Six.

39 Wallace Clement, "A Political Economy of Regionalism in Canada," in Daniel Glenday, Hubert Guindon, and Allan Turowetz, eds., *Modernization and the Canadian State* (Toronto: Macmillan, 1978), p. 89.

40 *Ibid.*, p. 94.

41 *Ibid.*, p. 99.

42 Ron Graham, "The Legacy of Joe Clark," *Saturday Night*, September 1983, p. 19.

43 The metropolitan–hinterland model dates from the work of economic historian Harold Innis.

See *Empire and Communications* (Toronto: University of Toronto Press, 1950).

44 J.M.S. Careless, " 'Limited Identities' in Canada," *Canadian Historical Review*, Vol. 50, 1969, p. 9.

45 This survey, conducted by the author in June 1982, encompassed 1,402 randomly selected respondents from the four western provinces.

46 Alan C. Cairns, "The Governments and Societies of Canadian Federalism," *Canadian Journal of Political Science*, Vol. 10, 1977, pp. 695–726.

47 Harold D. Clarke, Lawrence LeDuc, Jane Jenson, and Jon Pammett, *Political Choice in Canada* (Toronto: McGraw-Hill Ryerson, 1979). In feeling thermometer questions, respondents are handed a cardboard thermometer with values ranging from 0 (very negative) through 50 (indifferent) to 100 (very positive). They are then asked to locate various objects, such as Canada, their province or political leaders, on this scale. Although the thermometer may seem somewhat crude, it has proved to be a valuable tool in measuring the degree of respondent affect or emotional predisposition toward a wide range of political objects.

48 *Ibid.*, p. 64.

49 David J. Elkins, "The Sense of Place," in David J. Elkins and Richard Simeon, eds., *Small Worlds: Provinces and Parties in Canadian Political Life* (Toronto, Methuen, 1980), p. 16.

50 *Ibid.*, p. 21.

51 John W. Holmes, "Impact of Domestic Political Factors on Canadian–American Relations: Canada," in Annette Baker Fox, Alfred D. Herd, Jr., and Joseph S. Nye, eds., *Canada and the United States: Transnational and Transgovernmental Relations* (New York: Columbia University Press, 1976), p. 32.

52 Richard Allen, ed., *A Region of the Mind* (Regina: Canadian Plains Study Centre, University of Saskatchewan, 1973).

53 R. Douglas Francis, "Changing Images of the West," *Journal of Canadian Studies*, Vol. 17, No. 3 (Fall 1982), p. 5.

54 E.E. Schattschneider, *The Semi-Sovereign People* (New York: Holt, Rinehart and Winston, 1959).

55 In the 1984 federal election Tony Roman was elected as an independent in the Ontario riding of York North. Roman had earlier run for the Conservative nomination in the riding, and his campaign was openly supported by Conservatives opposed to their party's official candidate, incumbent John Gamble.

56 Richard Crossman, *Government and the Governed* (London: Christophers, 1939), p. 5.

57 Robert J. Jackson and Michael M. Atkinson, *The Canadian Legislative System*, 2nd ed. (Toronto: Macmillan, 1980), p. 113.

58 Mark MacGuigan, "Impediments to an Enlarged Role for the Backbencher," in Paul Fox, ed., *Politics: Canada*, 5th ed. (Toronto: McGraw-Hill Ryerson, 1982), p. 496.

59 Robert A. MacKay, *The Unreformed Senate of Canada* (Toronto: McClelland and Stewart, 1963), p. 44.

60 For examples only, see Roger Gibbins, *Senate Reform: Moving Towards the Slippery Slope* (Kingston: Institute of Intergovernmental Relations, Queen's University, 1983); Peter McCormick, Ernest C. Manning, and Gordon Gibson, *Regional Representation: The Canadian Partnership*, A Task Force Report prepared for the Canada West Foundation (Calgary, 1981); *Senate Reform*, The Report of the Special Joint Committee of the Senate and the House of Commons on Senate Reform (Ottawa, January 1984); and William J. Yurko, MP, *Renewed Federalism: Structural Reform of the Canadian Senate* (Ottawa, December 1982).

61 For an informative discussion, see William P. Irvine, *Does Canada Need a New Electoral System?* (Kingston: Institute of Intergovernmental Relations, Queen's University, 1979).

62 Reported in David J. Bell, "Regionalism in the Canadian Community," in Paul Fox, ed., *Politics: Canada*, 4th ed. (Toronto: McGraw-Hill Ryerson, 1977), p. 84.

63 David K. Elton, ed., *One Prairie Province?* (Lethbridge Herald, 1970).

64 For an overview of this line of argument, see Phillips, *Regional Disparities*.

65 For a discussion of this last point, see N.H. Lithwick, *Regional Economic Policy: The Canadian Experience* (Toronto: McGraw-Hill Ryerson, 1978), p. 144.

66 Phillips, *Regional Disparities*, p. 130.

67 Richard Simeon, "Natural Resource Revenues and Canadian Federalism: A Survey of the Issues," paper presented to the Conference on the Alberta Heritage Savings and Trust Fund, Edmonton, October 18–19, 1979, p. 2.

68 Speech at the Liberal Party of Canada Fund Raising Dinner, Vancouver, November 24, 1981.

69 Dalton Camp, *An Eclectic Eel* (Ottawa: Deneau, 1981), p. 84.

70 June 4, 1973. Cited in John A. Munro, ed., *The Wit and Wisdom of John Diefenbaker* (Edmonton: Hurtig, 1982), pp. 80–81.

CHAPTER FIVE

1 Government of Canada, *Income Security and the Social Services* (Ottawa, 1970), pp. 60, 68.

2 James J. Rice, "Social Policy, Economic Management, and Redistribution," in G. Bruce Doern and Peter Aucoin, eds., *Public Policy in Canada* (Toronto: Macmillan, 1979), p. 115.

3 *Ibid.*, p. 117. For a discussion of business support for and opposition to the rudimentary welfare state put into place between 1930 and 1945, see Alvin Finkel, "Origins of the Welfare State in Canada," in Leo Panitch, ed., *The Canadian State: Political Economy and Political Power* (Toronto: University of Toronto Press, 1977), pp. 344–70.

4 Donald Creighton, *The Passionate Observer: Selected Writings* (Toronto: McClelland & Stewart, 1980), p. 36.

5 Finkel, "Origins of the Welfare State," p. 345.

6 Rice, "Social Policy, Economic Management, and Redistribution," p. 109–10.

7 Richard M. Bird, in collaboration with Meyer W. Bucovetsky and David K. Foot, *The Growth of Public Sector Employment in Canada* (Montreal: Institute for Research on Public Policy, 1979), p. 49.

8 There is also an important distinction between transfer payments *to persons*, which are under discussion here, and *intergovernmental* transfers which are discussed later in the chapter.

9 Bird, *The Growth of Public Sector Employment in Canada*, p. 11.

10 *Ibid.*, p. 19.

11 For example, see Wallace Clement, *The Canadian Corporate Elite: An Analysis of Economic Power* (Toronto: McClelland & Stewart, 1975); and John Porter, *The Vertical Mosaic* (Toronto: University of Toronto Press, 1965).

12 National Council of Welfare, *1984 Poverty Lines* (Ottawa: Government of Canada, March 1984), p. 4. This document provides a good discussion of the technical complexities entailed in the construction of poverty lines.

13 *Ibid.*

14 *Ibid.*, p. 3.

15 Dennis Forcese, *The Canadian Class Structure*, 2nd ed. (Toronto: McGraw-Hill Ryerson, 1980), p. 64.

16 *Ibid.*, p. 37.

17 Joan St. Laurent, "Income Maintenance Programs and Their Effect on Income Distribution in Canada," in John Harp and John R. Hofley, eds., *Structured Inequality in Canada* (Scarborough: Prentice-Hall, 1980), p. 435.

18 Ingrid Bryan, *Economic Policies in Canada* (Toronto: Butterworths, 1982), p. 191.

19 *Ibid.*, p. 191.

20 It should be noted that there are even greater disparities in the distribution of *wealth* than in the

distribution of *income*. See Bryan, *Economic Policies in Canada*, p. 188 for a discussion of the distinction between the two terms.

21 Statistics Canada, *Income Distribution in Canada* (Ottawa, May 1984).

22 W. Irwin Gillespie, *The Redistribution of Income in Canada* (Toronto: Gage Publishing, 1980), p. 173.

23 *Ibid.*, p. 169.

24 St. Laurent, "Income Maintenance Programs," p. 430.

25 Donald Smiley, "Reflections on Cultural Nationhood and Political Community in Canada," in R. Kenneth Carty and W. Peter Ward, eds., *Entering the Eighties: Canada in Crisis* (Toronto: Oxford University Press, 1980), p. 37.

26 St. Laurent, "Income Maintenance Programs," p. 425.

27 W. Irwin Gillespie, "On the Redistribution of Income in Canada," in Harp and Hofley, *Structured Inequality in Canada*, p. 36.

28 Bryan, *Economic Policies in Canada*, p. 199.

29 Finkel, "Origins of the Welfare State," p. 354.

30 Estimates here vary within a fairly narrow range. Using 1969 data, Gillespie estimated that income taxes made up 30 percent of the tax load, with general sales taxes contributing 15 percent, corporate taxes 14 percent, property taxes 11 percent, excise taxes 10 percent, social security taxes 7 percent and a variety of other taxes 12 percent. ("On the Redistribution of Income in Canada," in Harp and Hofley, *Structured Inequality in Canada*, p. 29.) Richard Rose's estimate is 35 percent, which compares with 37 percent in the United States and 30 percent in the United Kingdom (*Understanding Big Government: The Programme Approach* (London: Sage, 1984), p. 107). The Vancouver-based Fraser Institute used 1983 data (*The Canadian Consumer Tax Index and You*, 1984) to estimate that income taxes make up 33 percent of the tax load faced by the average Canadian family.

31 Department of Finance, *Analysis of Federal Tax Expenditures for Individuals* (Ottawa, November 1981).

32 Linda McQuaig, "Rich Rewards," *The Globe and Mail*, National Edition, April 21, 1984, p. 1.

33 Statistics Canada, 1984.

34 Gillespie, *The Redistribution of Income*, pp. 30–66 and 172.

35 Bryan, *Economic Policies in Canada*, p. 188.

36 Forcese, *The Canadian Class Structure*, p. 153.

37 For example, see Clement, *The Canadian Corporate Elite*, and Dennis Olsen, "The State Elites," in Panitch, *The Canadian State*, pp. 199–224.

38 M. Janine Brodie and Jane Jenson, *Crisis, Challenge and Change: Party and Class in Canada* (Toronto: Methuen, 1980), p. 263.

39 *Ibid.*, p. 287.

40 See Douglas McCready and Conrad Winn, "Redistributive Policy," in Conrad Winn and John McMenemy, *Political Parties in Canada* (Toronto: McGraw-Hill Ryerson, 1976), pp. 206–27.

41 This conclusion holds whether class is measured by occupation, education, occupational prestige, or subjective assessments of class position. For a detailed analysis of the relationship between social class and voting behaviour in the 1965, 1968, and 1974 general elections, see Harold D. Clark, Jane Jenson, Lawrence Leduc, and Jon H. Pammett, *Political Choice in Canada* (Toronto: McGraw-Hill Ryerson, 1979), pp. 107–19. For supporting evidence see Donald Blake, "The Measurement of Regionalism in Canadian Voting Patterns," *Canadian Journal of Political Science* 5 (1972), pp. 55–81; and Jane Jenson, "Party Systems," in David J. Bellamy, Jon H. Pammett, and Donald C. Rowat, eds., *The Provincial Political Systems: Comparative Essays* (Toronto: Methuen, 1976), pp. 118–31.

42 Brodie and Jenson, *Crisis, Challenge and Change*, p. 299.

43 Their argument is developed at length in *Crisis, Challenge and Change*. A shorter synopsis appears as "The Party System" in Michael S. Whittington and Glen Williams, eds., *Canadian Politics in the 1980s*, 2nd ed. (Toronto: Methuen, 1984), pp. 252–70.

44 Brodie and Jenson, *Crisis, Challenge and Change*, p. 8.

45 *Ibid.*, p. 11.

46 *Ibid.*, p. 3.

47 Leo A. Johnson, "The Development of Class in Canada in the Twentieth Century," in Harp and Hofley, *Structured Inequality in Canada*, p. 99.

48 For some contrary evidence, see John C. Leggett, "The Persistence of Working-Class Consciousness in Vancouver," in John Allan Fry, ed., *Economy, Class and Social Reality* (Toronto: Butterworths, 1979), pp. 241–62.

49 E.M. Schreiber, "Class Awareness and Class Voting in Canada," *The Canadian Review of Sociology and Anthropology*, Vol. 17, no. 1, 1980, p. 37.

50 Variable 1383 in "The 1974–1979–1980 Canadian National Elections and Quebec Referendum Panel Study," Harold Clarke, Jane Jenson, Lawrence LeDuc, and Jon Pammett, principal investigators.

51 For a discussion of measurement problems, see Forcese, *The Canadian Class Structure*, pp. 14–20.

52 J. Goyder and P. Pineo, "The Accuracy of Self Assessments of Social Status," *Canadian Review of Sociology and Anthropology*, Vol. 14, No. 2 (May 1977), p. 236.

53 Such questions are addressed by the Marxist concept of "false consciousness," which attempts to explain why many individuals will incorrectly identify their class position or fail to recognize the class foundations of political life.

54 Anselm L. Strauss, *The Contexts of Social Mobility: Ideology and Theory* (Chicago: Aldine, 1971), p. xi.

55 *Ibid.*, p. 250.

56 Forcese, *The Canadian Class Structure*, p. 95.

57 Clement, *The Canadian Corporate Elite*, p. 365.

58 Herbert F. Quinn, *The Union Nationale: A Study in Quebec Nationalism* (Toronto: University of Toronto Press, 1963), pp. 192–93.

59 John Richards and Larry Pratt, *Prairie Capitalism: Power and Influence in the New West* (Toronto: McClelland and Stewart, 1979), p. 5.

60 Richard Simeon, "Regionalism and Canadian Political Institutions," in Richard Schultz, Orest M. Kruhlak, and John C. Terry, eds., *The Canadian Political Process*, 3rd ed. (Toronto: Holt, Rinehart and Winston, 1979), p. 294.

61 In the early part of this century, Canadian socialists themselves were often mired in imported models and ideas that had little relevance to Canadian experience. It has only been more recently that socialism has become "a viable and distinctive element in Canadian political thought." Norman Penner, *The Canadian Left: A Critical Analysis* (Scarborough: Prentice-Hall, 1977), p. 260.

62 Donald V. Smiley, *Canada in Question: Federalism in the Eighties*, 3rd ed. (Toronto: McGraw-Hill Ryerson, 1980), p. 165.

63 Anthony D. Careless, *Initiative and Response: Adaptation of Canadian Federalism to Regional Economic Expansion* (Montreal: McGill-Queen's University Press, 1977), p. 169.

64 See *ibid.*, p. 166 for a discussion.

65 Unconditional grants have no federal "strings" attached. The money can be spent as the provinces see fit, without the necessity of meeting federal program conditions or spending priorities.

66 Saskatchewan was in a state of transition between a "have-not" and a "have" status, which created the bookkeeping entry of a negative equalization payment. In fact, however, "have"

provinces do not face equalization payments *to* the federal government; equalization entails only payments from Ottawa to the have-not provinces.

67 T.W. Acheson, "The Maritimes and 'Empire Canada,' " in David Jay Bercuson, ed., *Canada and the Burden of Unity* (Toronto: Macmillan, 1977), p. 103. See also Donald V. Smiley, *Canada in Question: Federalism in the Seventies*, 2nd ed. (Toronto: McGraw-Hill Ryerson, 1976), p. 192.

68 Frank MacKinnon, "Prince Edward Island: Big Engine, Little Body," in Martin Robin, ed., *Canadian Provincial Politics* (Scarborough: Prentice-Hall, 1972), p. 256.

69 H.G. Thorburn, *Planning and the Economy: Building Federal–Provincial Consensus* (Toronto: James Lorimer, 1984), p. 150.

70 Bryan, *Economic Policies in Canada*, p. 210.

71 For a detailed discussion of DREE, see Careless, *Initiative and Response*.

72 Bryan, *Economic Policies in Canada*, p. 211.

73 Ross Laver, "Young and Out of Work," *Maclean's*, July 16, 1984, p. 38.

74 Supply and Services Canada, *Supply Administration Contracting Statistics*, Fiscal Year 1982–83 (Supply Information and Data Management Branch, 1984).

75 In 1976 the Department of Veterans Affairs was moved from Ottawa to a new $50 million headquarters in Charlottetown.

76 Herman Bakvis, *Federalism and the Organization of Political Life: Canada in Comparative Perspective* (Kingston: Institute of Intergovernmental Relations, Queen's University, 1981), p. 44.

77 Richard W. Phidd and G. Bruce Doern, *The Politics and Management of Canadian Economic Policy* (Toronto: Macmillan, 1978), p. 317.

78 Smiley, *Canada in Question*, 3rd ed., p. 184.

79 T.J. Courchene, "Interprovincial Migration and Economic Adjustment," *Canadian Journal of Economics* III, 1970, pp. 550–76; and Economic Council of Canada, *Living Together: A Study of Regional Disparities* (Ottawa: Supply and Services, 1977).

80 Bryan, *Economic Policies in Canada*, p. 207.

81 Thorburn, *Planning the Economy*, p. 120.

82 For an interesting linkage of gender politics to the themes of this chapter, see Elizabeth Wilson, *Women and the Welfare State* (London: Tavistock Publications, 1977).

CHAPTER SIX

1 J. Barlet Brebner, *Canada: A Modern History* (Ann Arbor: University of Michigan Press, 1960), p. ix.

2 Robert Frost, *The Poetry of Robert Frost*, ed. Edward Connery Lathem (New York: Holt, Rinehart and Winston, 1967).

3 Dale Posgate and Kenneth McRoberts, *Quebec: Social Change and Political Crisis* (Toronto: McClelland and Stewart, 1976), p. 19.

4 A.R.M. Lower, *Colony to Nation* (London: 1953), p. 109.

5 J.M.S. Careless, *Canada: A Story of Challenge*, rev. ed. (Toronto: Macmillan, 1963), p. 113.

6 Cited in Joseph Barber, *Good Fences Make Good Neighbours* (Toronto: McClelland and Stewart, 1958), p. 31.

7 *Ibid.*, p. 31.

8 *The Globe*, June 1, 1871. Cited in S.F. Wise and Robert Craig Brown, *Canada Views the United States: Nineteenth-Century Political Attitudes* (Toronto: Macmillan, 1967), p. 109.

9 Olivar Asselin, *A Quebec View of Canadian Nationalism* (Montreal, 1909), p. 19.

10 Henri Bourassa, *Great Britain and Canada* (Montreal, 1901), p. 7.

11 Cited in Jonathon Green, comp., *The Book of Political Quotes* (New York: McGraw-Hill, 1982), p. 59.

12 James Eayrs, "Sharing a Continent: the Hard Issues," in James Sloan Dickey, ed., *The United States and Canada* (Englewood Cliffs, N.J.: Prentice-Hall, 1964), p. 60.

13 Goldwin Smith, *Canada and the Canadian Question*, reprinted with an introduction by Carl Berger (Toronto: University of Toronto Press, 1971), pp. 223–24.

14 John W. Holmes, "In praise of national boundaries," *Saturday Night*, July 1974, p. 14.

15 Eayrs, "Sharing a Continent," p. 81.

16 Carl Berger, *The Sense of Power: Studies in the Ideas of Canadian Imperialism, 1867–1914* (Toronto: University of Toronto Press, 1970).

17 Denis Smith, "Political Parties and the Survival of Canada," in R. Kenneth Carty and W. Peter Ward, eds., *Entering the Eighties: Canada in Crisis* (Toronto: Oxford University Press, 1980), p. 139.

18 For extensive graphic illustrations of the extent and character of foreign investment in Canada, see Nydia McCool, *Canadian Facts and Figures* (Edmonton: Hurtig, 1982), pp. 85ff.

19 *Ibid.*, p. 156.

20 Jennifer Lewington, "Need for jobs puts FIRA's role in doubt," *The Globe and Mail*, National Edition, December 10, 1983, p. B1.

21 Stephen Clarkson, *Canada and the Reagan Challenge: Crisis in the Canadian–American Relationship* (Toronto: James Lorimer, 1982), p. 103.

22 *The Globe and Mail*, September 8, 1983, p. 8.

23 Clarkson, *Canada and the Reagan Challenge*, p. 127.

24 *Ibid.*, p. 129.

25 Statistics Canada report, cited in *The Globe and Mail*, National Edition, March 27, 1984, p. D2.

26 Ian M. Drummond, "The Implications of American Economic Nationalism," in Norman Hillmer and Garth Stevenson, eds., *A Foremost Nation: Canadian Foreign Policy and a Changing World* (Toronto: McClelland and Stewart, 1977), p. 13.

27 H.G. Thorburn, *Planning and the Economy: Building Federal–Provincial Consensus* (Toronto: James Lorimer, 1984), pp. 11 and 119.

28 Herbert Marshall, Frank Southard Jr., and Kenneth W. Taylor, *Canadian–American Industry* (Toronto: McClelland and Stewart, 1936, reprinted 1976), pp. 274–77.

29 Donald Creighton, *The Passionate Observer: Selected Writings* (Toronto: McClelland and Stewart, 1980), p. 45.

30 David W. Slater, "The Case for More Free Trade," *The Globe and Mail*, National Edition, September 16, 1983, p. 7.

31 *Ibid.*

32 Ozay Mehmet, "Managers for a New World," *Policy Options*, September 1983, p. 57.

33 John W. Holmes, *Life with Uncle: The Canadian–American Relationship* (Toronto: University of Toronto Press, 1981), p. 4.

34 *Foreign Ownership and the Structure of Canadian Industry: Report of the Task Force on the Structure of Canadian Industry* (The Watkins Report) (Ottawa: Queen's Printer, 1968); *Eleventh Report of the Standing Committee on External Affairs and National Defence Respecting Canada–U.S. Relations* (The Wahn Report) (Ottawa: Queen's Printer, 1970); *Foreign Direct Investment in Canada* (The Gray Report) (Ottawa: Information Canada, 1972).

35 *Statistics Canada*, Catalogue 61-210 (1980) Part 1.

36 H.E. English, *Industrial Structure in Canada's International Competitive Position* (Montreal: The Canadian Trade Committee, 1964).

37 For a discussion of the extraterritoriality issue, see David Leyton-Brown, "Canada and Multinational Enterprise," in Hillmer and Stevenson, *A Foremost Nation*, pp. 71–75.

38 Peter C. Newman, "The high cost of free trade," *Maclean's*, January 16, 1984, p. 38.

39 Kari Levitt, *Silent Surrender: The Multinational Corporation in Canada* (Toronto: Macmillan, 1970), p. 149.

40 George Ball, *Discipline of Power* (Boston: Little, Brown and Company, 1968), p. 113.

41 Lewington, "Need for Jobs," p. B1.

42 William Johnson, "Canada tests free trade waters," *The Globe and Mail*, National Edition, September 25, 1984, p. 10.

43 John W. Holmes, "Impact of Domestic Political Factors on Canadian–American Relations: Canada," in Annette Baker Fox, Alfred O. Hero, Jr., and Joseph S. Nye, Jr., eds., *Canada and the United States: Transnational and Transgovernmental Relations* (New York: Columbia University Press, 1976), p. 25.

44 For a cross-national comparison, see Nicholas J. Patterson, "Canada–U.S. Foreign Investment Regulation: Transparency Versus Diffusion," in Earl H. Fry and Lee H. Radebaugh, eds., *Regulation of Foreign Direct Investment in Canada and the United States* (Provo: Brigham Young University, David M. Kennedy International Center, 1983), pp. 47–62.

45 Lewington, "Need for jobs," p. B1.

46 Clarkson, *Canada and the Reagan Challenge*, pp. 87ff.

47 George Grant, *Lament for a Nation: The Defeat of Canadian Nationalism* (Toronto: McClelland and Stewart, 1965), p. 15.

48 *Ibid.*, pp. 69–70.

49 See "The NDP 'Waffle' Manifesto: For an Independent Socialist Canada," in Paul Fox, ed., *Politics: Canada*, 3rd ed. (Toronto: McGraw-Hill, 1970), pp. 242–45.

50 Arthur Siegel, *Politics and the Media in Canada* (Toronto: McGraw-Hill Ryerson, 1983), p. 1.

51 Holmes, "In praise of national boundaries," p. 14.

52 Eayrs, "Sharing a Continent," p. 89.

53 For a discussion of this debate as it relates to Canadian political science, see Alan C. Cairns, "Political Science in Canada and the Americanization Issue," *Canadian Journal of Political Science* VIII, 2 (June 1975); and David P. Shugarman, "The Problems of the Reluctant Nationalist: A Comment on Alan Cairns's," *CJPS* IX, 1 (March 1976).

54 In 1980 Canadian universities awarded 403 PhDs in the social sciences (19 in political science) compared to 166 (7 in political science) in 1969/70. Thomas H.B. Symons and James E. Page, *Some Questions of Balance: Human Resources, Higher Education and Canadian Studies*, Vol. III of *To Know Ourselves: The Report of the Commission on Canadian Studies, Association of Universities and Colleges of Canada* (Ottawa, 1984), p. 114.

55 *Ibid.*, p. 58.

56 Siegel, *Politics and the Media in Canada*, p. 183. Siegel also shows (pp. 180–81) that the French-language broadcast media is much more Canadian in content than is the English-language media.

57 Holmes, "In praise of national boundaries," p. 16.

58 Cited in Patrick Nagle, "Border disputes still pending," *Calgary Herald*, October 20, 184, p. A4.

59 Clarkson, *Canada and the Reagan Challenge*, p. 185.

60 Joseph S. Nye, Jr., and Robert O. Keohane, "Transnational Relations and World Politics: An Introduction," in Robert O. Keohane and Joseph S. Nye, Jr., eds., *Transnational Relations and World Politics* (Cambridge: Harvard University Press, 1972), p. ix.

61 John D. Redekop, "A Reinterpretation of Canadian–American Relations," *Canadian Journal of Political Science* IX:2 (June 1976), p. 237.

62 Government of Canada, *Foreign Policy for Canadians* (Ottawa, 1970). This was remedied somewhat by a special issue of *International Perspectives*, "Canada–U.S. Relations: Options for the Future," published in 1972.

63 Robert O. Keohane and Joseph S. Nye, Jr., *Power and Interdependence: World Politics in Transition* (Boston: Little, Brown and Company, 1977), p. 170.

64 Redekop, "A Reinterpretation," p. 233.

65 Holmes, *Life with Uncle*, p. 43.

66 Newman, "The high cost of free trade," p. 38.

67 Peter Moon, "Agents look out for Canada's interests," *The Globe and Mail*, National Edition, August 15, 1983, p. 5.

68 Leyton-Brown, "Canada and Multinational Enterprise," p. 81.

69 Holmes, *Life with Uncle*, p. 55.

70 Clarkson, *Canada and the Reagan Challenge*, p. 289.

71 Holmes, *Life with Uncle*, p. 7.

72 Eayrs, "Sharing a Continent," p. 66.

73 Clarkson, *Canada and the Reagan Challenge*, p. 261.

74 Michael Tucker, *Canadian Foreign Policy: Contemporary Issues and Themes* (Toronto: McGraw-Hill Ryerson, 1980), pp. 149–50.

75 Clarkson, *Canada and the Reagan Challenge*, p. 8.

76 Creighton, *The Passionate Observer*, p. 23.

77 Cited in Levitt, *Silent Surrender*, pp. 1–2.

78 *Ibid.*, p. 2.

79 Redekop, "A Reinterpretation," p. 230.

80 Eayrs, "Sharing a Continent," p. 93.

81 In the spring of 1980, a Gallup survey asked a national sample of Canadians which country they regarded as Canada's best friend. Across the country, 75 percent chose the United States, 7 percent Britain, 2 percent France, 3 percent some other country, and 13 percent couldn't say. When this question was asked in 1965, only 58 percent chose the United States while 24 percent chose Britain and 3 percent chose France. *The Gallup Report*, July 5, 1980.

82 Hans Kohn, *The Idea of Nationalism* (New York: Macmillan, 1944), p. 20.

83 See Roger Gibbins, "Models of Nationalism: A Case Study of Political Ideologies in the Canadian West," *Canadian Journal of Political Science* June 1977, pp. 341–73.

84 For a discussion of this theme's expression in Canadian literature, see Margaret Atwood, *Survival* (Toronto: Anansi, 1972).

85 Northrop Frye, *The Bush Garden* (Toronto: Anansi, 1971), p. iv.

86 *Vancouver Sun*, January 27, 1972, p. 6.

87 Margaret Atwood, *Second Words: Selected Critical Prose* (Toronto: Anansi, 1982), p. 380.

88 John Meisel, *Working Papers on Canadian Politics* (Montreal: McGill-Queen's University Press, 1973), p. 208.

89 J.R. Mallory, *The Structure of Canadian Government* (Toronto: Macmillan, 1971), p. 1.

90 Wise and Brown, *Canada Views the United States*, p. 94.

91 *Ibid.*, p. 96.

92 For an expansion of this point, see Roger Gibbins, *Regionalism: Territorial Politics in Canada and the United States* (Toronto: Butterworths, 1982), p. 196.

93 J.H. Dales, " 'National Policy' Myths, Past and Present," *Journal of Canadian Studies* 14:3 (Fall 1979), p. 93.

94 V. Seymour Wilson, "Federal–Provincial Relations and the Federal Policy Process," in G. Bruce Doern and Peter Aucoin, eds., *Public Policy in Canada* (Toronto: Macmillan, 1979), p. 197.

95 Levitt, *Silent Surrender*, p. 148.

96 Mason Wade, "The Roots of the Relationship," in Dickey, *The United States and Canada*, p. 44.

97 *Ibid.*, p. 53.

CHAPTER SEVEN

1 *Ninth Annual Report*, Alberta Department of Federal and Intergovernmental Affairs, October 1982.

2 Richard Rose, *Understanding Big Government: The Programme Approach* (London: Sage, 1981), p. 1.

3 Richard M. Bird, in collaboration with Meyer W. Bucovetsky and David K. Foot, *The Growth of Public Sector Employment in Canada* (Montreal: Institute for Research on Public Policy, 1979), p. 16.

4 H.G. Thorburn, *Planning and the Economy: Building Federal–Provincial Consensus* (Toronto: James Lorimer, 1984), p. 160.

5 See Roger Gibbins, *Regionalism: Territorial Politics in Canada and the United States* (Toronto: Butterworths, 1982), Chapter 4.

6 W.L. Morton, "Confederation 1870 to 1896," *Journal of Canadian Studies*, Vol. 1, 1966, p. 23.

7 Donald V. Smiley, *The Canadian Political Nationality* (Toronto: Methuen, 1967), p. 21.

8 Ivo D. Duchacek, *Comparative Federalism: The Territorial Dimension of Politics* (New York: Holt, Rinehart and Winston, 1970), p. 324.

9 Garth Stevenson, *Unfulfilled Union: Canadian Federalism and National Unity* (Toronto: Macmillan, 1979), p. 138.

10 Smiley, *The Canadian Political Nationality*, p. 41.

11 Donald V. Smiley, *Constitutional Adaptation and Canadian Federalism Since 1945*, Documents of the Royal Commission on Bilingualism and Biculturalism (Ottawa: Information Canada, 1970), p. 28.

12 Bora Laskin, *Canadian Constitutional Law*, 2nd ed. (Toronto: Carswell, 1960), p. 19.

13 J.A. Corry, "Constitutional Trends and Federalism," in J. Peter Meekison, ed., *Canadian Federalism: Myth or Reality* (Toronto: Methuen, 1968), p. 57.

14 Garth Stevenson, "Federalism and the Political Economy of the Canadian State," in Leo Panitch, ed., *The Canadian State: Political Economy and Political Power* (Toronto: University of Toronto Press, 1977), p. 75.

15 J.R. Mallory, *The Structure of Canadian Government* (Toronto: Macmillan, 1971), p. 342.

16 The "national dimension" criterion was established in 1882 by the JCPC ruling in *Russell v. the Queen*. It has since been used to uphold federal legislation relating to aeronautics, broadcasting, the regulation of the National Capital District, and the production of uranium. For a detailed discussion of the judicial interpretation of the Peace, Order, and Good Government clause, see Donald V. Smiley, *Canada in Question: Federalism in the Eighties* 3rd ed. (Toronto: McGraw-Hill Ryerson, 1980), pp. 24–25.

17 Frank R. Scott, "Our Changing Constitution," in W.R. Lederman, ed., *The Courts and the Canadian Constitution* (Toronto: McClelland and Stewart, 1967), p. 21.

18 Smiley, *The Canadian Political Nationality*, p. 20.

19 Martha Fletcher, "Judicial Review and the Division of Powers in Canada," in J. Peter Meekison, ed., *Canadian Federalism: Myth or Reality* (Toronto: Methuen, 1968), p. 157.

20 Alan C. Cairns, "The Living Canadian Constitution," in J. Peter Meekison, ed., *Canadian Federalism: Myth or Reality*, 3rd ed. (Toronto: Methuen, 1977), pp. 86–99.

21 Smiley, *The Canadian Political Nationality*, p. 54.

22 *Calgary Herald*, April 12, 1977, p. 7.

23 Gibbins, *Regionalism*, pp. 1–3.

24 Peter H. Russell, "The Political Purposes of the Canadian Charter of Rights and Freedoms," *Canadian Bar Review*, 1983, pp. 43–46.

25 Rainer Knopff and F.L. Morton, *Nation-Building and the Charter*, Research Report prepared for the Royal Commission on the Economic Union and Development Prospects for Canada, 1984, p. 90.

26 Frank MacKinnon, "The Establishment of the Supreme Court of Canada," in W.R. Lederman, ed., *The Courts and the Canadian Constitution* (Toronto: McClelland and Stewart, 1964), p. 112.

27 Mallory, *The Structure of Canadian Government*, p. 331.

28 For a review of the Supreme Court's record on federal–provincial disputes, see Peter W. Hogg, "Is the Supreme Court of Canada Biased in Constitutional Cases?," *Canadian Bar Review*, 1979.

29 Knopff and Morton, *Nation-Building and the Charter*, pp. 31–34.
30 During the Charter's first year, more federal statutes were challenged (171 cases) than were provincial statutes (31 cases), but provincial statutes were more prone to successful attack (55 percent) than were federal statutes (21 percent). The cases involving federal statutes were mostly legal rights challenges to the Criminal Code. F.C. Morton, "Charting the Charter—Year One: A Statistical Analysis," in *Canadian Human Rights Yearbook 1984* (Ottawa, 1984).
31 Reginald Whitaker, "Democracy and the Canadian Constitution," in Keith Banting and Richard Simeon, eds., *And No One Cheered: Federalism, Democracy and the Constitution Act* (Toronto: Methuen, 1983), p. 250.
32 Alan Cairns, "The Politics of Constitutional Conservatism," in Banting and Simeon, *And No One Cheered*, p. 53.
33 *Ibid.*, p. 55.
34 R.I. Cheffins, *The Constitutional Process in Canada* (Toronto: McGraw-Hill, 1969), p. 140.
35 Stevenson, *Unfulfilled Union*, p. 188.
36 Edwin R. Black, *Divided Loyalties: Canadian Concepts of Federalism* (Montreal: McGill-Queen's University Press, 1975), p. 101.
37 Government of Canada, "Dominion–Provincial Conference 1935," in *Dominion–Provincial Conferences 1927, 1935, 1941* (Ottawa: King's Printer, 1946).
38 Smiley, *Canada in Question*, p. 58.
39 Institute of Intergovernmental Relations, *Report: Intergovernmental Relations on Fiscal and Economic Matters* (Ottawa: Queen's Printer, 1969), p. 103.
40 Richard J. Van Loon and Michael S. Whittington, *The Canadian Political System: Environment, Structure, and Process*, 2nd ed. (Toronto: McGraw-Hill Ryerson, 1976), pp. 366–67.
41 V. Seymour Wilson, "Federal–Provincial Relations and the Federal Policy Process," in G. Bruce Doern and Peter Aucoin, eds., *Public Policy in Canada* (Toronto: Macmillan, 1979), p. 198.
42 Timothy B. Woolstencroft, *Organizing Intergovernmental Relations* (Kingston: Institute of Intergovernmental Relations, Queen's University, 1982), p. 9.
43 *Ibid.*, p. 2.
44 Woolstencroft argues that the degree of institutionalization is related directly to the degree of discontent with the federal status quo. Certainly this relationship appears to be borne out in the cases of Quebec and Alberta. (*Ibid.*, p. 5.)
45 Donald Smiley, "An Outsider's Observations of Federal–Provincial Relations Among Consenting Adults," in Richard Simeon, ed., *Confrontation and Collaboration: Intergovernmental Relations in Canada Today* (Toronto: Institute of Public Administration of Canada, 1979), p. 110.
46 Woolstencroft, *Organizing Intergovernmental Relations*, pp. 79–80.
47 H.G. Thorburn, *Planning and the Economy: Building Federal–Provincial Consensus* (Toronto: James Lorimer, 1984), p. 190.
48 Woolstencroft, *Organizing Intergovernmental Relations*, p. 15.
49 Provincial governments have an ambiguous position in international affairs. Any treaties signed by Canada which concern matters of provincial jurisdiction can only be implemented through provincial legislation. At the same time, the provinces are not recognized as states in international law, and therefore can only negotiate treaties or other state-to-state agreements through the Government of Canada even though such agreements may cover matters falling exclusively within provincial jurisdiction. See Mallory, *The Structure of Canadian Government*, p. 399.
50 *Calgary Herald*, October 4, 1983, p. A8.
51 Michael McDowell, "Quebec's quest for world identity still provokes rows," *The Globe and Mail*, National Edition, January 7, 1984, pp. 1 and 5.
52 A major but nonetheless isolated exception came in the constitutional negotiations when patriation proceeded without the consent of Quebec. In this case the Supreme Court had ruled that a federal–provincial consensus *but not unanimous consent* was required to amend the

constitution. Constitution amendment will now be handled through the amending formula contained within the Constitution Act, 1982, a formula which has no general applicability to First Ministers' conferences.

53 House of Commons, *Debates*, December 14, 1982, p. 21569.

54 Garth Stevenson, "Federalism and Intergovernmental Relations," in Michael S. Whittington and Glen Williams, eds., *Canadian Politics in the 1980s* (Toronto: Methuen, 1981), p. 288.

55 *Ibid.*, p. 289.

56 Speech at the Liberal Party of Canada fund-raising dinner, Vancouver, November 12, 1981.

57 Roy Romanow, John Whyte, and Howard Leeson, *Canada ... Notwithstanding: The Making of the Constitution 1976–1982* (Toronto: Methuen, 1984), pp. 212–14.

58 Richard Simeon, *Federal–Provincial Diplomacy: The Making of Recent Policy in Canada* (Toronto: University of Toronto Press, 1972).

59 Richard Simeon, "Regionalism and Canadian Political Institutions," in J. Peter Meekison, ed., *Canadian Federalism: Myth or Reality*, 3rd ed. (Toronto: Methuen, 1977), pp. 301–2.

60 Thorburn, *Planning and the Economy*, p. 242.

61 Stevenson, "Federalism and Intergovernmental Relations," p. 291.

62 Richard Simeon, "Some Suggestions for Improving Inter-governmental Relations," in Paul W. Fox, ed., *Politics: Canada*, 5th ed. (Toronto: McGraw-Hill Ryerson, 1982), p. 102.

CHAPTER EIGHT

1 Harold D. Clarke, Jane Jenson, Lawrence Le Duc, and Jon H. Pammett, *Absent Mandate: The Politics of Discontent in Canada* (Toronto: Gage, 1984), p. 10.

2 Richard J. Van Loon and Michael S. Whittington, *The Canadian Political System: Environment, Structure and Process*, 3rd ed. (Toronto: McGraw-Hill Ryerson, 1981), p. 307.

3 John Meisel, "The Party System and the 1974 Election," in Howard R. Penniman, ed., *Canada at the Polls: The General Election of 1974* (Washington, D.C.: American Enterprise Institute for Public Policy Research, 1975), p. 1.

4 The 1925 and 1926 elections are not included in this total. On October 29, 1925, the incumbent Liberals elected only 99 MPs compared to 116 for the Conservatives. Yet because neither party could form a majority government, the Liberal Prime Minister, William Lyon Mackenzie King, decided to stay in power until late June 1926, when King sought a dissolution of the House. The Governor General, Lord Byng, refused and instead asked the leader of the Conservative party, Arthur Meighen, to form a government. The Meighen government lasted only three days before it was defeated in the House. Meighen was then granted a dissolution, a general election was called for September 14, 1926, and the Liberals won a majority government with 128 seats, compared to 91 for the Conservatives.

5 Meisel, "The Party System and the 1974 Election," p. 14.

6 Seventy-six of the eighty-four total seats won by Social Credit candidates came from Alberta, where the party overwhelmingly dominated provincial politics from 1935 to 1971.

7 Cited in Joseph Wearing, *The L-Shaped Party: The Liberal Party of Canada 1958–1980* (Toronto: McGraw-Hill Ryerson, 1981), p. 1.

8 The Conservatives captured 78.5 percent of the House seats, whereas the 211 Conservative seats in 1984 constituted 74.8 percent of the seats in a slightly larger House of Commons.

9 For a discussion of the emergence of the Créditistes, see Maurice Pinard, *The Rise of a Third Party: A Study in Crisis Politics* (Englewood Cliffs, NJ: Prentice-Hall, 1971).

10 These figures are based on non-official returns, and are subject to minor revisions.

11 The term "government party" comes from Reginald Whitaker's *The Government Party: Organizing and Financing the Liberal Party of Canada 1930–58* (Toronto: University of Toronto Press, 1977).

12 The election statistics come from Loren M. Simerl, "A Survey of Canadian Provincial Election Results, 1905–1981," in Paul W. Fox, ed., *Politics: Canada*, 5th ed. (Toronto: McGraw-Hill Ryerson, 1982), pp. 658–69.

13 The pro-separatist Western Canada Concept, which captured 11 percent of the vote but no seats in the 1982 provincial election, provides a notable exception.

14 For a detailed analysis of the relationship between federal and provincial party support, see Wearing, *The L-Shaped Party*, pp. 81–86.

15 Van Loon and Whittington, *The Canadian Political System*, p. 319. For an extended discussion of the confederal nature of Canadian parties, see Donald V. Smiley, *Canada in Question: Federalism in the Eighties*, 3rd ed. (Toronto: McGraw-Hill Ryerson, 1980), Chapter Five.

16 There can be exceptions to this rule, as the above discussion of the 1925 election illustrates.

17 The Union Government is a unique case in that the Conservative party had a clear parliamentary majority before embarking upon the Union Government coalition with pro-conscription Liberals.

18 Brian H. Coulter, *Coalition Governments in Canada: A Comparative Analysis of Four Case Studies*, unpublished M.A. Thesis. University of Calgary, 1982.

19 Alan C. Cairns, "The Electoral System and the Party System in Canada, 1921–1965," *Canadian Journal of Political Science*, Volume 1 (1968), pp. 55–80.

20 For example, see William P. Irvine, *Does Canada Need a New Electoral System?* (Kingston: Institute of Intergovernmental Relations, Queen's University, 1979).

21 William Mishler, "Political Participation and Democracy," in Michael S. Whittington and Glen Williams, eds., *Canadian Politics in the 1980s*, 2nd ed. (Toronto: Methuen, 1984), p. 178.

22 Clarke et al., *Absent Mandate*, p. 35. Preliminary estimates place the 1984 turnout at 76 percent, which compares with 69 percent in 1980 and 76 percent in 1979.

23 Mishler defines political participation as "voluntary activities by citizens which are intended to influence the selection of government leaders or the decisions they make." "Political Participation and Democracy," p. 175.

24 Clarke et al., *Absent Mandate*, p. 37.

25 Harold D. Clarke, Lawrence LeDuc, Jane Jenson, and Jon H. Pammett, *Political Choice in Canada* (Toronto: McGraw-Hill Ryerson, 1979), p. 87.

26 Mishler, "Political Participation and Democracy," pp. 179–80.

27 *Ibid.*, p. 190.

28 Clarke et al., *Political Choice*, p. 137.

29 Partisanship was measured by first asking: "Thinking of federal politics, do you usually think of yourself as a Liberal, Conservative, NDP, Social Credit or what?" Respondents who mentioned a party were then asked: "How strongly (Liberal, Conservative or whatever) do you feel—very strongly, fairly strongly, or not very strongly?"

30 For a useful discussion of partisanship, see Clarke et al., *Political Choice*, Chapter Five.

31 *Ibid.*, p. 136.

32 Considerable debate exists as to the general strength and stability of partisan identifications in Canada. In summarizing this debate, Jon Pammett concludes that the majority predisposition is toward *flexible partisanship*, that about 60 percent of voters "... develop party loyalties that are either weak, changeable over time or different at the two levels of the federal system." See "Elections" in Whittington and Williams, *Canadian Politics in the 1980s*, 2nd ed., p. 276.

33 *The Globe and Mail*, National Edition, June 2, 1984, p. 1.

34 For an overview of both federal and provincial legislation, see Khayyam Z. Paltiel, "Canadian Election Expense Legislation: Recent Developments," in Hugh G. Thorburn, ed., *Party Politics in Canada*, 4th ed. (Scarborough: Prentice-Hall, 1979), pp. 100–110.

35 Bill C-169 was challenged in court by the National Citizens Coalition and as a consequence was not enforced in the 1984 federal election.

36 *The Globe and Mail*, National Edition, July 10, 1984, p. 5.

37 Wearing, *The L-Shaped Party*, p. 216.

38 Frederick C. Engelmann, "Canadian Political Parties and Elections," in John H. Redekop, ed., *Approaches to Canadian Politics*, 2nd ed. (Scarborough: Prentice-Hall, 1983), p. 225. For a general and informative discussion of the policy mandates of Canadian elections, see Clarke et al., *Absent Mandate*.

39 Clarke et al., *Absent Mandate*, p. 34.

40 For a discussion of the distinction between institutionalized and issue-oriented interest groups, see Paul Pross, "Pressure Groups: Adaptive Instruments of Political Communication," in Pross, ed., *Pressure Group Behavior in Canadian Politics* (Toronto: McGraw-Hill Ryerson, 1975), pp. 8–18.

41 *Ibid.*, p. 3.

42 The 1984 polls, which from early in the campaign indicated a Conservative landslide, arguably had at least three important though not necessarily decisive effects. First, they undercut morale within the Liberal campaign organization, making it difficult to attract financial support and volunteer assistance. Second, they undercut the Liberal campaign strategy in the West. There was little sense in voting Liberal to have an effective regional voice in government if the Conservatives were going to win. Third, they assured Quebec voters that a shift to the Conservative party would not isolate Quebec from the national government.

43 Van Loon and Whittington, *The Canadian Political System*, p. 313.

44 Cited in Mason Wade, *The French Canadians, 1860–1967*, Vol. II, pp. 524–25.

45 Elizabeth Armstrong, *The Crisis of Quebec, 1914–1918* (Toronto: McClelland and Stewart, 1937, reprinted 1974), p. 166.

46 *Ibid.*, p. 187.

47 *House of Commons Debates*, September 8, 1939, p. 36.

48 Although the voting returns did not distinguish between the two linguistic communities in Quebec, it is clear that the "no" vote among francophones alone was even higher.

49 George C. Perlin, *The Tory Syndrome: Leadership Politics in the Progressive Conservative Party* (Montreal: McGill-Queen's University Press, 1980).

50 George Grant, *Lament for a Nation: The Defeat of Canadian Nationalism* (Toronto: McClelland and Stewart, 1965), p. 20.

51 In the 1980 election, 102 ridings contained a francophone population of 10 percent or more. Of these, the Liberals won 100 and the Conservatives won two. As Mulroney argued in his 1983 leadership bid, "give the Liberals a 100 seat lead and they'll beat you ten times out of ten." Patrick Martin, Allan Gregg, and George Perlin, *Contenders: The Tory Quest for Power* (Scarborough: Prentice-Hall, 1983), p. 84.

52 Denis Smith, "Political Parties and the Survival of Canada," in R. Kenneth Carty and W. Peter Ward, eds., *Entering the Eighties: Canada in Crisis* (Toronto: Oxford University Press, 1980), pp. 142 ff.

53 Stein Rokkan, "Electoral Mobilization, Party Competition, and National Integration," in Joseph LaPalombara and Myron Weiner, eds., *Political Parties and Political Development* (Princeton: Princeton University Press, 1966), pp. 241–66; and Seymour Martin Lipset and Stein Rokkan, "Cleavage Structures, Party Systems, and Voter Alignments: An Introduction," in Lipset and Rokkan, eds., *Party Systems and Voter Alignments: Cross-National Perspectives* (New York: The Free Press, 1967), pp. 1–64.

54 G.A. Rawlyk and Doug Brown, "The Historical Framework of the Maritimes and Confederation," in G.A. Rawlyk, ed., *The Atlantic Provinces and the Problems of Confederation* (St. John's: Breakwater, 1979) p. 16.

55 Smith, "Political Parties and the Survival of Canada," p. 140.

56 Although the Confederation of Regions Western Party ran candidates in fifty-five of the seventy-

seven western Canadian ridings in the 1984 general election, it captured only 1.9 percent of the regional popular vote.

57 David E. Smith, *The Regional Decline of a National Party: Liberals on the Prairies* (Toronto: University of Toronto Press, 1981), p. 150.

58 The term "unrestricted reciprocity" refers to the reciprocal removal of tariff barriers to trade. The more contemporary term would be "free trade."

59 For a discussion of the 1891 and 1911 campaigns, see J.M. Beck, *Pendulum of Power* (Scarborough: Prentice-Hall, 1968), pp. 57–68 and 120–33.

60 *Ibid.*, p. 64.

61 *Ibid.*, p. 68.

62 Ramsay Cook, *The Maple Leaf Forever* (Toronto: Macmillan, 1971), p. 212.

63 Grant, *Lament for a Nation*, p. 12 and Chapter 3.

64 Clarke et al., *Absent Mandate*, pp. 20–21.

65 Clarke et al., *Absent Mandate*, p. 12.

66 Smiley, *Canada in Question*, 3rd ed., p. 146.

67 *Ibid.*, p. 148.

68 This point is developed in a comparative context by Ivo D. Duchacek in *Comparative Federalism: The Territorial Dimension of Politics* (New York: Holt, Rinehart and Winston, 1970), p. 329; and William H. Riker in *Federalism: Origin, Operation, Significance* (Boston: Little Brown, 1964), p. 129.

69 Donald V. Smiley, *Canada in Question: Federalism in the Seventies*, 2nd ed. (Toronto: McGraw-Hill Ryerson, 1976), p. 98.

70 Meisel, "The Party System," p. 2.

71 Ron Graham, "The Legacy of Joe Clark," *Saturday Night*, September 1983, p. 30.

72 Cited in Peter C. Newman, *The Distemper of Our Times* (Toronto: McClelland and Stewart, 1968), p. 57.

73 Wearing, *The L-Shaped Party*, p. 4.

74 F.R. Scott, "W.L.M.K.," from *Collected Poems of F.R. Scott* (Toronto: McClelland & Stewart, 1981), p. 78.

75 Whitaker, *The Government Party*, p. 141.

76 In the 1980 post-election study, the following rather difficult question was posed to respondents: "Take a moment to think over all the reasons why you decided to vote the way you did, and just briefly tell me the things that were most important to you." More respondents—30 percent—named a party leader or leadership than identified any other single factor. Twenty-three percent named a party, while ony 9 percent cited local candidates. Clarke et al., *Political Choice in Canada*, p. 273.

77 Walter D. Young, "Leadership and Canadian Politics," in John H. Redekop, ed., *Approaches to Canadian Politics*, 2nd ed. (Scarborough: Prentice-Hall, 1983), pp. 269–70.

CHAPTER NINE

1 Richard Needham, *You and All the Rest: The Wit & Wisdom of Richard Needham* (Toronto: M. Sutkiewicz Publishing, 1982), p. 35.

APPENDIX A

1 Between 1945 and 1976, Parliament passed only 2 percent of the 2,601 private members' bills introduced while passing 89 percent of the government bills. Colin Campbell, *Canadian Political Facts, 1945–1976* (Toronto: Methuen, 1977), pp. 56–59.

2 Eugene A. Forsey, *How Canadians Govern Themselves* (Ottawa: Minister of Supply and Services, 1982), p. 31.

3 Robert J. Jackson and Michael M. Atkinson, *The Canadian Legislative System*, 2nd ed. (Toronto: Macmillan, 1980), p. 111.

4 David Easton, *A Systems Analysis of Political Life* (New York: John Wiley and Sons, 1965), p. 21.

APPENDIX B

1 Michael M. Atkinson and Graham White, "The Development of Provincial Legislatures," in Harold D. Clarke, Colin Campbell, F.Q. Quo, and Arthur Goddard, eds., *Parliament, Policy and Representation* (Toronto: Methuen, 1980), p. 271.

2 C. Lloyd Brown-John, *Canadian Regulatory Agencies* (Toronto: Butterworths, 1981), p. 34.

3 There have also been a number of special appointments to the Privy Council including the premiers who signed the Constitution Act in 1982, the provincial premiers at the time of the 1967 centennial celebrations, NDP leader Edward Broadbent, veteran NDP MP Stanley Knowles, and Gordon Robertson, for years the Clerk of the Privy Council.

4 W.A. Matheson, *The Prime Minister and Cabinet* (Toronto: Methuen, 1976), p. 7.

5 *Ibid.*, p. 14.

6 Robert J. Jackson and Michael M. Atkinson, *The Canadian Legislative System*, 2nd ed. (Toronto: Macmillan, 1980), p. 102.

7 Philip Laundy, "Legislatures," in David Bellamy, Jon H. Pammett, and Donald C. Rowat, eds., *The Provincial Political Systems: Comparative Essays* (Toronto: Methuen, 1976), p. 293.

8 Atkinson and White, "The Development of Provincial Legislatures," p. 255.

9 Allan Kornberg, William Mishler, and Harold D. Clarke, *Representative Democracy in the Canadian Provinces* (Scarborough: Prentice-Hall, 1982), p. 173.

Index